Internet Environments
for Science Education

Internet Environments for Science Education

Edited by

Marcia C. Linn, *University of California, Berkeley*
Elizabeth A. Davis, *University of Michigan*
Philip Bell, *University of Washington*

 LAWRENCE ERLBAUM ASSOCIATES, PUBLISHERS
2004   Mahwah, New Jersey   London

Lawrence Erlbaum Associates, Inc., Publishers
10 Industrial Avenue
Mahwah, New Jersey 07430

Cover design by Kathryn Houghtaling Lacey

Library of Congress Cataloging-in-Publication Data

Internet environments for science education / edited by Marcia C. Linn, Elizabeth A.
  Davis, Philip Bell.
      p. cm.
    Includes bibliographical references and index.
    ISBN 0-8058-4302-7 (cloth : alk. paper) — ISBN 0-8058-4303-5 (pbk. : alk. paper)
    1. Science—Computer network resources. 2. Science—Study and teaching
  (Elementary)—United States. 3. Science—Study and teaching (Secondary)—
  United States. 4. Internet in education. I. Linn, Marcia C. II. Davis,
  Elizabeth A., 1967– III. Bell, Philip, 1966–

  LB1585.7.I58 2003
  507.1'2—dc21   2003051157
                                                                         CIP

Books published by Lawrence Erlbaum Associates are printed on acid-free paper,
and their bindings are chosen for strength and durability.

Printed in the United States of America
10 9 8 7 6 5 4 3 2 1

*We dedicate this book
to Matthew, Allison, Lucy,
Zoë, and Sophie.*

Contents

Part II: Curriculum Design Patterns for Knowledge Integration

Part III: New Partnerships

Part IV: Next Steps

Foreword

Doug Kirkpatrick
University of California, Berkeley

My first encounter with John, a resource student who had a reputation for violence, was before he was a student in my class. I had corrected John for a minor violation of the school behavior code and his teacher later commented to me that I was lucky he did not hit me as he had done with another teacher. Three weeks later, at the change of the semester, John became a student in my science class. The first few days we both had our defenses up, but because the projects and technology we were using allowed me to move out into the class and work with students on an individual or small-group level I was able to start to build a bridge with John. I began to notice that he would come up and talk to me on the playground, and then he started coming in frequently outside of class time to work on his projects. The resource aide that was assigned to work with him commented on the change of attitude toward his work that she had observed. Near the end of the semester I asked John, "What would you like to do in the future if you could pick anything?" His answer was, "I want to work with computers and science." When I asked, "Why?" he said, "I like computers and science is fun and about real stuff."

Using computers to carry out inquiry projects changed John's attitude toward school and learning, but I believe it had an even greater impact on me as a middle school science teacher. The technology freed me up to work with two students at a time, probing their understanding of the concepts and principles we set as learning goals for each project. As I move from group to group and observe the notes they are writing, the models they are constructing, and the discussions they are having, I am able to assess where the individual student or the class as a whole needs further guidance.

There are always those times in life when one says, "Why didn't someone tell me that when I was young?" The past 15 years of my teaching career, during which I had the opportunity to become part of a partnership with educational researchers interested in understanding how technology can impact student learning, has been filled with those experiences. This is illustrated by an event that occurred early in the partnership. The class had been doing a unit focused on principles of heat flow through conductors and insulators. Students were able to define a conductor on a written test, therefore, I made the assumption that they understood the concept. When one of the researchers interviewed individual students, it became obvious that they could not apply principles they were studying beyond the classroom to everyday events. The partnership group met to discuss this problem. We responded by setting the context of each activity in a real-life situation. We also asked the students to construct their own real-life prototypes that could be explained by the principles being studied. This change resulted in more meaningful and lasting learning.

As illustrated in the chapters of this book, the curriculum projects have continued to evolve based on both the research on student learning and new technologies as they become available.

Unfortunately, most teachers do not have the opportunity to be part of a partnership that brings educational researchers into their classroom. This reality presents a challenge to those involved in educational research at postsecondary institutions. Everyone recognizes the importance of taking advantage of new technologies and developing the pedagogy necessary to meet the needs of a changing student population. The challenge is how to provide teachers with this support on a large scale. How can programs enable all students to have the same opportunity that John had in my class? Developing partnerships between K–12 and postsecondary institutions is one of the most effective methods of supporting teachers as they begin to recognize the need to move from traditional to more integrated instruction. This book describes the impact of such a partnership between K–12 educators, educational researchers, and scientists on classroom learning and teaching.

Traditionally, science instruction in schools is done with outdated textbooks and laboratory activities that have been done the same way for years in spite of research that shows this to have little impact on student learning (e.g., Hart, Mulhall, et al., 2000). The new model, described in this volume, takes advantage of current technologies and the Internet to make learning science both accessible and relevant for students. As illustrated by the chapters in this text, this model must be based on extensive research, current science knowledge, and classroom trial and refinement. This new model impacts both the student and the teacher. For the student, the opportunity to investigate current scientific controversies, critique evidence, and create arguments for debate is more engaging and provides the skills and knowledge base needed to become lifelong learners of science. This model gives the student more autonomy and stresses not only the student to teacher role but also that of student to peer and student to community through the use of the Internet as a learning opportunity. For the teacher, this model provides a flexible environment that lends itself to more innovative instruction. Once the teacher leaves the front of the classroom to work with small groups or individual students, the needs of students with diverse capabilities and interests are better served.

The partnerships and research outcomes described in the following chapters changed the way I teach and enriched my understanding of how students learn. Having a group of multidisciplinary partners who are willing to challenge each other and to hold each other accountable for providing students with the best possible science learning environment has been a positive professional development activity for each member of the group. I do not know where John is today or if he has continued to follow his interest in computers and science, but I do know that he succeeded in one course, demonstrating his potential to be successful.

Introduction

Marcia C. Linn
University of California, Berkeley

Elizabeth A. Davis
University of Michigan

Philip Bell
University of Washington

Too many citizens fear, ignore, or distrust science, yet current dilemmas, often spurred by new technologies, require an attentive and thoughtful citizenry. Policy issues such as nuclear power or cloning call for an informed public. Environmental stewardship depends on individuals who can assess relative risk and understand scientific trade-offs. Citizens prepared to deal with personal dilemmas, such as selecting treatments for diseases or making energy efficient housing decisions, and ready to interpret the plethora of persuasive scientific messages found in every medium from news advertisements to Internet resources will succeed today.

The current science curriculum in the United States and many other countries generally fails to offer the preparation that students need to guide their own learning or take advantage of new or informal educational opportunities. Current courses often neglect contemporary issues in science as well as scientific topics of importance to students' lives. Most courses fail to engage students in the kinds of experiences they will encounter in their adult lives such as interpreting persuasive messages, searching for information on the Internet, or finding the answers to everyday science problems. No wonder so many students complain about the relevance of science courses and report forgetting the material they studied.

This book offers a road map for reforming the educational enterprise to produce lifelong science learners who continue to make sense of science for personal and professional goals throughout their lives. We seek to create learners who can guide their own inquiry in science. We describe *inquiry instruction* as engaging students in the intentional process of diagnosing problems, critiquing experiments, distinguishing alternatives, planning investigations, researching conjectures, searching for information, debating with peers, seeking information from experts, and forming coherent arguments. *Internet Environments for Science Education* provides a guide for reform of science education inquiry project by inquiry project.

OPPORTUNITIES FOR EVERYONE

We describe a research program intent on spreading inquiry across the science curriculum. Our approach features projects lasting 1 or more weeks, conducted with technology supports, and matched to the goals of each science course. We hope that students will perform at least one project each semester that they study science. If precollege students studied science every year for 12 years, they would complete 24 inquiry projects and spend about 48 weeks—more than one school year—on inquiry. We describe how this might occur and why it would achieve our goal of transforming every student into a lifelong science learner.

Internet Environments for Science Education offers teachers, professional development leaders, curriculum designers, cognitive researchers, technologists, policymakers, science educators, and natural scientists the opportunity to work together to convert students into lifelong science learners one inquiry project at a time. This book provides starting points so each of these groups can contribute to a coordinated effort.

Internet Environments for Science Education advocates leveraging inquiry and technology to reform the full spectrum of science education activities—including instruction, curriculum, policy, professional development, and assessment. We have researched mutually supportive combinations of inquiry and technology that extend throughout the complex educational system and sustain new practices.

We offer those concerned about reform of science instruction the following contributions:

- The **knowledge integration perspective on learning** featuring the interpretive, cultural, and deliberate natures of the learner (Linn, Eylon, & Davis, chap. 2).

- The **scaffolded knowledge integration framework** on instruction featuring metaprinciples and pragmatic principles designing inquiry instruction (Linn, Davis, & Eylon, chap. 3).
- A series of **learning environments** including the Computer as Learning Partner (CLP), the Knowledge Integration Environment (KIE), and the Web-based Inquiry Science Environment (WISE; Linn, Davis, & Bell, chap. 1) that designers can use to create new inquiry projects or customize existing projects.
- **Curriculum design patterns for inquiry projects** that establish activity sequences to promote critique (Davis, chap. 5), debate (Bell, chap. 6), design (Hoadley, chap. 7), and investigation (D. Clark, chap. 8) in science.
- A **partnership model** establishing activity structures that allow groups of teachers, researchers, and technologists to guide iterative refinement of inquiry instruction (Shear, Bell, & Linn, chap. 12).
- A **professional development model** that implements our educational philosophy based on mentoring by an expert teacher (Slotta, chap. 9).
- A **model for using contemporary controversy** to communicate the nature of science (Bell, chap. 10).
- A **customization process** to help teachers adapt inquiry projects to their own students, geographical characteristics, curriculum framework, and personal goals (Baumgartner, chap. 11).
- **Design principles and associated methods for design-based research studies** (Linn et al., chap. 3; Bell, Hoadley, & Linn, chap. 4; Linn, Bell, & Davis, chap. 13).

OUR PHILOSOPHY—KNOWLEDGE INTEGRATION

Our knowledge integration perspective on learning stems from two central findings. First, learners hold multiple conflicting ideas about virtually any phenomenon (diSessa, 2000; Eylon & Linn, 1988; Linn, 2001; Linn & Hsi, 2000), which may be connected to the context in which the phenomenon is being considered. For example, students may believe that objects in motion come to rest on the playground but remain in motion in science class. Second, learners invest intellectual energy in sorting out, linking, connecting, critiquing, reconsidering, prioritizing, selecting, and organizing their ideas (Piaget, 1971; Vygotsky, 1962).

This perspective on learning incorporates research in education, psychology, sociology, and related disciplines. The perspective has emerged from investigations in varied learning contexts and disciplines.

We build on a core set of views on instruction called the *scaffolded knowledge integration framework*, along with design principles that reflect this perspective (Linn & Hsi, 2000). These principles, supported by extensive research in both college and precollege classrooms, give us a head start on creating powerful learning environments to support inquiry.

The knowledge integration perspective on learning led us to speculate about effective instructional supports and to test our speculations by creating learning environments and studying how students respond. These technology-enhanced learning environments enable researchers to consistently vary the conditions of instruction. For example, we can design versions of a project that systematically vary forms of feedback, student activities, or access to resources yet can be taught by the same teacher without imposing an undue burden.

OUR METHODS—DESIGN-BASED RESEARCH STUDIES

New opportunities to teach inquiry, new technologies, and increased understanding of how teachers and their students learn, accompanied by the clear evidence that education is a complex system, suggest the need for new research methods suited to the investigation of a complex, systemic, inertia-laden educational enterprise. We have evolved design-based research to both determine successful interventions and identify ways to improve instruction. Our studies typically involve comparing one version of instruction to another to investigate the customization, localization, and generalization of educational innovations. Our research results in the development of design principles that can guide future work.

OUR APPROACH—LEVERAGING TECHNOLOGY

Science classrooms have historically been information-lean environments. Students and their teachers rely on textbooks, audiovisual materials, library books, carefully orchestrated experiments, and occasional contemporary materials. These resources, selected to streamline the presentation of content and reduce controversy, tend to privilege established findings and silence debate.

In the last decade we have witnessed an unprecedented explosion of information access for everyone who has access to a web browser and a network connection. We seek to take advantage of these global, networked information resources to support student learning and at the same time to prepare learners to deal with questionable, persuasive, inaccurate material found in online sources.

The term *information ecologies* refers to the vast information resources that have become available considered in tandem with the interactions with and about them (Card, Robertson, et al., 1996). Invoking the notion of an ecology is meant to help reify the rich, highly variable range of information available. This book explores ways to use these vast information ecologies used to help students learn science.

More now than ever, the networked information resources of the Internet are becoming commonplace in school settings (National Center for Education Statistics [NCES], 2001; Rodger, 1998). Almost 75% of all youth 12 to 15 years of age make use of the Internet. Over 90% of the connected youth have sent or received e-mail. By 2000, 98% of public schools in the United States had Internet connectivity compared to 35% in 1994. By 2000, 77% of instructional rooms had direct connections compared to only 3% in 1994. The proportion of instructional rooms connected decreases as the proportion of students in poverty increases, although access to the Internet does not.

This trend can be expected to continue as the world approaches universal access to the Internet in public schools and libraries. However, what impact will this massive infusion of information technologies really have on schools? How can educators support student learning with this networked information ecology? How should educators be prepared for this endeavor? Detailed educational research conducted in school settings should factor into any serious response to these questions.

Increasing engagement with science information ecologies brings the challenge (and responsibility) to make sense of more and more diverse information. Today, the simple click of a mouse brings a wealth of information on just about any topic. The information students may find will be extremely varied in terms of quality and is often only tangentially related to the original line of inquiry. Judging the veracity of that information and determining its relevance are increasingly difficult challenges. Yet, information technologies are here to stay for the foreseeable future. Knowledge integration has become not a choice but a necessity.

The noise of daily bombardments of information demand increased attention to beliefs about the nature of knowing and learning. Students need ways to interpret conflicting ideas and they need to appreciate the iterative nature of scientific research. Learners also need to understand the utility of engaging in sustained sense-making on specific topics while, at the same time, respecting the parsimony of scientific principles.

Although many view the Web as a vast electronic science encyclopedia, this framing does not resonate with reality. A significant amount of the information on the Web is dubious from a scientific perspective. By supporting students in developing an integrated understanding of science, we harness this resource and prepare lifelong learners. We report on the design of inquiry projects that enable students to make sense of diverse information and sort out compelling arguments.

PLAN OF *INTERNET ENVIRONMENTS FOR SCIENCE EDUCATION*

In *Internet Environments for Science Education* we build on over 25 years of research on inquiry instruction. We describe our philosophy and methods in Part I, present our curriculum design patterns in Part II, discuss extensions to new partnerships in Part III, and summarize our findings as well as look to the future in Part IV.

Part I: Starting Points

In Part I, "Starting Points," we introduce the challenge of inquiry instruction, describe our knowledge integration philosophy, articulate the mechanisms associated with knowledge integration, explain our approach to instruction, and characterize our research methods.

Chapter 1, "Inquiry and Technology," by Linn, Davis, and Bell, describes the learning environments that support inquiry. We designed and tested features for learning environments using findings from cognitive and social research and refined them. These features take advantage of computer and Internet technologies to amplify learning and enhance teacher effectiveness. Although computer technology could compound the problem of teaching science inquiry, research shows that new technologies can support inquiry projects by providing guidance, collaborative supports, real-time display of data, online interactions with experts, analytic tools, visualizations, simulations, and access to information through databases or Web sites. We have incorporated these features into learning environments that enable students to work independently and free teachers to interact more closely with students.

Chapter 2, "The Knowledge Integration Perspective on Learning," by Linn, Eylon, and Davis, looks at knowledge integration through two lenses supported by somewhat distinct research programs. From the science learning lens we identify the interpretive, cultural, and deliberate nature of the learner. From the cognitive process lens we describe the learner as recognizing new ideas, generating connections, and monitoring progress.

Chapter 3, "The Scaffolded Knowledge Integration Framework for Instruction," by Linn, Davis, and Eylon, looks at knowledge integration through the science instruction lens. We draw on diverse research programs to identify the scaffolded knowledge integration framework. We engage the framework around four metaprinciples (Linn & Hsi, 2000): Make science accessible, make thinking visible, help students learn from others, promote autonomy and lifelong learning. These metaprinciples synthesize the main themes in numerous views of instruction. We elaborate the metaprinciples with 14 pragmatic pedagogical principles that define specific research programs. Taken together, these principles give designers a head start in creating inquiry projects in science.

Chapter 4, "Design-Based Research in Education," by Bell, Hoadley, and Linn, introduces design-based research studies as an emerging form of educational inquiry that weds the design and orchestration of complex interventions with empirical research and theorizing about educational phenomena. These methods support investigations in the settings where learning occurs—classrooms, museums, workplaces, homes. The methods capture the complexity of these enactments and inform the revision of curriculum designs. We introduce the *design narrative* as an important genre for describing the intentions, results, conditions, and findings of iterative studies of designed materials in varied settings.

Part II: Curriculum Design Patterns for Knowledge Integration

In Part II we use the notion of design narrative to describe the design and refinement of projects that address four main images of scientific inquiry: critique, debate, design, and experimentation. We summarize the promising activities for each image in curriculum design patterns.

In chapter 5, "Creating Critique Projects," Davis reports on a set of studies that investigate the role of reflection and prompts for reflection in helping students engage in critique activities and knowledge integration. Davis finds that reflection can help students engage in the identification of weaknesses in their own knowledge at the same time as it helps them identify weaknesses in materials they are presented with—thus, reflection plays a role in critique at multiple levels. The work also points to effective patterns for promoting reflection for students with different characteristics. The chapter closes with a discussion of the design principles that emerged from the work and the implications of those design principles for curriculum design patterns.

In chapter 6, "Promoting Students' Argument Construction and Collaborative Debate in the Science Classroom," Bell discusses the role of debate and argumentation in science learning. Bell posits that argumentation and debate represent forms of intellectual activity that can wed an exploration of information to the purposes of science education and to those of the broader democratic society. The chapter presents a narrative account of the designs, lessons, and findings associated with a research program focused on argumentation and collaborative debate involving Internet resources. Design principles and curriculum design patterns for argumentation and collaborative debate are presented that connect the use of particular tools and resources to particular activity structures, classroom norms, and collaborative practices.

In chapter 7 "Fostering Productive Collaboration Offline and Online: Learning From Each Other," Hoadley describes the deliberate evolution of a set of tools and patterns to help students collaborate effectively in a student design project. These studies illustrate ways to embed inquiry in social contexts and create a culture of collaboration. Both software and activities were refined to improve the ways students learned through collaboration. The chapter provides principles and patterns that describe lessons learned from this work.

Chapter 8, "Hands-on Investigation in Internet Environments: Teaching Thermal Equilibrium," Clark analyzes the process of iteratively refining a hands-on laboratory in an Internet environment to make thinking more visible to students. The chapter describes iterative refinement of curriculum design patterns delivered using Internet learning environments that enhance hands-on activities to make the critical ideas and connections more visible. The chapter traces the genesis of visualizations and online discussions as they contribute to experimentation to their roots in the Computer as Learning Partner (CLP) project.

Part III: New Partnerships

In Part III, "New Partnerships," we describe projects that use the curriculum design patterns from Part II to extend the research program. The research, described in Part II, took place in an *ameliorative con-*

text—a classroom in which we had previously worked extensively and that was supportive of our efforts. Typically, innovations developed in ameliorative contexts are next tested in challenging contexts to determine whatever will be robust enough to succeed in a difficult, entrenched, or complicated setting. Our approach is different. While designing and testing instruction in the ameliorative context, we identified specific principles that synthesize empirical tests of the designs as well as curriculum design patterns that represent the essential elements of each inquiry project. In Part III, we test these patterns in challenging contexts and study ways to tailor and customize the instruction to the primary contextual factors in the new environment. As the research reported here suggests, these studies reveal substantial advantages to customizing and tailoring design patterns to each setting rather than assuming that innovations developed in one setting will work in another. Perhaps one of the biggest disadvantages and legitimate complaints about educational research today concerns the limits of its generalizability. As is discussed in the following chapters, our design-based research studies, curriculum design patterns, and specific principles guide the tailoring of understanding.

These chapters address customization and tailoring of inquiry projects to challenging contexts, curriculum frameworks, and varied accountability systems. The chapters expand our focus to issues of professional development, curriculum design, and partnership practices. We show how the knowledge integration perspective can inform all aspects of our endeavor to transform science instruction one inquiry project at a time.

In chapter 9, "The Web-Based Inquiry Science Environment (WISE): Scaffolding Knowledge Integration in the Science Classroom," Slotta describes the WISE learning environment and a professional development model informed by the scaffolded knowledge integration framework. The chapter describes the challenge of extending inquiry learning to a whole school. Every science teacher in a suburban middle school used inquiry projects. A detailed case study compares two seventh grade life science teachers who differ substantially in their interactions with students. The analysis shows that the WISE technology and pedagogy combined with intensive professional development supports this diversity of practice.

In chapter 10, "The Educational Opportunities of Contemporary Controversies in Science," Bell explores the challenge of engaging a community of students, teachers, scientists, and citizens in argumentation about contemporary controversies in the natural sciences. The Science Controversies Online: Partnerships in Education (SCOPE) project extends the curriculum design pattern for debate (Bell, chap.

6) to contemporary scientific controversies. The chapter provides empirical evidence for design principles that develop controversy-focused learning opportunities and foster virtual communities to explore the controversial topics.

In chapter 11, "Synergy Research and Knowledge Integration: Customizing Activities Around Stream Ecology," Baumgartner describes work from the Center for Innovative Learning Technologies Synergy project that explores ways to support the customization of water quality projects in diverse contexts and settings. A team of researchers, scientists, and high school teachers collaborated to transform their existing water quality instruction into a 2-week, technology-rich inquiry unit. This chapter showcases the challenges of using research to inform customization of innovative curriculum by researchers and teachers. Customization, as opposed to dissemination, takes advantage of a knowledge integration framework to create robust, effective innovations.

In chapter 12, "Partnership Models: The Case of the Deformed Frogs," Shear, Bell, and Linn describe a partnership that teamed urban middle school teachers, educational researchers, and natural scientists in a project to codesign, implement, and refine an inquiry project about a current science controversy. The chapter describes a set of structured activities that promoted successful collaboration among students in an urban school with three classes, including a Russian bilingual classroom. The partnership negotiated goals, designs, and classroom activities in support of student learning. The chapter offers a set of guiding principles for design partnerships.

Part IV: Next Steps

In Part IV, "Next Steps," we synthesize our findings and discuss how to create a community of researchers that continuously improves the field. We structure all the design principles introduced in the book. We define new research questions.

In chapter 13, "Specific Design Principles: Elaborating the Scaffolded Knowledge Integration Framework," Linn, Bell, and Davis synthesize the four levels of design principles. *Specific principles* capture the impact of a feature of a learning environment—often relying on the results of a compelling comparison. These are the principles that emerge from studies like those described in Part II. *Pragmatic principles* described in chapter 3 combine similar specific principles into a more general statement and illustrate the idea with multiple features from distinct learning environments as well as empirical findings.

These principles often characterize a research program such as investigation of the role of reflection in knowledge integration or studies of curriculum design patterns for debate projects. *Metaprinciples* capture results from cognitive research in multiple research programs and from studies in laboratory, classroom, and distance learning contexts. These principles resonate with recommendations from many research programs but lack the specificity needed for curriculum design. *General principles* approach the status of laws of science and represent constraints and opportunities that underpin student learning such as limitations on processing capacity. The cognitive processes discussed in chapter 2 fit this category.

In chapter 14, "Closing Thoughts: Internet Environments for Science Education," Linn, Davis, Bell, and Eylon reflect on progress in the field of science education. Transforming science learning one inquiry project at a time requires marshaling all the elements described here—learning environments, knowledge integration perspectives and frameworks, curriculum design patterns, inquiry projects, mentored professional development, design-based research studies, and design principles.

WAYS TO USE THIS BOOK

The results summarized in the principles presented throughout the book depend on findings from multiple educational contexts. Too often claims for what have been called *quick fixes* in education stem, at least in part, from studies showing success in ameliorative contexts. Teachers have rightfully become weary of grandiose claims for innovations because they understand the difficulty of transferring an innovation from one context to another. Rather than assume innovations have an integrity that only requires minor adjustments in new settings, it seems much more fruitful to view educational settings as varied along important dimensions and to focus on taking advantage of those settings by using flexibly adaptive technological innovations and by customizing instruction to the students and teachers. We call on those interested in lifelong science learning to join in this effort.

We designed this book to meet the needs of diverse audiences. We recommend that all readers start with the Introduction and chapter 1. We suggest that those primarily interested in research on inquiry continue with chapters 2, 3, and 4. In contrast, we suggest that those primarily concerned with effective inquiry instruction turn to Part II before reading chapters 2, 3, and 4. All readers, we imagine, will select among the topics in Part III depending on their particular interests.

Those concerned with design of instruction might start with partnership practices in chapter 12, whereas those concerned with professional development might start with the whole school study in chapter 9 and with the customization research in chapter 11. Those interested in the epistemological underpinnings of science might start with chapter 10. All readers, we imagine, will find chapter 14 helpful. We recommend chapter 13 on design principles to designers, researchers, and those interested in methods of research synthesis.

We provide a Web site for those interested in learning more. The site includes, among other things, more detailed information on our learning environments, an annotated bibliography of papers by members of our partnerships, an elaboration of the principles we present in the book, and pointers to the curriculum materials as well as the design principles database.

ACKNOWLEDGMENTS

Our research program, matched to the complexity of the educational enterprise, features a partnership that represents all the forms of expertise relevant to science education reform. Partnerships guide a cohesive, robust research program that captures the complexity of education. Participants support each other's professional development and jointly gather evidence about their designs. Partnerships bring all the stakeholders together to understand the multiple agendas and to develop common norms and criteria for interpreting the performance of programs in complex settings.

One of the core features of this approach is that partnership activities contribute to the knowledge integration of the group. For example, as a group we engage in classroom observations, reviews of software designs, interpretation of student responses to interview questions, collaborative grading of student work, semiannual planning meetings, regular presentations of work in progress, reviews by advisors, discussions with classroom teachers, critical review of practice talks, and feedback on writings.

The partnership described here began in 1994 at the University of California, Berkeley as a partnership of classroom teachers, cognitive scientists, natural scientists, software designers, precollege students, and pedagogy researchers. Since that time, many of our partners have moved on to other locations, but we continue to benefit from our work together. We appreciate the contributions of all the partners including the following:

Postdoctoral scholars: Eric Baumgartner, Doug Clark, Helen Clark, Sherry Hsi, Yael Kali, Eileen Lewis, Jim Slotta, and Michelle Spitulnik.

Middle and high school science teachers: Mimi Bisson, Brenda Davis, Jennifer Gordon, Doug Kirkpatrick, Lawrence Muilenberg, Ramona Muniz, Staci Richards, Judy Smith, Laura Telep, Ronna Voorsanger, and Richard Weinland.

Natural scientists and engineers: Alice Agogino, Julie Froehlig, Igal Galili, Pamela Hines, John Layman, Duncan Parks, Fred Reif, David Samuel, Bob Tinker, David Wake, and Bill Wood.

Pedagogy, technology, and science education researchers: Steve Adams, Flavio Azevedo, Britte Cheng, Doug Clark, Helen Clark, Alex Cuthbert, Brian Foley, Chris Hoadley, Sherry Hsi, Jacquie Madhok, Alan Li, Brian Levey, Kristine Romano, Dawn Rickey, Christina Schwarz, Sherry Seethaler, Linda Shear, Stephanie Sisk-Hilton, Mariko Suzuki, Ricky Tang, Mark Thomas, Lydia Tien, Richard Weinland, Erika Whitney, and Michele Williams.

Software designers: Fred Beshears, Ben Berman, Brian Foley, Jeff Morrow, Greg Pitter, and Judith Stern.

We appreciate insights and comments from project advisors and critical friends including Sasha Barab, Carl Berger, Paul Black, Phyllis Blumenfeld, Jane Bowyer, John Bransford, Sean Brophy, Nick Burbules, Joe Campione, David Chen, Micki Chi, Michael Clancy, John Clement, Allan Collins, Lyn Corno, Andrea diSessa, Danny Edelson, Bat-Sheva Eylon, Barry Fishman, John Frederiksen, John Gilbert, Bob Glaser, Fred Goldberg, Louis Gomez, Rogers Hall, David Hammer, Sherry Hsi, Paul Horowitz, Yasmin Kafai, Joe Krajcik, Alan Lesgold, Cathy Lewis, Shirley Malcom, Ron Marx, Jim Minstrell, Annemarie Palinscar, Roy Pea, Peter Pirolli, Michael Ranney, Mitch Resnick, Bill Rohwer, Brian Reiser, Bill Sandoval, Geoffrey Saxe, Marlene Scardamalia, Alan Schoenfeld, Elliot Soloway, Nancy Songer, Sid Strauss, Iris Tabak, Robert Tinker, John Thomas, Ron Thornton, Susan Williams, Barbara White, and Richard White.

We appreciate the support and encouragement of our program officers at the National Science Foundation including Chris Dede, Eric Hamilton, Eammon Kelley, Michael Martinez, Nora Sabelli, Gerhard Salinger, Larry Suter, Elizabeth VanderPutten, and Lee Zia. This book draws on research supported by the National Science Foundation under the following grants to members of our partnerships:

MDR–9155744 (CLP).
MDR–9453861 (KIE).

REC–9805420 and REC–0128062 (WISE).

REC–0087832 (Synergy Communities: Aggregating Learning about Education).

REC–9873180 (SCOPE).

CDA–9720384 and EIA–0124012 (Center for Integrative Learning Technologies).

EEC–9053807 (SYNTHESIS; Agogino, co-principle investigator [co-PI]).

EHR–9554564 (Science and design; Linn, diSessa, and Ranney, PIs).

EEC–9908328 (Collaborative Learning in Engineering; Hoadley, co-PI).

This monograph also draws on research supported by the Spencer Foundation, including grant Number 200100273 (Hoadley, PI). Additionally, portions of chapters 4 and 7 were previously published in Hoadley (2002). This material was partially prepared while Marcia C. Linn was a Fellow at the Center for Advanced Study in the Behavioral Sciences with financial support provided by the Spencer Foundation. Any opinions, findings, and conclusions or recommendations expressed in this publication are those of the authors and do not necessarily reflect the views of the National Science Foundation, the Spencer Foundation, or other collaborators. We greatly appreciate the support, encouragement, patience, and sage advice of Naomi Silverman, our editor at Lawrence Erlbaum Associates. Thanks to all who helped with collection of data, analysis of data, production of reports, creation of graphics, and development of this book, including David Crowell, Scott Hsu, Kathy Lin, and Lisa Safley. We appreciate the support and encouragement of our families.

I

STARTING POINTS

1

Inquiry and Technology

Marcia C. Linn
University of California, Berkeley

Elizabeth A. Davis
University of Michigan

Philip Bell
University of Washington

We view science learning as ubiquitous, uncertain, sustained, perplexing, commonplace, visual, inviting, technological, intriguing, logical, controversial, contradictory, frustrating, rewarding, and unrelenting. We worry that current courses, high-stakes testing programs, texts filled with terms, standards packed with topics, tedious assignments, cookbook laboratories, and downtrodden teachers turn science into hostile territory—or worse—an intellectual wasteland. We see students unable to find a way into the excitement of science and instead finding numerous paths out of science.

We offer teachers, their students, and whole communities a recipe for transforming science one inquiry project at a time. Realizing the promise of inquiry instruction in science can convert students into lifelong learners—eager to revisit topics studied in science class and willing to learn new topics just in time for the next election, job, or personal decision. We address this challenge by leveraging technology and inquiry, connecting to everyday resources such as Internet sites and news articles, addressing pressing societal problems such as global warming, and coalescing the efforts of the entire enterprise including curriculum designers, natural scientists, computer scientists, cognitive scientists, classroom teachers, administrators, and students.

USING INQUIRY TO PROMOTE SCIENCE, TECHNOLOGY, AND LANGUAGE LITERACY

Converting students to lifelong learning one inquiry project at a time calls for new curriculum and new pedagogy that addresses the needs of today's learners. As noted in the introduction, we define *inquiry* as the intentional process of diagnosing problems, critiquing experiments, distinguishing alternatives, planning investigations, researching conjectures, searching for information, constructing models, debating with peers, and forming coherent arguments. In science inquiry projects, students communicate about scientific topics, evaluate scientific texts, conduct investigations, ask questions about science or technology policies, create designs, and critique arguments, often using technology resources.

We designed four types of inquiry projects and refined curriculum design patterns for each type. Debate projects such as "How Far Does Light Go?" (Bell, chap. 6, this volume) or "What Causes Frog Deformities?" (Shear, Bell, & Linn, chap. 12, this volume) emphasize distinguishing alternatives, searching for information, forming arguments, and debating with peers. Critique projects such as "All the News" (Davis, chap. 5, this volume) emphasize critiquing evidence and claims, researching ideas, and forming arguments. Design projects such as "Houses in the Desert" (Hoadley, chap. 7, this volume) emphasize using scientific evidence to support the principled design of artifacts. Investigation projects such as "Thermal Equilibrium" (D. Clark, chap. 8, this volume) emphasize diagnosing problems, researching conjectures, planning investigations, constructing models, and forming arguments. Ideally, students would perform at least one inquiry project each semester.

Inquiry projects demand new teaching methods and technology offers promising solutions. Supporting 15 small groups engaging in a new practice rather than one larger group following established routines means that teachers need to develop new techniques to keep track of progress and responding to questions. Learning environments can amplify the effectiveness of teachers by handling routine requests as well as offering new representations, models, collaborative activities, complex resources, and learner supports.

Using inquiry to prepare lifelong learners takes attention away from weekly tests and high-stakes assessments and focuses instruction on what everyone needs to know to succeed in their life. This intentional process succeeds when students engage in what we call *knowledge integration*—adding, linking, connecting, sorting out, questioning, and coalescing diverse forms of evidence, arguments, and perspectives to continuously develop a more coherent view. The knowledge integration perspective on learning (see Linn, Eylon, & Davis, chap. 2, this volume) involves cognitive processes like recognizing and adding new ideas, generating connections, and monitoring progress.

Today science, technology, and language literacy go hand in hand to support inquiry. Many contemporary science topics including cloning, nuclear power, global warming, and DNA testing require understanding of how science and technology interact. Furthermore, success rests on communicating about science as well as reading to learn about science—essential aspects of language literacy.

As technology becomes integral to science and society, students need technological literacy or fluency with information technology (Snyder et al., 1999) so that they can take advantage of technological advances in their personal and professional lives. Teaching science as inquiry can enhance science, technology, and language literacy and prepare students to recognize when their science learning applies to a new problem.

Science Literacy

Science literacy today requires an intentional approach to inquiry, including such activities as reconsidering scientific ideas, making sense of persuasive messages, testing conjectures, interpreting data collected using modern technologies, and seeking more and more coherent understanding. Projects connected to relevant issues such as space exploration, environmental stewardship, and wilderness survival can set students on a path toward lifelong learning by providing inquiry opportunities and enhancing connections to topics and materials students may encounter spontaneously.

Technology Literacy

We define *technology literacy* as the ability to use relevant technologies, critique technology-based arguments, and learn new technologies just in time for the next job, course, or activity. Reports on essential aspects of technology literacy (American Association of University Women [AAUW], 2000; diSessa, 2000; Kafai & Resnick, 1996; Snyder et al., 1999) call for infusing technology projects across the curriculum. Following the National Academy of Sciences report on fluency with information technology (Snyder et al., 1999), our projects target three complementary aspects of technology fluency—capabilities, skills, and concepts. First, students become capable of using technology in complex, sustained problem solving, identifying unanticipated consequences, searching for relevant information, communicating, collaborating, and critiquing. Second, students learn contemporary skills such as using e-mail, searching the Internet, word processing, and computing with spreadsheets. They are prepared to learn the next generation of skills to succeed in future courses and the workplace. Third, students continuously refine their understanding of concepts of technology such as modeling, simulation, intellectual property, and algorithms.

Language Literacy

Language literacy for science is defined as critical reading of science material, effective communication about science issues, and clear writing about science topics (Heath, 1983). Language literacy is essential for lifelong science learning and includes the construction and interpretation of syntactically correct and semantically coherent explanations and arguments that are used in communication about science topics and projects. Teachers often observe that students need to read more critically and write more cogently in science than they do in many other courses—often including English. To respond to rapid increases in science knowledge, frequent job changes, and consequential policy debates, citizens must constantly interpret science texts as well as critique and evaluate contradictory or persuasive messages.

Leveraging technology to promote inquiry learning raises researchable questions and invites experimentation to try new ideas and trash unsuccessful solutions. Technology is a moving target, continuously offering new opportunities.

INQUIRY AND SCIENCE STANDARDS

Most standards (American Association for the Advancement of Science, 1993; AAUW, 2000; National Research Council, 1996; Snyder et al., 1999) mandate teaching science and technology as inquiry, yet 90% of courses use other methods (Alberts, 2001; Becker, 1999). Why is inquiry neglected? In many American states curriculum frameworks mandate over 50 topics such as genetics, the rock cycle, or electricity per year, leaving no time for inquiry (Schmidt, Mc-Knight, et al., 2001).

High-stakes tests featuring multiple-choice questions send the wrong message about inquiry. These tests tempt textbook authors and teachers to provide information at the same grain size and level of connection as found on the test. Administrators and parents may reinforce these decisions, worrying that college admissions or advanced placement tests require extensive factual knowledge of numerous topics and rarely assess inquiry. These forces oppose research-based innovations and push the complex educational system back toward the status quo.

Even advocates of inquiry note that unless curriculum, professional development, and high-stakes tests are aligned, few will implement inquiry. In addition, policymakers need better understanding of the benefits of technology-leveraged science instruction so they can distinguish among competing solutions and shape educational programs. We offer some evidence for the value of technology in this volume.

Advocates of inquiry also emphasize that students cannot possibly learn all the science they will need in their lives and therefore must learn how to make sense of new topics just in time for new jobs, personal health decisions, or science policy decisions. This view resonates with research evidence showing that students who engage in science inquiry projects are more successful in subsequent courses and projects (Linn & Hsi, 2000). Research shows that devoting time to inquiry does not diminish performance on high-stakes tests (Cobb & Bowers, 1999; Shymansky & Kyle, 1992; Walker & Schaffarzik, 1974).

Technology offers a flexible and customizable opportunity to transform science instruction with inquiry projects that improve science, technology, and language literacy. Designers can provide teachers with an opportunity to create personalized and customized instruction, to study the impact of these changes, and to store customized units for future use. Learning environments can provide windows on knowledge integration in the making (Barab & Luehmann, 2003; Blumenfeld et al., 2000; Krajcik, Blumenfeld, Marx, & Soloway, 1994; Songer, Lee, et al., 2003; Squire, MaKinster, et al., 2003).

Curriculum materials that take advantage of new technologies can use these same technologies for innovative assessments. Embedded assessments can record the sequence of student activities, capture student thinking at crucial points in the learning process, track performance of complex tasks such as solutions to algebra problems (Anderson, 1983; Anderson, Corbett, et al., 1995), and keep a record of how teachers communicate electronically with their students. These artifacts of complex student work are accessible to students as indicators of strengths and weaknesses, to teachers as checks on the adequacy of instruction, and to evaluators as evidence about the effectiveness of innovations.

DESIGNING INSTRUCTION FOR INQUIRY

Technology-enhanced curriculum materials can include flexibly adaptive features that allow instructors to customize materials in ways not supported by traditional curriculum materials such as textbooks. Using Internet-based learning environments, for example, teachers can reformulate instruction to connect to prior units, incorporate current events, and target local geological features, weather patterns, or bodies of water. New technologies such as simulations, Internet resources, real-time data collection, or modeling environments offer designers new opportunities to create materials that are responsive to the needs of society, teachers, and students. Designers can create materials that meet needs of diverse learners and disparate assessment programs.

Designers and teachers using technology-enhanced learning environments can carry out a program of continuous improvement. Designers can test their innovations with users and refine the innovation based on failures, misunderstandings, or missed opportunities. Once an innovation is reasonably stable, teachers can test it in their schools and classrooms and modify the innovation by customizing it to their own needs. In reformulating an innovation, for example, teachers might modify the order of activities, add online discussions, change writing assignments, tailor to students' own locale, or connect the project more closely to their curriculum.

These opportunities come with responsibilities. They require new partnerships of designers, educational researchers, policymakers, and classroom teachers to work closely together. Creating effective learning environments that permit teachers to make appropriate customizations demands careful testing with a broad range of user groups.

Instruction featuring technology and inquiry calls for new forms of professional development programs to help teachers take advantage of new features, develop skill in customizing materials, and provide feedback to designers so that the innovation achieves its full potential. Technology can contribute to effective professional development by supporting a community of geographically distributed teachers, providing tools that allow teachers to show their customizations to peers, and enabling participants to serve as critical friends who discuss challenges and problems.

INQUIRY, TECHNOLOGY, AND EQUITY

Virtually every aspect of education faces equity challenges. The population of students and their teachers has become substantially more diverse. Today in California, no single cultural group predominates, and in many schools fewer than one in five students goes home at night to speak English (see http://www.cde.ca.gov/demographics). Students bring a far broader range of cultural backgrounds and experiences to classrooms today, and by and large, our curriculum and professional development programs fail to take advantage of this cultural diversity.

Access to technology has advanced substantially over the past 20 years but remains unevenly distributed. Initially, few individuals had home access to technology and schools tended to offer very limited technological opportunities for their students. Today schools still provide very limited access to technology, but out-of-school technology access has increased dramatically and may reach saturation in the next 20 years.

When we started our research program, a small number of schools were experimenting with computer technology, mainly funded by grants. The first grants were often Apple II® computers or IBM PCs with external disk drives and the capability of running the BASIC programming language. Schools enthusiastically embraced these technologies, and given the alternatives, began by attempting to include programming courses in the curriculum. Most schools using these technologies made the assumption that programming instruction enhanced inquiry by improving general critical thinking ability (Papert, 1993).

Our early work and that of others showed that in most precollege computer programming classes students worked in groups of two to four on these computers in classes that met for 45 min a day, often for only one semester to ensure that all the students had a chance to use the technology. This meant that if a group of four worked for five 45-min periods per week, each individual student averaged less than 1 hr per week controlling the technology. In a course that typically lasted for 14 weeks, an individual student would have at most 14 hr of experience with technology. To the surprise of no one, these programs had little impact on students' understanding or use of technology, and they stimulated a huge equity issue because students who had out-of-school or home access to technology could gain greater experience with the machine on a single weekend (Linn, 1985).

Our early research revealed enormous discrepancies between students with home and school access to computers, especially because home users typically had expert parents to guide their interactions (e.g., Mandinach & Linn, 1987). Furthermore, early courses designed to teach about technology or engage students in using technology suffered from limited understanding of the best way to use these technologies to enhance student learning and understanding. Nevertheless, schools and universities often collaborated to experiment with alternative approaches to programming instruction (Linn, 1985; Linn & Dalbey, 1985; Mandinach & Linn, 1987; Pea & Kurland, 1987; Sloane & Linn, 1988).

These studies reached two main conclusions. First, pedagogy for teaching with technology needed substantial improvement. Supporting students as they worked in small groups on computers demanded new approaches. New techniques for class instruction, such as guiding groups of students through activities, were needed. Many humorous events arose, including situations in which each student typed the same information at the same time, crashing the local server. Teachers sought effective pedagogical strategies to take advantage of the considerable power of technology. Developing skill in monitoring small groups and tutoring individuals as needed required experimentation.

A second major finding from these studies concerns the discipline specificity of inquiry strategies. Students who learned to program in BASIC struggled to apply their knowledge to other programming languages. Reflection on these findings revealed that techniques such as generating and comparing alternatives were highly specific to the discipline and not readily transferred from one discipline to another. Generating alternative ways to solve a programming problem, for example, involves fairly deep understanding of the strengths and limitations of the language used for solving the problem. Solutions that depend on list processing, for example, are cumbersome and difficult to implement in Pascal but much easier in Scheme. Eventually, criteria for good programming solutions emerged, including such factors as self-documenting code, ease of reuse, or modularity, that could generalize to new programming languages. Applying problem-solving approaches from programming to other scientific endeavors such as biology raises new issues. Criteria important in programming were not readily applicable to, for example, the design of an investigation of fruit fly genetics. Inequitable access to technology combined with unrealistic expectations about its benefits led to frustration, confusion, and often a backlash against technology.

Two groups lag in technology access today. First, older individuals who failed to gain experience with technology in the past have difficulty both learning to use technology and gaining access to it. Nevertheless, the largest growing segment of technology users today are older Americans. Second, individuals at or near the poverty line have considerably less access to technology than their more affluent peers.

Because most technology uses require substantial amounts of access, ultimately personal computing tools will be essential to ensure that all citizens achieve technology literacy. Educational institutions have a special obligation to provide access to technology for the least economically advantaged segments of our population. To fully meet this challenge, schools must offer students more than a computer laboratory that can be visited once a day or once a week. Teachers and students need to be able to use technology both frequently and regularly, and it must be integrated into teaching and learning in every discipline. As libraries, community centers, faith communities, senior centers, and other institutions increase access to technology, we can begin to meet this considerable need and obligation.

USING INQUIRY TO TAKE ADVANTAGE OF TECHNOLOGY

Responding to the mandate for inquiry teaching and the potential of lifelong learning, our research partnership has followed a process of iterative refinement to leverage technology to improve science learning one inquiry project at a time. We have continuously reformulated not only the innovations designed for science education but the titles of the research programs creating these innovations to introduce inquiry into science instruction.

Our first effort in the 1980s to incorporate inquiry and technology into science education—the Computer as Laboratory Partner—involved the use of real-time data collection programs to improve science laboratory investigations. We researched the role of temperature-sensitive probes connected to Apple II computers in science laboratories. We soon documented considerable intellectual benefits for this technology (Linn & Songer, 1991) and proposed a new project called the Computer as Learning Partner (CLP). This semantic change reflects a deeper philosophical change because our work had begun to suggest that the technology could do more than record laboratory data from science inquiry; it could also support students as they learned complex scientific concepts such as the difference between heat and temperature (Linn & Hsi, 2000).

The CLP research revealed detailed information about how students respond to new software, often captured by the technology itself, when students made predictions and responded to experimental results. These studies underscored the multiple ideas students bring to science class and the struggles they have reconciling the many views of a complex topic like thermodynamics. Students had ideas about why objects felt warmer or colder than each other at room temperature while at the same time they suspected that objects might approach, or even reach, the same temperature as their surroundings. We synthesized this process of holding multiple ideas, sorting them out, and returning to them later as the *knowledge integration perspective* on learning (see Linn et al., chap. 2, this volume).

Our work revealed that some instructional activities worked better than others in promoting knowledge integration. We synthesized our ideas about instructional design in a set of design principles called the *scaffolded knowledge integration* framework (see Linn, Davis, & Eylon, chap. 3, this volume). This framework captures the crucial interactions of curriculum, technology, and classroom activity needed to support students' efforts to make sense of new and established ideas.

With the advent of the Internet, our partnership sought to take advantage of growing understanding of learning and rapid advances in technology. We proposed what we called the *Knowledge Integration Environment* (KIE) employing the first Internet platform called *Mosaic*. The KIE project, using Netscape® by the time funding arrived, developed a learning environment and tested it in a series of iterative refinement studies reported in Part II of this book. We define a *learning environment* as the combination of curriculum, technology supports, and classroom activity structures orchestrated jointly by a teacher and a computer-delivered program.

Increased attention to the potential benefits of the Internet led to the Web-based Integrated Science Environment (WISE), a program that focused on bringing together the broad range of disciplines represented on the World Wide Web and taking advantage of the learning environment features from KIE. Study of students learning integrated science underscored the centrality of inquiry and the benefit of a learning environment for authoring new inquiry projects. These studies illuminated the strength of technology to support inquiry and led in multiple directions as reported in Part III of this book.

We proposed the Web-based Inquiry Science Environment (still WISE) to research inquiry projects and professional developments (see Slotta, chap. 9, this volume). At the same time we emphasized the epistemological basis for inquiry and the importance of science controversy in inquiry instruction. The Science Controversies Online: Partnerships in Education (SCOPE) project expanded our efforts to support contemporary scientific controversies both in inquiry projects and at a Web site bringing together all the constituencies represented in our partnership, including discipline experts, policymakers, classroom teachers, and instructional designers (see Bell, chap. 10, this volume).

To explore the process of knowledge integration among classroom teachers using inquiry projects, we initiated a new project called *Synergy Communities: Aggregating Learning about Education* (SCALE). SCALE seeks to support teachers as they engage in continuous improvement of their instruction. SCALE studies the design of science inquiry projects that bend but do not break (see Baumgartner, chap. 11, this volume), taking advantage of learning environments that support flexibly adaptive designs, technology features that support customization, and professional development programs to help teachers customize innovations to the systemic complexities of their own settings.

CLP

The CLP project began with Apple II computers in 1980 and pioneered a partnership model of research (Linn, 1987; Linn & Hsi, 2000; Shear et al., chap. 12, this volume). The research team consisted of a partnership of technologists, classroom teachers, educational researchers, discipline specialists, and policy analysts guiding investigations of how technology could enhance the science curriculum using successive versions of Apple technology and varied software in a semester-long course about energy.

The CLP partnership developed and tested eight versions of the course. The first version of the CLP curriculum resulted in a mere 12% of students achieving the most sophisticated understanding of the difference between heat and temperature. Eight versions later, a 400% increase in success was recorded. About half the students achieved the most sophisticated understanding of heat and temperature. At the same time, virtually every student gained substantial understanding of the difference between insulators and conductors, the nature of thermal equilibrium, and the direction of heat flow. The project included a longitudinal study that provided a unique corpus of information about how lifelong science learning proceeds. This study demonstrated substantial benefits for the semester-long coverage of energy and documented the long-term implications of this curriculum on students (D. Clark, 2000; Linn & Hsi, 2000; Linn & Muilenburg, 1996).

This research program led to a set of design principles to guide through designing inquiry instruction (see Linn et al., chap. 3, and

Bell, Hoadley, & Linn, chap. 4, this volume). The principles are organized under four tenets or metaprinciples: (a) make science accessible, (b) make thinking visible, (c) help students learn from others, and (d) promote autonomy and lifelong learning. The CLP partnership abstracted these principles from the iterative refinement process and added pragmatic pedagogical principles in a book titled *Computers, Teachers, Peers: Science Learning Partners* (Linn & Hsi, 2000). We build on these principles in this book by adding specific principles that emerge from new research studies. We connect the principles from past work with these new, specific principles (see Linn, Bell, & Davis, chap. 13, this volume).

The first metaprinciple calls for *making science accessible*. CLP pioneered the process of seeking an appropriate level of analysis for the scientific content so that students can restructure, rethink, compare, critique, and develop more cohesive ideas. For thermodynamics, we researched models at various levels of abstraction and ultimately settled on a heat-flow model rather than a molecular-kinetic model because it did a better job of connecting to students' knowledge about heat and temperature (Linn & Muilenburg, 1996; Linn & Songer, 1993). This principle also leads to making the inquiry process visible in a checklist first introduced in CLP (see Fig. 1.1).

The second metaprinciple underscores the benefits of *making thinking visible*. Inquiry instruction can make scientific ideas and arguments visible using animations when teachers offer compelling explanations as well as when students write answers to complex science concepts. CLP started by designing visualizations to illustrate complex science concepts such as heat flow (Foley, 1999; Lewis, 1996). CLP also used prompts and notes to motivate students to make their thinking visible.

The third metaprinciple advocates *helping students learn from others*. Inquiry instruction can motivate students to collaborate, discuss ideas, and debate consequential science questions such as the causes of the declining population of amphibians in North America. These discussions enable students to make their own thinking more visible and also provide explanations that more readily connect to the ideas of students. Student explanations succeed because they use vocabulary that students understand and because peer accounts of scientific ideas may be easier for students to connect to their own thinking (A. L. Brown & Campione, 1994; Hoadley, 1999; Hsi, 1997).

The fourth metaprinciple emphasizes the value of *promoting autonomy and lifelong learning*. To become lifelong learners students need investigatory skills that they can use throughout their lives. CLP guides students to make predictions, test their predictions online, compare

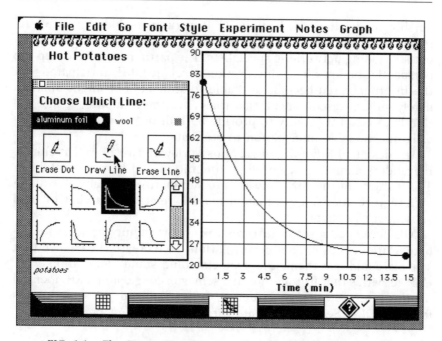

FIG. 1.1. The Computer as Learning Partner interface and features.

graphs of their predictions and the outcome, and reconcile their ideas with the outcome. To promote autonomy, inquiry instruction can also help students reflect on their progress and learn to critique their own ideas and those of others (Davis, chap. 5, this volume; 2003).

The scaffolded knowledge integration framework and principles that emerged from the design of the CLP curriculum were used to create KIE. These principles jointly lead to the design of inquiry projects that enable students to compare and contrast the various ideas that they have about a scientific phenomenon as well as new ideas that might be introduced when the instruction makes them visible. Such instruction helps students engage in the process of reconceptualizing ideas, an activity that leads to lifelong learning. Following the principles, designers provide curricular supports, social supports, and technological supports to ensure that the curriculum is maximally successful in promoting knowledge integration.

KIE AND BEYOND

When the partnership created the KIE, the National Science Foundation proposal called for converting Internet resources into knowledge integration partners for science learning. KIE reformulated the part-

nership model first used in the CLP work to include cognitive researchers, pre-college teachers, computer scientists, and natural scientists, adding networking specialists. The partnership elaborated the
perspective on knowledge integration in science. KIE anticipated that
the Internet would become available to students but might unfortunately serve to discourage, rather than encourage, knowledge integration because of its ability to provide both disorganized and scientifically questionable information to students.

The design of KIE built on previous work with CLP as well as emerging understanding of knowledge integration and how to scaffold it.
The features of the KIE software are summarized in Table 1.1 along
with their relationships to metaprinciples, related research, CLP, and
subsequent projects.

KIE developed a set of features to support inquiry projects for debate, critique, design, and investigation. To increase the chance that
schools could use them, the projects could stand alone, unlike the
CLP activities that fit together in a semester-long course. KIE focused
on the interpretation of evidence rather than on the experiments
found in CLP. See the Web site for a list of current projects.

KIE TOOLS PALETTE: GETTING HELP
WITH COMPLEX TASKS

KIE built on the successes of the CLP software by incorporating guidance (or scaffolding) for students as they worked on projects. The CLP
software, for example, used a simple checklist to help students manage their work. The checklist, combined with its associated guidance
that helped students know how to accomplish the tasks it listed, allowed the teacher to spend more time interacting productively with
students. The teacher spent considerably less time answering queries
such as "What do we do next?" or "How do we do this?" and more time
discussing science concepts with students.

KIE provided a tools palette that built on understanding of the
guidance students need when engaging in complex work (Bell & Davis, 2000). This palette appeared for all projects and always remained
on the screen (see left side of Fig. 1.2). The "Checklist" lists the activities that students need to do to complete the project. The students' current activity is highlighted. A "Details" button provides access to detailed information about precisely how to use the software
to complete the activity; the Details button also provides informa-

TABLE 1.1

KIE's Features and Their Relations to the Literature, CLP, WISE, and SCOPE

KIE Feature	Metaprinciple and Relevant Research	Antecedents from CLP	Descendants in WISE and SCOPE
KIE tools palette and checklist	Make science accessible ThinkerTools inquiry cycle (White & Frederiksen, 1998) Scientists in Action	Checklist	Process map Inquiry map
Mildred hints and prompts (Fig. 1.3)	Promote autonomy and lifelong learning CSILE prompts (Scardamalia & Bereiter, 1991b)	Prompts Predictions, principle construction, prototype explanations, conclusions	Varied forms of hints Varied forms of prompts
NetBook	Promote autonomy, and lifelong learning Storage of student work in collaborative notebooks or portfolios (CoVis; Edelson, 1999)	Automatic file storage and retrieval	Student project work stored and available for display in a portfolio
Evidence database (Fig. 1.4)	Make thinking visible Students access public Web pages	Pragmatic scientific principles and prototypes Evidence front pages pointing to evidence in the database	Web pages constructed by students, scientists for SCOPE, and whole classes
Evidence annotations (Fig. 1.4)	Make thinking visible Partnership adds annotations or elaborations by varied individuals.		Student, teacher, and researcher annotations of evidence
SenseMaker (Fig. 1.5)	Make thinking visible (Hickey & Zuiker, 2003; Kuhn, 1970; Lesgold, Lajoie, et al. 1992).	Worksheets to organize arguments	SenseMaker continues to evolve and is used in WISE, SCOPE, and so forth
SpeakEasy (Figs. 1.6, 1.7, 1.8)	Help students learn from others CSILE (Scardamalia & Bereiter, 1991a) CaMILE (Guzdial & Turns, 2000)	Multimedia Forum Kiosk (Hsi, 1997)	COOL system WISE forum
KIE inquiry projects	Promote autonomy and lifelong learning Case studies (Kolodner, 1993; Linn & Clancy, 1992)	CLP projects	WISE, SCOPE projects

Note. KIE = Knowledge Integration Environment; CLP = Computer as Learning Partner; WISE = Web-based Inquiry Science Environment; SCOPE = Science Controversies Online Partnerships for Education; CSILE = Computer Supported Intentional Learning Environments; COOL = Collaborative Opportunities for Online Learning.

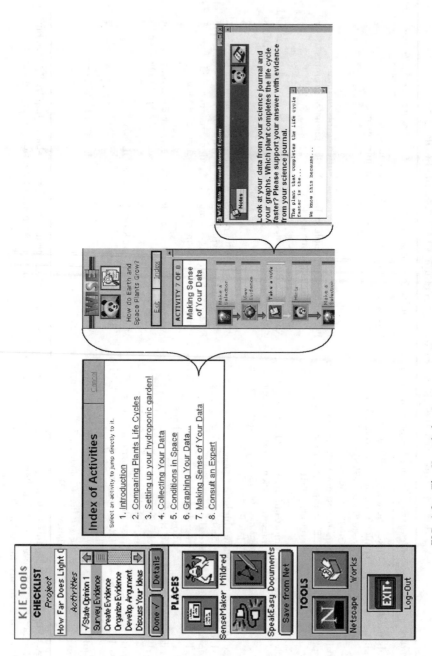

FIG. 1.2. The Knowledge Integration Environment (KIE) and Web-based Inquiry Science Environment (WISE) tool palette and inquiry map.

18

tion on why students are working on a particular task. Students use the "Done" button to check off a completed activity.

Most of the activities listed in the checklist require the use of the software tools available in KIE. The second area of the tools palette window then provides buttons to access the KIE custom-made software (Mildred, SenseMaker, SpeakEasy, and Documents) as well as a feature that allows them to save information on Web sites they want to remember. The third area contains buttons that open the commercial applications that KIE uses (Netscape®, ClarisWorks), and the fourth logs out of KIE. This interface proved confusing and cumbersome.

WISE streamlines and improves the KIE model of providing help and guidance. WISE provides a single inquiry map that captures the nonlinear, iterative nature of scientific inquiry (see right side of Fig. 1.2). The map represents the inquiry process and thus meets the scaffolded knowledge integration metaprinciple of making thinking visible. By incorporating tools, guidance, and hints into a single set of steps, WISE makes navigation far easier.

MILDRED: GETTING COGNITIVE GUIDANCE AND SUPPORT

KIE provides guidance about how to do things as well as information about what to do next. KIE tailors the guidance to the different projects and activities students engage in, the evidence they investigate, the claims they develop and consider. Mildred (the bovine science guide) provides guidance about how to do science in KIE (see Fig. 1.3). In Mildred, students can request hints and take notes (including rating aspects of the evidence). Using *guidance on demand*, students can ask for hints about the current activity, a particular piece of evidence, or a scientific claim relevant to the topic. Mildred also suggests relevant issues for each activity, piece of evidence, or claim. Finally, Mildred also prompts students to reflect on their learning. The Mildred software promotes autonomy by encouraging students to choose when they need what kind of guidance. Mildred also aims to make both experts' and students' thinking visible. We found that Mildred's guidance influenced student knowledge integration (Davis, chap. 5, this volume; Davis & Bell, 2001). Mildred could help learners but required considerable effort on the part of students.

In WISE, Mildred the Cow morphed into Amanda the Panda. Amanda continued to provide the hints for which Mildred had become known. Prompts, explanations, and other Mildred functions were

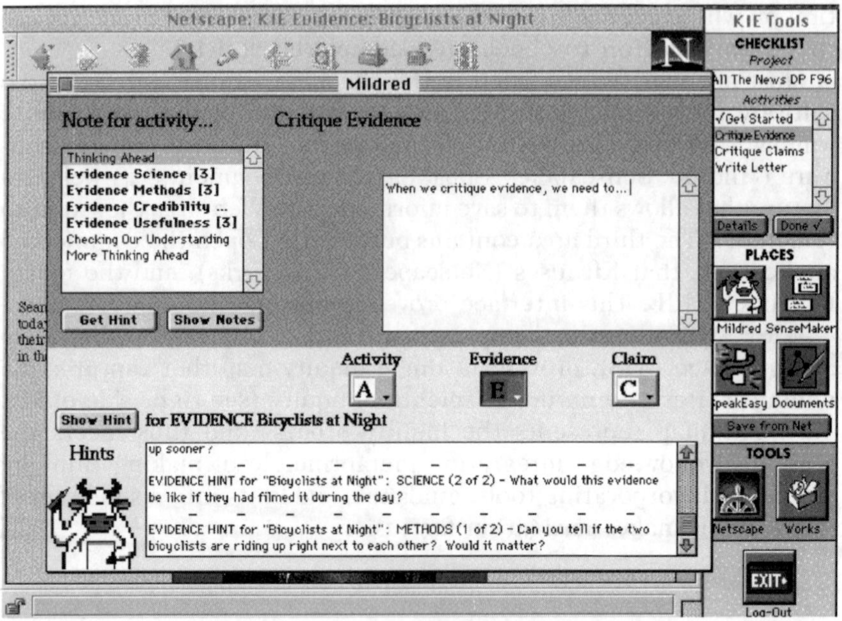

FIG. 1.3.   Mildred, the bovine guide to the Knowledge Integration Environment (KIE).

transferred to the inquiry map to better represent the distinction between the inquiry process and the advantages of help seeking (see Fig. 1.2). WISE simplified and streamlined this function.

STUDENT DOCUMENT NETBOOK

In CLP, students stored their work electronically on their computer. The software automatically generated a laboratory report containing all the work students had done, including their predictions, experimental results, and conclusions. We found that this automatic generation reduced the amount of time students had to spend on nonproductive tasks like organizing and neatening their papers; therefore, they had more time to spend on the important cognitive work of scientific inquiry. We built on this design idea in creating the KIE NetBook.

In some KIE activities, students open and edit specific documents using the Documents window in the NetBook (Bell et al., 1995). Double clicking opens the document in the appropriate application. The NetBook keeps track of work, helps make students' thinking visible, helps students become autonomous learners, and encourages students to become cumulative learners. Even with these features, students had difficulty keeping track of their work.

In WISE, all student work is stored on a remote server. Students can revise their work by going to the step in the inquiry map where they did the work originally. They can use the "show all work" feature to view their whole project or to make their work visible to other students.

KIE EVIDENCE DATABASE: EXPLORING COLLECTIONS OF SCIENTIFIC EVIDENCE

The KIE project exploits the Internet to provide rich, varied scientific evidence in a departure from CLP, which was mainly laboratory-based (Bell et al., 1995). KIE Evidence was designed by teachers, KIE developers, students, and others to add provoking and controversial ideas. Evidence pages generally provide an advance organizer, directing students to central parts of a Web site created by some other group or individual, and connected to the Mildred software for hints on the topic (see Fig. 1.4). The evidence was designed to make sci-

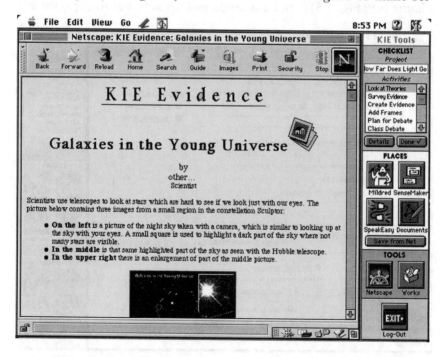

FIG. 1.4. Knowledge Integration Environment (KIE) evidence page organizing a Web page about the Hubble telescope and connecting to the tool palette.

ence accessible to students. Additionally, specific guidance (provided through Mildred) helps students interpret each piece of evidence. Often Mildred made more sophisticated thinking about the evidence visible to the students.

In WISE, the emphasis on evidence continued. WISE added more integrated links between inquiry and evidence. In chapter 6, Bell (this volume) describes intermediate versions of these connections (see Figs. 6.6 and 6.7). Eventually, to complement KIE's use of evidence with CLP's emphasis on experimental work, WISE added a fourth type of project—encouraging students to combine evidence from the Internet with investigations (see Clark, chap. 8, this volume).

SENSEMAKER: MAKING SENSE OF EVIDENCE AND CLAIMS

To support argument construction using the KIE evidence database, the KIE SenseMaker helped students make sense of evidence and claims (see Fig. 1.5). Students could use SenseMaker to organize evi-

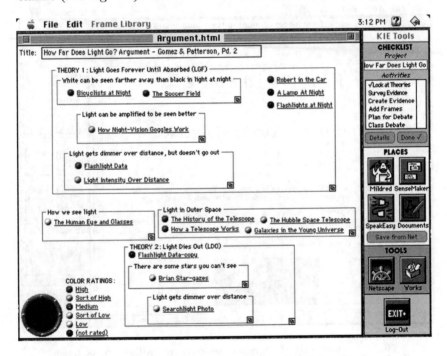

FIG. 1.5.   Knowledge Integration Environment (KIE) SenseMaker software for argument construction.

dence into categories (e.g., for different theories, stages of planning, or design features) and to formulate arguments. Students click and drag to move evidence dots into category boxes (called *frames*). They could create new frames themselves. From SenseMaker they could also jump directly to Evidence pages and take notes in Mildred. Finally, they could add evidence they created or found to their representation.

Students constructed SenseMaker artifacts to organize their arguments for a debate project or their resources for a design project. WISE found that SenseMaker helped students understand and use the diverse range of information found on the Web (Bell, 1997). SenseMaker made student thinking visible in a way that textual arguments could not (see Bell, chap. 6, this volume, Figs. 6.3, 6.4, and 6.5).

WISE continued to use SenseMaker as an argument-building tool and to refine the software as we gained more and more understanding of students' scientific argumentation (see Fig. 10.5 in Bell, chap. 10, this volume; 1997). SenseMaker supports students and scientists in learning about scientific controversies in the SCOPE project (see Bell, chap. 10, this volume).

SPEAKEASY DISCUSSION TOOL: ENGAGING IN SCIENCE CONVERSATIONS

In the later years of the CLP project, the Multimedia Forum Kiosk provided a first step toward having students engage in online discussions (see Fig. 1.6; Hsi & Hoadley, 1997). The *kiosk*, as it was called, was a stand-alone machine hosting discussions of science topics relevant to current investigations. These discussions became a critical complement to the face-to-face, in-class discussions. Most students participated in the kiosk compared to fewer than 15% in a face-to-face class discussion (Hsi, 1997). In addition, the kiosk motivated more coherent arguments and made student thinking visible to teachers. The kiosk visually represented students' discussions as discussion trees, using their pictures (or other icons) to identify their comments.

As part of KIE, students started exchanging their scientific ideas using SpeakEasy, a Web-based structured discussion tool (see Fig. 1.7; and see Hoadley, chap. 7, this volume). Students used SpeakEasy to communicate with other students (in the same class or other classes around the world) about science topics relevant to their projects (see Hoadley, chap. 7, this volume). SpeakEasy built on the work with the kiosk and made science more accessible by personalizing ideas in so-

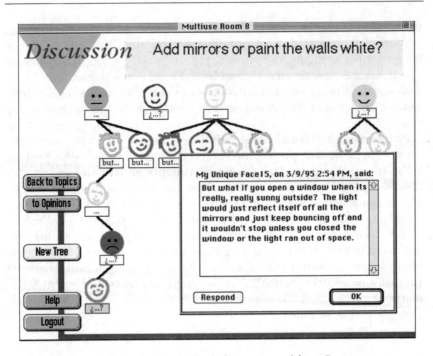

FIG. 1.6.   Multimedia Forum Kiosk discussion tool from Computer as
Learning Partner.

cially relevant representations. These social supports in SpeakEasy
made the thinking of peers and experts visible and helped students
better integrate their knowledge (Hoadley, 1999; Hoadley & Linn,
2000).

WISE has tested and refined several versions of online discussions.
The Collaborative Opportunities for Online Learning (COOL) System
incorporated many of SpeakEasy's features and was designed to explicitly promote collaboration online (see Fig. 1.8). The WISE discussion
tool refines COOL and directly connects to the inquiry map (see
Slotta, chap. 9, this volume).

CONCLUSIONS

In this chapter and in this book, we describe a program of research to
improve science instruction inquiry project by inquiry project. We
draw on research exploring how technology can contribute to education, reporting on an iterative process that has revealed many unin-

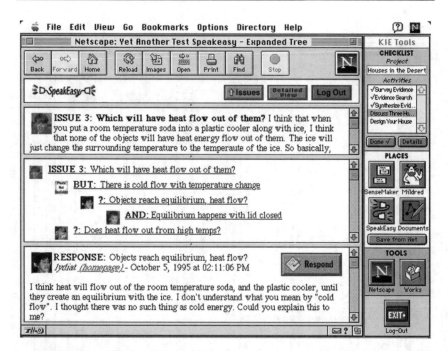

FIG. 1.7. The SpeakEasy asynchronous discussion tool used in Knowledge Integration Environment (KIE).

tended and unanticipated consequences of efforts to utilize technology in education. We seek a continuously improving enterprise to harvest the tremendous benefits that technology can offer while at the same time dealing with the pitfalls and problems that technology produces. We are beginning to synthesize the activity structures of our projects in curriculum design patterns (Linn, Clark, et al., 2003).

The evaluation of our software from CLP to KIE to WISE takes advantage of changing technologies along with improved models of learning. Whereas Apple II computers lacked support for labeling of axes in graphs, today's software can provide individualized feedback and tomorrow's software will take voice input and suggest neglected evidence. We expect to continue to try new approaches and to encounter pitfalls as well as failures.

When we started we wondered how to deal with clear evidence that students held multiple conflicting ideas about every science topic. Today we have numerous strategies to help students take advantage of their diverse views. We have begun to recognize how to design evidence so that students generate more sophisticated and cohesive

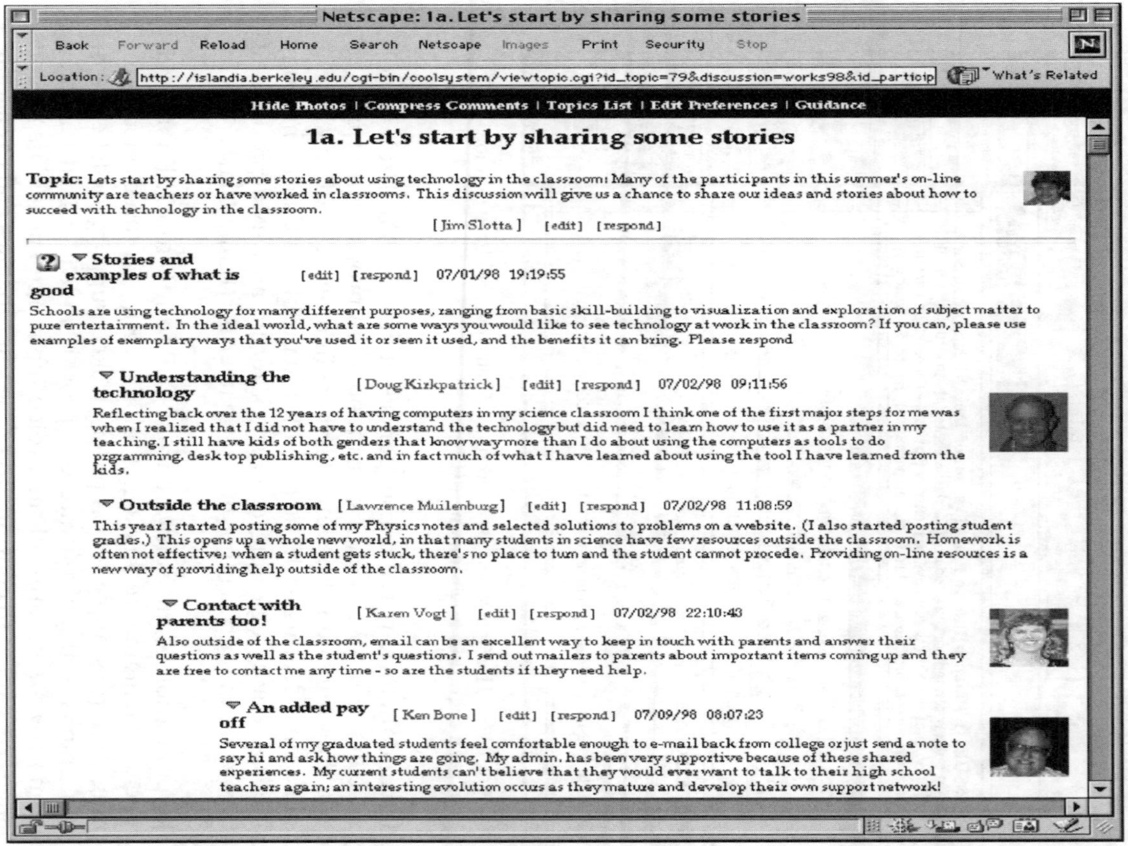

Back Forward Reload Home Search Netscape Images Print Security Stop

Location: http://islandia.berkeley.edu/cgi-bin/coolsystem/viewtopic.cgi?id_topic=79&discussion=work398&id_particip   What's Related

Hide Photos | Compress Comments | Netscape | Topics List | Edit Preferences | Guidance

1a. Let's start by sharing some stories

Topic: Lets start by sharing some stories about using technology in the classroom. Many of the participants in this summer's on-line community are teachers or have worked in classrooms. This discussion will give us a chance to share our ideas and stories about how to succeed with technology in the classroom.

[Jim Slotta]   [edit] [respond]

Stories and examples of what is good   [edit] [respond] 07/01/98 19:19:55

Schools are using technology for many different purposes, ranging from basic skill-building to visualization and exploration of subject matter to pure entertainment. In the ideal world, what are some ways you would like to see technology at work in the classroom? If you can, please use examples of exemplary ways that you've used it or seen it used, and the benefits it can bring. Please respond

Understanding the technology   [Doug Kirkpatrick]   [edit] [respond] 07/02/98 09:11:56

Reflecting back over the 12 years of having computers in my science classroom I think one of the first major steps for me was when I realized that I did not have to understand the technology but did need to learn how to use it as a partner in my teaching. I still have kids of both genders that know way more than I do about using the computers as tools to do programming, desktop publishing, etc. and in fact much of what I have learned about using the tool I have learned from the kids.

Outside the classroom   [Lawrence Muilenburg]   [edit] [respond] 07/02/98 11:08:59

This year I started posting some of my Physics notes and selected solutions to problems on a website. (I also started posting student grades.) This opens up a whole new world, in that many students in science have few resources outside the classroom. Homework is often not effective; when a student gets stuck, there's no place to turn and the student cannot procede. Providing on-line resources is a new way of providing help outside of the classroom.

Contact with parents too!   [Karen Vogt]   [edit] [respond] 07/02/98 22:10:43

Also outside of the classroom, email can be an excellent way to keep in touch with parents and answer their questions as well as the student's questions. I send out mailers to parents about important items coming up and they are free to contact me any time - so are the students if they need help.

An added pay off   [Ken Bone]   [edit] [respond] 07/09/98 08:07:23

Several of my graduated students feel comfortable enough to e-mail back from college or just send a note to say hi and ask how things are going. My admin. has been very supportive because of these shared experiences. My current students can't believe that they would ever want to talk to their high school teachers again; an interesting evolution occurs as they mature and develop their own support network!

FIG. 1.8. The Collaborative Online Opportunities for Learning system used in Web-based Inquiry Science Environment.

views. We are crafting guidelines and principles to help designers and teachers create more efficient instruction that enables more and more students to become lifelong learners.

In the following chapters we describe our knowledge integration perspective on learning and the scaffolded knowledge integration framework for instruction. We provide evidence for many of our design decisions. We synthesize our results in design principles and curriculum design patterns to give those creating new technology-enhanced learning environments a head start in designing inquiry projects.

2

The Knowledge Integration Perspective on Learning

Marcia C. Linn
University of California, Berkeley

Bat-Sheva Eylon
The Weizmann Institute of Science

Elizabeth A. Davis
University of Michigan

In this chapter we explore the nature of learning in general and science learning in particular to develop what we call the *knowledge integration perspective on learning*. Investigations of the systemic, complex nature of science education require a perspective on learning matched to the rich, dynamic classroom experience. We combine views of learning from two lenses motivated by rather distinct research traditions. First, we look at learning through the *science learning lens*, drawing on investigations of the development of expertise in the science disciplines, including in-depth studies of individuals performing complex tasks and longitudinal studies of individuals developing understanding of concepts and of the nature of science itself. Second, we look at learning through the *cognitive process lens*, drawing on investigations of memory, skills, and reasoning often conducted under well-controlled conditions. Much of this cognitive research is carried out in laboratory settings with college students using tasks that limit or constrain the role of prior knowledge. Combining these two lenses brings together studies that rely on quite different time frames: Studies of science learning typically elicit views developed over a period of weeks, months, or years, whereas studies of memory and skill development often capture the process of learning over a period of seconds, minutes, or hours. Remarkably, these lenses, although drawing on somewhat unique investigations, offer a more coherent perspective on learning.

By combining these lenses we leverage the strengths of both these research traditions.

In chapter 3 (Linn, Davis, & Eylon, this volume) we explore the design of instruction. We add the *science instruction lens* to draw on studies of curriculum design, the social context of classrooms, learning environment design, and other aspects of instruction in widely varied contexts or settings. We translate our perspective on learning into the *scaffolded knowledge integration framework for instruction*. This framework synthesizes research on science instruction including research on design of technology-enhanced learning environments.

DEFINITION OF KNOWLEDGE INTEGRATION

Knowledge integration refers to the process of adding, distinguishing, organizing, and evaluating accounts of phenomena, situations, and abstractions. Many theorists describe this process although they may emphasize different aspects of it (e.g., Dewey, 1900; Piaget, 1971; Schwab, 1978; Vygotsky, 1962). The knowledge integration view of learning resonates with extensive research and theorizing in the learning sciences (Bereiter, 1994; Bransford, Brown, et al., 1999; Bransford, Sherwood, et al., 1990; Carey, 1985; diSessa, 2000; Hawkins, 1991; Krajcik, Marx, et al., 2000; Pea & Gomez, 1992, 1993; Reiser, Copen, et al., 1994; White & Frederiksen, 1998). It incorporates over 25 years of investigations by our research partnership in the rich, diverse settings where learning occurs (Linn, 2001; Linn & Hsi, 2000). We define the repertoire of ideas and the knowledge web to facilitate communication about knowledge integration.

Repertoire of Ideas

We refer to the varied, potentially conflicting views of the same phenomena held by students as a *repertoire of ideas*. Knowledge integration involves both developing a repertoire of ideas and sorting out the web of connections among the ideas. Students add some ideas spontaneously, often from observations of the world. They infer views from interactions with peers, teachers, family, and groups. Newspapers, television, courses, books, experiments, and investigations provide additional examples. Analyses at varied grain sizes such as microscopic or policy interpretations provide additional views. Learners end up with a repertoire of ideas about any topic including concepts, principles, procedures, examples, conjectures, and experiences. Ideas in the repertoire may connect to specific contexts or types of analysis and often conflict with each other.

Individuals studying how students interpret scientific phenomena observe that learners generally possess a fragmented, fragile, or incoherent repertoire of ideas about specific scientific topics (Chi & Slotta, 1993; diSessa, 1988, 1993, 2000; Eylon & Linn, 1988; Slotta, Chi, et al., 1995). Research suggests that the repertoire expands or contracts depending on the context of investigation—often students respond to questions by narrowing the contexts to which their ideas apply. For example, students may conclude that insulators work for hot materials but not for cold materials (Linn & Hsi, 2000). Learners establish the context of application for their ideas and may modify the context to achieve coherence rather than seeking to make their ideas coherent across contexts.

In chapter 3 (Linn et al., this volume) we discuss how effective science instruction introduces ideas that help students organize their existing ideas, sort out the most promising views, and refine the context of application for the idea. For example, we discuss how well-designed additions to the repertoire can motivate students to broaden the context of application and create a more cohesive repertoire of ideas.

Knowledge Web

We refer to the relations among ideas in the repertoire as *knowledge webs*. Students may connect ideas based on surface features or on scientific principles (Chi, Feltovich, et al., 1981; Eylon & Linn, 1988; Reif & Larkin, 1991). Connections may come from proximity in a course, experiment, or anecdote or from critical analysis of similarities and differences (Bagno & Eylon, 1997). Students may base connections on empirical evidence or on conjecture.

In chapter 3 (Linn et al., this volume) we discuss how well-designed instruction helps students strengthen the connections among ideas in their web, develop criteria for adding new connections, make connections across contexts or settings, and create knowledge webs that make it easy to incorporate new ideas. Strengthening the web often includes distinguishing contexts of explanation—such as microscopic and macroscopic depictions or causal and descriptive models. Effective science instruction enables students to make their web of ideas more robust and cohesive.

SCOPE OF KNOWLEDGE INTEGRATION

The knowledge integration perspective on learning applies equally to precollege and college students (e.g., Linn, 1995; Linn & Hsi, 2000), preservice and inservice science teachers (e.g., Davis & Petish, 2001; Shear, 1998; Slotta & Linn, 2000; Williams & Linn, 2002), as well as researchers and curriculum designers (e.g., Linn, 1987, 2001). We see parallels in the ways individuals and groups gain understanding of the complexities of science and in the ways novices and experts make progress. We argue that the field of educational research holds a repertoire of ideas and that individual research programs follow a process of knowledge integration that bears resemblance to the processes followed by individuals.

SCIENCE LEARNING LENS ON KNOWLEDGE INTEGRATION

The science learning lens on knowledge integration draws on a broad and diverse set of investigations conducted by science educators, classroom teachers, educational psychologists, natural scientists, technologists, sociologists, methodologists, policymakers, and others. We err on the side of including studies that have both science learning and cognitive aspects in this section. As discussed in chapter 1 (Linn, Davis, & Bell, this volume), many of these research programs involve partnerships that include members of all these groups. These investigations emphasize three natures of learning that jointly contribute to knowledge integration.

We refer to these natures of learning as interpretive, cultural, and deliberate (Linn, 2001). Students spontaneously generate interpretations of the world around them and bring these interpretations to science class. Often learners develop descriptive accounts of phenomena such as a source–receiver model of electricity based on their everyday experiences—electricity seems to come out of the wall and into the lamp. Students carry out their efforts to make sense of science in a cultural context that shapes their norms and standards for evidence as well as for intellectual activity. The culture communicates views of scientists, the nature of science, and the practices that succeed in science learning. Students make deliberate decisions about the which scientific activities, courses, and careers to choose. Often students avoid science because they fail to identify ways to connect it to their lives, neglect opportunities to monitor their progress, or cannot anticipate how effort put into understanding today will benefit them in the future (Linn & Hsi, 2000).

INTERPRETIVE NATURE OF LEARNING

The interpretive nature of learning captures the generative propensity of humans to explore new information, identify patterns, and sort out alternatives (Shonkoff & Phillips, 2000). Vygotsky (1962) and Piaget (1929/1951) identified the spontaneous ideas students develop about the natural world and speculated about their origins. Researchers interested in the interpretive nature of learning have studied the spontaneous ideas of learners, the development of scientific understanding, and the acquisition of expertise.

Spontaneous Ideas About Science

Many studying what have been called misconceptions, preconceptions, alternative ideas, and phenomenological primitives have documented the ideas that students form in their efforts to make sense of natural phenomena (diSessa, 1988; Driver, Guesne, et al., 1985; Eylon & Linn, 1988; Gordin et al., 1994; Pfundt & Duit, 1991). For example, students can articulate the benefits of sweaters as insulators but interpret their experiences to conclude that sweaters warm people up and could not keep ice cream cold (Linn & Hsi, 2000). Students integrate both personal experiences and school activities. Ben-Zvi et al. (1986) showed how students interpret models of atoms in chemistry courses—often believing that individual atoms have color, conduct electricity, and are malleable, although these properties only characterize multitudes of atoms.

Studies of students who participated in traditional secondary school courses on tasks involving electric circuits show systematic problems with relatively straightforward tasks. For example, when asked to explain what would happen when one of the bulbs in a circuit with two bulbs in parallel was removed, students confuse voltage and current and neglect systems thinking. They conceive of batteries as providing electric charges (current) that get used up by the bulbs rather than seeing the batteries as part of a system that distributes energy to the components of the circuit. In particular, students do not think about circuits as systems with reciprocal relations among their elements. These interpretations lead to inaccurate predictions and to non-normative explanations of electrical circuit phenomena (Cohen, Eylon, et al., 1983; Eylon & Ganiel, 1990).

In numerous case studies Linn and Hsi (2000) and Clark (2000) have shown that students often fail to resolve apparent discrepancies in their observations and explanations, consistent with the view that students hold a repertoire of incoherent ideas and add new ideas more readily than they generate connections to existing ideas. D. Clark (2000) charted the connections learners make among their ideas over time and showed that some students primarily add ideas, whereas others both add and sort out their ideas. Carey (1985), in studying the trajectories of young children as they seek to distinguish living and nonliving things, drew on the distinction between normal and revolutionary science put forth by Thomas Kuhn (1970). Carey concluded that students' reasoning generally proceeded along the lines of normal science in which students added ideas to elaborate or refine their views rather than along the lines of revolutionary science in which students made paradigm shifts based either on new information or on some developmental accomplishment. Carey did identify individual students who responded to an unusual event by making a revolutionary reorganization of their ideas. In general, learners seem more inclined to add ideas about scientific phenomena than to sort out those that are inconsistent with others (Carey, 1985; Case, 1985; Inhelder & Piaget, 1970; Siegler, 1978; Singer et al., 2000; Smith et al., 1994).

Development of Scientific Understanding

Piaget (Inhelder & Piaget, 1970) postulated processes of accommodation and assimilation to explain how learners interpret their experiences. Learners accommodate to some ideas—adding, for example, the idea that the earth is round. Learners assimilate other ideas, adjusting views to incorporate the new information. For example, learners may assimilate information about the earth being round to their perception of the earth as flat by determining that the earth must be round like a pancake (Nussbaum, 1985; Vosniadou & Brewer, 1992). In another example, many students rely primarily on their tactile information to determine the temperature of objects in a room. Thus, at room temperature they conclude that metal objects are actually colder than the room temperature and that wooden objects may actually be warmer than the room temperature. Students show the power of the interpretive process when asked to explain what they would use to wrap a drink to keep it cold in their lunch. Frequently, students choose aluminum foil, a form of metal, and argue that metals with their ability to impart cold would have an advantage in keeping a drink cold in their lunch (Lewis & Linn, 1994). Thus, students exercise the interpretive process but reach a non-normative account of insulation. In this example, students also fail to link their solution to the context of metal and wood in a hot car or on a sunny day at the beach where metal items would feel far warmer than wooden items.

Several research programs endeavor to explain the interpretive nature of the learner. Many developmental theorists argue that reasoning ability develops with age. They point to evidence of similar patterns of reasoning among learners of the same age to support this view (e.g., Clement, 1988; diSessa, 2000; Driver, Guesne, et al., 1985; Piaget, 1969). DiSessa (2000) described what he called *phenomenological primitives*—ideas about the natural world that emerge among most individuals as they observe natural phenomena. For example, most students conclude that light dies out or that heat and temperature are the same. Students base these views on observation and interpretation of a relatively limited set of linguistic and experiential information sources.

Piaget (e.g., Inhelder & Piaget, 1958/1972; Piaget, 1929/1951) put forth a powerful account of biological development of logical reasoning based on extensive interviews of students about scientific phenomena. Piaget (1929/1951) described students as progressing from concrete operations to formal operations. Piaget (Inhelder & Piaget, 1958/1972) argued for adjusting expectations for student scientific understanding based on biological limits on reasoning abilities, suggesting that full logical reasoning ability emerged around age 15. Several recent accounts of students' scientific reasoning offer similar cautions (Slotta, Chi, et al., 1995; Vosniadou & Brewer, 1992). These findings have led some to call for instruction in critical thinking. Others argue that critical thinking instruction can only succeed when enacted in the disciplinary context (e. g., Hawkins & Pea, 1987; Linn, Clement, et al., 1989).

Several followers of Piaget have explained the reasoning limitations of children in terms of developing capacity for processing information, taking advantage of basic psychological research on processing capacity (Atkinson & Shiffrin, 1968; Miller, 1956). Researchers have argued that reasoning capacity increases with age, and they have distinguished the forms of reasoning possible with greater capacity (e.g., Case, 1985; Pascual-Leone et al., 1978; Scardamalia, 1977; Siegler, 1978). These researchers show that students, as they mature, can handle more information efficiently and therefore solve more complex scientific dilemmas. This research program assumes that learners use similar strategies for solving these problems at different ages and rely

primarily on increased processing capacity to perform in a more sophisticated fashion. Research shows that instruction designed to reduce processing demands can enable students to use more powerful
reasoning strategies. For example, Case, Griffin, et al. (1999), working with young children learning mathematics, devised instruction
that helped students sort out the complex relations that contribute to
basic mathematics manipulations and demonstrated that with this
form of instruction students can solve problems requiring more sophisticated mathematics. Likewise, Metz (1995) described how, with
appropriate supports, even preschool children can engage in scientific
inquiry. Researchers have also sought to identify appropriate sequences of ideas based on developmental research (e.g., Chi, 2000)
and to determine the mix of ideas that would help students develop sophisticated understanding (e.g., Linn & Hsi, 2000).

Although students can use logical reasoning strategies starting at a
young age, they often neglect opportunities to do so. Research shows
that students often add new ideas to their repertoire that contradict
existing ideas without reconciling the apparent discrepancies (e.g.,
Smith et al., 1994). Researchers following the Piagetian tradition have
created discrepant events to enhance learning (Piaget & Inhelder,
1974; Reif & Heller, 1982). For example, to provoke understanding of
conservation of weight, followers of Piaget present two balls of clay,
weight them on a pan balance, make one into a pancake, and ask
learners to predict what the balance will do when the ball and the pancake are weighed. Young children predict that the pancake will weigh
more; when contradicted, they conclude that this clay is special, that
pancakes with other shapes would weigh more, or that the pancake
might weigh more the next time. These studies confirm that students
may consider the new examples as augmenting rather than contradict-
ing existing ideas and end up with a less cohesive repertoire than they
had when they started the course.

Acquisition of Expertise

Researchers studying the acquisition of expertise note that experts
spend thousands of hours mastering a field and become qualitatively
different from novices (e.g., Chase & Simon, 1973; Reif & Larkin,
1991). Study of how experts acquire knowledge show that individuals
add information and organize it to solve more and more complex problems (Anderson, 1982; Eylon & Reif, 1984; Gagne, 1965; Glaser,
1976). Over time, experience with a complex domain such as mechanics enables experts to represent and organize their knowledge around

principles and foci that improve reasoning. Thus, expert physicists organize their information about mechanics around abstract ideas, whereas novices rely on formulas (e.g., Larkin & Reif, 1979). These expert methods, however, may depend on extensive experience and other knowledge that novices lack—making it difficult to untangle the necessary and sufficient conditions of learning.

Longitudinal case studies support the notion that logical reasoning and disciplinary knowledge go hand in hand in science learning (D. Clark, 2000; Linn & Eylon, 1996; Linn & Hsi, 2000). For example, D. Clark (2000) demonstrated that students started middle school with a broad range of disconnected ideas about thermal equilibrium and only after extensive opportunities to revisit their ideas in a concentrated curriculum were they able to sort out these ideas and develop more robust, cohesive, and normative views. Students often used sophisticated forms of reasoning to defend their non-normative ideas, including creative interpretations of the role of materials such as metal. For example, students reported that metals could keep things cold because they felt cold. They preferred non-normative ideas due to compelling empirical evidence such as the feel of metal and wood objects and ignored contradictory results established using such tools as thermometers to measure the room temperature of objects.

In a similar vein, research has shown the difficulty that students face when asked to transfer a concept from one context to another (Bransford, 1979; Gick & Holyoak, 1980; Holyoak, 1985). Students struggle to recognize ideas in new contexts and often fail to connect evidence from experiments conducted at different grain sizes (like microscopic and macroscopic) or from a dynamic rather than a more static perspective (e.g., Linn & Hsi, 2000; Scardamalia & Bereiter, 1991a; Slotta, Chi, et al., 1995). Students often isolate contexts of investigation—using a source–receiver account of electricity when describing how a toaster works but talking about circuits when describing a battery, wire, and bulb—rather than seeking to integrate these ideas (e.g., Driver, Guesne, et al., 1985).

Davis and Petish (2001) reported on a case study of a preservice teacher developing a unit plan for teaching energy concepts. The teacher, drawing on text, personal experience, and lecture material, adds both scientifically normative and non-normative principles to her repertoire. For example, the teacher adds the view that absorbed light is converted to heat energy but does not attempt to connect this idea to other ideas about either heat or light. The teacher makes more connections between personal experience and the topics, linking the principle that light needs to be reflected off an object for us to see it to her personal experience in a dark house. The interpretive nature of science learning is reflected in these connections, but the connections are not yet cohesive.

These research programs contribute three important dimensions to the understanding of the interpretive nature of learning. First, students bring diverse ideas to science class that emerge from a process of generating interpretations of experience. Second, recognizing and adding ideas to the repertoire of views does not ensure that new ideas connect to existing ideas—indeed, students often contextualize their ideas such that existing and new ideas can exist side by side. Third, students rarely spontaneously sort out the ideas in their knowledge web and often lack criteria for evaluating new ideas.

The interpretive nature of the science learner has many implications for instruction as detailed in chapter 3 (Linn et al., this volume). For example, designing ideas to add to the mix of views can stimulate knowledge integration by showcasing potential links to related contexts, drawing attention to salient aspects of the scientific phenomena, and leaving irrelevant details underspecified. Tracking the trajectories of learners as they revisit and revise their web of connections has tremendous potential for science learning and deserves additional attention in the research community.

CULTURAL NATURE OF LEARNING

Learning takes place in a complex, influential sociocultural environment. Individuals learn norms for behavior, dress, argumentation, and aspiration from the practices in their cultural setting. Students infer views about scientists, the nature of science, and science learning as well as specific ideas about the natural world by observing their parents, peers, teachers, and others interpreting scientific information (Bell & Linn, 2002; Cole, 1996; Collins, Brown, & Holum, 1991; Davis, 2003b; Dewey, 1900; Lave & Wenger, 1991; Linn, Songer, et al., 1996; Means & Coleman, 2000; Means, Middleton, et al., 1996; Songer & Linn, 1991; Vygotsky, 1962).

Views of Scientists

Cultural influences on science learning shape students' development of beliefs about scientists and about who can participate in science (American Association of University Women [AAUW], 2000; Wellesley College Center for Research on Women, 1992). Using the draw a scientist test, researchers demonstrate that students view scientists as male, wearing laboratory coats, and having a beard or moustache (Chambers, 1983). Research on perceptions of scientists reveal both articulated and subtle stereotypes about who can become a scientist and about the personalities of scientists (e.g., Bargh, 1997; Tversky, 1977). Many expect scientists to hold strong opinions, argue vehemently, and look down on those without scientific training.

The media, including television shows, books, advertisements, and news accounts of disputed science findings provide an image of scientists as engaged in controversy that stands in sharp contrast to accounts of science in textbooks. Students have little opportunity to gain insight into how scientists sort out complex and uncertain results and determine the most fruitful research directions (Latour, 1998). Published accounts of scientists efforts often gloss over the complexities, personal disputes, or arguments in favor of an account of innovation that depicts scientific knowledge as unfolding in a logical progression. In their courses, students may come to believe that everything in the science textbook is true (Linn & Hsi, 2000; Songer & Linn, 1991) or that science progresses in a linear fashion (Driver, Leach, et al., 1996). In reading news accounts of current scientific disputes, students might conclude that scientists have their own opinions about whether to follow a high-fiber, high-fat, low-fat, or high-protein diet. These diverse experiences lead to a contradictory repertoire of views about scientists.

Views of the Nature of Science

Scientific research takes place in a cultural context (e.g., Latour, 1998; Stokes, 1997). The cultural context provides students with multiple accounts of how scientific work proceeds. For example, in the quest for a cancer treatment, scientists may privilege experimental results and policymakers may privilege human risks. Recent publicity about clinical trials that have been stopped due to unanticipated deaths illustrate the repertoire of views of the nature of science and raise public awareness of the complexity of scientific decision making.

Students typically develop a repertoire of views about the nature of science, some of which interfere with knowledge integration (Bell & Linn, 2002; Halloun & Hestenes, 1985; Hofer & Pintrich, 1997, 2002). News accounts of controversy clash with classroom laboratories that emphasize cookbook approaches to investigation and minimize interpretation of aberrant or surprising findings. Distinctions between research and application or between basic and applied research often confuse rather than inform. Although these distinctions blur in most research programs (Stokes, 1997), interpreters of science often use them to reinforce artificial boundaries.

Even within a domain of science, explanations occur at multiple levels from macroscopic, to microscopic, to policy, and to design. Scientists establish the scope of their argument and therefore the ideas they connect based on their research questions. Representatives of advocacy groups such as environmentalists or consumers develop conflicting accounts of many scientific dilemmas because they consider aspects of the problem that others neglect. For example, ideal calculations of friction, motion, and the behavior of metals require reformulation in design of structures intended to withstand earthquakes. A research area linking these domains is essential for solving the important problem of creating safe buildings.

Students gain understanding of the nature of science by observing others making this process visible. Exhibits at museums, zoos, and science centers offer alternative ideas about the processes and practices of science and about norms or standards for evaluating scientific information. From parents or peers who disparage science or report forgetting all they have learned, children may learn to distrust science or to distrust their ability to make sense of science. For example, many students conclude that memorizing scientific information succeeds more often than understanding scientific material, based on perceptions of science as a body of facts.

Views of Science Learning

Learning science involves making sense of varied images of science as well as remaining ready to reformulate connections among ideas based on new information. Students' views of science learning contribute to the motivation they have for learning science and the desire they have for creating a cohesive knowledge web. Memorizing as a strategy for science learning is reinforced by textbooks that emphasize recall of facts and standardized, multiple-choice tests that emphasize details of science (Linn & Hsi, 2000).

When learners encounter new information that varies in level of analysis, certainty, representation, context of applicability, or source, they can coherently connect the new material in their knowledge web or just add the idea to their repertoire. Even experts sometimes isolate their practical knowledge rather than connecting it to their theoretical ideas (Lewis & Linn, 1994).

Students may decide to memorize information for science class and to understand or interpret information relevant to personal decision making. Learners who instead consider varied perspectives and attempt to apply their knowledge in novel settings are more likely to distinguish central and peripheral aspects of the topic and to recall information in the future (Linn, 1986; White, 1993b).

Students may fail to integrate ideas across cultural contexts because generating connections is difficult. For example, textbooks may represent scientific ideas in formulas, animations, visualizations, or experimental results that might not easily connect to each other or to more personally relevant situations (Chi, Feltovich, et al., 1981; Lewis, 1991; Reif & Larkin, 1991). In addition, learners may allocate their intellectual energy based on their beliefs about the relevance of science to their lives. When instruction fails to emphasize connections to problems individuals will encounter, then students will have difficulty recognizing connections in the future.

Students also may fail to integrate ideas because they may lack personal autonomy for their science learning. Instead of identifying weaknesses in their own knowledge, for example, these students may expect others (e.g., teachers, peers, or parents) to do so for them (Davis, 2003b).

Students generate their ideas about science based on their own experiences, yet science learning involves managing a complex set of information from diverse sources, in distinct formats, of varied validity, at different levels of analysis, and at different time scales. Because students have difficulty interpreting information from one context in a new setting, students may not test ideas from, for example, media or peers against the ideas they gained in science class.

Sometimes peers translate societal stereotypes into classroom norms about who belongs in science and may exclude some classroom members from scientific discourse and discourage some individuals from pursuing careers in science (Steele, 1997; Wellesley College Center for Research on Women, 1992). Research shows that White male students predominate in classroom scientific discussions, providing less opportunity for others to participate in scientific discourse (AAUW, 2000; American Institutes for Research, 1998). Because science typically involves considerable discussion of alternative views, students benefit from developing communication skills early in their scientific studies.

The cultural nature of learning contributes important ideas to our perspective on knowledge integration. Cultural experience can introduce stereotyped ideas about scientists, the nature of science, and the process of science learning. Although learners might benefit from contrasting the cultural perspectives of varied groups, these stereotypes can also motivate learners to eschew connections. In chapter 3

(Linn et al., this volume), we discuss how effective instruction can help students develop a more generative perception and coherent repertoire of views about the cultural aspects of science.

DELIBERATE NATURE OF LEARNING

The deliberate nature of learning concerns the process of translating intentions, goals, values, and expectations into action. Many argue that science courses would succeed if students had greater motivation. The deliberate component of science knowledge integration unpacks motivation into a variety of dimensions.

Learners make decisions about their science learning, including decisions about whether to include a particular idea in the mix they consider for a given problem, whether to explore ramifications of an issue, whether to study hard for a course, whether to take the next more advanced course, and whether to consider a science career. To make these decisions, learners can monitor their progress, reflect on their own learning, and select learning practices.

Monitoring Progress

Students can monitor their own learning by comparing their progress to some set of norms or standards. Often science classes set norms that deter knowledge integration. Linn and Hsi (2000) reported on students who argue that they do not have to understand because memorizing enables them to succeed. Students make deliberate decisions about whether or not to monitor their own science learning behavior. They can deliberately limit or expand their opportunities for complex and cohesive scientific knowledge integration.

Research on the deliberative nature of the learner (e.g., Scardamalia & Bereiter, 1991a, 1992a) emphasizes that most students need support or guidance to learn to monitor and guide their own science learning. Studying how students intentionally make sense of scientific topics shows why their process is easily derailed. For example, when students participating in the Computer Supported Intentional Learning Environments program attempt to determine what questions they have about a scientific passage, they often report confusion. Similarly, Davis (2003b) investigated the intentions students have when carrying out a complex science project and found that less than one third spontaneously took responsibility for their own learning. Engaging students in sustained, complex projects that place learners in charge of the investigation can succeed but requires extensive redesign of instruction (Lehrer et al., 2000; Metz, 2000).

Reflecting on Learning

Many researchers (e.g., A. L. Brown & Campione, 1994; Chi, 2000; Davis & Linn, 2000; Scardamalia & Bereiter, 1992b; Songer, 1996) have investigated how reflecting on learning influences knowledge integration. Chi (2000) reported that some students spontaneously generate self-explanations and identify connections or contradictions among ideas. These learners are more successful than those who do not try to explain to themselves the meaning of the material they encounter.

Songer and Linn (1991) surveyed learners about their reflection practices and distinguished those who viewed learning as dynamic from those who viewed learning as static or unchanging. Songer and Linn found that successful students reported reflecting on their learning more often.

Linn and Eylon (2000) reported that students who believe that science learning involves reflection and reconsideration of ideas succeed as often as other students on immediate indicators of progress when studying displaced volume. However, when asked similar questions several months later, these reflection-oriented students outperform their peers. These studies suggest that a disposition to reflect leads to more durable understanding.

Selecting Learning Practices

Research suggests that more students engage in knowledge integration about topics that have personal relevance for learners. Students make more connections when science topics connect to their personal interests and concerns (Krajcik, Blumenfeld, Marx, et al., 1994; Linn & Hsi, 2000; Scardamalia & Bereiter, 1991a). Anchoring instruction in contexts that students care about and creating authentic science projects increases connections and sustains participation (e.g., Cognition and Technology Group at Vanderbilt, 1997). In anchored instruction and problem-based learning, students start with a complex, realistic situation and a driving question. They gather information about a local pond or stream, the likelihood of an earthquake at their house, or prevention of a local epidemic to discover a path for the solution of a problem or the explanation of a phenomenon. The instructional materials provide guidance and support to help students connect their ideas and to solve problems in this meaningful context. Students can readily revisit these topics in their daily lives.

The deliberate nature of science learning sheds light on what motivates students to persist in science courses and to carry out independent projects. Students who monitor their progress, reflect on their ideas, and alter their practices based on these ideas learn more than others and develop more durable understanding. Interest in science in general contributes to successful learning, but specific personally relevant problems seem even more effective in promoting knowledge integration. Inquiry learning in which students carry out authentic projects has the potential to elicit deliberate attention to learning as discussed in chapter 3 (Linn et al., this volume).

COGNITIVE PROCESS LENS ON LEARNING

Psychological research on memory and skill acquisition (e.g., Gardner, 1985; Sternberg, 1977, 1985) highlights three cognitive processes that occur naturally and contribute to learning. Understanding these processes strengthens the analysis of knowledge integration from the science learning lens.

First, learning involves recognizing and adding new ideas to the repertoire of views. Learners spontaneously identify new ideas, often without considering whether the new idea resembles or augments an existing idea. Learners may also dismiss new ideas as identical to currently held views or irrelevant to the context instead of adding them to the repertoire. Research on long-term memory and skill acquisition shows that often learners cannot distinguish new ideas from ideas that were introduced previously, helping to explain why individuals may develop a repertoire of views (Baddeley & Longman, 1978). Work on the context effect in memory helps explain why learners isolate their new ideas or connect ideas based on superficial features (R. C. Schank, Fano, et al., 1993/1994). Research on the role of priming and stereotype threat in social psychology sheds light on how the interpretive nature of learning works in practice. Learners may be primed by context to select ideas not considered in other contexts.

Second, learning involves generating connections among ideas. Learners vary in their tendency to generate connections and in the types of connections that they develop. Many learners rarely transfer information from one context to another and therefore rarely generate connections across contexts or across instances of the same idea (Gick & Holyoak, 1980; Sternberg, 1977, 1985). As a result, learners might treat a new context as a new idea or fail to revisit ideas when they reoccur. Investigations of the interpretive nature of the learning and of the process of generating connections have considerable overlap in studies of science learning and of interpretation of text. Recent research on desirable difficulties suggest some promising areas for further collaboration (e.g., Bjork, 1994; Kintsch, 1998).

Third, knowledge integration involves self-monitoring—evaluating the ideas in the repertoire and the connections among ideas in the knowledge web and promoting the most promising ideas. Ideally, students would seek a cohesive knowledge web that distinguishes normative ideas, conjectures, and views at diverse levels of analysis and that spans all the contexts where the topic might arise. Learners who monitor their progress end up revisiting their ideas more often and develop more durable understanding (Bjork, 1999). Research on the deliberate nature of the learner connects to psychological research on self-monitoring (e.g., Bjork, 1999; Chi, 2000; diSessa, 2000; Linn & Hsi, 2000) and suggests new areas for investigation.

We summarize these natural propensities of recognizing new ideas, generating connections, and self-monitoring as cognitive processes because they appear to be ubiquitous. All learners do these things to varying degrees and with unique consequences. As we discuss in chapter 3 (Linn et al., this volume), instructional designers face the challenge of harnessing these cognitive processes to improve scientific ideas and to promote a lifelong quest for more cohesive and powerful accounts of natural phenomena.

CONCLUSIONS

Students develop expertise in science, we argue, by integrating their understanding. By looking at learning through the science learning lens and the cognitive process lens we identify common findings from diverse research programs and define open research questions. Research reveals three natures of science learning: interpretive, cultural, and deliberate. To a large extent these natures resonate with the general cognitive processes of recognizing and adding new ideas, generating connections, and self-monitoring.

The knowledge integration perspective on learning elaborates how the cognitive processes work in science. Learners apply these processes as part of the interpretive, cultural, and deliberate nature of learning. Learners may add notions that conflict with normative views, connect science to memorizing, and remain complacent about their progress. The connections between the cognitive processes and the natures of science learning are depicted in Table 2.1. As the table il-

TABLE 2.1
The Knowledge Integration Perspective on Learning

Cognitive Processes	Natures of Learning		
	Interpretive	Cultural	Deliberate
Recognizing and adding new ideas	Prior experience and knowledge determines which ideas appear new and which appear redundant or irrelevant.	Cultural beliefs, group norms, and societal expectations promote some ideas and demote others.	Interests, goals, and values establish the relevance of scientific ideas to courses and future activities.
Generating connections	Experience, prior knowledge, and context make some connections salient and others invisible.	Cultural beliefs and values highlight some connections and interfere with formation of other connections.	Goals and values focus attention on forming connections relevant to personal agendas.
Monitoring progress	Experience, norms, and expectations determine markers of progress and signals of success.	Personal, institutional, and societal norms and standards determine what counts as evidence of progress.	Goals, interests, and values motivate the frequency and procedure for monitoring progress.

lustrates, students' spontaneous knowledge integration activities rely on the processes of recognizing ideas, generating connections, and monitoring progress. These processes can encourage or hamper the interpretive, cultural, and deliberate nature of the learner.

By viewing learning and instruction in all settings and for all learners through the same lenses, we strengthen our understanding of these processes. Indeed, this approach of linking and connecting research from a broad set of studies follows exactly from our original premise—that learning involves a process of knowledge integration and that learners bring a rich, diverse set of ideas to novel problems.

Translating our perspective on the science learner into the design of instruction raises dilemmas because there are many holes in our knowledge. We add the third lens—research on science curriculum and instruction—in chapter 3 (Linn et al., this volume) and discuss how the knowledge integration perspective on learning can inform design of instruction.

3

The Scaffolded Knowledge Integration Framework for Instruction

Marcia C. Linn
University of California, Berkeley

Elizabeth A. Davis
University of Michigan

Bat-Sheva Eylon
The Weizmann Institute of Science

The scaffolded knowledge integration framework translates our knowledge integration perspective on learning into guidance for those designing science instruction. Taken together, the scaffolded knowledge integration framework, the knowledge integration perspective on learning, and the cognitive processes offer three lenses for understanding science learning and instruction. These three lenses allow researchers to combine the results from a variety of research endeavors and will ultimately, we hope, lead to a more robust understanding of learning in general and of science learning and instruction in particular.

Science learning environment designers have begun to represent and communicate design knowledge and theoretical insights as design principles that emerge from research with the goal of informing future design activities (see Bell, Hoadley, & Linn, chap. 4, this volume, for discussion of the epistemological status of design principles). Design principles can synthesize the pragmatic aspects of practice, capture results from compelling comparisons, and inform theories of learning (Kali, 2002).

As a first step toward communicating design knowledge, we articulated a framework with four tenets based on instructional research in several contexts (Linn, 1995). Here we refer to these tenets as *metaprinciples* because they capture the results from multiple research programs. These metaprinciples are (a) make science accessible, (b) make thinking visible, (c) help students learn from others, and (d) promote autonomy and lifelong learning. These metaprinciples connect both to the science learning lens and the cognitive process lens introduced in chapter 2 (Linn, Eylon, & Davis, this volume; see Fig. 2.1). By relating the metaprinciples to the cognitive processes introduced in chapter 2 (Linn et al., this volume) we can take advantage of cognitive research and identify promising directions for design research. We illustrate these connections in Table 3.1.

The pragmatic pedagogical principles identified by Linn and Hsi (2000) are each associated with a metaprinciple (see Tables 3.2–3.5). These principles capture results from research programs in science learning. For example, one pragmatic pedagogical principle says "encourage students to investigate personally relevant problems and revisit their science ideas regularly." This pragmatic pedagogical principle summarizes a research program aimed at defining what makes a science problem personally relevant, distinguishing reasoning about such problems from reasoning about textbook problems, and investigating how instruction featuring personally relevant problems enables students to recognize ideas in new contexts. The research associated with this principle also shows how personally relevant problems help students learn to revisit and refine their science ideas (Linn & Hsi, 2000). Pragmatic pedagogical principles are informed and elaborated by results from individual research studies and by classroom investigations of new technology-enhanced features of instruction.

The metaprinciples of scaffolded knowledge integration and the pragmatic pedagogical principles associated with them rely on a large body of research. Here we describe a representative set of research programs for each metaprinciple, focusing primarily on investigations that take advantage of technology to explicate design knowledge for science instruction.

MAKE SCIENCE ACCESSIBLE

The first metaprinciple emphasizes making science accessible, an idea that resonates with the work of Piaget (Inhelder & Piaget, 1958/ 1972), Vygotsky (1978), and Dewey (1901). Making science accessible contributes to knowledge integration by building on what students know. To make science accessible, instructors design materials that connect to students' ideas and encourage students to reconsider their existing ideas.

Making science accessible connects to the three natures of learning. First, to take advantage of the interpretive nature of learning, de-

TABLE 3.1
Illustrative Connections Between Metaprinciples and Cognitive Processes

Cognitive Processes	Metaprinciples for Scaffolded Knowledge Integration			
	Make Science Accessible	*Make Thinking Visible*	*Help Students Learn From Others*	*Promote Autonomy and Lifelong Learning*
Recognizing and adding new ideas	Design pivotal cases that link existing ideas to more normative views.	Design representations of new ideas that illustrate dynamic, sequential, visual, or complex aspects of science knowledge.	Create social interactions that enable learners to hear ideas in words of peers, experts, and members of diverse cultural groups.	Design ways for students to devise new explanations and arguments in context of complex projects.
Generating connections	Ask learners to explain personally relevant situations and connect their ideas to more normative views.	Design tools that allow learners to construct representations of connections among ideas, depict arguments, or link elements of a process.	Ask learners to describe the connections between their ideas and those of others and to critique connections proposed by others.	Encourage students to organize ideas, construct arguments, add new evidence, and revisit phenomena in new contexts.
Monitoring progress	Design ways for students to encounter feedback that motivates continuous revisiting of relevant contexts.	Design assessments that elicit student ideas and enable teachers to evaluate progress as well as provide feedback.	Design ways for students to establish criteria for scientific explanations, to evaluate their own progress, and to analyze the progress of others.	Enable students to devise personal goals, seek feedback from others, interpret comments, and adjust behavior accordingly.

TABLE 3.2
Pragmatic Pedagogical Principles for Making Science Accessible

Pragmatic Pedagogical Principle	Examples of Research Evidence	Examples of Learning Environment Features
Build on student ideas: Encourage students to build on their scientific ideas as they develop more and more powerful and useful pragmatic scientific principles.	Studies comparing the impact of varied examples support design of pivotal cases that connect student ideas to more normative instructional goals (Linn, in press).	Well-designed evidence pages and animations can introduce pivotal cases or relevant contexts.
Study personally relevant problems: Encourage students to investigate personally relevant problems and revisit their science ideas regularly.	Courses featuring real-world problems make learners aware of the relevance of science to their lives (Linn & Hsi, 2000).	Projects about earthquake prediction, environmental stewardship, or design of picnic coolers that keep food safe.
Scaffold inquiry: Scaffold science activities so students participate in diverse inquiry tasks and practice productive inquiry.	Combinations of examples and scaffolds can guide productive inquiry (Linn & Eylon, 2000).	Scaffolds such as the inquiry map, inquiry cycle, and associated guidance can instantiate inquiry patterns.

signers need to find problems, examples, and contexts that engage learners in connecting new and existing ideas. Second, to take advantage of the cultural nature of learning, designers need to pay attention to the epistemological views students bring to science class and engineer environments to promote fruitful interactions among diverse learners. Third, to take advantage of the deliberate nature of science learning, designers can capture student interest and motivate additional study.

Table 3.2 describes the pragmatic pedagogical principles (see Linn & Hsi, 2000) associated with making science accessible. The table provides illustrative evidence and features of learning environments.

Build on Student Ideas

Designers often make science inaccessible by selecting abstract, expert examples rather than choosing examples consistent with student understanding. Texts and lectures written by natural scientists typically employ the models they find illuminating rather than ideas that resonate with the experiences of students. When students encounter such abstract or incomprehensible models, they often revert to a memorization approach to learning and isolate the new ideas rather than connect them to existing ideas (Linn & Hsi, 2000).

Students' epistemological ideas about science dictate their techniques for developing understanding of science and suggest additional aspects of the learner that need consideration in instructional design (Bell & Linn, 2002). By illustrating the wrong paths, shaky assumptions, and inadequate interpretations that have contributed to science historically, we help students expand their understanding of cultural influences on science and make a broader set of science ideas accessible.

Piaget's (Inhelder & Piaget, 1958/1972) clinical interviewing method illustrates ways that instruction can stimulate reinterpretation of ideas. In these interviews, students were often asked to connect their views to those of their peers. For example, a teacher might say, "A child told me that if you had a really small rock, it might float. What do you think?" This may force the learner to generate an explanation that shows why their ideas will hold up under new circumstances or in different settings. They may also reveal dimensions of the situation that the learner had neglected. In the rock example, the question asks about the mass of the rock rather than the density. A small stone has small volume and small mass, therefore students find it difficult to think about its density. Contrasting rocks with popcorn can cause density to become salient, helping the learner to defend a position and sort out ideas.

Researchers from many traditions call on designers to create more accessible examples including "benchmark lessons" (Minstrell, 2000), "bridging analogies" (Clement, 1993) or "anchored instruction" (Cognition and Technology Group at Vanderbilt [CTGV], 1997). Likewise, diSessa (2000) described the critical role that those intuitive ideas play in how students make sense of science. With technology, in fact, ideas that were once considered far beyond students' ken are now feasible to teach in middle school (e.g., Newtonian physics—see White, 1993a) or high school (e.g., thermodynamics—see Staudt & Horwitz, 2001).

Researchers including Bruner (1979), Kintsch (1998), Linn (in press), and Stigler and Heibert (1999) have all argued that designing problems at the right level of complexity such that they both encourage students to generate alternative solutions and help students distinguish among those solutions have advantages for lifelong learning. Examples can both promote and discourage knowledge integration.

Psychological research illustrates the difficulties that result from poorly designed examples. Research on the Luchins Water Jar problem, for example, shows that students can learn procedures and fail to reanalyze their appropriateness—in this set of problems students continue to engage in a multistep process even when a single-step process could succeed. Schoenfeld (1987) extended this finding to mathematics instruction showing that students often apply procedures rather than an inquiry process. Reif and Larkin (1991) demonstrated that students often learn to manipulate formulas without insight. These examples or problems discourage knowledge integration.

Provide Personally Relevant Examples

To make science accessible to students and encourage students to revisit their science knowledge web, the Computer as Learning Partner (CLP) research grounded instruction in personally relevant problems. This research showed that students reason about personally relevant problems such as determining how to keep a drink cold more effectively than laboratory problems such as cooling a beaker of water because they contrast their own ideas with class ideas (Linn & Hsi, 2000; Songer & Linn, 1991).

Clement (1991, 1993) studied how students interpret examples including depictions of Newton's first law—objects in motion tend to remain in motion. Often texts describe a car driving on an icy road. Many students in the United States have difficulty connecting this example because they have not experienced icy roads and lack driving licenses. A more connectable example might ask students to compare a ball rolling on mud, grass, and pavement. Clement (1993) referred to successful examples as *bridging analogies* because they help students connect scientific ideas to more familiar situations they encounter in their lives.

This work resonates with research on the advantages of complex examples. The Vanderbilt group (CTGV, 1997) showed the advantage of anchoring mathematics problems in a realistic situation such as a rescue mission and offering students a challenge based on the anchoring situation (Bransford, Sherwood, et al., 1990; CTGV, 1997).

Making the ideas of science accessible is a good first step, but students also need to participate in the process of inquiry to integrate their ideas. Krajcik, Blumenfeld, et al. (1998) used "driving questions" to ground students' investigations in personally meaningful, sustainable, and challenging inquiry contexts. Songer and Linn (1991) and Linn and Hsi (2000) have shown the benefit of asking students to predict, test, and reconcile their ideas about complex phenomena such as the design of picnic coolers. To place examples in more complex contexts, educators in mathematics (Cobb & Bowers,

1999; Lampert & Blunk, 1998), computer science (Kolodner, 1993; Linn & Clancy, 1992), business (Yin, 1994), teacher education (Lundeberg et al., 1999), and other fields cite similar strengths for authentic case studies.

Memory research reinforces the need to scaffold inquiry. Complex, confusing examples compared to straightforward examples can encourage students to reconsider the connections in their knowledge web with appropriate scaffolding. Bjork (1999), Kintsch (1998), and others have shown that when students encounter verbally presented information that seems straightforward and logical they recall less than when the information takes more effort to understand. For example, when an outline aligns perfectly with a text it helps learners immediately; an outline that aligns poorly with the text elicits more inquiry and ultimately enhances long-term recall (Kintsch, 1998). Similarly, students learn material such as foreign language vocabulary better when they practice, perform an intervening task that results in some forgetting, and then practice some more rather than when they skip the complex, intervening task (Bjork, 1994). In both of these examples, the successful condition required students to spend time testing their ideas and resolving apparent discrepancies.

Linn and Eylon (2000) found that students were more successful in learning the scientific idea of displaced volume when scaffolded to interpret examples. They contrasted a principle condition with an enhanced experimental condition. In both conditions, students encountered the full range of examples. Students in the principle condition connected their ideas to examples with and without feedback and wrote principles to summarize their results, thus making connections at multiple levels of analysis. Students in the investigations' experimental condition performed multiple experiments, including experiments they designed themselves, and explained their results but did not abstract principles. The two conditions were equally successful immediately. The principle condition was more successful on the delayed posttest, supporting the advantage of scaffolding inquiry to encourage connections at several levels of analysis. Similarly, Eylon and Helfman (1984) found that students who were scaffolded to construct principles across the full range of examples were more successful than students who performed multiple experiments or those who encountered a subset of the examples.

This discussion illustrates the contribution of well-designed examples combined with scaffolding that incorporates a representative range of contexts to promote knowledge integration. The scaffolding spurs comparisons, reorganizations, and even critiques of views in the repertoire of ideas.

Pivotal cases (Linn, in press; Linn & Hsi, 2000) are complex examples that enable students to reorganize and sort out their ideas and
come up with a more cohesive and normative account of a scientific
phenomena. Research to date suggests four criteria for pivotal cases.
First, pivotal case designers should provide a compelling comparison
distinguishing two situations to illustrate the key ideas and central
variables. For example, a pivotal case for thermal equilibrium involves
contrasting the perceived temperature of wood and metal in a cool
room and on a hot day—at room temperature metal feels cooler than
wood, but on a hot day metal feels hotter than wood, drawing attention to the human sensory system. (See D. Clark, chap. 8, this volume,
for further discussion of this pivotal case.) In another example from
the CLP research, the Heat Bars simulation (www.CLP.Berkeley.edu)
allowed students to compare rate of heat flow in different materials
such as wood and metal and helped students visualize the process of
heat flow (Foley, 1999; Lewis, 1991; Linn, in press).

Second, designers need to place inquiry in an accessible, relevant
environment. If the context is too esoteric, students may miss the central idea. For example, a pivotal case for students considering the
worldwide threat of malaria concerns the role of DDT. Students who
contrast the benefits of DDT for preventing infant mortality with the
hazards of biomagnification of DDT in the diets of birds reconsider
their ideas about environmental stewardship.

Third, designers should provide feedback to promote pro-normative
self-monitoring. If students cannot monitor their progress they take
too many wrong paths. For example, the thermal equilibrium software
(Clark, chap. 8, this volume) provides spontaneous feedback to students in the form of temperature readings and tactile input.

Fourth, designers should enable narrative accounts of science.
When students reconstruct their ideas in an argument they recognize
gaps in their knowledge and elaborate the connections among their
ideas. For example, the DDT case allows students to recount historical
events leading to policy decisions and to incorporate new information
from sources such as the international debate about the ban on use of
DDT. Work on argumentation shows how designers can scaffold the articulation of complex ideas in narrative form (Bell, chap. 6, this volume; Osborne, 1996).

These results illustrate the difficulty of designing effective examples, cases, or views to add to the repertoire of ideas in the knowledge
web and at the same time makes it clear that well-designed examples
are necessary but not sufficient for successful knowledge integration.
All of the successful studies described previously also design the inquiry conditions under which students interact with these new ideas.

These studies show that to make science accessible instructional designers have to design the scientific content they offer students rather than necessarily choosing the most sophisticated ideas or the most attractive illustration. Designers have the responsibility of selecting the scope of knowledge integration, the examples, the sequence of topics, and the context of generalization. As discussed in chapter 4 (Bell et al., this volume), the examples often require refinement based on trials in classrooms.

In summary, making science accessible also depends on the goals of instruction. Too often science instruction in the United States mandates more science topics than students can integrate. As a result, when compared to other countries, the United States curriculum has been described as an inch deep and a mile wide (Schmidt, McKnight, et al., 1997). National standards and benchmarks (American Association for the Advancement of Science, 1993; National Research Council, 1996) encourage teachers to cover many science topics each year. Research shows, however, that allowing students to explore topics in depth enables many more connections, ultimately leading to more coherent and linked understanding (D. Clark, 2000). This type of instruction may set students up for improved learning even in areas they have not yet experienced in school (Linn & Muilenburg, 1996). Reducing the number of topics covered in any given course then works in tandem with designing the examples and activities students study to make science more accessible to all students.

Thus, making science accessible involves adding ideas to the mix that students bring to science class, scaffolding the inquiry process so that students generate new connections, and providing supports that move students in a normative direction. It also involves ensuring that students connect ideas in a web such that they are prepared to revisit science in everyday life rather than isolate school science. Finally, making science accessible means ensuring that students get feedback on their reasoning that motivates them to continue to learn science rather than to either give up on understanding science or on taking more science courses.

MAKE THINKING VISIBLE

The second metaprinciple of scaffolded knowledge integration, making thinking visible, involves modeling and evaluating how ideas are connected and sorted out to form new knowledge webs (Bransford, Brown, et al., 1999; Collins, Brown, & Holum, 1991; Linn, 1995). This metaprinciple connects to the three natures of learning described in

TABLE 3.3
Pragmatic Pedagogical Principles for Making Thinking Visible

Pragmatic Pedagogical Principle	Examples of Research Evidence	Examples of Learning Environment Features
Model scientific thinking: Model the scientific process of considering alternative explanations and explaining mistakes.	Case studies improve understanding of complex problem solving and prepare students for complex projects (Kolodner, Crismond, et al., 1998).	Case studies that depict reasoning of experts or peers can ask students to add solutions as well as critique.
Scaffold students to make their thinking visible: Scaffold students to explain their ideas to teachers, peers, experts, and themselves.	When students articulate their views, they can monitor their own progress (Davis, chap. 5, this volume) and permit teachers and peers to comment (Hoadley, 2002).	Embedded assessments using varied response formats can invite teachers to send personal comments to students.
Provide multiple representations: Provide multiple visual representations from varied media.	Animations, visualizations, and interactive models permit students to interact with complex, dynamic systems (D. Clark, chap. 8, and Baumgartner, chap. 11, this volume).	Interactive models of scientific phenomena such as stream ecology, mechanics, or thermodynamics can illustrate ideas.

chapter 2 (Linn et al., this volume). Teachers, scientists, students, and technology can all model knowledge integration (Linn & Hsi, 2000). Making thinking visible both adds new perspectives to the mix considered in the knowledge integration process and makes explicit the interpretive process of combining perspectives to form more coherent knowledge webs. When role models succeed, they often help learners understand the nature of scientific research as well as the cultural characteristics of scientific communities. By making their ideas visible, students can inspect their own knowledge integration processes and engage in linking, distinguishing, or reconciling ideas as appropriate to deliberately guide their learning. Findings about making thinking visible result in pragmatic pedagogical principles (see Linn & Hsi, 2000) articulated in Table 3.3.

Model Scientific Thinking

Many projects model the process of scientific thinking. For example, in our research on computer programming, we developed case studies in which experts modeled the process of selecting among alternatives

(Linn & Clancy, 1992). Palincsar, Magnusson, et al. (2001) asked students to interpret scientific notebooks designed by experts to model the process of carrying out complex science investigations. When students can select among varied models of the process, they have the opportunity to compare alternative approaches to the problem.

When expert scientists serve as role models, they represent their cultural group as well as their particular methods for making sense of science. Scientists can show students how they discover new views to add to their mix of ideas, but they are even more effective if they also show students how they detect failures, deal with negative feedback, and communicate with others. Reif and Scott (1999) showed how this process can be implemented using a computer to make expert use of problem-solving strategies visible for students. Role models can encourage students to distinguish among their notions, interpret feedback from others, reconsider information in light of experimental findings, and develop a commitment to scientific endeavor. Some role models discourage learners by depicting science in ways that do not connect to the views of the individual or by only telling success stories instead of also recounting frustrations and mistakes. Cognitive apprenticeship (Collins, Brown, & Holum, 1991) emphasizes the benefits of learning from more able others based on Vygotsky's (1978) notion of the zone of proximal development. Programs based on cognitive apprenticeship make the thinking of experts visible. These programs structure activities to encourage students to behave more and more like experts. Many designers have followed this approach, creating instructional programs to support students as they emulate the practices of experts (Kozma et al., 1996).

Making expert thinking visible is much more easily advocated than accomplished. Textbooks generally give the right answer or the conclusion rather than clarify the interpretive process, including pitfalls, wrong paths, and misunderstandings that occur along the way. Scientific papers typically report only on the results leading to the ultimate conclusion rather than also describing all of the frustrations and dead ends that led to the reported findings. Often limits on classroom time motivate teachers to simplify the process of thinking that leads to a conclusion. Making time for thinking available in the curriculum by including inquiry projects has proven difficult.

Scaffold Students to Make Their Thinking Visible

When students make their own thinking visible, as in essay assessments, they make visible the ideas about science topics that they bring to science class. For example, prompts can reveal surprising alternative views, as described by Davis (chap. 5, this volume). Designers of prompts can use sentence starters to help students describe scientific inquiry activities and to promote planning, monitoring, and reflection. Teachers can use what they learn when students respond to inform the ways they make their own thinking visible.

Software such as SenseMaker, described in detail by Bell (chap. 6, this volume), allows students to group Internet evidence they have surveyed into frames and to lay out an argument. Designers creating materials for SenseMaker need to carefully select materials that enable students to make their arguments visible and therefore inspectable. Instructional designers can create advance organizers in the form of evidence pages to help students navigate the material and incorporate it into their reasoning process.

Similarly, the causal mapping tool described by Baumgartner (chap. 11, this volume) allows learners to make their thinking about scientific models visible. Instructional designers need to support students in making sense of the factors that come into play in scientific models.

Part of making thinking visible involves inspecting and reorganizing one's knowledge web. Learners reconcile ideas when they reorganize knowledge webs to resolve incompatibilities. They might promote one element while demoting another to create a new, more integrated web. For example, Davis and Petish (2001) described how a preservice teacher needed to reconcile the incompatible scientific principles that black objects absorb all light (a non-normative principle) and that light needs to be reflected off an object for us to see it (a normative principle). When learners subordinate ideas to other ideas, they recognize that an element previously viewed as unique is instead a special case. For example, D. Clark (2000) illustrated how students classify Styrofoam® and wood as both being insulators and reconcile these ideas by linking the notion of slowing heat flow to the meaning of an insulator.

Students strengthen their knowledge web when they distinguish their ideas in a new context. They strengthen the knowledge web by augmenting existing links and enriching the contexts where the element applies. For example, Linn and Hsi (2000) reported on situations in which students suddenly distinguish between the features of an oven and conclude that "an oven is just like a room, everything has the same temperature."

Ultimately learners benefit from making their thinking visible by creating their own representations. DiSessa (2000) showed benefits when a small class of students generated and critiqued their own representations of motion under the guidance of an expert teacher. Maher and Martino (2001) showed that when students design representations about combinatorial reasoning using cubes, numeric systems, and illustrations and explain their thinking to their peers, they develop a notion of mathematical proof.

Design studies show that students with proper support can develop the ability to make their own thinking visible. Students learn more when they monitor their own progress, stop and reflect, critique their own methodologies, and invent and refine representations of their experimental findings (Chi, de Leeuw, et al., 1994; Davis & Linn, 2000; diSessa, 2000; White & Frederiksen, 1998).

Provide Multiple Representations

Computer animations, modeling programs, dynamic representations, and scientific visualizations make scientific processes and ideas visible by illustrating how elements of the situation interact. Design of examples to take advantage of symbolic, episodic, visual, verbal, kinesthetic, and other types of memory can improve learning because recall of one type of representation can support recall of another type of representation of the same material (Baddeley & Longman, 1978).

Researchers have designed learning environments to introduce models of many phenomena including water quality (Krajcik, Blumenfeld, Marx, et al., 1998), mechanical systems (White & Frederiksen, 1998), and chemical systems (Kozma et al., 1996). These models require scaffolding to succeed.

Visualizations and representations can lead to understanding as well as to confusion (e.g., Hegarty, Quilici, et al., 1999; Tversky, 1977). Learners need opportunities to understand the visualization and to conduct their own experiments with the visualization. Foley (1999) reported that representing heat flow with color, although it sounds intuitive, actually makes less sense to students than when heat is represented using shades of gray. Collecting and displaying data using real-time data collection also contributes to successful inquiry and benefits from iterative design studies. Linn and her colleagues (Linn & Hsi, 2000; Linn & Songer, 1991) have researched real-time graphing of data (Lewis & Linn, 1994), analog-to-digital probeware (Linn & Songer, 1991), and interpretation of graphical representations; they found that students benefited far more from real-time graphing if they first predicted the outcome and then tested their predictions than when they only did the tests.

Making thinking visible involves illuminating and modeling the processes of knowledge integration. Students can demonstrate their own thinking for themselves, their peers, and their teachers (e.g., Davis, chap. 5, this volume). Classroom teachers can illustrate the complexity of scientific thinking (e.g., Bell, chap. 6, this volume). Technologists can devise mechanisms for capturing complex interactions in visualizations (e.g., D. Clark, chap. 8 and Baumgartner, chap. 11, this volume) and for displaying arguments (e.g., Bell, chap. 6, this volume). Natural scientists can make their thinking visible to students in online forums and other venues (e.g., Bell, chap. 10, this volume). Partnerships can negotiate instruction that offers students a repertoire of these approaches matched to curricular goals (e.g., Slotta, chap. 9, Baumgartner, chap. 11, and Shear, Bell, & Linn, chap. 12, this volume). To some extent visible thinking can empower students to seek coherence and to consider all the alternatives. Students may also find the efforts at visible thinking inaccessible and end up avoiding knowledge integration. Models can also deter students from critical thinking and problem solving by either providing an illusion of comprehension or encouraging memorizing.

In summary, making thinking visible provides valuable opportunities for students to exercise the interpretive process of knowledge integration. This process requires careful attention to the views added to the repertoire of ideas and to the context for generation of explanations. Designers may be tempted to revise instruction to overly simplify learning, but limiting opportunities to interpret complex ideas may interfere with learning (e.g., Kintsch, 1998). Designers can take advantage of the propensity of learners to monitor progress by providing feedback linked to articulation of views.

LISTEN AND HELP STUDENTS LEARN FROM OTHERS

The third metaprinciple of scaffolded knowledge integration, helping students learn from others, takes advantage of the collective knowledge in the classroom community. First, encouraging students to analyze and build on ideas from peers can introduce new perspectives and motivate students to interpret their own ideas. Second, when students interact, they connect to the cultural aspect of learning by bringing to light the alternative views held by learners and the criteria used to interpret ideas. Third, by enabling students to question peers and authorities, social supports can encourage the deliberate nature of learning. These insights result in pragmatic pedagogical principles (see Linn & Hsi, 2000, p. 40) associated with helping students learn from each other in Table 3.4.

TABLE 3.4
Pragmatic Pedagogical Principles for Helping
Students Listen and Learn From Others

Pragmatic Pedagogical Principle	Examples of Research Evidence	Examples of Learning Environment Features
Encourage listening to others: Encourage students to listen and learn from each other.	When teachers design discussions to require responses to others, they can improve learning (Hoadley, chap. 7, this volume).	Group learning software allows teachers to monitor interactions and customize activities to meet needs of their students.
Design discussions: Design technology-enhanced activities to promote productive and respectful interactions.	Group composition, group size, availability of resources, group leadership, and group goals all impact the success of collaborations (e.g., Cohen, 1984).	Discussion tools enable students to take roles, participate anonymously, and think before acting.
Highlight cultural norms: Scaffold groups to consider cultural values and to design criteria and standards.	Groups form norms and values that impact their comments and critiques (Hoadley, chap. 7, this volume).	Discussion tools enable groups to articulate and revise their norms and standards.
Employ multiple social structures: Employ multiple social activity structures.	Individuals benefit from learning to communicate in discussions, debates, essays, and other formats (Hoadley, chap. 7, this volume).	Learning environments vary social activities and enable teachers to adjust groups, change topics, and establish rewards.

Encourage Listening to Others

Many researchers have stressed how communities of learners can help students become more deliberate learners with better ability to monitor their progress (Bereiter & Scardamalia, 1993; A. L. Brown & Campione, 1994; Cohen, 1984; Heller, Heller, & Heller, 2001; Pea, 1987). Cohen (1984), for example, described the complex interactions that take place between pairs of students and identified interaction mechanisms that succeed and fail. Communities of learners, like individuals, can make progress using knowledge integration mechanisms. D. Clark (chap. 8, this volume) develops collaborations to promote learning. Aronson (1978) described the jigsaw in which groups of individuals specialize in different aspects of a complex domain and follow a process of forming new groups from the prior groups to jointly compare and contrast their ideas and assertions to build a broader and more comprehensive understanding of the situation. Design principles summarized in the reciprocal teaching approach to instruction (Palincsar & Brown, 1984) encourage students to compare ideas about complex situations. In reciprocal teaching, communities of learners have the opportunity to observe good role models engaging in the process of making sense of complex situations and to have guided practice in emulating the practices of these role models. Heller, Keith, et al. (1992) combined context-rich problems with cooperative activity structures to scaffold the process of listening to peers.

Design Discussions

Many argue that students can learn from each other in class discussions, but others complain that discussions often involve only a few students who dominate the discourse (Hsi, 1997; Wellesley College Center for Research on Women, 1992). Frequently participants are primarily males who enthusiastically shout out answers. Females and individuals who are less interested in science may end up feeling unwelcome in scientific discourse (American Association of University Women, 2000; Mayberry, 1998).

Online, asynchronous discussion tools such as the Multimedia Forum Kiosk (Hoadley, chap. 7, this volume; Hsi, 1997; Hsi & Hoadley, 1997; Yerushalmi & Eylon, 2000), when properly designed, can encourage all learners to participate. Classroom assignments to contribute to online discussions typically have far more success than do similar assignments when used for class discussion.

In online discussion, students have time to reflect, incorporate ideas of others, and compose their contributions carefully rather than rapidly forming imperfect arguments. Often in class discussions students pay little attention to the contributions of others and make contributions that lack reflection or connection to classroom evidence. In online discussions students may consider more ideas generated by peers, provide more warrants for their ideas, and articulate their norms for evidence more carefully (e.g., Hsi, 1997).

Hoadley (2002) showed how design studies can refine discussion tools to increase the opportunity of students to learn from each other. As Hoadley and Linn (2000) reported, students can learn complex material from discussion alone, but they are more successful when the distinct views of experts are attributed to separate scientists than when all the comments are attributed to a teacher-like guide. Furthermore, groups vary in their success—some discussions have few participants and limited impact, whereas others engage all the learners. Research suggests that there is no straightforward connection between participating in discussion and learning—some students profit from minimal contact with the discussion and others who participate frequently fail to gain understanding (e.g., Cuthbert, Clark, et al., 2002).

Design challenges include ensuring that persuasive, unproductive, or unfruitful ideas are balanced with alternative views (Linn & Burbules, 1993), providing equitable opportunities for students to participate in scientific discourse (A. L. Brown & Campione, 1994; Lave & Wenger, 1991; Lemke, 1990; Sadker & Sadker, 1994) and enabling communities to devise agreed-on norms or criteria (e.g., Saxe, Gearhart, et al., 1993).

Highlight Cultural Norms

To help students sort out culturally constructed perspectives, we have studied the criteria students evoke in classroom discussions. D. Clark and Slotta (2000) reported design studies that investigate how students assess the validity of Internet sites. A well-established finding in the psychology literature concerns "cite amnesia" in which citizens, scientists, students, and others frequently pay more attention to the information reported in a communication than the authorship (Jacoby & Dallas, 1981). Thus, individuals might quote statements from advertisements as authoritative. When asked, these respondents do not recall that the material they now take as established was originally in a persuasive message. Working in groups, students can help each other by questioning the authority of Internet sites and by discussing criteria for validity. For example, students might jointly agree that evidence requires more than testimonials from so-called experts before being incorporated into an argument or ask their peers to back up assertions with data.

To become a community of learners, students negotiate shared criteria for scientific reasoning and shared standards for scientific argument. Developing shared criteria for science projects can improve group progress on scientific understanding (White & Frederiksen, 1998). For example, when students devise principles to explain scientific phenomena and then discuss their productions with their peers, they learn more than when they only generate principles (H. C. Clark, 1996).

Employ Multiple Social Structures

Technology can support a broad range of group learning activities. The knowledge integration environment's "How Far Does Light Go?" project takes advantage of social supports in a debate. Students work in pairs to engage in a range of activities: they create arguments using the SenseMaker tool, discuss alternatives, present their debate argument, compare their views, and critique each other. We designed the debate so all students learn from others by asking some students to present arguments and some to ask questions. The teacher helps by modeling good questions (Bell, chap. 6, this volume).

Software can help groups get critical appraisals of their work by allowing students to post intermediate results and monitor who can view the information. Tools such as the inquiry map can guide students to follow the jigsaw method or use other patterns of interaction (Aronson, 1978; Songer, 1996).

In summary, class discussion, peer collaboration, online discussion, and class debate can help students learn from others and learn about the varied norms, argument preferences, and beliefs associated with the cultural nature of knowledge integration. To take advantage of the learners' propensity to add ideas, discussions need participants with varied expertise. To help students generate connections, discussions profit from scaffolds to encourage critique and linking of ideas. Discussions can help students learn to ask for help when they are confused and enable students to recognize unproductive ideas—activities that are likely to direct the propensity to self-monitor in a productive direction.

PROMOTING AUTONOMY
AND LIFELONG LEARNING

The fourth metaprinciple of scaffolded knowledge integration, promoting autonomy and lifelong learning, involves establishing a rich, comprehensive inquiry process that students can apply to varied problems both in science class and throughout their lives. Students need to guide their own learning, recognize new ideas, and develop a view of effective inquiry to become autonomous science learners. This metaprinciple connects to the three natures of learning explicated in chapter 2 (Linn et al., this volume). To become responsible for their own learning in carrying out projects, students need to recognize new ideas and to de-

TABLE 3.5
Pragmatic Pedagogical Principles for Promoting
Autonomy and Lifelong Learning

Pragmatic Pedagogical Principle	Examples of Research Evidence	Examples of Learning Environment Features
Encourage monitoring: Engage students in reflecting on their own scientific ideas and on monitoring their own progress in understanding science.	Students who spontaneously reflect or explain their ideas learn more (Chi, Bassok, et al., 1989). When students are prompted to reflect, more individuals benefit from monitoring progress (Chi, de Leeuw, et al., 1994; Davis, 2003a).	Multiple, diverse opportunities for students to reflect on their ideas and create representations of their views
Provide complex projects: Engage students in varied, sustained science project experiences.	Many complex forms of reasoning only occur in the context of projects.	Scaffolds for students to perform projects and inspire students to continue on their own
Revisit and generalize inquiry processes: Establish a generalizable inquiry process suitable for diverse science projects that supports revisiting of ideas.	Gaining a robust understanding requires revisiting of ideas in new contexts.	Representations of inquiry so that the similarities between distinct projects become apparent
Scaffold critique: Engage students as critics of diverse scientific information and to establish generative norms.	When students understand the reciprocity between generation and critique of knowledge, they learn more (Davis, chap. 5, this volume).	Patterns to engage students in generation and critique

cide whether these ideas make sense. Instruction that elicits provocative ideas takes advantage of the interpretive nature of learning even when the ideas lack credibility by motivating learners to distinguish them from powerful ideas. Autonomous learners guide their interactions with peers and need the ability to identify cultural factors that motivate diverse opinions. One can take advantage of the deliberate nature of the learner by developing the ability to monitor progress and shaping it in the direction of promoting knowledge integration.

We summarize the pragmatic pedagogical principles (see Linn & Hsi, 2000, p. 40) associated with promoting autonomous lifelong learning in Table 3.5.

Encourage Monitoring

Requests to monitor progress and respond to feedback promote knowledge integration by motivating learners to review the connections in their knowledge network and evaluate their success (Chi, de Leeuw, et al., 1994; Davis, 2003a). When students make predictions prior to performing an experiment, for example, they are more likely to connect the results to their knowledge network than when they perform the experiment without making connections. Students who review their connections can look for incongruities, identify gaps, and establish a plan for their own future activities. Feedback from instructors or learning environments can motivate reorganization and focusing of ideas. Unambiguous feedback in the form of, for example, specific organizations for information may derail personal monitoring and stand in the way of individually constructed networks.

Generating a summary, account, outline, or set of questions about a topic can contribute to monitoring of progress (Bjork, 1999; Kintsch, 1998). Generating reflections on the topic helps students develop a more robust understanding of the material (Davis, 1998; Linn & Hsi, 2000). When learners perform a generation task, they make their own connections and have a chance to refine these connections. For knowledge integration, opportunities to generate a response succeed when learners make connections between the topic, their own ideas, and the ideas they have studied.

Optimal instruction balances feedback with opportunities for students to evaluate their own ideas. Instruction that helps groups form norms for their networks or explanations can improve the monitoring process. Crouch and Mazur (2001) engaged university physics students in making predictions, answering diagnostic questions, and using feedback to become better at explaining their ideas and developing understanding.

Too much or poor feedback appears to deter students from thoughtful consideration of their own network of ideas (Anderson, 1982; Davis, Linn, et al., 1995). For example, Schoenfeld (1987) reported that mathematics learners come to rely on established practices instead of monitoring progress. To promote monitoring, designers need to balance independent and scaffolded work.

Provide Complex Projects

Designing instruction to develop an autonomous stance toward science knowledge integration involves helping students carry out their own inquiry projects by distinguishing ideas, seeking comprehensive ideas, and recognizing unique cases that reveal special features. Projects that engage students in sustained inquiry need to address consequential, central topics in science and to connect to future learning.

Numerous supports for sustained inquiry in complex settings exist. For example, in case-based learning (Kolodner, Crismond, et al., 1998; Schank, Fano, et al., 1993/1994) the instructor provides students with the opportunity to study and analyze complex cases of innovations, designs, or problem solutions relevant to their own concerns. Students are scaffolded to learn from these cases and use the materials that they have studied to design solutions to new, personally compelling problems. Another project, BGuILE (Reiser, Tabak, et al., 2001), also supports sustained reasoning—for example, about Galapagos finches—and provides powerful scaffolds such as partially completed charts to help students carry out a generative study (Reiser, Tabak, et al., 2001).

Socratic dialogues also promote sustained inquiry. When someone plays the devil's advocate, they provoke new explanations.

Ultimately, students need to become deliberate guides in their efforts to solve complex projects. To help students get started, research shows the benefit of prompts for reflection (Davis & Linn, 2000; Linn, 1992a; Scardamalia & Bereiter, 1991a). Linn and Clancy (1992) demonstrated the impact of prompts for reflection in programming case studies. Davis (2003a) and Chi, de Leeuw, et al. (1994) have shown that autonomous students engage in more effective reflection than do their less autonomous peers.

Creating a complex project involves balancing large and small questions. In projects, students link ideas in effective and in unproductive ways. For example, linking principles to real-world experiences is very desirable because one of the central goals of learning science is to enrich understanding of the world by using the scientific principles. Yet very often students do not make such links. McDermott (1990) reported that in many domains of physics (optics, electricity, motion, etc.) students cannot connect their science learning to principles. Bagno and Eylon (1997) showed that both students and their teachers rarely generate relations within domains of physics. When teachers fail to connect topics such as electric circuits and electrostatics or when they teach concepts of fields and potentials studied in mechanics and electromagnetism as two unrelated domains, they fail to model this process for students.

Researchers from a behaviorist tradition have frequently argued against complex cases and problems and for a more controlled instructional setting that prevents students from going down wrong paths or elaborating flawed ideas. ACT theory (Anderson, 1982) called for analyzing student problem solving and intervening whenever students made flawed inferences. Anderson's Geometry, Lisp, and Algebra Tutors, devised following this tradition, inhibit generation of unsuccessful steps in problem solving. The Algebra Tutor (Koedinger & Anderson, 1998) has successfully taught large numbers of students in conjunction with traditional instruction. Observers find that the tutor inhibits wrong paths, but students regularly explore these paths in traditional activities. In addition, evaluation of the instruction suggests that the tutor enhances learning by providing a coherent, accessible set of examples, extensive feedback, and a consistent pace of progress.

Nevertheless, the packed curriculum in the United States means that students cannot finish all the topics in the algebra course in the available time. These findings illustrate the advantages of directing the process of generating explanations and also demonstrate that fundamentally knowledge integration takes instructional time that is often not available.

A variety of studies illustrate the benefits of asking students to generate explanations to develop autonomous reasoning ability. Relating knowledge gained in solving problems to the repertoire of relevant principles and concepts can be enhanced by asking students to identify this repertoire and to explicitly represent the relations in the web of concepts and principles. Such activities improve problem solving and recall of main ideas in the domain (Bagno, Eylon, et al., 2000).

By developing concentrated, cohesive knowledge webs students can deal with the more dilute ideas that arise naturally. By *concentrated* we mean webs that have links to all the nuances of the situation and that clarify the central and peripheral notions of the topic. When students already have some comprehensive ideas, they are more likely to connect new ideas to more powerful ideas, and they also can begin to develop a set of criteria for their own organization of ideas. To succeed in developing such webs, students need to engage in sustained reasoning, to encounter ideas in multiple contexts, and to prepare themselves to recognize ideas in familiar contexts.

Revisit and Generalize Inquiry Processes

Students need a repertoire of approaches to inquiry that they can reuse. By labeling and highlighting repeated aspects of inquiry, such as critiquing perspectives, designing experiments, making predictions, interpreting perspectives, and forming arguments, one can help students recognize some general inquiry skills that apply to most situations. These are often called *critical thinking* or *problem solving*.

Learners who revisit a topic review the connections between perspectives associated with the topic, strengthening some and relaxing others. Learners who revisit topics as part of learning develop an orienting response to the topic and potentially become more receptive to connections to the topic in the future. By making revisiting of ideas part of instruction, designers mimic the experience of lifelong learning in which students might encounter an instructed topic outside of class.

When learners revisit a topic, they reuse their inquiry process with customization to the new contexts. Research shows that retrieval of information has a greater impact on learning than additional study of the same information (e.g., Bjork, 1994). Revisiting, when successful, has the effect of strengthening the connections to the retrieval process and therefore increasing the likelihood of retrieval in the future. Instructors can take advantage of the deliberate nature of the learner by orchestrating the revisiting of topics.

Research by Bell (1997) contrasts two approaches with equal instructional time for researching the question, "How far does light go?" Students are more successful when they develop arguments for both the light goes forever and the light dies out viewpoints. By switching between these two viewpoints, students gain a more linked understanding and develop a more normative view of the topic than when they only study one of the views. To study both, students need to revisit each one after doing some research on the other topic.

Revisiting enhances the knowledge web by adding connections to the contexts where revisiting takes place. Revisiting can add new perspectives to the knowledge web as well as stimulate connections to events that occurred between when the first learning took place and when the revisiting happened. Even when revisiting does not result in retrieval, it has the potential of motivating additional study of the topic (Linn & Hsi, 2000).

A 3-year program for middle school students in chemistry shows the benefits of revisiting complex science (Margel et al., 2003). During these years students revisited the particulate model of matter in three different modules. Each module involved a different context built on the knowledge gained in the previous one and used a very different approach to teaching. The relation was explicitly formed through common vocabulary and other organization aids. Students' understanding of the particulate model was refined, and they retained the understanding long-term.

To make inquiry revisiting visible, designers devised software supports like the *checklist*, a sequence of classroom activity structures, or the inquiry map to scaffold revisiting of inquiry strategies. The CLP project used the checklist to portray the reusable pattern of activities. Subsequent partnerships and projects continue the process (Linn, Clark, et al., 2003; Reiser, Tabak, et al., 2001; Sherwood et al., 1998). Students who learn these patterns can become autonomous learners who use multiple activity structures (rather than memorization) to reach coherent understanding.

In designing instruction for revisiting inquiry processes, selecting the scope of knowledge integration influences success. Selecting an appropriate level of analysis and meaningful specific examples allows students to make connections rather than isolating and forgetting science ideas.

Scaffold Critique

Learners identify weaknesses in perspectives when they seek to clarify, revise, or add links. Davis (2003a) described how this knowledge integration process, a form of metacognition, promotes all the other processes. Davis (chap. 5, this volume) reports that those who identify weaknesses in their own perspectives are better at critiquing ideas of others.

Conflict among ideas can promote knowledge integration and learning when used appropriately, but conflict can also cause students to isolate ideas. When conflicts reveal new relations, they can be resolved with more connections. To engage students in the deliberate process of learning, Davis and Linn (2000) investigated prompts for reflection. In a series of studies they found that embedded prompts in Knowledge Integration Environments (KIE) projects varied in their effects and their effectiveness. As Davis and Linn (2000) illustrated, creating effective prompts can be difficult. Not all prompts result in the knowledge integration desired. Some prompts derail the knowledge integration process leading students in unfruitful directions, whereas others promote knowledge integration. Carefully designed prompts can help students begin to ask themselves questions and look at scientific claims critically. Davis (chap. 5, this volume; 2003a) has also shown that students need to add new ideas to their repertoire but also need opportunities to identify weaknesses in their knowledge. This identification, promoted by productive reflection, helps them engage in other knowledge integration processes such as linking ideas and distinguishing among others.

In summary, to promote autonomy and lifelong learning, students need opportunities to generate and recognize new ideas and to connect them to existing ideas; they need to learn to monitor their prog-

ress so that they gain more cohesive understanding. They need to engage in sustained project work so they can connect personally relevant
problems to class topics and reflect on experience using a robust inquiry process in diverse contexts. Instruction should help students become autonomous by providing varied supports and communicating a
robust inquiry process.

CONCLUSIONS

To characterize knowledge integration we look at learning and instruction through three mutually supportive lenses: the science instruction lens described in this chapter as well as the science learning
lens and the cognitive process lens described in chapter 2 (Linn et al.,
this volume). We depict connections among these lenses in Table 3.1
as well as chapter 2, Table 2.1. The lenses inform the design of instruction but are not sufficient to resolve all the questions that arise.

In Part II, we employ what we call *design narratives* to capture the
empirical process of designing, testing, and refining instruction
aimed at knowledge integration. We discuss how these lenses influenced the design of the KIE as introduced in chapter 1 (Linn, Davis, &
Bell, this volume) and show how the lenses influenced the iterative
process of curriculum design. From these design studies come insights that improve our knowledge integration perspective on learning and our scaffolded knowledge integration framework for instruction. The reciprocal relations between the continuous refinement of
the knowledge integration view of learning and instruction and the
improvement of instruction reflect the rich system of interactions
that exist in the field of education.

The design narratives, shaped by the three lenses, also yield curriculum design patterns for instructional activities in the areas of critique
(Davis, chap. 5, this volume), debate (Bell, chap. 6, this volume), design (Hoadley, chap. 7, this volume), and investigation (D. Clark,
chap. 8, this volume). These patterns form starting points for design
groups interested in creating new activities because they already capture much of our instructional framework and have benefited from iterative refinement.

From these reciprocal relationships emerge specific principles to
guide designers of new curriculum materials, of professional development programs, of design activities, and of educational policies. Each
chapter in Part II and most chapters in Part III identify specific principles backed by empirical work. These specific principles are summa-

rized and connected to the metaprinciples and the pragmatic pedagogical principles in chapter 13 (Linn, Bell, & Davis, this volume).

Finally, from the design narratives, the application of design principles, and the critical appraisal of activities in new contexts come methods for research that match the complex, systemic nature of the field of education. We discuss starting points for the emerging field of design-based studies in chapter 4 (Bell et al., this volume).

In summary, the lenses summarized in chapters 2 (Linn et al., this volume) and 3 (Linn, Davis, & Eylon, this volume) both inform and are informed by the design-based studies reported in the following chapters. From this work emerges curriculum design patterns, design principles, and design narratives that offer a diverse group of individuals interested in improving science education starting points for their efforts.

4

Design-Based Research
in Education

Philip Bell
University of Washington

Christopher M. Hoadley
The Pennsylvania State University

Marcia C. Linn
University of California, Berkeley

Design-based research studies respond to the systemic, complex nature of education and align well with the goal of promoting inquiry in science courses. The current theoretical frameworks for learning and instruction lack the detail necessary to guide all aspects of the design of science education programs. Design-based research studies draw on the full range of social science research methods to improve designs for instruction and advance understanding of learning. The reciprocal relation between curriculum improvement and advances in theoretical frameworks distinguishes this type of research program from earlier work.

Research programs using these methods engineer instructional materials including technology-enhanced learning environments and curriculum projects as well as study the educational phenomena that emerge from the enactment of the curriculum. These designs are informed by educational goals such as promoting inquiry and guided by instructional frameworks such as knowledge integration. Researchers test the designs in authentic settings and gather evidence about the impact of the materials. The research partnership then analyzes the results of the investigation, reformulates the instructional materials, and reconceptualizes the theoretical framework guiding the research.

Design-based research studies continue a tradition begun over 100 years ago. At the laboratory school at the University of Chicago, Dewey (1896) pioneered a research model that employed the systematic study of teaching and learning associated with the enactment of complex educational interventions. As Dewey (1929) later explained in detail, he sought to make the act of teaching less ad hoc and mystical. Research traditions that follow in Dewey's footsteps include design experiments (A. Brown, 1992; Collins, 1992), design studies (Bell, in press; Linn & Hsi, 2000), local sciences research (diSessa, 1991), teaching experiments (Steffe & Thompson, 2000), and design-based research in education (Design-Based Research Collective, 2003; Hoadley, 2002). We refer to these and other interventionist research efforts as *design-based research studies* or *design studies* for short and illustrate relevant methodologies.

Design studies respond to the need to study complex interventions that include a range of intentionally designed features and materials such as curriculum sequences, technological tools, social norms, instructional approaches, activity structures, and cognitive assessments in complex settings. Design studies capture the iterative exploration and refinement of these educational elements in the varied places where learning occurs. This research tradition also allows for the appropriation and customization of such materials and approaches by specific learning communities.

We illustrate our research program in the next sections of this book. In our investigations, we carry out multiple iterations of projects in diverse classrooms and summarize the results. We present the results of these iterations as design narratives to provide a detailed history of the research questions, the corresponding studies, the resulting design knowledge, and the research findings. We represent the sequence of activities in successful projects in curriculum design patterns. We synthesize promising design practices in design principles. Additionally, we combine the results of these studies with research by others to reformulate the knowledge integration perspective on learning and the scaffolded knowledge integration framework for instruction.

Design studies put the development of educational approaches in a reciprocal relation with research that involves theorizing about learning, cognition, and development. Design-based research thereby affords the opportunity to develop detailed design knowledge (e.g., design principles, curriculum design patterns) while simultaneously advancing theoretical knowledge of learning and cognition (diSessa, 1991). As researchers, we seek to make our research increasingly cumulative, cohesive, repeatable, and inspectable.

RATIONALE FOR DESIGN-BASED
RESEARCH IN EDUCATION

Our research group elected to engage in design-based research to work toward the ultimate goals of promoting innovation in diverse educational contexts, surfacing educational phenomena of interest for detailed study, and keeping apace with the changing fields of the natural sciences as well as the educational possibilities of computer technology.

The systemic nature of education combined with rapid, often unanticipated, changes in the context of teaching and learning calls for new methods to conduct interventionist research in naturalistic settings. We draw on established research paradigms in cognitive anthropology (e.g., Hutchins, 1995; Lave, 1987), cognitive psychology (e.g., Anderson & Schunn, 2000; Bjork, 1999; Kintsch, 1998), and action research (e.g., Masters, 1995) while also investigating new approaches for data collection and analysis as necessitated by the research. Controlled laboratory studies of learning and cognition in the cognitive psychology tradition can only partially inform the systemic and enduring issues in education. Detailed observational studies of "cognition-in-the-wild," as found in the cognitive anthropology tradition, add to our understanding but fall short of embracing the designed nature of real-world contexts and typically lack the interventionist mandate associated with design-based research. Action research can be considered an established design-based research approach that weds research activities to the concerns of practice (Masters, 1995), although it has been stereotyped (fairly or unfairly) more as political action rather than research.

Educational innovations typically exist as collections of materials, activities, and practice (A. L. Brown & Campione, 1994; Salomon, 1996). They respond to the systemic nature of education—with some features coming from intentional design, whereas others emerge during enactment. Unanticipated consequences emerge from the interacting aspects of the situation. This systemic quality of education makes innovations quite difficult to design, cultivate, enact, and study. Features of the design (and the underlying design principles) are often contingent on one another and interact in unpredictable ways. To better promote the diffusion of innovation (cf. Rogers, 1995), researchers need to develop a better understanding of innovative educational programs and of how participants customize them in varied settings. By attempting to coordinate the use of innovative educational programs, one can identify educational phenomena for study and also learn about systemic connections that exist within the learning environments.

CUSTOMIZATION

Several realities push researchers toward a design-based approach that respects enactment and customization (Baumgartner, chap. 11, this volume). Student populations vary greatly in terms of experience, fluency with language, technology, and science, as well as cultural norms for communication and learning. This diversity leads to many educational opportunities and challenges with regard to the promotion of innovation. It calls for creative customization of innovations and contradicts a one-size-fits-all approach to curriculum, instruction, and assessment. Educational designers and teachers can leverage off of the characteristics and practices of specific communities, although significant effort is typically involved. Still, design studies allow for the sensible local customization and appropriation of materials, tools, and approaches originally designed for use with other participants.

To respond to the rapid expansion of scientific knowledge, educational designers and teachers need to regularly refine curriculum for future scientists and nonscientists alike. The avalanche of findings in the natural sciences significantly shapes the activities and policies of society. Providing a firm foundation for integrating unanticipated impacts of contemporary scientific research requires new, more responsive curricular materials. Design studies allow one to explore new educational opportunities and the concomitant issues associated with advances in one's understanding of the natural world. For example, in chapter 10 Bell (this volume) explores the educational opportunities associated with contemporary controversies in science.

New technological possibilities outstrip the ability to research their implications for education. As the Internet reaches more and more schools and families, the possibilities for engaging with information and for interpersonal interaction increase. Beyond proving the feasibility of new learning technologies, researchers need to understand how new forms of technology can be productively embedded into larger systems of human activity (curricula, intellectual investigations, group activities, disciplinary inquiry). Design-based approaches provide for such contextualization and integration of technology in educational practice.

Clearly, the complexity of these settings, multiple interacting trajectories, pressing societal problems, and the new possibilities represented by emerging technologies justify design-based research. These studies use methods matched to the complexity of the endeavor. They help understand and distinguish real-world contexts of learning.

DESIGN-BASED RESEARCH METHODS

Design-based research in education includes testing theoretical accounts of learning, cognition, and development by using the theory to design or engineer instruction and conducting empirical studies of the instruction in a naturalistic setting. Design studies result in designed innovations as well as theoretical insights about learning, cognition, and development (diSessa, 1991). Chapters in Parts II and III report on design studies.

Partnerships guide design-based research studies. *Partnerships* are interdisciplinary teams that include teachers, technologists, educational researchers, and disciplinary experts who bring diverse but relevant expertise to the effort (see Shear, Bell, & Linn, chap. 12, this volume; also see Linn, Shear, et al., 1999; Linn, 1990; Radinsky et al., 2001). Successful partnerships respect each other's expertise, contribute to each other's professional development, and over time negotiate a common perspective on learning, instruction, technology, and innovation. The partnerships develop shared criteria for the activities they are conducting and develop approaches for further modifying the materials and instruction. These mutually beneficial partnerships (to use the terminology of Radinsky et al., 2001) strongly resemble participatory design efforts in computer science and stand in contrast to other curriculum development and evaluation efforts in which decreed materials are mandated for use by teachers without their active codesign (e.g., Linn, Songer, et al., 1996).

Design-based research activities are inherently iterative and take place in naturalistic learning settings. At the course level, these studies involve cycles of design, enactment, and detailed study. At a more fine-grained level, these phases are somewhat less distinct (cf. Cobb, 2001). That is, partnerships may conduct ministudies within the design phase (e.g., to test usability of interfaces or pilot test instruments), microcycles of design during the enactment phase to respond to local features of the setting, as well as redesign during the detailed study phase.

Design research also includes what we call *compelling comparisons* in which two forms of the innovation are enacted under otherwise similar conditions (e.g., Davis, chap. 5, Bell, chap. 6, and Hoadley, chap. 7, this volume; see also Linn, in press). Variations in the innovation used during such compelling comparisons test hypotheses about learning embedded in the designs. Compelling comparisons test hypotheses with strict methodological techniques such as controlled comparisons with random assignment, double-blind coding of outcomes, and longitudinal studies. These techniques yield more benefit when accompanied by rich understanding of the context of the research (Linn, in press). Such comparative experimentation can provide important insights about learning.

Design-based research can focus on creating generalizable innovations, customizing instruction to specific contexts, or testing design principles. In chapter 11, Baumgartner (this volume) illustrates customization research for a water quality project. In chapter 12, Shear et al. (this volume) illustrate the varied forms partnerships take, showing how customization can be primarily guided by local teachers and how technological innovation might primarily be guided by pedagogy experts. Balancing the proportion of partnership participants should align with the research questions and issues faced by the investigation.

DESIGN NARRATIVES: A MISSING GENRE
FOR EDUCATIONAL RESEARCH

Although reports of experiments should include enough information to permit others to repeat the experiment, this is often impossible in educational research for two reasons. First, because our interventions as researchers are culturally embodied the complexity of human nature may prevent us from adequately and completely describing our research context. This problem is well explored in the field of ethnography, and researchers turn to richer and richer descriptions (so-called thick descriptions) of a research setting to communicate factors that may be relevant. A second, related idea is that educational research is often naturalistic and may be quasi-experimental, correlational, or descriptive. Researchers rarely control every variable, every aspect of experience in and around a classroom, much less the out-of-school experiences students and teachers bring to their classroom lives. Because researchers cannot precisely engineer learning contexts, replications vary many factors. There is an art to identifying relevant aspects of the research context and to communicating results that include potentially relevant factors.

Although findings are not universal in the tradition of physical science research, they are often helpful to others in similar (but distinct) contexts. As Linn, Davis, and Eylon point out in chapter 3 (this volume), rather than uncovering inviolable laws, the goal is to conduct research that leads to locally grounded theories and findings, and through application by experienced practitioners in other contexts, to uncover just how localized or generalizable the findings are. Design principles are one important way of providing these findings, but by themselves they often fail to help educational designers interpret others' experience and apply it to new problems. Likewise, educational researchers need more information to understand, question, test, and refine these principles.

Design-based research can meet the challenge of replicability by adequately describing research contexts. In design narratives researchers describe the tools they have designed, the learning context, the activities and practices offered to the users, and most important, the evolution of the context over time in response to the tools. Design narratives also critically evaluate the assessments and outcomes and reflect on whether or not the measures used in the research adequately capture the results.

Design narratives encourage deeper attention to cultural questions in education. Too often, consumers of research want simple answers to questions that require more serious study such as, "What is the added value of technology?" or worse yet, "Is learning with technology better than without technology?," irrespective of how technology is used. Rich descriptions of the context, use, and outcomes of instructional studies help consumers appreciate the measures of research studies.

Design narratives tell the story of the events leading up to, during, and following the investigation. Design narratives help make sense of design studies by including compelling comparisons as well as more informal research.

Narratives may omit details, but important agents, events, causes, and results are relayed. A design narrative describes the history and evolution of a design over time. It abstracts the wealth of information available such as videotapes of the entire design process and all uses of the designed artifacts. It communicates compactly and effectively how a design came into being and succeeded in the classroom. It is broader than a design rationale, which provides only the reasons for the current state of the design; a good design narrative should describe failed design elements as well as successful ones and should relate the warrants used for making changes to the design over time. By relating the design changes over time, a design narrative can help make explicit some of the implicit knowledge the designer or research partnerships used to understand and implement the intervention.

Another important advantage of a design narrative is that it helps promote adoption of both principles and packages. A design narrative clarifies which elements of the program are intentional and which were accidental. Often narratives can say which elements were responses to local constraints that may not apply in other settings. Additionally, because so many design decisions involve trade-offs, narratives can explore why certain trade-offs were made so that people who customize may choose different trade-offs if their values or their situation demand it.

Established educational, psychological, and instructional theory helps inform these decisions. Often the detailed examples and rationale provided in a design narrative help illustrate the origins and nature of the design principles that are reported. When design principles are proposed, an account of their origins can help others who might refine those principles attempt to account for the data that led to their proposal in the first place. The scaffolded knowledge integration research program articulates locally grounded theories and findings, encourages the use of these results by experienced practitioners in other contexts, and attempts to capture the localized or generalized character of the work. Design principles are one important way of capturing these findings. Educational researchers need detailed information about research so they can understand, question, test, and refine these principles.

By reflecting on the evolution of designs over time, partnerships can uncover important regularities. These regularities may be locally applicable design principles or important overarching findings that help isolate relevant factors in technologies. Reflections help achieve better alignment between theories, interventions, and assessment (Cronbach, 1975), thereby increasing the validity, especially consequential validity (Gray, 1997).

The goal of this book is to provide design narratives of varied methodological rigor and present many of the studies that informed the design, to give the general shape of the design process, and to describe what was learned in the large. In covering several years of development work, some of the detailed description is left out. For instance, Hoadley (2002) described not only how the design of a collaboration tool evolved over time but also how specific experiences the designers had in the classroom helped inform the design. The narrative illustrates how observations prevented misinterpretation of the experimental data. This type of narrative is important because it helps others avoid the same pitfalls, and it also demonstrates the added benefit of the design-based approach. The minimal descriptions of a single study often reprinted in journals rarely capture theoretical reframing or customizable components of the innovation. Design narratives help report, honestly and credibly, a refinement in understanding rather than a replacement. In much classroom research, to really understand what happened—or what could be made to happen—requires a story.

REPRESENTING DESIGN KNOWLEDGE
IN DESIGN PRINCIPLES

In education, it is becoming increasingly common to represent design knowledge and theoretical insights as design principles that emerge from research with the goal of informing future design activities. Design principles speak to the pragmatic aspects of practice while also informing theories of learning. The research on scaffolded knowledge integration has developed design principles that span the continuum from being localized to specific aspects of learning or the setting to being more general principles that span across contexts or guide the more universal contours of instruction.

Design principles have a long history. Early human factors research identified specific principles or guidelines for design of interfaces (e.g., Card, Moran, et al., 1983). Recent designers have continued the tradition (Nielson, 2000). Building on this tradition, some educational researchers have developed generic design principles (e.g., Merrill & Twitchell, 1994; Reigeluth et al., 1993). Recent commentators have compiled specific examples of effective designs into books (e.g., Tufte, 1997). Other researchers have devised guidelines for specific disciplines or tasks (e.g., Kolodner, 1993). Recently, Kali (2002) led a group at the Center for Innovative Learning Technology to create a database of contemporary design principles harvested from researchers conducting a plethora of diverse studies.

Design principles vary a great deal (as demonstrated in this volume). Some are like general laws of physics and others are like specific opportunities. Rather than try to define a unitary class of design principles, they are established in this book at different levels of localized specificity (e.g., principles tied to a learning community, cultural group, or a more general aspect of cognitive processing) and generality.

Taken together, the general cognitive principles introduced in chapter 2 (Linn, Eylon, & Davis, this volume), the metaprinciples and pragmatic pedagogical principles introduced in chapter 3 (Linn et al., this volume), and the specific principles described in chapter 13 (Linn, Bell, & Davis, this volume) capture the knowledge integration view of learning and instruction. We define the four types of principles as follows.

General Cognitive Principles

These principles describe cognitive processes. Many of these principles emerge from research on memory and skill acquisition generally conducted in laboratories with undergraduates who respond to tasks using materials that minimize prior knowledge. In chapter 2, Linn et al. (this volume) identify three general processes that underlie the performance of all learners: (a) recognizing and adding ideas, (b) generating connections among ideas, and (c) monitoring progress toward self-generated goals.

Metaprinciples

These principles capture the results from multiple research programs in science learning and instruction. Linn and Hsi (2000) identified four metaprinciples in prior work: (a) make science accessible, (b) make thinking visible, (c) help students learn from others, and (d) promote autonomy and lifelong learning.

Pragmatic Pedagogical Principles

These principles are each associated with a metaprinciple. They emerge to capture a research program in science education and typically apply across instructional settings. Linn and Hsi (2000) identified 14 of these principles in prior work and the authors of this book report on how these research programs have progressed.

Specific Principles

These principles synthesize results from specific design-based research studies and may or may not generalize beyond the setting from which they emerge. Specific principles offer starting points for new design partnerships as well as individual teachers working in specific settings. In chapter 13, Linn et al. (this volume) summarize the specific principles introduced in earlier chapters and connect them to pragmatic pedagogical principles.

As noted in chapters 2 (Linn et al., this volume) and 3 (Linn et al., this volume), learning and instruction are looked at through three lenses that roughly align with the research programs in cognition, science learning, and design of science instruction. Although these lenses have much in common, they each offer unique insights and jointly inform each other.

In chapter 2, Linn et al. (this volume) articulate connections between research on cognitive processes and research on science learning; in Table 2.1, they show how the general cognitive processes connect to the knowledge integration perspective on learning.

In chapter 3, Linn et al. (this volume) summarize the connections between research on cognitive processes and research on the design of effective science instruction. The connections between the meta-principles and the general cognitive processes are depicted in Table 3.1. Tables 3.2, 3.3, 3.4, and 3.5 (Linn et al., chap. 3, this volume) illustrate how the pragmatic pedagogical principles extend understanding of the metaprinciples. These tables provide pointers to research programs investigating the pragmatic pedagogical principles. The tables also describe learning environment features that implement the pragmatic pedagogical principles.

In chapter 13, Linn et al. (this volume) capture the specific principles resulting from research reported in this volume; they describe evidence supporting each of the specific principles and also show how designers have used the specific principles to create curriculum materials.

USING DESIGN PRINCIPLES TO IMPROVE INSTRUCTION

Design principles require interpretation. Design principles might lead to approaches that are most easily afforded by technology tools; however, the principles generally inform instructional activities whether or not technology is directly employed. Much in the way design principles or patterns in architecture do not fully determine the design of a house but rather can serve to guide the process in the hands of a skilled architect (Alexander et al., 1977), researchers view design principles as an intermediate step between scientific findings, which must be generalized and replicable, and local experiences or examples that come up in practice.

Because of the need to interpret design principles, they are not as readily falsifiable as scientific laws. The principles are generated inductively from prior examples of success and are subject to refinement over time as others try to adapt them to their own experiences. In this sense, they are falsifiable; if they do not yield purchase in the design process, they will be debated, altered, and eventually dropped.

Principles become stronger when they have a tight link to empirical research, and the work in this volume illustrates this synergy. This research began by incorporating cognitive models of conceptual change and adding sociocultural models of collaborative learning, scaffolding, and debate. Each of these perspectives brought theory to bear on the design processes involved in creating curriculum, shaped the types of research questions that were being addressed, and engendered dialogue on how the designs and design principles embodied hypotheses about learning. The principles in this book link to theories of learning and draw support from studies of the impact of designs as well as from more traditional research findings.

Design principles are established, communicated, and refined for them to help inform future educational design work. For that reason, it is necessary to carefully demarcate when particular principles might apply to design activities or how principles are systemically connected (i.e., mutually constitutive) so that they can be applied in appropriate clusters.

Design knowledge finds its way into design practice in many ways. Principles might become embedded in artifacts that are reused either as intact elements or as metaphors for further innovation. Design knowledge might be represented in a design trade-off reported in a case study of an innovation. We fully expect the principles we propose to be discussed, refined, and rescoped as others attempt to put them into practice. For this reason we have borrowed from other design fields that have leveraged design narratives to further communicate the origin and application of design principles for particular purposes. Simultaneously, we have made our assumptions and trade-offs clear in the narrative account.

CONCLUSIONS AND FUTURE DIRECTIONS

Design studies require further refinement and formalization to fully guide educational inquiry.[1] Researchers trained in this emerging tradition are applying it to novel educational contexts such as teacher professional development, the design of educational tools used in informal learning contexts (Stevens et al., 2002), and the district-wide scaling of educational reform efforts (Confrey et al., 2001). Graduate methods courses in design studies are introducing the associated research practices to students in colleges of education.[2]

Design narratives depict the orchestration of productive partnerships between classroom teachers, learning scientists, and natural scientists. In the sense of participatory design, further exploration is needed of the mechanisms for involving participants in design-based research. Teachers and scientists should explore how to more deeply involve stakeholders such as parents, administrators, and policymakers in this work.

The epistemological basis of design narratives and their products, including design principles and other forms of design knowledge, deserves further scrutiny. How can design knowledge systematically inform educational design and teacher practice? How can such knowledge become integrated into the day-to-day practices of designers? Other fields such as architecture and engineering have evolved rich design-based traditions and practices. More work is needed to explore productive forms of design knowledge for the field of education. Researchers need to make further progress on how they communicate the nature of design activities and research to others. Design principles, case studies, project histories, narrative accounts, and detailed ethnographic descriptions of designs in use represent some specific forms that could be further explored for this purpose.

Design-based research represents a compelling and distinct form of educational inquiry with roots in Dewey's (1896) work at the laboratory school in Chicago. The chapters in this book showcase a range of approaches while taking advantage of closely related learning environments. This interventionist and iterative research yields design principles, comparison studies, and designed artifacts to advance understanding of learning with technology.

Although there is room to further formalize the range of methods associated with design-based research, it is an emerging paradigm for educational inquiry sitting alongside other established research methodologies (historical, experimental, philosophical, anthropological). One can expect design-based research to be applied to diverse corners of the education landscape in the coming years.

ENDNOTES

1. We are aware of two funded efforts to promote the formalization of design-based research in education. The Spencer Foundation funded a group of scholars to engage in such work starting in 2000 (http://designbasedresearch.org/). The National Science Foundation funded a 3-year research project in 2001 to explore similar issues (http://gse.gmu.edu/research/de/).

2. A two-quarter research methods course was taught during the 2001–2002 academic year at the University of Washington to support students in applying the practices of design-based research to questions and issues of their own interest (http://faculty.washington.edu/pbell/courses/design-methods). Analogously, a one-quarter course on research-based design methods has been taught to future practitioners at Stanford's School of Education since 1998.

II

CURRICULUM DESIGN PATTERNS FOR KNOWLEDGE INTEGRATION

5

Creating Critique Projects

Elizabeth A. Davis
University of Michigan

The Internet has become a tremendously important resource for science teaching. However, students often accept information as valid just because they see it in print. One of the goals in the Knowledge Integration Environment (KIE; Bell, Davis, et al., 1995; Linn, Davis, & Bell, chap. 1, this volume) is to help kids develop a critical eye in using materials on the World Wide Web. Critique is a crucial scientific practice; scientists apply criteria to help them differentiate between high- and low-quality claims and evidence. Using KIE, students think critically about evidence and use it to build arguments. Another primary goal of KIE is to help students integrate their conceptual knowledge. By *knowledge integration* (Linn, Eylon, & Davis, chap. 2, this volume; cf. also Linn, 1995; Smith, diSessa, & Roschelle, 1994) I mean, at its most basic level, the process of linking scientific ideas together to develop a robust, coherent, conceptual understanding. Knowledge integration is a view of how students learn. Specifically, I am interested here in how students learn science.

The studies I report in this chapter investigated ways of prompting students to foster engagement in productive thinking—most notably reflection—as they engage in critique and knowledge integration. I use the term *reflection* to refer to both metacognition and sense making. For example, reflection can focus on goals or on one's own thinking (metacognition) or on content itself (sense making). I look at reflection facilitated by sentence-starter prompts that explicitly call for this special kind of thinking.

I take as an assumption that reflection can help students undertake the other processes of knowledge integration as well as the practice of critique. Knowledge integration processes include expanding one's repertoire of ideas, distinguishing between ideas, making links between them, and identifying weaknesses in one's current knowledge (Linn et al., chap. 2, this volume; Linn, 1995). I characterize reflection as *poor* or *unproductive* when it seems unlikely to promote knowledge integration and as *more productive* when it is more likely to foster knowledge integration. For instance, students who, when they reflect, recognize weaknesses in their current understanding are more apt to engage in the other knowledge integration processes of linking and distinguishing ideas. These students who critique their own ideas may also be more likely to critique the ideas of others. Characterizing how reflection may promote knowledge integration and critique is one goal of the series of studies I report in this chapter.

The research I report here takes place in an eighth-grade physical science classroom using the KIE software and curriculum. Success using KIE is measured both by conceptual understanding and by ability to critique and use evidence. Although in more traditional science classes a student can often succeed without reflection, in this classroom reflection plays a paramount role because it helps students set goals and monitor (and improve) their understanding.

Through this research, I identify characteristics of prompts that most effectively promote productive learning outcomes and describe how those outcomes may be mediated by reflection. I also identify the conditions in which particular kinds of prompts are most effective. Toward this end, I describe studies of prompts for justification, explanation, planning, monitoring, and reflection. Together, these results inform the field's understanding of knowledge integration. Furthermore, the results can be used in designing instruction in classrooms to foster in all students the knowledge integration processes that happen naturally for some students and to help students learn to engage in these processes autonomously over time—whether good prompting is embedded in a teacher's instructional practice or in educational software.

PROMPTING IN KIE: HISTORY AND RATIONALE

How did my colleagues and I come to design the particular types of prompts used in the studies reported here? The KIE software and curricula have developed directly out of Linn's extensive research on designing curricula and technology for middle school science teaching and learning, especially the Computer as Learning Partner (CLP) project (see, e.g., Linn & Hsi, 2000; Linn & Songer, 1991). The prompts used in KIE build on the CLP experiences as well as those of other researchers (e.g., Chi, de Leeuw, et al., 1994; Palincsar & Brown, 1984; Scardamalia & Bereiter, 1991a; Tabak et al., 1998). However, KIE projects are more open-ended than CLP laboratories. KIE projects are aimed more squarely at synthesis of prior knowledge than is most work in self-explanations. They are less activity driven than summarizing a passage in reciprocal teaching. Also, they are more directed than the knowledge building of Computer Supported Intentional Learning Environments (CSILE). Thus, KIE requires prompts that explicitly encourage students to make explanations and to reflect at selected points as they work on complex projects (see Davis, 2003a). Table 5.1 summarizes the kinds of prompts used in KIE in various instantiations; I describe the studies in which the prompts were investigated in later sections.

Prompts for sense making, explanation, and justification can take the form of questions or sentence starters to be responded to verbally (A. L. Brown & Palincsar, 1989; Chi, 2000; Chi, de Leeuw, et al., 1994; Hogan, 1999; Palincsar & Brown, 1984; van Zee & Minstrell, 1997) or in writing (Linn & Songer, 1991; Recker & Pirolli, 1995; Rothkopf, 1966; Scardamalia & Bereiter, 1991a; White & Frederiksen, 1995, 1998). Regardless of delivery mechanism or format, prompts like these can promote understanding and conceptual change. *Activity prompts* in KIE prompt students for explanations and justifications as well as task completion and are organized around the KIE ontology of activities, evidence, and claims. For example, an activity prompt focused on the critique of evidence is, "How good are the methods for this evidence? The methods for this evidence. . . ." Building on work done in CLP (Linn & Songer, 1991) and by other groups (e.g., Chi, Bassok, et al., 1989; Chi, de Leeuw, et al., 1994; Palincsar & Brown, 1984), these prompts are intended to help students engage in the necessary steps of a scientific inquiry, including making explanations. (Like all the prompts in KIE, the activity prompts are sentence starters to which students respond in writing.) The activity prompts were studied explicitly in Studies 1 and 2 and are included in every KIE project (including the one in Study 3).

Explicitly metacognitive prompts, delivered in various ways, can encourage students to reflect on their problem-solving processes, inquiry methods, laboratory work, and explanations (e.g., Coleman, 1998; Collins, Brown, & Holum, 1991; Gunstone, Gray, et al., 1992;

TABLE 5.1
Examples of Prompts Used in Knowledge Integration
Environment During Studies 1, 2, and 3

Prompt Type	Goal	Subtypes	Examples	Study in Which Investigated
Activity prompts	Explanations and justifications; task completion	Activity prompts	"The letter says we need to. . . ."	Study 1; Study 2
		Evidence prompts	"How good are the methods for this evidence?" "The methods for this evidence. . . ."	
		Claim prompts	"In thinking about how to change this claim to be more valid, we think. . . ."	
Self-monitoring prompts	Planning and monitoring	Plan ahead	"In thinking about doing our design, we need to think about. . . ."	Study 1; Study 2
		Look back	"Our design could be better if we. . . ."	
Directed prompts (evolved from self-monitoring prompts)	Reflection	Thinking ahead	"When we critique evidence, we need to. . . ."	Study 3
		Checking our understanding	"Pieces of evidence we didn't understand very well included. . . ."	
Generic prompts	Reflection	n/a	"Right now, we're thinking. . . ."	Study 3

Note.   n/a = not applicable.

King & Rosenshine, 1993; Lan, 1996; Schoenfeld, 1987; Tien et al., 1999; White & Frederiksen, 1995, 1998). Prompts focused on planning and monitoring can improve students' understanding (e.g., Bielaczyc et al., 1995; A. L. Brown & Palincsar, 1989; Palincsar & Brown, 1984; Scardamalia & Bereiter, 1991a). Planning can benefit writing (Flower & Hayes, 1980), and students who perform consistently well on learning tasks do more monitoring than do poor performers (e.g., Chi, Bassok, et al., 1989; Recker & Pirolli, 1995). Thus, KIE has used *self-monitoring prompts* focused on planning and monitoring; Studies 1 and 2 investigated these prompts. An example of a self-monitoring prompt from Study 1 is, "Our design could be better if we. . . ."

The *directed prompts* for reflection used in Study 3 were refined versions of self-monitoring prompts that elicited the best responses in earlier trials. The scaffolded knowledge integration framework (Linn et al., chap. 2, this volume; Linn, 1995) supported interpretation of the effects of the prompts and design of new investigations to better understand those effects. As a result, the directed prompts used in Study 3 benefited from many iterations on both their practical application and theoretical foundation.

The self-monitoring and directed prompts both give students hints about what to think about; for example, "what to include in the report" or "pieces of evidence we do not understand." These prompts may act as a "more able other" (Vygotsky, 1978), prodding the students to consider issues they may not have considered otherwise. Specifically, these prompts are intended to elicit planning and monitoring. Directed prompts aimed at planning are called *thinking ahead prompts*, and those aimed at monitoring are called *checking our understanding prompts*. (The analogous self-monitoring prompts were called *plan ahead prompts* and *look back prompts*.) An example of a thinking ahead prompt is, "When we critique evidence, we need to . . ."; an example of a checking our understanding directed prompt is, "Pieces of evidence we didn't understand very well included. . . ." Although the directed prompts are intended to elicit planning and monitoring, a range of ideas from instructional goals to scientific concepts can be addressed. Thus, these prompts may promote productive planning and monitoring or alternatively they may constrain students by explicitly encouraging a particular type of reflection.

The checking our understanding directed prompts used in Study 3 ask students to assess their own understandings and in particular to identify what they do not currently understand. The monitoring prompts were designed this way to provide students with explicit opportunities to identify weaknesses and gaps in their own knowledge—an important component process of knowledge integration (Linn, 1995; cf. also Chi, Bassok, et al., 1989). The name *self-monitoring prompt* was changed to *directed prompt* in part because students responded to the self-monitoring prompts in varied ways. Because not all the responses indicated self-monitoring per se, it seemed more appropriate to call the prompts according to the approach (attempting to guide students in a particular direction) as opposed to according to the goal (which evolved to be promoting reflection more generally as opposed to self-monitoring specifically, with reflection acknowledged to comprise both metacognition and sense making).

Much of the research points to the value of specific, contextualized prompts over abstract prompts (e.g., A. L. Brown & Palincsar, 1989; Chi, de Leeuw, et al., 1994; Linn & Clancy, 1992; Recker & Pirolli, 1995). When a prompt is specific and contextualized, it points students toward performing a specific desired action (e.g., explaining) and is contextualized within a particular learning activity (e.g., reading a passage of text). Self-monitoring and directed prompts not only attempt to focus students' attention on specific types of reflection. Most also are contextualized within specific activities; that is, they are developed with a particular activity, such as critiquing evidence, in mind.

However, specific and contextualized prompts must be very carefully designed so they do not confuse students. In programming, for example, students can be derailed by confusing or complex error messages that attempt to direct students' attention to features that may not be salient to the students (Davis, Linn, et al., 1995). Thus, specific and contextualized prompts may have drawbacks as well—especially when they are delivered by a computer rather than a person and when they are one size fits all rather than being tailored to individuals.

The specificity and contextualization of directed prompts for reflection distinguishes them from *generic prompts* for reflection, which do not direct students' reflection in specific ways and do not explicitly highlight particular activities within the project, although their proximity to particular activities makes them implicitly contextualized.[1] Study 3 compared directed prompts to generic prompts. The generic prompts, in contrast to the self-monitoring and directed prompts, encourage students to stop and think without providing instruction in what to think about. An example of a generic prompt is, "Right now, we're thinking. . . ." Students can choose to focus on their own subject matter understanding, their understanding of the project goals, or their own learning and thinking. By being open-ended, generic prompts for reflection provide a nondisruptive opportunity for students to express their thoughts and contemplate their understanding. Generic prompts act as a way to encourage thinking aloud and at the same time give the students a written record of those thoughts. It may be, however, that not all students are able to reflect in this way without more guidance than generic prompts provide.

Prompts are typically provided to students while they are engaged in a learning activity—for example, a student is asked for a self-explanation while reading a passage of text (Chi, 2000; Chi, de Leeuw, et al., 1994). KIE's activity prompts are provided during learning activities. Even examples involving planning and monitoring (e.g., Bielaczyc et al., 1995; A. L. Brown & Palincsar, 1989) are usually embedded within a particular learning activity. On the other hand, White and

Frederiksen's (1998) prompts for self-assessment in inquiry occur regularly after each learning activity. Other than the work on planning in writing (Flower & Hayes, 1980), none of the prompts reviewed previously occur explicitly before learning activities. KIE's self-monitoring prompts and later the directed and generic prompts for reflection were provided before and after the learning activities. The reflection prompts in Study 3 were used in conjunction with (rather than as replacements for) the activity prompts. Thus, students received interleaved prompts before, during, and after each learning activity embedded in a KIE project.

Research Questions in These Design Experiments

In this brief review, I highlight some of the complexities involved in prompting students effectively. Empirically studying the effects of different prompts helps promote better understandings of these complexities. The series of studies I discuss in this chapter investigate a set of complementary research questions:

Study 1: Are eighth graders able to plan and look back on their progress? Do prompts for planning and looking back help students in their work?

Study 2: Building on and extending Study 1, what are the effects of a refined set of prompts in a different project? How do students' responses in the different contexts compare to one another? What are the specific effects of activity and self-monitoring prompts, especially on students' knowledge integration? What are these prompts' individual strengths and weaknesses?

Study 3: Building on and extending Studies 1 and 2, do students just need to be reminded to reflect or do they needed guidance in determining good directions for their reflection? That is, what are the specific effects of generic and directed prompts for reflection given that these prompts differ in their specificity? What kinds of reflection are most productive? How do reflection prompts support students in engaging in critique (as well as knowledge integration)?

Design experiments typically consist of a series of learning and design studies like these. These studies are embedded in instruction that is dependent on particular classroom settings, curriculum materials, and in this case computer software. I describe these aspects of the studies' context next.

RESEARCH CONTEXT: THE CLASSROOM SETTING

This research took place in 6 eighth-grade physical science classes of no more than 32 students each. The classes used the KIE (Bell, Davis, et al., 1995; Linn et al., chap. 1, this volume) and CLP (Linn et al., chap. 1, this volume; Linn, 1992a; Linn & Hsi, 2000) software and curricula. The basic curriculum for the 1-semester course was identical for each of the six classes and focused on heat, temperature, and light. The same experienced teacher taught each class during a single semester; the teacher has won numerous teaching awards and at the time of this study had been teaching for more than 30 years. The school is located in a small city in the San Francisco Bay Area. The student population is mostly middle class and is ethnically diverse with some recent immigrants from the former Soviet Union, East Asia, Israel, and India.

CLP and KIE are both computer-based learning environments that afford investigation of how students learn science. Both encourage a deep understanding of science concepts rather than memorization of a collection of scientific facts and help students apply the science principles they have learned in class, integrate those principles with other knowledge, and extend their understanding to new situations (Davis & Linn, 2000; Linn, Bell, et al., 1998; Linn & Hsi, 2000). The KIE projects used in the CLP and KIE classroom have been designed to complement the CLP curriculum and serve as capstone experiences for a series of related CLP laboratories. CLP laboratories involve hands-on components and visual computer-based simulations. Students apply principles from these laboratories to real-life situations. KIE projects scaffold students in making sense of complex information from the World Wide Web. Students critique scientific evidence and claims and use evidence to build scientific arguments and create designs.

A typical CLP and KIE class involves some brief opening remarks from the teacher followed by the students working in pairs on a CLP laboratory or a KIE project. In laboratories and projects, the teacher works with pairs of students individually, asking probing questions and making suggestions. The students' work is largely self-paced, although each laboratory or project has a distinct start and endpoint. Students are scaffolded in this process in part by the software, which increases the teacher's role in students' learning by allowing greater opportunity to interact with individual students about conceptual issues.

KIE PROJECTS: ALIENS ON TOUR
AND ALL THE NEWS

Each study took place in a different semester with different students. Two different KIE projects—"Aliens On Tour" and "All The News"— served as focus projects for the design studies on prompting. These projects both benefited from several cycles of design and resulted in what can be called curriculum design patterns for critique projects (see Bell, Hoadley, & Linn, chap. 4, this volume; Linn, Clark, et al., 2003).

In Study 1, students did a design project called Aliens On Tour. In this project, adapted from the version developed by Songer (1989) who was a founding member of the CLP project, students design houses and clothing for three sets of cold-blooded aliens with different climate requirements. The students review a range of evidence (from an advertisement to a table of R values). They then create their designs combining the evidence with ideas from CLP laboratories on insulation, conduction, energy conversion, and heat flow.

One of the pieces of evidence in the KIE version of Aliens was an advertisement for the "Anti-Heat Shirt," which purported to be made of "ice cloth" and to be treated with a special "anti-heat sauce." To the surprise of the research group, students working on the Aliens project accepted this evidence at face value, not questioning the science even in light of their semester-long curriculum about heat and temperature. This highlighted the power (for good or evil) of Internet materials and prompted the curriculum developers in the group to begin a new focus on the practice of critique. The All The News project was the group's first foray into designing a critique project to help promote understanding of critiquing scientific evidence and claims.

In Studies 2 and 3 then, students worked on the All The News critique project. After Study 2, the project was revised slightly for instructional purposes, but the overall instructional goals and design remained the same for Study 3. For both studies, All The News took place approximately in the middle of the semester at the conclusion of a series of laboratories and projects focusing on heat flow, thermal equilibrium, energy conversion, and the nature of light. The instructional goals of All The News are twofold. First, students should improve their understanding of the science concepts involved in the project. At the same time they should develop an understanding of critiquing evidence and claims.

In the All The News project, students critique evidence cited by a fabricated news article about energy conversion and elementary thermodynamics. The students are told that a "science tabloid" wants to become a respected science journal and has requested the students' help in doing so. The project follows a curriculum design pattern that incorporates successful elements of past critique projects. It involves (a) reading the article to be critiqued and looking at its concomitant evidence about heat flow, energy conversion, and thermal equilibrium; (b) critiquing the evidence being used; (c) critiquing the claims being made; and (d) writing a letter to the imaginary editor with a synthesized critique and giving guidelines for future use of evidence. Thus, the four main activities include getting started, critiquing evidence, critiquing claims, and writing the letter.

Both the evidence and the claims are designed to need improvement. Students critique the six pieces of evidence based on their science, methods, credibility, and usefulness. For example, one piece of evidence, "T-shirts on the Beach," shows a scenario with two people wearing white and black clothing on the beach; among other things, students could critique the methods of the evidence because one person wears a T-shirt and the other a dress (i.e., variables are not controlled) and the hypothetical experimenter does not take actual temperatures, relying instead on the participants' self-reported feelings (i.e., the evidence depends on anecdotal data). Furthermore, one piece of evidence—the "Benches" evidence—is included as a pivotal case (cf. D. Clark, chap. 8, this volume; Linn et al., chap. 2, this volume; Linn & Hsi, 2000). The Benches evidence helps students pivot or shift their ideas about thermal equilibrium and conductivity to be more sophisticated.

Students critique the three claims based on the claims' validity; they also write claim changes notes saying what changes should be made to the wording of the claims. Two of the claims are scientifically invalid. These claims state that, "Energy conversion principles indicate that black objects attract heat" (the energy conversion claim), and "Some materials are naturally cold" (the thermal equilibrium claim). I hoped that students would apply their scientific knowledge to determine that more appropriate claims would approximate these: "Energy conversion principles indicate that black objects absorb more light and convert that light to heat energy," and "Materials in the same environment come to the same temperature unless an object is a heat source; some materials just feel different." (In critiquing the thermal equilibrium claim, students may also bring in rate of heat flow through different materials.)

Students are supported in working on KIE projects by the teacher, who talks with pairs of students as they progress through the project, and by their peers. As described more fully in Davis and Kirkpatrick (2002), completing the project takes about 8 days (about 1½ days for getting started, 2½ days for critiquing evidence, 2 days for critiquing claims, and 2 days for writing the letter), during which the students' work is largely self-directed as guided by the KIE software, another important support in the classroom.

KIE comprises a blend of commercial and custom software (Bell, Davis, et al., 1995). The basic elements include a tool palette, which provides a checklist of activities involved in the current project and also facilitates navigation among the other tools. The commercial tools include a Web browser and a word-processing and graphics application. The custom tools include a guidance system, an argument editor, and a Web-based discussion tool. (See, e.g., Bell, 1997; Bell & Davis, 2000; and Hoadley & Linn, 2000, for discussions of scaffolding provided in the KIE software.) I describe the guidance system that presented the prompts to the students next.

SOFTWARE SUPPORTING KNOWLEDGE INTEGRATION: MILDRED THE SCIENCE GUIDE

A prominent component of the KIE software is a guidance-on-demand system called *Mildred* designed explicitly to help provide the support students need to integrate their ideas. (*Mildred* is the name of the cartoon cow who provides the guidance.) Over the course of several years, Mildred evolved from a fairly simple guidance system that provided hints to an integrated resource in which students could receive all the cognitive guidance built into the projects—both hints and prompts (Davis & Bell, 2001). Much of the explicit scaffolding in KIE is embedded in Mildred. The details of the hints and prompts are at the discretion of the curriculum designer developing a specific project. Mildred's design was influenced by other successful learning environments including CSILE (Scardamalia & Bereiter, 1991a), CLP (Linn & Songer, 1991), and others (e.g., Linn & Clancy, 1992; Tabak et al., 1998).

The features of Mildred support the tenets of the scaffolded knowledge integration framework (Linn et al., chap. 2, this volume). For example, hints make expert thinking visible, and notes allow the students to make their own thinking visible. Hints also help students connect the science ideas to their own experiences. As students work together on their project, Mildred also acts as a catalyst for getting students to talk to one another and exchange ideas. Last, by providing prompts, Mildred helps students to engage more freely in knowledge integration; by designing Mildred as a guidance-on-demand system in which students choose when they want a hint rather than receiving automated hints, Mildred promotes autonomy as well.

Given the potential complexity of Web sites that students could be exploring in KIE projects and the research team's knowledge of students' difficulty in interpreting computer help (Davis, Linn, et al., 1995), the team realized immediately that it would be important to have a means by which to provide students with meaningful conceptual and strategic hints. Initially Mildred provided a set of three hints (about the project, the activity, and the evidence) when students requested help. In a completely separate word-processing software component, students were prompted to take notes about the evidence and activities. As noted previously, KIE prompts appear in the form of sentence starters. Students respond by writing one or several sentences. They could easily change the words in the prompt, although relatively few students chose to do so. (In Studies 1 and 2, the activity prompts and self-monitoring prompts were included in word-processing files students worked with as part of the project rather than in Mildred.)

By the fourth trial semester of KIE, the team had separated the different types of cognitive guidance by making visible the KIE ontology of activities, evidence, and claims rather than providing a set of hints and expecting students to sift through the hints to find one relevant to their current thinking. A new notes feature was implemented by Semester 5, changing Mildred into an integrated cognitive guidance tool. In parallel to the hints, the notes were now associated with the KIE ontology of activity, evidence, and claims and contextualized to the students' current work. Furthermore, the notes were linked to the SenseMaker argument tool (Bell, chap. 6, this volume).

The final instantiation of Mildred thus provides three types of hints—on activities, evidence, and claims (see Fig. 1.3 in chap. 1). *Activity hints* in a critique project would, for example, provide definitions and examples of the critique criteria of science, methods, and credibility. *Evidence hints* are more specific, providing help in thinking about a particular piece of evidence. (Figure 1.3 shows two evidence hints.) Likewise, *claim hints* help students think about a particular claim. A student working on a critique of a piece of evidence could receive converging evidence on both the act of critiquing and the specific evidence being critiqued and could later receive a hint about a particular claim to be critiqued as well.

However, the real emphasis in Mildred has shifted from the hints to the prompted notes. The final version of Mildred includes notes focused on the KIE ontology of activities, evidence, and claims (collectively referred to in these studies as *activity prompts*). Activity prompts not aimed at evidence or claims focus students' attention on particular tasks involved in an activity. *Evidence prompts* focus instead on aspects of the evidence students are reviewing. *Claim prompts* are similar to evidence prompts except they are instead specific to claims or theories. (Refer back to Table 5.1 for examples of each of these kinds of prompts.) The activity, evidence, and claim notes are integral parts to the activities themselves; as described previously, they are provided during the learning activities.

The last type of notes encourage students to be more reflective. As described previously, Mildred gives two types of reflection prompts. Generic prompts for reflection represent a view that asking students to stop and think will encourage reflection. Directed prompts for reflection assume that students need guidance in determining how to reflect. Mildred gives directed prompts oriented toward planning and monitoring: Thinking ahead prompts encourage planning for future activities, whereas checking our understanding prompts ask students to monitor their understanding. Figure 1.3 shows a thinking ahead note selected on the left side and the prompt, "When we critique evidence, we need to . . ." appears on the right. (Again, see Table 5.1 for examples of the prompts.) Reflection prompts (like the self-monitoring prompts used earlier) fall before and after the activity itself and are not integral to completing the project. Thus, the sequence for a critique evidence activity might be first a thinking ahead prompt, second the evidence prompts for critiquing the evidence, and third a checking our understanding prompt.

A SERIES OF STUDIES OF PROMPTING

In three studies, I investigated the effects of the different kinds of prompts. Collectively, the studies help educators better understand the complexities of prompting students effectively and the role of prompts in knowledge integration and critique.

Study 1: Comparison of Self-Monitoring Prompts and Activity Prompts

In Study 1, I compared the effects of self-monitoring prompts and activity prompts on project success (Davis & Linn, 2000). I investigated whether eighth graders are able to plan and look back on their progress and whether planning and looking back help students in their work. As students completed each design, they saw an activity prompt asking why their design would work well for the different types of aliens. This prompt, along with the general instructions given, helped students think about the justification necessary to demonstrate to others the quality of their design. The activity prompt stated, "Our design will work well because. . . ." In addition, half of the students received a total of seven specific self-monitoring prompts, including plan ahead and look back prompts. The plan ahead prompts asked them to think about the activity on which they were embarking. A plan ahead prompt used in the design activities was, "In thinking about doing our design, we need to think about. . . ." The look back prompts asked them to reflect on what aspects of the activity were still confusing to them or how their designs could be better. A look back prompt used was, "Our design could be better if we. . . ." I evaluated students' responses to the two types of prompts and rated their final designs.

Although the groups who received only activity prompts had more time for their reports, they did not create better designs. However, students who received self-monitoring prompts along with the activity prompts gave fewer purely descriptive explanations and were significantly more likely to use at least one scientific principle in their designs, $\chi^2(2, N = 65) = 8.92, p < .05$ (Davis & Linn, 2000). For example, one pair of students wrote a descriptive explanation with no scientific principles:

> The first floor will be like a lobby. . . . The second floor is where the Kulebeings will stay. . . . On each side of the floor we will cover with a half inch layer of stucco. We will also [have] a carpet made of wool. For the walls we will use 8" of concrete blocks which is framed and lined with polystyrene boards which is then layered with half an inch of stucco. . . . The third floor is where the Equilibs will stay. Because of their adaptability the walls will be made of 8" of brick layered with half an inch of stucco. . . . [continues on in this vein, with more and more materials being used and layered together.] On the outside of the house we will cover with stucco and paint it yellow.

In contrast, another pair wrote a principled (and more succinct) clothing design:

> The clothing for the Sizzle Persons will be made of black wool and it will be tight against their bodies. The clothings should be rather thick. . . . The Kulebeings will also wear tight clothing in thick wool. The wool suits [for the Kulebeings] will be covered with cloth to reflect the light energy off of them. The wool will also be white. . . . The Kulebeings should have thick wool suits because it will help to keep the heat energy out of their bodies. . . . This [design] will keep the Kulebeings cold be-

cause wool is a good insulator and not much light energy is absorbed by the suits.

These findings led to the first specific design principle that emerges from this work:

Including prompts for planning and monitoring may promote the use of better (i.e., not purely descriptive) explanations. Prompts should focus students' attention on being reflective.

However, in the context of Study 1, which took place in the very first semester in which KIE was tested, the research team also discovered that students accepted evidence from the Internet (such as the anti-heat shirt advertisement) at face value. Thus, the second specific design principle that emerges from this work, supported by careful classroom observation of students' emergent uses of the KIE software and curriculum, is the following:

Students may need scaffolding in knowing to—and how to—critique materials they view on the Web.

In sum, Study 1 led me to see the promise of self-monitoring prompts and to want to test their effects more carefully and in a new context of a project focused explicitly on critique.

Study 2: Extension and Replication of Comparison of Activity and Self-Monitoring Prompts

Study 2 was undertaken for three purposes: to test a refined set of prompts in a different project with the intent of comparing students' responses in different contexts, to investigate separately the activity and self-monitoring prompts to identify their individual strengths and weaknesses, and to create activities that would allow students in each condition to spend comparable amounts of time on the actual project work itself (Davis & Linn, 2000). Study 2 also introduced the scientific practice of critique.

As I gained a better understanding of their effects, I improved the prompts used. In Study 2, unlike Study 1, the activity prompts included not just prompts for justification but for all the steps necessary to do a good job on the critique project. For example, students were prompted for a discussion of the article with the prompt, "Readers would get more from the article if the article. . . ." I also refined the self-monitoring prompts to include thinking types before each prompt, similar in nature to those used in the CSILE program (Scardamalia & Bereiter, 1991a), to cue students as to what kinds of planning and reflection are important. Examples of thinking types included "thinking ahead," "checking our understanding," and "how we spent our time." (These were modifications of the plan ahead and look back prompts from Study 1, which were less explicit in the interface.) One self-monitoring prompt for planning the letter to the editor was, "Specific things we need to think about as we write our letter include. . . ." One monitoring prompt from that activity was "In looking back at what the editor wanted, we think she will like our letter because. . . ."

In Study 2, one group received activity prompts and another group received self-monitoring prompts. The total number of prompts was kept constant across conditions. To provide the most direct scaffolding, the activity prompt group was explicitly prompted with sentence starters for each part of the letter to the editor. The self-monitoring prompt group received only the section headings and some prose discussing each piece. The headings and prose were present for each of the groups.

First, I determined through classroom observation and investigation of students' critiques that students could indeed engage in the scientific practice of critique. This led to a third specific design principle:

Focusing students' attention on criteria of science, methods, credibility, and usefulness helps them identify weaknesses and strengths of evidence.

Second, analysis indicated that overall project completion varied by condition. Most of the students (78%) in the activity prompt condition completed all pieces of the project as compared to 32% of the self-monitoring prompt group (Davis & Linn, 2000). Although I expected a difference in completion rates, the degree to which the conditions performed differently was unexpected. The activity prompts had a clear positive effect in helping students do the aspects of the tasks that I, as the project designer, highlighted as important. The fourth specific design principle then is the following:

Including prompts that remind students of the pieces of the project may promote completion of the project.

However, students in the self-monitoring prompt condition were significantly more likely than those in the activity prompt condition to explain phenomena using a principle and one or more other types of cites such as everyday experiences or laboratories done in class. (I had decided to modify the outcome measure used in Study 1 to account for integration of ideas and called the new measure *principled knowledge integration*.) In contrast, the activity prompt group gave significantly more principle-only explanations, $\chi^2(3, N = 60) = 7.83, p < .05$ (Davis & Linn, 2000). From this finding, a fifth specific design principle emerged:

> *Including prompts for planning and monitoring may promote principled knowledge integration. Again, prompts should focus students' attention on being reflective.*

Thus, Studies 1 and 2 show that self-monitoring prompts encourage students to integrate their knowledge. In Study 1, students who received self-monitoring prompts were more likely to cite at least one principle, and in Study 2, the self-monitoring prompt group was more likely to link those principles to other ideas.

Study 3: Comparison of Generic and Directed Prompts for Reflection

It was clear from Studies 1 and 2 that it was important for students to receive both activity prompts (to promote project completion) and some form of prompts for reflection (to promote knowledge integration). Yet the question still remained whether students just needed to be reminded to reflect or if they needed guidance in determining good directions for their reflection. As previously discussed, researchers have long emphasized the importance of encouraging students to reflect (e.g., Bloom, 1956; A. L. Brown, Bransford, et al., 1983; Flower & Hayes, 1980; Rothkopf, 1966). Yet we know little about how reflection can lead to learning (Resnick, 1987; Van Lehn, 1999) nor how best to promote reflection in classrooms. In keeping with the idea of scaffolding, explicitly telling students what to reflect on seems sensible. On the other hand, being too directive may derail or constrain some students' thought. Building on Studies 1 and 2, in Study 3 I investigated these issues directly.

I also still wondered about what kinds of reflection were most productive. Studies 1 and 2 found that students make choices about what to write in response to even specific prompts—some students focus mainly on science content, for example, whereas others focus more on instructional goals (Davis & Linn, 2000). Furthermore, I wondered how reflection prompts supported students in engaging in critique as well as knowledge integration because I already had reason to believe that these prompts would promote knowledge integration. Thus, in Study 3 I compared generic and directed prompts for reflection and investigated the kinds of reflection the prompts elicit as well as the relations between reflection and success in critiquing and knowledge integration (Davis, 2003a).

Students in the generic prompt condition received generic prompts; those in the directed prompt condition received a directed set. All students in the generic prompt condition received identical sets of 11 generic prompts, which were intended to be indistinguishable from one another. All students in the directed prompt condition received identical sets of 11 directed prompts: 6 thinking ahead prompts, 4 checking our understanding prompts, and 1 thinking back prompt. In each condition, prompts occurred at exactly the same placements. For example, if the directed prompt condition involved 1 prompt at the beginning of an activity and 2 at the end of the activity, the generic prompt condition would have this setup as well. Students' responses to the reflection prompts were coded as "productive" or "less productive." In addition, various aspects of the quality of students' project work were investigated. Here, the focus is on students' *overall critique quality* score, which measures how well students critiqued the claims and evidence.

A more complete discussion of the results, including how reflection prompts were related to students' knowledge integration, is presented in Davis (2003a). Here the emphasis is on how the prompts promoted critique, and therefore two types of students are highlighted: *elaborators* who write lengthy responses to reflection prompts and *poor reflectors* who reflect unproductively in response to reflection prompts—especially in response to directed prompts intended to promote self-monitoring. These groups of students emerged as important for further investigation based on earlier analyses of the data (Davis, 1998).

Elaborators' Critique Quality.   To compare how much they elaborated their responses, students were grouped using the top quartile, middle two quartiles, and bottom quartile of the number of words students wrote in their responses to prompts. Students who elaborated their responses achieved significantly higher overall critique quality scores than did those who were less elaborative (Fisher's PLSD p = .0311 for low elaboration vs. high elaboration; p = .0459 for middle vs. high). Highly elaborative students responding to directed prompts tended to write better critiques than did any other group of students, including highly elaborative students responding to generic prompts (effect size = .46) and students responding to directed prompts who were in the middle group of elaborators (effect size = .98). The discussion in the next section shows how this finding fits into a larger pattern demonstrating the importance of engaging in productive reflection.

These students who elaborate take advantage of the opportunities to reflect that are inherent in the directed prompts—they identify weaknesses with their understanding and places where distinctions and links can be made. Other analyses show, in fact, that elaborating in response to both types of directed prompts was highly predictive of successful critiquing but that elaboration of checking our understanding prompts was also negatively correlated with less productive responses to those prompts (Davis, 1998). In other words, short responses to prompts for monitoring tended to not include productive reflection. Encouraging elaboration in response to directed prompts, if less productive responses to checking our understanding prompts could be discouraged, would be an especially appropriate instructional goal. However, as the reader sees, the productivity of students' responses can be particularly problematic.

A sixth specific design principle then is the following:

Encouraging lengthy responses to prompts—especially directed prompts for planning and monitoring—may promote the development of high-quality critiques.

An example will illustrate the finding. Compare two pairs' responses to the same checking our understanding prompt:

[Nonelaborators responding to checking our understanding prompt:] Claims in the article we didn't understand very well included nothing, we understand basically all 3 claims.

[Elaborators responding to checking our understanding prompt:] Claims in the article we didn't understand very well included the fact that if you were in a room with lots of marble and metal in it, you would stay cooler. Perhaps if you were touching something marble or metal, you would stay cooler, but I'm not so sure what the results would be in a room. Also, the anti-heat shirt confuses me. What chemical is this shirt dipped in and how can it affect one's body temperature? How does it work? Does such a thing really exist?

The first pair writes a terse (and nonreflective) response to the call for monitoring. This pair ends up developing a poor critique. The second pair, by contrast, writes an elaborated response to the prompt. They develop a very high-quality critique. In fact, the second pair starts to critique the evidence and claims even here in their reflection prompt response; the prompt primes them to think about the kinds of things they will include in their critique later, and in fact the effects of that reflection are seen later in the project itself.

Poor Reflectors' Critique Quality.   However, simply elaborating without reflecting productively seems unlikely to support students' knowledge integration. In Studies 1 and 2, informal investigation showed that students responded quite differently even to the same prompts. This led me to investigate more systematically the focus of students' reflection in response to reflection prompts and in particular to characterizing students' reflection as more or less productive. One group that emerged as worthy of further investigation was the group of students who reflected less productively in response to prompts. These students wrote responses such as, "Claims in the article we didn't understand very well included . . . none, we understood them all." (The science involved in the All The News project is quite complex, and students are unlikely to understand it all—especially with regard to how it applies to real life or to the evidence in the project. Furthermore, the evidence and claims in the project are scientifically problematic; therefore, if students actually understood the evidence and claims, they would likely comment on their concerns about them.)

Factorial analyses of variance (ANOVAs) demonstrate that students who received directed prompts engaged in less productive reflection significantly more often than did those in the generic prompt condition, $F(1, 89) = 14.000$, $p = .0003$ (Davis, 2003a). Students did not write responses to the generic prompts such as, "We understood all the evidence." Instead, responses to the generic prompts were coded as "no problem" if the students wrote that they had no new ideas since the previous prompt. These (infrequent) responses were coded in the same category as the "no problem" responses to directed prompts because they too seemed to indicate less productive reflection.

Students in the directed prompt condition wrote these "no problem" responses significantly more often for checking our understanding prompts than for thinking ahead prompts, $t(43) = 5.365$, $p < .0001$ (Davis, 2003a). In fact, 21% of students' responses to checking our understanding prompts were coded as "no problem," in contrast to none of their responses to thinking ahead prompts. (Only 2% of students' responses to generic prompts overall were coded as "no problem.")

This pair of findings led me to develop a seventh specific design principle:

Prompts for monitoring do not necessarily promote productive reflection; students need support in monitoring their understandings. Prompts should not allow students to develop or articulate an illusion of comprehension.

Students were characterized as poor reflectors if they displayed an above-average proportion of "no problem" responses to checking our understanding prompts or if they gave any "no problem" responses to generic prompts; these students misjudged their own level of understanding or otherwise reflected poorly or avoided opportunities to reflect productively. ANOVA analysis indicates that poor reflectors responding to directed prompts achieved significantly lower overall critique quality scores than did (a) better reflectors responding to directed prompts (effect size = .85) or (b) poor reflectors responding to generic prompts (effect size = .78), $F(1, 1, 1, 85) = 4.757, p = .0319$ for the interaction between the poor reflectors group and condition (Davis, 2003a).

When poor reflectors critiqued evidence, they often wrote summaries rather than critiques. These students did not assess their own understanding as problematic. Learners are often poor at monitoring their own understanding (e.g., Glenburg & Epstein, 1987; Pirolli & Recker, 1994). Perhaps these students lacked an understanding of the purpose of critiquing (as exemplified by their propensity to summarize instead) or perhaps they were equally unlikely to assess a claim or piece of evidence as flawed as they were to see a flaw in their own understanding of the claim or evidence.

A final specific design principle that emerged from this work was the following:

When prompts allow students to develop an illusion of competence, the students do not identify weaknesses in their own or in others' ideas. Prompts should provide opportunities for students to identify weaknesses in their knowledge.

DISCUSSION AND CONCLUSIONS

The series of studies on prompting and reflection informs the field's understanding of design and learning. What have educators learned about design? Table 5.2 summarizes the main findings from the three studies and the specific design principles that follow from the findings. As discussed in Bell et al. (chap. 4, this volume) and Davis and Bell (2001), these specific design principles are contextualized—in the context of the CLP and KIE classroom, the KIE (and especially Mildred) software, and the curricular projects of Aliens On Tour and All The News. Nonetheless, they provide pointers to potentially effective design decisions that can be implemented and tested by others working in new contexts. Furthermore, these specific design principles are supported by a range of evidence, from extensive classroom observation to careful analysis of multiple forms of data.

These principles build on the more generalized and generalizable design principles (or pragmatic pedagogical principles) articulated by Linn and Hsi (2000) based on their extended work in the CLP project. For example, in describing how to promote students' autonomy, Linn and Hsi (2000) discussed the importance of engaging students in "reflecting on progress and ideas" (p. 187) and having them act "as critics of diverse scientific information" (p. 185). Clearly these two pragmatic pedagogical principles provide the premise for the entire body of work reported here; the specific design principles summarized in Table 5.2 provide further nuances about specific ways in which educators may be able to promote students' autonomy through reflection and critique.

The findings of the series of studies point to the importance of careful design of prompts. Some prompts (such as the self-monitoring prompts of Studies 1 and 2 that evolved into the directed prompts of Study 3) are linked with positive learning outcomes in some situations, yet less positive outcomes in other situations. Is this due to a difference in the prompts themselves, in the context, or in the specifics of individuals that only become apparent with more analytic investigation? One cannot assume that a well-designed prompt intended to promote reflection will necessarily promote the productive reflection its designers intend—which leads to the second, related implication of this work: The effects of scaffolds designed for technology-mediated learning environments must be investigated carefully through classroom observation and detailed analysis to determine their actual effects. In this study, generic prompts were linked with more positive learning outcomes along some measures (Davis, 2003a), but the results highlighted in this chapter show the nuances behind both the generic prompts and the directed prompts. Only careful empirical analysis can bring such nuances to the surface.

What have we as educators learned about learning? This series of studies helps us better understand the processes of knowledge integration. In particular, the series of studies demonstrates the importance of students identifying weaknesses in their knowledge—that is, of critiquing their own knowledge—at the same time as they critique others' knowledge (or the materials that represent that knowledge,

TABLE 5.2
Summary of Findings and Specific Design Principles

Findings	Specific Design Principles
Study 1	
The students in the self-monitoring prompt condition gave fewer purely descriptive explanations and were significantly more likely to use at least one scientific principle in their designs.	Including prompts for planning and monitoring may promote the use of better (i.e., not purely descriptive) explanations. Prompts should focus students' attention on being reflective.
In the context of a design project, students accepted at face value evidence that they received via the Internet.	Students may need scaffolding in knowing to—and how to—critique materials they view on the Web.
Study 2	
In the context of a critique project, which includes criteria for critiquing, students can critique scientific evidence.	Focusing students' attention on criteria of science, methods, credibility, and usefulness helps them identify weaknesses and strengths of evidence.
Most of the students in the activity prompt condition completed all pieces of the project, whereas a smaller proportion of the self-monitoring prompt group completed the project.	Including prompts that remind students of the pieces of the project may promote completion of the project.
Students in the self-monitoring prompt condition were significantly more likely to engage in principled knowledge integration. In contrast the activity prompt group gave significantly more principle-only explanations and did not link principles to other cites.	Including prompts for planning and monitoring may promote principled knowledge integration. Again, prompts should focus students' attention on being reflective.
Study 3	
Students who elaborated their responses achieved significantly higher overall critique quality scores than did those who were less elaborative; the effect was particularly strong for students who wrote long responses to directed prompts.	Encouraging lengthy responses to prompts—especially directed prompts for planning and monitoring—may promote the development of high-quality critiques.
Students who received directed prompts reflected poorly significantly more often than did those in the generic prompt condition. Furthermore, students in the directed prompt condition reflected poorly significantly more often in response to checking our understanding prompts than for thinking ahead prompts.	Prompts for monitoring do not necessarily promote productive reflection; students need support in monitoring their understandings. Prompts should not allow students to develop or articulate an illusion of comprehension.
Poor reflectors responding to directed prompts achieved significantly lower overall critique quality scores than did (a) better reflectors responding to directed prompts or (b) poor reflectors responding to generic prompts.	When prompts allow students to develop an illusion of competence, the students do not identify weaknesses in their own or in others' ideas. Prompts should provide opportunities for students to identify weaknesses in their knowledge.

such as evidence or claims). This series of studies highlights criteria that can help students critique evidence and claims yet does not yet help educators know the best ways of supporting them in critiquing their own knowledge. Although generic prompts were less likely to allow students to develop the illusion of competence the directed prompts allowed, they still need further investigation. Might different directed prompts be more helpful? Again, empirical analysis might help identify whether different prompts would help more students—or whether generic prompts are not just a local peak but a global peak. Also, of course, context again matters: The generic prompts here were tested within the context of a highly scaffolded environment, and therefore it would be impossible to make claims, from this study, of their efficacy in a less scaffolded environment. That said, these studies do show the importance of helping students to identify weaknesses in knowledge and point to productive directions for future research.

For example, this work demonstrates the importance of researching the synergistic effects of various types and forms of scaffolds. The researchers involved in the projects described in this book consider the classroom as a complex system with scaffolds provided by the teacher, the curriculum, the software, and the students' peers (Salomon, 1996). Investigating how all these scaffolds interact is an important area of work. One could ask, how are scaffolds in other software components (like SenseMaker, described in Bell, chap. 6, this volume, and SpeakEasy in Hoadley, 2002) similar to and different from those in Mildred? How do the various scaffolds in KIE complement each other in the cognitive actions they promote? How do those actions all interact to promote the knowledge integration processes? The teacher plays an especially important role in supporting students' learning in environments like KIE. What do teachers need to know and be able to do to support students in engaging in critique and in reflection? Finally, based on the results from this set of studies, how might the scaffolds in KIE be made generic? What needs to be specific, and what can be generic?[2] What are the affordances of different levels of specificity? How are these answers different from student to student?

Other questions emphasize learning over design. Studies 2 and 3 emphasized the scientific practice of critique. How is learning to critique similar to learning to develop arguments (Bell, chap. 6, this volume), to use evidence in designs (Hoadley, chap. 7, this volume) or to engage in hands-on science experiments (D. Clark, chap. 8, this volume)? How does knowing about critique help students as they engage in these practices?

Future work should extend this investigation of prompt specificity to test different directed prompts and to test generic and directed prompts in a less scaffolded environment. However, in addition, future work should extend the investigation of reflection and of knowledge integration more generally. Research should continue to investigate what kinds of reflection are most productive for students with different characteristics. Also, research should extend the field's understanding of reflection to teacher learning. In my newest work, I ask how does teacher reflection differ from student reflection? What kinds of critique (e.g., of instructional materials such as lesson plans) are supported by reflection on the part of teachers? How does teacher knowledge integration differ from student knowledge integration? Also, what kinds of curriculum projects, supports, and scaffolds are most helpful for promoting teacher learning? Answering all these questions will help researchers in developing an integrated understanding of learning across learners and subject areas.

ENDNOTES

1. Thus, the directed reflection prompts are directed relative to the generic prompts but not on an absolute scale. The activity prompts from Studies 1 and 2, on the other hand, are quite directed; they are much more specific than either the directed or generic reflection prompts.
2. Allan Collins raised this question in a session at which I presented my work with Philip Bell, at the meeting of the American Educational Research Association, April 2001, in Seattle, Washington.

6

Promoting Students' Argument Construction and Collaborative Debate in the Science Classroom

Philip Bell
University of Washington

The focus of this chapter is to detail how students were supported in argumentation and debate as they explored information from the Web and what was learned in the process. Students were provided with various forms of educational infrastructure to support their argumentation and debate. To the degree possible, connections are made between the design that was enacted in the classroom and the outcomes observed. In this way, readers will be able to understand what in the learning environment contributed, in complex ways, to the observed student learning and interaction.

Argumentation and collaborative debate are central features of intellectual inquiry in the natural sciences; however, they rarely find their way into the science curriculum (Newton et al., 1999). I distinguish collaborative debate from other popular forms of debate used in school (e.g., Lincoln–Douglas style debates associated with high school speech classes) by emphasizing that the debates that proved to be most beneficial to science learning were focused on the collective exploration of issues and evidence by the group of students—and not on norms associated with winning at all costs or never admitting weaknesses from a theoretical perspective. The program of research I describe in this chapter has explored how argument construction and collaborative debate could be promoted in the science classroom for the dual purpose of having students learn science while also learning about the nature of science.

LEARNING SCIENCE WHILE ENGAGING
IN THE EPISTEMICS OF SCIENCE

Historically, approaches to science education have often explored the teaching of science content and process as separate educational endeavors. The results have not been particularly satisfying. Frequently, students learn scientific content quite removed from learning about the nature of scientific inquiry. Not surprisingly, they develop a view that scientific knowledge is immutable and that inquiry is always a straightforward process. Students are frequently asked to engage in generalized forms of a scientific method quite apart from specific lines of inquiry, leaving them unable to understand how inquiry and understanding are intertwined pursuits. In the last 10 years science educators have investigated ways of not separating the learning of science into dichotomous content and process experiences (Krajcik, Blumenfeld, Marx, Bass, et al., 1998; Linn, 2000b; Reiser, Tabak, et al., 2001). These integrated approaches successfully engage students in forms of scientific inquiry as they simultaneously develop scientific knowledge that is grounded and relevant to scientific and personal life situations. The scaffolded knowledge integration framework (Linn, Bell, et al., 1998; Linn & Hsi, 2000) informs the development of curriculum that interleaves the exploration and refinement of conceptual knowledge as students are engaged in appropriate, derivative (or prototypical) forms of the epistemics of science.

A powerful outcome of this kind of integrated approach is that students develop rich conceptual knowledge while also learning about the epistemics associated with the nature of science. Students rarely understand the degree to which scientific knowledge changes over time (Collins & Shapin, 1986; Songer & Linn, 1991); however, a knowledge integration approach focused on argumentation and debate provides compelling educational contexts in which to develop an understanding of the dynamic nature of scientific knowledge production and refinement (Bell & Linn, 2001).

MAKING THE DYNAMIC NATURE
OF SCIENCE VISIBLE TO STUDENTS

Scientific knowledge is precious to our global society. For better and for worse, knowledge from the natural sciences has increasingly influenced our activities, health, and livelihood over the last century. It is formulated, tested, applied, refined, and rejected in complex ways that are highly dynamic and socially mediated. Debate and argumentation are constituent mechanisms associated with this knowledge work of science.

Typical science instruction can easily promote static views of scientific knowledge (Collins & Shapin, 1986; Songer & Linn, 1991; also see Bell, chap. 10, this volume, for a further exploration of these issues). Certainly efforts to standardize learning outcomes—which serve to focus educational outcomes mostly on specific content to be learned—reinforce this static depiction of scientific knowledge. Given the dynamic and social nature of the scientific enterprise, this is an unfortunate outcome. Students should learn how scientific understanding unfolds over time and intersects with the interests and arenas of society. As described in the following design narrative, formulating instruction as argument construction and collaborative debate offers the possibility to promote a dynamic and social view of scientific knowledge construction in ways that bear more epistemic fidelity to the intellectual mechanisms of the natural sciences.

DESIGN NARRATIVE: LEARNING ABOUT THE NATURE OF LIGHT THROUGH ARGUMENTATION AND DEBATE

From a subject matter perspective, it is difficult to overstate the importance of understanding the electromagnetic spectrum, of which visible light is only a minor subset. Light is an exceedingly complex natural phenomenon; however, humans' everyday reliance on it makes it an ideal focus for the science curriculum. The Computer as Learning Partner (CLP) project had elected to focus about one fourth of its curricular time on the topic of light. Through scaffolded experimentation (Linn & Hsi, 2000), students learned about light sources and receivers, light intensity over distance, reflection, absorption, scattering (diffuse reflection), and energy conversion. To further promote students' integrated understanding of light as a unique and virtually ever-present form of energy, the research group decided to culminate the 5-week curriculum sequence with an overarching debate activity (Weinland, 1993). The substantive focus of this debate project—called "How Far Does Light Go?"—was on an exploration of evidence related to the farthest extent of light's propagation from sources of illumination. In its original form, it was a worksheet activity including a dozen evidence items that were anecdotal descriptions consisting of one to three sentences. After being used, studied, and refined over several iterations, this version of the How Far Does Light Go? curriculum project was converted into the Internet format of the Knowledge Integration Environment (KIE). The light debate was the first KIE project to be used in the classroom (Bell, Davis, et al., 1995).

The KIE version of the How Far Does Light Go? debate project takes about 8 to 10 days to run in the classroom. Students explore a dozen relevant multimedia evidence items—including movies, simulations, complex Web pages of information, and some of the original anecdotal accounts—construct explanations and arguments about how the evidence relates to the debate topic, and then engage in a whole-class debate about the issues, claims, and evidence.

Iterative Refinement of the Collaborative Debate Activity

The evidence focus for the KIE research project was strongly influenced by several CLP curriculum activities that supported students in working with pieces of potential evidence as a form of scientific inquiry. The line of research described in this chapter began with the observation and analysis of the mature paper-based version of the light debate activity from the CLP curriculum.[1] Having observed significant promise for integration with information technology, I selected the debate project as a long-term focus of research and conducted five subsequent design research iterations. I detail all six iterations in the following sections.

Observational Iteration 1: Short and Simple Paper Design. The original paper-based version of the How Far project ran in three 50-min class periods. Students were initially presented with the debate topic (how far light can travel) along with two competing theories that were used to frame the debate—the scientifically normative theory that "light travels forever until absorbed" and the intuitively aligned theory that "light dies out as you move farther away from a light source." Students stated their initial position in the debate and then, working in pairs, they explored the collection of 12 anecdotal evidence items over the course of a class period or two. Students created an argument by selecting pieces that supported and contradicted their stated position. Evidence consisted of brief, textual evidentiary items such as "Brian looks up at one part of the sky on a clear night, and doesn't see any stars. When he looks through his telescope, however, he can see stars." The activity culminated in a student debate in which pairs would present the evidence they had identified that supported their stated position and responded to questions from other students. Students then individually had the opportunity to state their final position in the debate.

The selection of the two competing theories for the debate was carefully done. The normative position makes sense—educators want students to ultimately consider and understand the scientific perspective on the debate. The light goes forever position was framed at an intermediate level that was accessible to the students. The other intuitively aligned theory bears further discussion. The light dies out perspective succinctly frames a theoretical position that seems defensible in a superficial sense; it is a position that many students find compelling. It was crafted to fit with humans' phenomenological experience with light—as we move farther away from a light source, the intensity of the light drops off and the illumination seems to disappear or die out. In a manner that builds on student's prior knowledge, the light dies out theory allows students to connect and build on their current understanding of light. Overall, the debate topic was framed such that an explanation aligned with the normative theory necessitates an integration of knowledge about light from the CLP curriculum—knowledge of light intensity over distance, reflection, absorption, and energy conversion. That is, the overall framing of the debate project was aligned with the pedagogical focus of the curriculum: the integration of understanding.

Observational Iteration 1: The Social Dynamics of Classroom Debate. Research about this initial iteration focused on the social dynamics of the classroom debate: the role of the teacher during the debate, the nature of student questions and responses, patterns of interaction about the subject matter, and dimensions of the talk that seemed to promote or hinder learning. The research methods used to analyze the debate discourse involved a psychological coding of discourse moves made by participants (cf. Resnick, Salmon, et al., 1993) and a weak form of conversation analysis in which segments were analyzed in an attempt to understand the perspectives and meanings of the participants.

Students generated over 90% of the turns of talk during the classroom debate; it was a student-centered discussion. Given that the teacher only accounts for about 10% of the turns of talk during a classroom debate, it is possible that his role could be underestimated with that statistic. In contrast, analysis of the debate discourse showed that the teacher was playing several fundamental roles during the debate. First, they were framing the nature of the task to the student pairs and moderating the discussion for participation and consideration of ideas to be as equitable as possible. Second, they asked many questions initially during the question-and-answer portions of the debate to model the nature of appropriate questioning for students. Third, the teacher inquiries were balanced and probing questions for both of the theoretical sides of the debate; they did not play favorites or indicate directly which theoretical position was more valid. However, they did allow for a consensual view to emerge and to be elaborated in the public space over the course of the debate. These findings lead to the following design principle for orchestrating collaborative debates in the classroom:

> *Specific design principle: The role of the teacher during a classroom debate should be to moderate equitable interactions, to model appropriate question asking, to probe theoretical positions of the debate in equal measure, and to serve as a translator between students—all in the fewest turns of talk as possible.*

The paper-based debate activity allowed students to engage collaboratively in a prototypical form of scientific debate. The conversation analysis indicated that students asked relevant, probing questions of each other and brought out-of-school experiences into the discussion as evidence; these questions often led to elaborated explanations for student ideas and positions. Students were regularly elaborating, testing, refining, warranting, and possibly discarding their ideas about the debate topic. The following principle captures the purposes of the classroom debate with respect to the students' interactions:

> *Specific design principle: When engaged in a collaboratively focused debate discussion, students can safely share, explore, test, refine, and integrate their scientific ideas.*

The primary drawback associated with this paper-based iteration of the project hinged on the nature and entailments of the anecdotally derived evidence. Compared to what would subsequently be used, the evidence was quite simple—although it was personally relevant and somewhat compelling to the students. The pieces of evidence did not allow for any inclusion of data—only briefly described hypothetical experiences related to the debate topic. The sparse pieces of evidence led to impasses consisting of stated differences of opinion that were not resolvable because data or detailed information was not associated with the evidence. Subsequent versions of the project in KIE moved away from these simple depictions of scientific evidence.

Iteration 2: Multimedia Representations of Evidence and the First KIE Learning Environment.   The How Far Does Light Go? debate was the first KIE curriculum project developed and used in a classroom. In keeping with the design of the KIE learning environment, students would explore the Web-based evidence items. As an adaptation of the paper-based activity, I developed multimedia evidence items (in collaboration with other research group members) to parallel the anecdotal, textual items from the previous successful version. Figure 6.1 shows stills from one of the KIE multimedia evidence items created called "Bicyclists at Night." Generally, the multimedia evidence included data and detail related to the evidence item that was an elaboration of the notion of evidence in the paper-based version of the project.

For each piece of evidence students were prompted (using Claris-Works template files) to state its relevance to the debate. The KIE system did not easily allow for the customization of prompts for each piece of evidence—a feature that the research group would build into the next generation Web-Based Inquiry Science Environment

FIG. 6.1.   Frames from the "Bicyclists at Night" movie evidence used in the light debate project.

(WISE) environment—so students were responding to generic, sentence-starter prompts for causal explanation of the form "This evidence is relevant to the debate because. . . ." However, students could receive any number of conceptual hints specifically relevant to each piece of evidence—available through the Mildred bovine science guide component.

Iteration 2: The Mystery of Media Representation on Interpretation. The transition from paper- to Internet-based inquiry allowed for a comparison study to be conducted that analyzed how students interpreted evidence in different media formats and marshaled the pieces in their arguments. The multimedia evidence items created—which included stills, movies, and interactive simulations—were designed to be as conceptually isomorphic to the original textual items as possible. Half the students received a blend of textual and multimedia evidence items and the other half received the complementary set (which was also a blended set).

Because each isomorphic text–multimedia evidence pair was conceptually similar, one might expect students to work with the items in a similar manner. However, dramatic differences were found. Students marshaled the evidence in support of different ideas and even positions in the debate. This media effect was fueled by common, idiosyncratic differences in terms of how the evidence pairs were interpreted. Figure 6.2 shows one of the more dramatic differences of in-

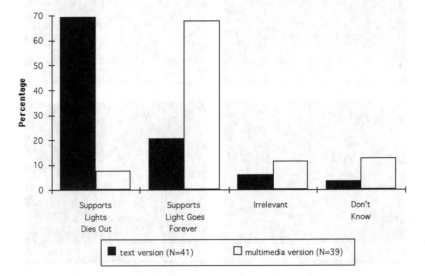

FIG. 6.2. Difference in interpretation of two conceptually isomorphic evidence pieces rendered in text and multimedia (the media effect).

terpretation (in terms of how the evidence supports one theory or the other).

There are many possible reasons why the media effect seemed so prevalent from the paucity or prevalence of data in the items to the epistemological stance of what counts as compelling scientific evidence to students (e.g., a telescope image being more compelling than an anecdotal description of the same). Perhaps the most compelling reason for the media effect is to associate the effect with a more established phenomenon from the assessment literature—the sensitivity of interpretation to surface characteristics of items (see Pellegrino et al., 2001, for more about this phenomenon). Although the underlying conceptual ideas were designed to be isomorphic, the surface characteristics were sometimes different. Students seemed to be taking these surface details into account as they worked with the evidence. We as educators learned that significant care needed to be taken in terms of understanding precisely how students would interpret and work with specific evidence presented in KIE, leading to the following design principle. For this reason, we have often needed to pilot evidence items and analyze written evidence explanations to understand how students generally engage with the piece and then decide if that fits within the overall purposes of the curriculum project in question:

Specific design principle: The media representation of scientific evidence significantly influences the interpretation of that evidence by students.

The conversion of the project from the paper-based format to presentation within the Internet learning environment was largely successful. Learning gains measured through conceptual items indicated the same degree of conceptual change during the project (Bell, 1998). In addition, students were having the opportunity to engage with more sophisticated pieces of evidence and were prompted (e.g., by Mildred, the bovine science guide described by Davis, chap. 5, this volume) to think more deeply about the evidence and apply more sophisticated criteria to the evidence items. Although over the course of the six iterations the research team never dramatically improved the number of students that developed an integrated understanding about the specific debate topic—about 20% of the students started with a deep understanding of how far light goes and about 40% more students developed that deep understanding as a result of the debate project—almost all students made conceptual progress (Bell, 1998; Bell & Linn, 2000).

The analytical phase of this iteration also included a facet-based analysis (Minstrell, 1989, 2001) of the chunks of student reasoning involved in their written evidence explanation (see Bell, 1998, for details). This led to several dozen regularly occurring facets associated with student thinking about light. A cluster analysis of the co-occurrence of specific facets within the evidence explanations indicated that distinct, logically consistent sets of ideas were associated with the defense of the two theoretical positions (i.e., they each had a distinct facet cluster). This analysis provided details into the array of conceptual ideas and the interconnected knowledge that students typically possess about the light propagation topic. It provided a pedagogically useful description of the conceptual change landscape involved with the particular subject matter at hand. This "cluster map" was used to inform the further shaping of the How Far Does Light Go? debate instruction.

During Iteration 2, it seemed clear that students were overly focused on particular evidence items during the project. Rather than consider the entire corpus of available evidence—similar to the Popperian notion of the epistemics of science in which all evidence is considered and counterevidence sheds important light on the status of theories—students would fixate on one or two pieces they believed strongly supported their perspective. In addition, the arguments constructed seem to be relatively thin—students would categorize evidence relative to the two debate positions, but they were not elaborating on what the theoretical stances actually meant from their perspective. This led me to imagine the introduction of a new software tool, SenseMaker, which included a particular knowledge representation to support students in argumentation with more epistemic fidelity to arguments in science.

Iteration 3: Introducing Representational Infrastructure for Making Thinking Visible During Argumentation. To respond to the evidence fixation issues identified in the prior iterations, I designed, prototyped, and tested the SenseMaker argument editor as part of the light debate project. As shown in Fig. 6.3, SenseMaker provides an overview (or a "helicopter view") of the entire corpus of evidence associated with the project. It is a knowledge representation tool that allows for the coordination of claims (boxes) and evidence (dots) to create parsimonious argument maps. From the perspective of the epistemics of science, the tool was designed to reinforce the evidence–claim distinction, promote their coordination, and support students in working with the entire evidence corpus. SenseMaker is an argument editor that can be seeded with theo-

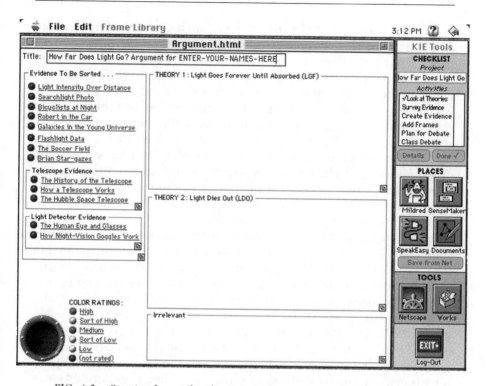

FIG. 6.3. Starting layout for the SenseMaker argument map used by students to represent coordinations of claims (boxes) and evidence (dots) associated with the debate topic.

retical positions at the start of the project as a scaffold. It is a structured inscriptional system that allows students to express their personal understanding of the evidence.

Iteration 3: Unanticipated Uses of the Helicopter View of Argumentation. The tool was introduced to students in a lock-step activity structure—they organized evidence with claims after having already explored all of the evidence individually and having crafted corresponding evidence explanations (described in more detail in Bell, 1998, in press). The SenseMaker argument maps were a novel representation from the perspective of the students. It became immediately clear that it needed more of an introduction than was possible in this iteration. Students needed to become fluent with the intended use of the argument map representation. However, students were still largely successful in categorizing the evidence relative to the theoretical positions of the debate in this initial use, and a few student groups created a new conceptual frame of their own design to add to their argument maps.

The categories created were not what had been originally intended. It was thought that students would represent their conceptual ideas (e.g., "light gets dimmer over distance") as organizing, nested claim frames in the argument map. In practice, only one third of the students created frames of this kind. Another one third created categorical frames (e.g., "binocular evidence"), and the last one third created frames that were logistically useful to the authors during the debate (e.g., "good to avoid during debate"). Although all of these frames could be considered useful, for the goal of promoting conceptual change it was thought that conceptually focused frames would be the most useful in that it would make student thinking the most visible within the argument representations. Subsequent iterations addressed this issue as I describe following.

In this iteration, however, it did become evident that the introduction of the SenseMaker argumentation infrastructure was supporting many students in considering the entire corpus of evidence associated with the project. Other research has shown that students tend to predominantly focus on single instances of evidence—when they attend to it at all—to inform their claims and arguments (see Driver, Leach, et al., 1996, for a discussion of this phenomenon). Before the use of SenseMaker, students had often been basing their personal opinion on individual pieces of evidence they found to be compelling, often ignoring other contradictory pieces of evidence. Unless there are grounds for excluding specific pieces of evidence, a central epistemological goal in the natural sciences is for theoretical knowledge to account for the entire corpus of empirical evidence relevant to a topic. A compelling goal for science education would be to help students develop an understanding of the mechanics of developing an argument that attempts to take into account a corpus of empirical evidence along with an appreciation of why such an epistemic practice is beneficial with regard to the construction of a causal, theoretical explanation of phenomena of the natural world. By exploring an evidence collection and being asked to represent and coordinate the set in the SenseMaker argument representation, students are encouraged to not fixate on individual pieces. Figure 6.4 shows a completed SenseMaker argument map created by a student pair working on the How Far Does Light Go? project. Developing an argument that involves making sense of an evidence collection is an affordance of the argument map representation used in SenseMaker (Bell, 1998) and another argumentation tool called *Belvedere* (Toth et al., 2002). Thus, these knowledge representation tools support the epistemic practices associated with having students make sense of patterns in all relevant data as they coordinate

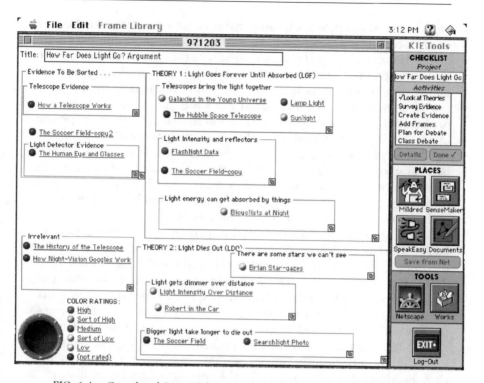

FIG. 6.4. Completed SenseMaker argument map showing how one student pair interpreted the evidence corpus and theorized about the debate topic.

theory and evidence in their constructed arguments, as summarized in the following design principle:

> *Specific design principle: Make evidence collections visible. When students attend to evidence in their argumentation, they tend to fixate on individual pieces. Argument representations promote student consideration of a corpus of evidence during argument construction.*

SenseMaker was designed to promote students' theorizing, to support evidence–theory coordination, and to make their thinking visible during classroom debate. There are a couple of relevant trade-offs involved with its design and use that are worth mentioning. First, I settled on presenting a particular representational form to students for them to become fluent with and use for their argument-building efforts. This did not need to be the case. One can imagine supporting students in developing their own epistemic representations that could easily look quite different and be more personally meaningful to students. However, given the desire to allow students to easily compare their constructed argument maps with those of other students and due to time constraints in most classrooms (especially involving the use of computers), a standardized form for the argument maps was preferred in this case. A second trade-off has to do with the representation selected. It is best thought of as an intermediate, or prototypical, form of scientific argumentation. A representation could have been employed that has greater fidelity to the nature of scientific explanation or was elaborated for other means, but I gravitated to an intermediate representation that would have a milder learning curve without sacrificing the epistemic goals at hand.

Most importantly, the use of this principle is contingent on a larger system of design decisions that involve supporting science learning through scaffolded evidence-based inquiry (see Bell & Linn, 2000, for more details). The focus on the corpus of evidence only makes sense in that pedagogical context. The argument map representation itself has been used for a variety of topics with diverse fields within the natural sciences; it is quite general as a scientific knowledge representation in that regard. (This design principle, as embodied in variations of the SenseMaker argument map representation, is currently being studied in the support of students' historical inquiry; more specifically, variations on the argument map representation appear to be well suited for microhistorical controversies, although some changes were needed to account for the multiple causality more typical of historical explanations.)

As important as it is to represent a collection of evidence in an argument representation, I have found it useful for that collection to consist of a shared corpus for students to explore as part of the curriculum project. An alternative would be to allow pairs of students to explore different collections of evidence. It is likely that this alternative approach could be used to promote the development of distributed expertise within the classroom (A. L. Brown, Ash, et al., 1995).

What are the possible benefits of using a shared evidence corpus for all students in a class? First of all, a shared corpus allows the classroom teacher to develop pedagogical content knowledge relevant to supporting students with their engagement with the evidence and thinking about the project topic (Wilson et al., 1990). Predictably, each piece of evidence cues prior knowledge somewhat systematically from the students. Pieces of evidence of different forms also benefit from particular interpretation practices associated with understanding that piece. For example, an evidence item that depicts a specific laboratory experiment calls for an interpretation of details from the experiment and the associated data generated.

Another important consequence associated with using a common corpus of evidence is that it helps establish common ground for discourse in these learning communities as they explore and debate the project topic (Edwards & Mercer, 1987). That is, the corpus allows groups of students along with the teacher to work toward a shared understanding of the same phenomena and theoretical ideas. In a related manner, students will often invoke common life experiences as a form of evidence in their verbal arguments to make their arguments more compelling and understandable. For this very reason, I also have students extend the shared corpus of evidence with instances of this evidence from their own personal life experiences. It also allows students to connect the project topic to their own lives and develop more of an integrated understanding of the topic:

> *Specific design principle: Shared corpus of evidence. Engaging classes of students with a common corpus of evidence will allow the teacher to more quickly refine usable pedagogical content knowledge and instructional strategies related to the topic. It will also help establish an increased degree of common ground during classroom discussions.*

Iteration 4: Activity Structures for Argument Construction. SenseMaker was still not being used in a sophisticated manner by most of the students as of the third iteration of the project; there were only select instances of innovative uses. The fourth iteration attempted to better introduce the idea of argument map representations and more systematically support students in using the argumentation tool during their argument construction process to get broader compelling use of the tool by students. It was thought that more extensive use of the argument map representation was necessary: A 2-day curriculum project was developed that simply introduced students to SenseMaker, and the How Far Does Light Go? project was amended to fully integrate the use of the SenseMaker tool into the activity structure whereby students survey each piece of evidence.

Iteration 4: Fostering Causal Argumentation Incrementally. Designing the software for a new learning technology tool is only the first step of the necessary educational design process. For tools in which specific uses are imagined or desired, it then becomes necessary to design instructional experiences and activity structures that help students develop fluencies related to the desired use of the tool.

In this particular case, the lock-step activity structure used in the third iteration was thought to be somewhat problematic. Students segmented the use of the tool from their work with the evidence because work with the evidence items and the argument map were in sequence. In the fourth iteration, the SenseMaker argument maps became the central organizing representation of the argumentation process. In this integrated activity structure, students surveyed evidence from the argument map, created their evidence explanations, and categorized the evidence before moving on to the next piece. The argument map was thereby slowly constructed over the course of days in an incremental fashion in conjunction with their interpretation of the evidence and their authoring of evidence notes. Students developed their argument maps more slowly over time. These three activities became an integrated intellectual experience for most students, leading to a more coherent and refined argument:

> *Specific design principle: Students created more elaborated arguments when an activity structure was promoted whereby the use of the knowledge representation tool was integrated into their interpretation and theorizing about evidence.*

Yet what is the quality of the arguments being created by students? Is it unreasonable to expect middle school students to know how to productively coordinate evidence and theory? That is, do students have an epistemological facility for engaging in such evidence–theory coordination if they were to receive appropriate supports and enculturation? Researchers have documented how students do not come to science class understanding this type of argumentation (Driver, Leach, et al., 1996; Kuhn, 1991). However, structural analysis of the arguments created by students revealed that students regularly coordinate evidence and theory when provided with these supports during instruction (see Bell, 2002; Bell & Linn, 2000).

At least in part, I believe that it is because both evidence (dots) and theoretical claims (frames) are components of the ontology of the SenseMaker software. The active coordination of evidence and theory in the representation also supports the epistemic goals of knowledge being the object of inquiry in science and the importance of understanding the reciprocal relation between theory and data. This creation and tethering of evidence and theory is the inquiry students are engaged in during these controversy-focused debate projects. Through this particular depiction of scientific argumentation (which is an intermediate form, as mentioned earlier), students are being introduced to an important form of scientific knowledge—another goal associated with epistemic understanding.

This principle is motivated by the image of science represented in the epistemic goal that students understand the reciprocal relation between theory and data. The epistemic game of interest here focuses on a coordination of evidence and theoretical claims associated with the topic of inquiry:

> *Specific design principle: Theory–evidence coordination. Left to their own accord, middle school students rarely incorporate instances of evidence into their arguments about science. Argument representations should promote theory and evidence presence, distinction, and coordination.*

Yet how exactly are students coordinating evidence and theory? Are these coordinations descriptive connections or causal conjectures or something else? Actually, structural analyses of student arguments showed that 70% to 80% of the evidence explanations composed by students involve trying to use or establish causal warrants related to the debate (Bell, 1998; Bell & Linn, 2000). Only 15% of the explanations on average relied on phenomenological description to try and establish a connection between evidence and theory, leading to the following design principle:

> *Specific design principle: Causal theorizing. Students produce arguments that predominantly include causal conjectures connecting empirical evidence and theoretical conclusions when they are supported in a process of authoring prompted explanations. Such theorizing is further supported when it becomes the focus of community discussion in the classroom.*

Iteration 4: Room for Improvement.   In the fourth iteration students were introduced to the SenseMaker argumentation tool during a 2-day activity in which they constructed arguments based on the scientific principles and evidence (interpreted data) associated with their laboratory experiences with light. It was thought that building an argument about their prior laboratory work would help promote further knowledge integration by bringing it all together into one argument map. At the same time, I hoped they would learn about argument map representations. It was a plausible approach, but it did not pan out as desired. Students were still generally confused about the argument map representation and were not accustomed to revisiting all of their prior classroom activities in this kind of synthesis effort.

Apart from some early learning of the SenseMaker interface, it was not thought that students developed any significant fluency with the tool or the representation through this introductory activity. This still left this strand of research with a palpable problem: how best to introduce students to the possibilities and features of the knowledge representation tool.

Iteration 5: Exploring the Past to Argue About the Present. I decided to try modeling expert use of the SenseMaker tool to the students. The 2-day introductory project was redesigned and expanded to a 3-day exploration of a historical debate: a hypothetical argument between Johannes Kepler and Sir Isaac Newton about the relation between light and color. Not only was the project a reasonable subject matter extension of the light curriculum, but it introduced the nature of expert arguments, the personal nature of theorizing and interpretation of evidence, and the historical prevalence of argumentation and debate in science.

Kepler theorized that light and color were distinct phenomena—that colors were produced when pure white light picked up and actually carried colors (which were a natural kind of their own). Through experimentation Newton developed a theoretical alternative: that white light is composed of different specific colors of light. For the brief curriculum project, several relevant pieces of historical evidence were authored. Students were asked to interpret arguments of Kepler and Newton—presented as SenseMaker argument maps—and then author their own new argument map using SenseMaker with the same pool of evidence.

This modeling of expert use of the SenseMaker tool proved to be quite beneficial. Students learned a bit about light and color while coming to understand argument maps in a relatively complex way and learning the software interface. The project modeled the desired prototypical form of scientific argument—the coordination of knowledge claims and evidence—and demonstrated the personal creative act involved with interpreting evidence and making conjectural claims about a topic. Fluency with this prototypical representation is quite attainable but is contingent on a broader emphasis on how knowledge is constructed and refined in science. To this end, care needs to be taken to promote a disciplinary understanding of the nature of evidence, theory, and explanation in science as it varies from everyday reasoning. Importantly, the project also showed that two scientists could disagree about pieces of evidence based on their own ideas about the subject matter. This seems to have allowed students more expressive freedom in representing their own ideas and coordinations of evidence in their argument maps:

> *Specific design principle: Introducing argumentation through the exploration of a historical debate between scientists allows students to understand aspects of scientific argumentation and the creativity involved with theorizing and coordinating with evidence, as well as how individual ideas can shape one's interpretations of evidence and constructed arguments.*

Iteration 5: Promoting a Blended Argument Representation. Building on the principled focus on evidence–theory coordination through an engagement with an evidence collection that is shared, I now describe how SenseMaker can serve as an inscriptional system for representing students' scientific ideas, notions, conjectures on one hand and various perspectives (hypotheses, positions, solutions, or propositions) about the controversy topic associated with the project. Although both dimensions of this knowledge—student and topical—come to be represented, they become interrelated (or blended) in the actual representation. This is typically an interaction of how the representation was originally designed by the project developer or teacher and how the students represent their understanding and conjectures visibly in the representation.

Before the project begins in the classroom, the SenseMaker representation is set up with some initial theoretical structure built into it in the form of competing claim frames. In this regard, it is useful to map out the competing perspectives associated with the controversy. In the How Far Does Light Go? project, there are claim frames for each of the theories and for irrelevant evidence (as shown in Fig. 6.3). Note that apart from looking to the topic for guidance in the initial design of the representation, it has also been useful to represent positions that will resonate with students initial thinking about the topic—to give them a way to easily represent their personal understanding in their argument map. The blend of the student thinking within the perspectives associated with the topic can promote active sense making and perspective taking on the part of students (see Bell, 1998, for details):

> *Specific design principle: Represent student thinking and topical perspectives. Promote the use of the argument representation as a blended representational medium that depicts (a) students thinking and theorizing about the controversial topic (based on their*

prior and evolving understanding) and (b) different perspectives associated with the controversy.

Iteration 5: Room for Improvement. As described in Iteration 4, it was observed that students were very savvy at authoring causal warrants for evidence. Interestingly, they were still having difficulties creating frames in their SenseMaker arguments. Due to the causal theorizing in their evidence explanations, I knew it was not due to a lack of ideas—it seemed like they could not abstract the embedded ideas into more general conceptual frames. During the fifth iteration of the How Far Does Light Go? project, I experimented with the use of a frame library—a list of conceptual ideas that students could consider making into frames in their argument maps. Because the goal was to just promote theorizing, the frame-library list includes scientifically normative as well as alternative conceptions. It provided further modeling as to what was desired in the argument maps along with some specific suggestions. The frame-library list proved to be useful enough to students that I built the library into the SenseMaker software for use in the sixth trial.

Iteration 6: Perspective Taking Promotes Argumentation and Learning. Given the educational goals of the KIE research group, the How Far Does Light Go? curriculum project was running pretty well at this point. Also, with most of the educational package developed, refined, and integrated in this curriculum sequence, it was now possible to pose a theoretical question through a compelling comparison of two hypothesis-driven variations in the educational package. Were students better off developing an argument for their original position in the debate, or was it more helpful to support students in thinking about both perspectives in the debate? These two alternatives became the "personal scope" and the "full scope" conditions in the sixth iteration of the project. Three of the six periods of students were in the "personal scope" condition and were told they would defend the theoretical position they initially identified with about how far light goes. The other three periods of students—who were in the "full scope" condition—were told that they should prepare to defend either theoretical perspective as they constructed their argument. When the debate arrived, the teacher and I allowed students to defend the theoretical position they believed in at the time, as we had not had luck in a previous iteration asking students to defend a position they did not believe in.

Did the perspective-taking activity structure influence students' learning, or did students learn more by being asked to bolster their initial position? The results were compelling. In the "full scope" condition that promoted perspective taking, there was a gain of 57% of students who developed a full scientific understanding of light propagation by the end of the semester compared to a gain of 39% of students doing the same in the "personal scope" condition (Bell, 1998). Further, I found that students with a low prior knowledge of light actually benefited more from the perspective-taking activity structure than students who had some knowledge of light. Being in the "full scope" condition led to more conceptual theorizing in student argument maps, especially among students who initially were aligned with the non-normative light dies out perspective. This indicates a powerful effect of perspective taking: that the activity structure scaffold better supported the development of an integrated understanding than asking students to just explore, refine, and be responsible to their initial opinions about the debate topic:

> Specific design principle: Compared to allowing students to refine their initial position in a debate, students engaged in a perspective-taking activity structure theorize more in their argument maps and evidence explanations and develop a more integrated understanding of the subject matter in the process.

Iteration 6: Promoting Scientific Discussion During Classroom Debates With Argument Maps.   In the How Far Does Light Go? curriculum projects (and other WISE and Science Controversies Online Partnerships for Education debate projects), students present their scientific arguments constructed in small groups during a culminating whole-class debate after they have investigated the corpus of shared evidence. Without the use of argument map representations, most students rely on a rather straightforward rhetorical strategy as they participate in the debate: They present just their strongest pieces of evidence to the class, trying to bracket the discussion to those particular evidentiary pieces and the related reasoning. There is good reason for students to begin their argument with the pieces of evidence they found to be most compelling. However, for reasons discussed during the third iteration, students should be accountable for the corpus of evidence available for a given topic (with obvious caveats pertaining to time constraints).

The SenseMaker representation has been used in a number of classrooms as supplemental intellectual infrastructure for argument construction and debate activities. In addition to scaffolding the argument construction of individuals or pairs of students (as described previously), the resulting argument maps can also be used as collaborative, comparative artifacts with each one representing the understanding, albeit only partially and abstractly, of particular participant groups during the culminating debate activity (see Bell, 2002, for more detail). In the sixth iteration the argument map representations were incorporated into whole-class debates in science classrooms and their influence on the discourse dynamics has been studied using conversation analysis methods. More specifically, as student pairs present their argument to the class, their argument map was web-casted to all of the computers spread around the room. Students in the audience could then compare their printed argument maps with that of the presenting group (see Fig. 6.5 for a symbolic representation of this setup).

When argument maps were used in this manner, the discourse patterns involved with the classroom debate shifted. Student presentations still took the form of highlighting their strongest pieces of evi-

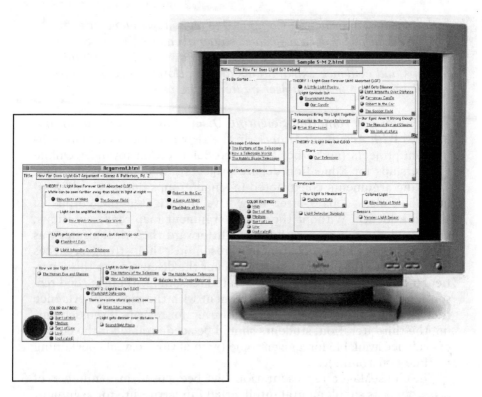

FIG. 6.5. Picture detailing the comparative use of argument maps during whole-class debate presentations and discussions. Students compare their own printed argument map (left) to the map created by the presenters projected on computer screens in the room (right).

dence. However, questions from students in the audience focused largely on evidence *not* mentioned by the presenters. After some initial modeling by the teacher and researcher, students regularly engaged in the practice of asking student presenters about evidence that they had ruled as being irrelevant to the debate or had theoretically interpreted differently than others in the classroom. The argument maps became representational infrastructures that allowed students to compare interpretations of evidence (or underlying scientific ideas). Audience members used the maps to hold presenters more accountable to the corpus of evidence involved with the project. The maps provided a social mechanism for the unpacking of student thinking in a very focused way. Students had spent days building their scientific arguments about the evidence, basically amassing intellectual capital about the topic that was cashed in during the debate discussions in ways that established learning opportunities around the epistemological and conceptual issues involved:

> *Specific design principle: Debate infrastructure. Use argument map representations comparatively during whole-class debate presentations to promote accountability to the body of evidence under consideration.*

Iteration 6: Promoting Epistemological Sophistication Through Argumentation and Debate.   One might wonder if all of this argumentation and debate lead to the same degree of understanding of the debate topic, then why bother with the KIE approach. In short, it is because students are learning about the nature of science in significant detail in addition the their development of integrated conceptual understanding. During the sixth iteration, I posed epistemological questions to students about argumentation and debate in science to gauge their degree of epistemological sophistication before and after the How Far Does Light Go? debate project. Categorical coding of student responses indicated that students developed a greater understanding of the evidentiary basis of scientific argumentation, the general connection between argumentation and learning, and the social refinement of their own integrated understanding during the debate activity (see Bell & Linn, 2000, for details).

Given that students seem to have difficulty understanding the evidentiary nature of scientific argumentation (Koslowski, 1996; Kuhn, 1993) and the social dimensions of science (Driver, Leach, et al., 1996), this documented statistical shift is an important mark of epistemological sophistication that should be considered an important educational outcome of the same importance, if not greater, as the conceptual understanding of some particular subject matter. With this increased degree of sophistication, students are more likely to approach scientific information and sense making in productive ways. Debate in science will less often be perceived as arbitrary, unproductive, or mysterious.

CONCLUSIONS

Argumentation and Debate as Core Intellectual Practices of the Natural Sciences

How does scientific knowledge progress over time? One might think that the settled, factual knowledge of science simply accumulates. Certainly new experiments lead to new knowledge about the natural world. Yet new knowledge often displaces old knowledge. Relativity offered a significantly different alternative to the Newtonian model of motion. Accumulation is not a sufficient epistemological model in and of itself. At the cutting edge of scientific knowledge, there are often competing notions or models being explored. Technology and experimental design is brought to bear on the issues. Arguments are mounted and debates come about.

I frame debate and argumentation as the exploration of a theoretical controversy involving the coordination of evidence with theoretical ideas. It seems incontrovertible that argumentation and debate are central mechanisms that drive the advancement of scientific knowledge (as well as knowledge in other disciplines). The history of science is full of accounts in which competing hypotheses and models have been explored around a specific scientific topic through theoretical and experimental means. Kuhn (1970) described how different theories attempting to describe the same phenomena can advance until the approaches are incommensurable in terms of the language and concepts used. Such distinctions can lead to paradigm shifts in scientific fields as a debated topic is resolved.

In the natural sciences, argumentation and debate operate at many different time scales and in numerous formal and informal venues. Controversies can span generations or be resolved in a matter of days or months. Latour (1987) documented scientific debates occurring on specific scientific hypotheses over the course of years, months, or even days. For example, he described in detail how two research laboratories explore competing notions of growth hormones. Therefore, there is reason to believe that in addition to being a historical lens on which to view scientific events across generations (i.e., the Kuhnian sense), debate is also an active, day-to-day, operational construct for scientists. Indeed, Latour (1987) spent significant time documenting the competitive nature of science. One need only investigate accounts of current controversies in science to see central aspects of debate represented. I explore this idea in depth in chapter 10 (Bell, this volume).

Scientific debates play out within the formal venues of the primary and secondary scientific literatures. They surface publicly in scientific society meetings and privately in informal research group meetings and bar room gatherings of scientists. They partially, and frequently imperfectly, show up in the mainstream press. The research in this chapter is predicated on the assumption that argumentation and debate are central features of substantive intellectual work in the natural sciences. An entailment of this assumption also needs to hold in that argumentation and debate in the natural sciences need to follow epistemic rules and norms of practice that allow for their characterization—at least at a level of detail that might be characterized as a prototypical form appropriate for students. Of course, such systematic characterizations of argumentation are somewhat commonplace in philosophy (e.g., Toulmin, 1958). Such forms have been characterized by Collins and Ferguson (1993) as epistemic forms.[2] With these assumptions in mind, the focus of this research then becomes how students can be educationally engaged in such prototypical forms of argumentation and debate such that they can make sense of diverse information sources and develop a more integrated understanding of science.

Supporting Student Learning Through Argumentation and Debate—Mission Impossible or a Matter of Scaffolding?

Student argument maps can serve as learning artifacts that provide a window onto their thinking about the science as well as about the nature of science. I have used analyses of these artifacts to understand student learning from the designed curriculum as well as the nature of their epistemological sophistication (Bell, 2002; Bell & Linn, 2000). Most middle school students have not experienced a structured debate activity in school. They probably experience argument construction mostly within the confines of their English and social study classes. Fostering argumentation and debate in the classroom can seem like unknown pedagogical territory to middle school science ed-

ucators. Developmental psychologists studying the growth of argumentation strategies and abilities (Koslowski, 1996; Kuhn, 1991,
1993) have highlighted that several dimensions of the intellectual activity prove to be quite difficult for adolescents, including the coordination of evidence and theory, consideration of multiple perspectives,
the construction of rebuttals, and other metacognitive features of argument. It is important to realize that most of these developmental
studies are conducted under information-lean and relatively unscaf-
folded conditions. In contrast, the program of research I described in
this chapter has indicated that compelling arguments and generative
debate experiences can be scaffolded in middle school science classrooms. Students may not have been able to spontaneously engage in
these performances, but when they are tuned into the epistemic game
at hand and supported in their inquiry, they can indeed engage in such
intellectual activities and develop a more integrated understanding of
complex science topics in the process.

EPILOGUE: PUSHING THE LEARNING
ENVIRONMENT THROUGH THE BROWSER

Over the course of the software and curriculum iterations in KIE, the
World Wide Web—as it was described at the time with some cumber-
someness—continued to thrive and mature as a technical platform.
When Netscape® Version 3.0 showed up (with integrated Javascript-
ing), we realized that it would be possible to push more of the KIE
learning environment functionality through the web browser directly.
Rather than relying on the careful coordination of half a dozen local
Macintosh® applications, it started to become possible to embed more
of this functionality into the web experience itself. This shift in the
technological implementation cannot be understated with regard to
the corresponding technical support issues. The minimum technical
requirements would become a recent browser with decent simulta-
neous browsing capabilities for all the machines to be used.

Building on the new scripting functionality and support for frames
in the Netscape browser, I developed a web-centric version of the How
Far Does Light Go? debate that is still in use at the time of this writing, although the research group has improved upon it a couple of
times more with the development of versions of the WISE environment. Figure 6.6 shows what is called the "WebKIE" version of the
How Far Does Light Go? debate.

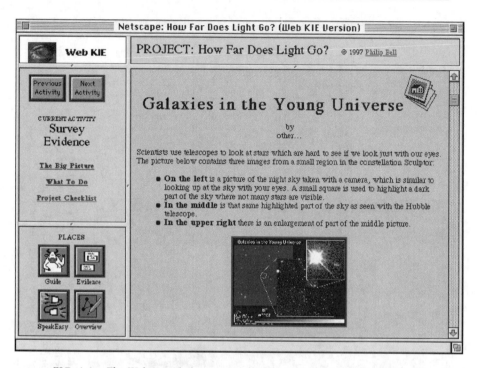

FIG. 6.6.   The Web Knowledge Integration Environment (KIE) implementation of the How Far Does Light Go? debate project provided some of the core
KIE functionality directly through the Web browser rather than using custom
software components.

The WebKIE implementation was like taking a step backward with
regard to some of the functionality that had come to be present in the
full KIE suite of tools; this was necessary given the instabilities of the
technical platform and the approach taken at the time. However, once
this implementation direction proved sound, the KIE research group
conducted a series of design meetings to come up with an approach
whereby we could include more of the evolved functionality of KIE and
even extend it further. Based on those group design meetings, I implemented the first prototype for what would become WISE (see Slotta,
chap. 9, this volume, for more details on the design of WISE) within
the context of the Deformed Frogs curriculum development partnership (described further in Bell, chap. 10, and Shear, Bell, & Linn,
chap. 12, this volume). Figure 6.7 shows this early precursor to the
WISE environment (which has gone on to be used by tens of thousands
of students). It includes the first time that the inquiry map provided
procedural scaffolding—an elegant, although perhaps somewhat
static, solution to the scaffolding of student inquiry and to the orches-

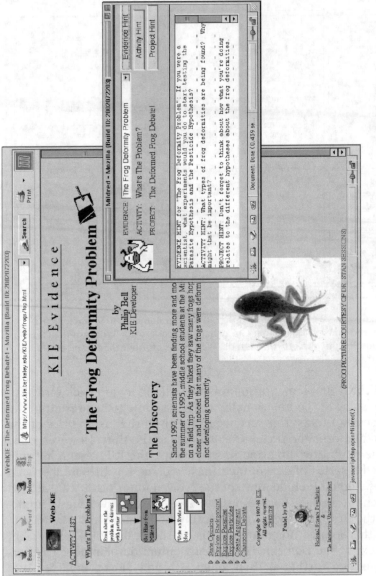

FIG. 6.7. The Web Knowledge Integration Environment (KIE) implementation of the deformed frogs mystery project was the immediate precursor to the Web-Based Inquiry Science Environment learning environment. It included a clickable inquiry map for procedural scaffolding and provided integrated access to different tools (e.g., Mildred, the bovine science guide component).

tration of numerous tools and information resources without having to resort to a strictly sequenced interface. All these versions of the debate activity refined the underlying curriculum design pattern. Each new version took advantage of the prior work with the pattern.

These environments proved to be incredibly productive educational resources to fuel argumentation and debate in the science classroom. As I have described in this chapter, many details of the design and appropriation need to be carefully considered as they are systemically and culturally rooted within a specific learning community. Further research on supporting student learning through the exploration of scientific controversy with information technologies built on and refined these design principles and research findings (see Bell, chap. 10, this volume, for details). I believe this line of research is still compelling given the new forms of access to information ecologies via cell phones to personal digital assistants to wireless communicators, and the promises and complications of research from the natural sciences seem only to be becoming more prevalent. Educators need to understand how to support individuals and groups in developing an integrated understanding of controversial issues of science and make sense of the diverse pieces of scientific information they encounter across the breadth of their life activities.

ENDNOTES

1. The development and refinement of the original paper-based version of the "How Far Does Light Go?" project was conducted by Weinland (1993) in collaboration with the other members of the CLP group.
2. It is certainly worth mentioning that argumentation and debate are likely to vary across disciplines and even subfields within the natural sciences. The prototypical forms put forth in this research should not be taken to be any sort of universal grammar for argumentation and debate in the natural sciences. In fact, given that much empirical work in the various corners of scientific practice remain to be conducted, the prototypical form model presented should at best be taken to be an initial educational treatment.

7

Fostering Productive Collaboration Offline and Online: Learning From Each Other

Christopher M. Hoadley
Pennsylvania State University

This volume describes a number of innovations in the field of Internet-based education from a research group that helped invent the general approach. Some readers may have come upon this volume hoping that it would contain simple prescriptions on how to use the Internet for learning as determined by simple either–or comparisons, the "hard research" that is so lauded by experimental traditionalists. However, as any teacher who has tried to implement a research-based innovation knows, there are no simple answers. Research is important, and the defining characteristic of research is an empirical stance, a willingness to "listen to the data" and to look for patterns that hold true across time and space. Our work as researchers certainly fits this bill. However, as is true with most educational research, the simple studies and simple answers ("Which is best, A or B?") are notably backgrounded in the work. The tricky part of doing educational research is that the devil is in the details—interventions may take on widely varying forms depending on the teacher, the classroom context, and even the particular geographic location. In technology research in particular, many ask questions that belie the role of context. The question, "Is tool A better than tool B?" is foolish if one doesn't ever examine what is done with tools A and B or why. In all of the work reported in this volume, these so-called horse race studies are backgrounded. They are used to answer important questions, but any experimental comparisons are highly embedded in a tapestry of efforts that blends creative technology and curriculum generation, proactive implementation, and iteration. This cycle of activities makes sure that the comparisons examined make sense—that they are compelling—and that the interventions tested represent the best possible examples of their kind that could be provided.

One of the most valuable lenses with which to examine work in this volume is the idea of design-based research (Bell, Hoadley, & Linn, chap. 4, this volume; Design-Based Research Collective, 2003; Hoadley, 2002). This stance of design as integral to the work was especially important in the creation of collaborative tools and activities. Like many of the visualization and modeling activities in the Knowledge Integration Environment (KIE) that drew on years of experience in the Computer as Learning Partner (CLP) research and the CLP classroom, my work with collaborative technologies in KIE was grounded in years of prior work on creating collaborative tools and, equally important, *collaborative contexts*, or activities and cultural norms that supported collaboration leading to learning.

DESIGN AS A CONTEXT OF RESEARCH

When we as researchers discuss design, we imply certain ideas about the character of the activities we engage in. First and foremost, design is purposeful and creative. As researchers, our purpose was fundamental to our approach: We weren't merely developing theories about learning but were also seeking ways to ensure that young students (in our case, 12- to 14-year-olds) were able to learn science. We were troubled by the deficits that seemed rampant, including disconnected knowledge that students might parrot but didn't understand and certainly couldn't apply to their own lives. This actually set us apart from pure technologists in that our major goal was not to find application of technology but to enhance learning.

A second defining feature of design is that design is open ended. This is usually thought of as what makes design challenging (as compared to, for instance, problem solving; Greeno & Simon, 1988; Simon, 1969). However, open-endedness proves to be an advantage in educational technology research because it means researchers' designs are well suited to the types of open-ended questions the research addresses, such as "How can we best use technology to support reasoning in thermodynamics?" (in contrast to, "Are computers better than filmstrips?").

Good design is iterative. The process of creating something to address a goal is repeated many times as the designed artifact or process is tested, observed, and refined. The iterative nature of design is often missing in research but is vital in testing researchers' interventions. By repeatedly creating, implementing, enacting, and improving our interventions, we as researchers begin to understand intuitively and empirically what works and what doesn't and also which features of the design are essential and which are irrelevant to our goals. In typical design, especially typical software design, this type of refinement is an informal way of doing research—user testing can encompass experimentation that would pass muster with the most stringent research methodologists, but usually it is far more informal. The sage researcher uses mixed methodologies combining informal and formal methods according to costs and benefits (Neilsen, 1994). In our case, we used this refinement cycle as an opportunity to listen to the data and to conduct studies that were robust because they were meaningful and were grounded in the extensive contextual knowledge that came from participating in the design process that created the intervention in the first place. As with scientific research in general, we used studies to test hypotheses and to ground us as we constructed falsifiable models and theories from the data.

One of the tenets of the scaffolded knowledge integration framework (Linn, Davis, & Eylon, chap. 3, this volume) is the development of social supports for learning. This chapter provides a design narrative on how we as researchers studied what types of collaboration might support learning and how technology can enhance this collaboration.

Elsewhere, I (Hoadley, 2002) reported how design-based research can lead to better alignment between theories, experimental interventions, and outcome measures, a lesson learned while studying scientific discussion online and the "SpeakEasy" collaboration tool (Hoadley, Berman, et al., 1995; Hoadley, Hsi, et al., 1995). A design narrative of this explicitly collaborative tool is available in Hoadley (1999, 2002). However, by labeling tools either *collaborative* or *noncollaborative*, one oversimplifies things (Hoadley & Enyedy, 1999). Here, I provide a contrasting design narrative, one that shows how social supports for learning are important even when one is not designing groupware.

DESIGNING FOR COLLABORATION

This chapter is about some designs of technologies and activities that fostered collaborative aspects of learning. The discussion in chapter 4 (Bell et al., this volume) of design-based research and design narratives can and does apply to other aspects of the research reported in this volume. Research on collaborative learning, however, presents some unique challenges that underscore the importance of a design-sensitive report of the work. In other work, Hsi, Hoadley, et al. (1995) discussed how collaboration research adds design complexity. Collaboration research is particularly sensitive to variations in context, and any intervention reverberates through the setting changing both the individuals and the social context. Time is required to see how the intervention settles into a steady state as both individuals' practices and the group practices adapt to the new tools.

Here, I give a design narrative for one particular innovation that began as a curricular unit to address specific learning needs. It provided a rich context for studying how technology could scaffold student learning and knowledge integration in science. Through this saga, I try to point out ways that the research team learned to provide social supports for learning and how technology, activity, and local culture interrelated in these studies.

DESIGN NARRATIVE: THE HOUSES IN THE DESERT ACTIVITY

In this design narrative, I describe how a student Internet project in a middle school physical science classroom was refined through four iterations. Although the curricular project was not initially thought of as a collaboration project, social concerns ended up being an important part of the learning experience and shaped the uses of technology in the project. The project, named "Houses in the Desert," or Houses for short, asked students to apply their knowledge of thermal equilibrium, heat energy, and light energy to the problem of designing a house in a desert environment. Like capstone design projects in engineering education, we hoped this final project in the classroom curriculum would help solidify student understanding of analytic concepts in energy and thermodynamics, and might serve as a performance assessment for student learning over the course of the semester.

This project is an example of the design genre of Internet project created in KIE. In some ways, the design of student design projects is the most difficult. As instructional, curricular, and technology designers, we had to be clear about the similarities and differences between our own design practices and student design practices. Even our choice of language was a challenge; "learning through design" was the phrase we selected that most accurately represented our goals. The students were learning to design, but this was subsidiary to the real goal of learning science content and scientific reasoning (as opposed to design skills). Design is also naturally a very open-ended activity, which left us many choices and few examples to follow in helping the students. Whereas some research has been done on teaching students design skills (in domains such as computer programming, architectural design, and engineering in which design is a part of professional practice), few have studied use of design activities specifically as a pedagogy for knowledge that is not inherently design based. Kafai (1995) and Carter Ching (2000) are the most notable exception to this rule, having studied how design activities may be used in elementary school mathematics. These efforts and those of our contemporaries like Kolodner (Kolodner, Crismond, et al., 1998) and Baumgartner (2000; Baumgartner & Reiser, 1998), inspired the research group to seek a role for design in the KIE environment.

As in prior chapters, the first project in the genre took considerable time and effort to polish. Unlike the theory comparison (Bell, chap. 6, this volume) and critique (Davis, chap. 5, this volume) genres, this genre did not have significant representation in the existing CLP curriculum. Indeed, the refinements of our design-based project were intimately intertwined with the design and redesign of the KIE software; software interfaces that made sense for claims didn't necessarily have as much relevance in a design context where decisions or constraints were more central. Likewise, as the collaborative technology of the SpeakEasy was a part of the project, our experiences with Houses in the Desert informed uses of the SpeakEasy tool in other contexts and some of the redesigns of this tool. However, in this narrative I focus more closely on how we structured the design activity than on changes to the overall KIE interface or to SpeakEasy. As is seen, although collaboration was not a central feature of this project in the beginning, through iterative refinement we came to understand how structuring collaboration was the most powerful way of scaffolding the students' science learning in the design.

Goals for Design Curricula

Design-based curricula appeared to offer some important benefits that initially attracted us to the genre. Through the use of design-based activities, we as designers hoped to help students apply and integrate their knowledge in the context of a real-world problem with relevance to the students. Design problems are by nature open-ended and for this reason are an important class of problems suitable for problem-based learning (Boud & Feletti, 1991; Sherwood et al., 1998). Commonplace examples such as the "mousetrap car" activity found in physics classrooms worldwide point to design activities as motivating. Furthermore, by applying their knowledge to a real context, the designers hoped that students would be better able to apply their knowledge of thermodynamics and light energy, integrate their understanding through reconciling the various principles with a single designed artifact (the house plans), and bring in real-world experiences they had living in houses in a somewhat desert-like climate. (This research site was in a warm, inland valley in California, which had hot, dry weather.)

The context for which the activity was developed was Doug Kirkpatrick's eighth-grade physical science classroom. As described earlier in this volume, Kirkpatrick was a member of the research and development team and had been working previously with the same research group at the University of California at Berkeley on the CLP project, a research and development effort that helped study student science learning and developed a semester-long curriculum on energy, especially heat and temperature.

The Houses project was developed with the help of other members of the KIE team. The initial creation of the project in 1994 was based on a much shorter CLP activity called "Aliens on Tour" in which students designed clothing to keep cold-blooded aliens comfortable at different temperatures; this project was originally created as a performance assessment by Nancy Songer in the late 1980s and later revised by Eileen Lewis and Elizabeth Davis. I led the creation of Houses with help from Sherry Hsi and Alex Cuthbert, and Cuthbert helped in subsequent runs. Kirkpatrick had enormous input throughout the design process. Considerable work has been done by Cuthbert refining the design project approach in multiple classrooms using the new Web-Based Inquiry Science Environment (WISE) platform since this initial phase of development in KIE, although it is not reported here (for more information, see Cuthbert, 2002; Cuthbert & Hoadley, 1998a, 1998b).

Challenges for Learning Through Design

Because our goal was to foster good learning experiences rather than good designs, the designers of Houses faced several challenges. The biggest challenge was that we wanted the activity to engage students in the scientific principles involved in the problem. In the case of

Houses, students were not expected to learn architecture in this course or elsewhere, nor did we have time to teach the basics of architectural design. Many of the reasons that the problem we posed was engaging made it easy for students to focus on superfluous aspects of the house design problem. Students were highly motivated to invent personal spaces and would have happily done so to the exclusion of the heat and temperature problems related to the design task (Kolodner, Crismond, et al., 1998).

Another challenge we as designers faced was how to constrain the task enough to prevent students from floundering. Our task was easily open ended enough to take the entire semester. We didn't want to lose the sense of an open-ended problem, but we also didn't want students wasting their time on unprincipled guessing as a design strategy (Baumgartner & Reiser, 1998; Williams & Bareiss, 1998).

A third challenge was to encourage students to refine their ideas. Certainly in a less project-based unit, students would practice their ideas through a number of exercises. Here, students could really only make a few major strategy choices about how their house would address the heat and temperature needs of its occupants. If they made these choices early on and if they made poor choices, they would have little opportunity to explore the scientific concepts or improve their design. Thus, avoiding design fixation (Jansson & Smith, 1991) was an important goal to help students in thinking through numerous examples (Linn & Songer, 1993; Linn, Songer, et al., 1996; Reiser, Ranney, et al., 1989).

Each of these goals was a design goal for the other Houses designers and me in creating the project, with justification from both the literature and theories of productive discussion. However, implementing these goals proved challenging and took several iterations. The focus of the design narrative that follows is how the KIE team came to achieve these goals in our setting by iteratively refining not only the technology tools but also the activities around them. For each iteration of the project, I characterize shortcomings of the design and how we remediated them in the next run. Again, the point of this chronicle is not merely to show that we put work into improving our intervention but rather to demonstrate the degree to which providing social supports for learning was a part of creating a successful project, even though it wasn't initially perceived to be a project in which collaboration would be central. Also, by conveying some of the deliberate design choices and the justifications for them, I hope that this design narrative will enable others who wish to create projects for learning through design.

Iterative Refinement of the Design Activity

In this narrative, I focus on the first four iterations of the full project (there was a partial pilot test of the project before this story begins), one each semester in the same classroom. Research on the SpeakEasy discussion tool (Hoadley, Berman, et al., 1995) was also occurring in the classroom at the same time. SpeakEasy was one of the first two web-based discussion tools (predating the introduction of Netscape®) and scaffolded students' online discussion akin to the Computer Supported Intentional Learning Environments system developed earlier by Scardamalia and Bereiter (Scardamalia, Bereiter, et al., 1989). Although SpeakEasy was one of the four main software components of KIE (including the Mildred cognitive guide software, the SenseMaker argument and evidence organization tool, and the KIE Tools Palette for organizing and structuring student use of the other tools), Speak-Easy predates the KIE project and was in use as a stand-alone system for learning and for educational evaluation; it had been developed as a next-generation version of the Multimedia Forum Kiosk software (Hoadley & Hsi, 1992). More complete histories of this tool and the research on it are available elsewhere (Hoadley, 1999, 2002; Hoadley, Hsi, et al., 1995). SpeakEasy provided several novel features; it was designed to maximize social cues in discussion and used semantic labels to help scaffold participants' contributions. SpeakEasy discussions were topical, with a question or proposition introduced by a topic author; in this classroom, students mostly used SpeakEasy as an adjunct to the topics they were studying in class and participated in the discussion over a period of weeks as an ongoing homework assignment.

The Houses project included a SpeakEasy component specifically tied to the project, again completed primarily as homework, whereas this project was conducted primarily in class. Although this online collaboration did play a role in the project, it was face-to-face collaboration that illustrates our point about how social supports for learning are an important (perhaps inevitable) design concern in any project. Students participating in the project were following the model in this course to which they had become accustomed: work in pairs or triples, mostly in class, over an extended period of time. This project was slightly longer than most; the students usually did 3-day to week-and-a-half-long projects, whereas this project took over 2 weeks. Because the project took place near the end of the semester, it was interrupted by testing and field trips slightly more than other projects (especially during spring semester); therefore, it took nearly 3 weeks of calendar time.

The research method was based on iterative refinement in the design experiment tradition (A. Brown, 1992; Collins, 1992), although I did have at least one planned compelling comparison between class periods with slightly different treatments each semester the curriculum was run. Initially, student design practices and motivation were the primary research focus, but eventually social configurations were the predominant theme in the research, as we designers tried to effectively link work occurring at individual, dyadic, and whole-class scales.

As noted elsewhere in this volume, the entire KIE team was aiming at a moving target. The relation students had to technology, particularly the Internet, changed radically during the course of the research project; whereas our initial runs of KIE involved instructing students in what blue, underlined text signified, later runs had students bringing not only surfing skills but also strong preconceptions about the Internet to class. In addition, this project, as the last one of the semester, was heavily influenced by the developing culture of scientific discussion and evidence that was the hallmark of KIE in those years. Although we did not initially envision learning about claims and evidence as one of the central features of KIE, by the end of the research program it was one of the defining features of our approach; this project then was a product of this evolution of goals. On a related note, the role of resources (typically called *evidence* in the classroom[1]) was one that shifted in the classroom culture both throughout the semester-long curriculum and in this project. We refined our presentation of resources to try to encourage students to make use of them in a way that was consistent with the goals of a learning-through-design project. The "How Far Does Light Go?" project discussed earlier (Bell, chap. 6, this volume) was a driving force in this direction of using scientific argumentation as a core aspect of the KIE software and KIE projects, as was our need to make effective use of the information resources on the Internet despite their varying applicability, appropriateness, and trustworthiness.

Historical reconstruction is always tricky, but luckily there are a lot of primary sources to consult. Each semester, the overall structure of the project and of the resources was built into the KIE software files for the project, allowing a more accurate than usual reflection on exactly what changed at each iteration. The titles I give each iteration represent my own post hoc characterization of the project at that time, although the overall description is consistent with discussions of the project at the time. Students began with the introductory screen shown in Fig. 7.1, which remained essentially unchanged throughout the iterations.

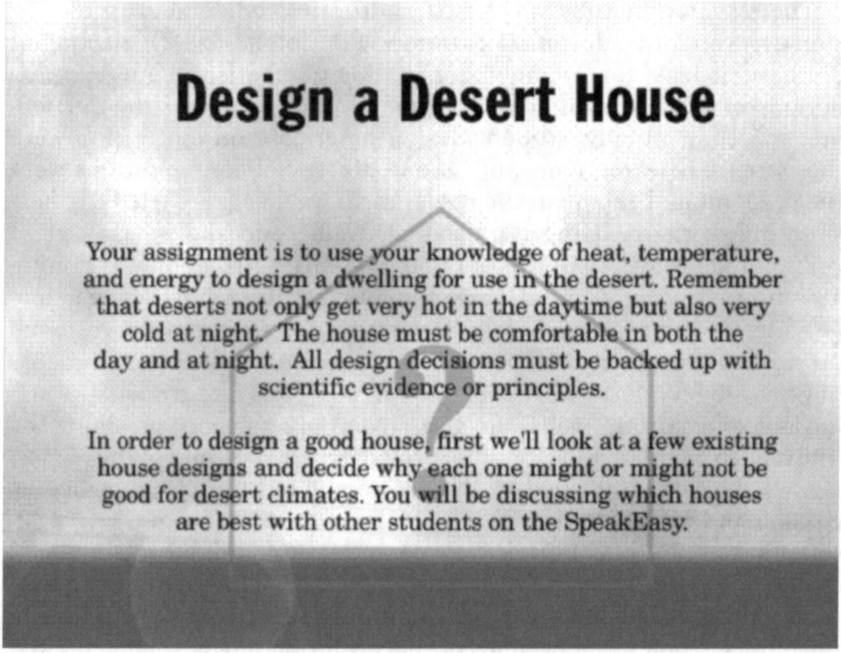

Design a Desert House

Your assignment is to use your knowledge of heat, temperature, and energy to design a dwelling for use in the desert. Remember that deserts not only get very hot in the daytime but also very cold at night. The house must be comfortable in both the day and at night. All design decisions must be backed up with scientific evidence or principles.

In order to design a good house, first we'll look at a few existing house designs and decide why each one might or might not be good for desert climates. You will be discussing which houses are best with other students on the SpeakEasy.

FIG. 7.1.   Opening screen for the "Houses in the Desert" project.

The Nature of the Task: Maintaining Comfort in the Desert

Before exploring the nature of the student activity, it is informative to examine the nature of the design task set before the students. The main design goal is to maintain a comfortable temperature inside the dwelling, even though deserts have extremely high temperatures in the daytime and extremely cold temperatures at night. The main design constraint is that we told students not to rely primarily on fuel-consuming heaters and air conditioners.

In the real world, there are several strategies used to solve this problem. Heat gets in and out of a house through three primary methods—conduction, radiation, and convection—and houses' properties for each kind of heat transfer can be manipulated. In modern buildings such as office buildings, conductive insulation is an important strategy. Greater insulation of the building allows any powered heating, ventilation, and air conditioning systems present to be more effective. Another important strategy is to manage the impact of radiant heat. For instance, lighter colors can be used to reflect more radiant heat energy in the daytime, or darker colors can be used to absorb more light energy in preparation for cold nights. Radiant heat transfer is the reason for foil coatings on fiberglass insulation materials; whereas foil is highly conductive, it also reflects radiant heat that the house would otherwise radiate or absorb. Windows may be used to create a greenhouse effect for heating (light energy enters and is converted to heat) or may be specially coated to avoid this effect if overheating is a concern. In preindustrial and traditional architectural styles, the primary way to accommodate daily temperature swings is to use thermal inertia (a concept only briefly touched on in the curriculum). For instance, adobe houses in New Mexico have a very high heat capacity; the walls take a long time to heat up in the daytime, and they radiate heat (taking a long time to cool) in the nighttime. The ultimate heat capacity strategy is used by cave dwellers such as some of the Native Americans in the American Southwest; the earth, with its nearly infinite heat capacity, helps maintain a constant temperature inside the dwelling. Other important strategies include use of natural ventilation or evaporative cooling to help cool houses (or their inhabitants) when they are uncomfortably hot.

As designers, our hope for the students was that they would approach this problem armed with the concepts they had previously been working with: They had spent a great deal of time studying thermal conductivity and insulation and the role of temperature differentials in heat flow (i.e., heat flows from hot to cool materials, and insulative materials slow this process.) We also hoped they would apply their understanding of how light is converted to heat energy when it is absorbed (although students had not studied radiant transmission of heat through infrared light, they were taught that visible light is converted to heat when it is absorbed by nonreflecting materials such as black construction paper; this was the subject of several in-class laboratory investigations and was further emphasized in another KIE project; Davis, chap. 5, this volume).

Iteration 1: Deductive Model

In the first iteration, the Houses design team viewed the design project largely as problem solving with some extra opportunities for creativity. Given what students had learned, we expected them to be able to come up with a highly insulated house as a solution, and our activities were focused on hinting to students that this might be sensible. Almost as an afterthought, we added in a small amount of information about heat capacity and specific heat, anticipating that high-achieving students might make use of this information as well.

Survey Evidence (Read Science Information, Three Examples). The survey evidence activity was the initial activity and involved reading web pages and advance organizers for those pages from the KIE evidence database. The first three evidence pages were built by the Houses team as examples of houses; one was a poorly insulated wooden house with specific discussion of how hard it was to heat in the winter, the second was a straw bale house being built by a group of students at Swarthmore (with description of how straw houses are exceptionally well insulated), and last a house of mud with information about the Native American Mandan tribe and the mud dwellings they constructed in the Dakotas. We also included evidence pages about the R value (insulating properties) of various materials, a summary of a laboratory the students had done previously on conduction and insulation, and two examples of the relation between light and heat (a story of what happens when leaving a car at the beach with closed windows and a story about wearing white vs. black T-shirts at the beach). Students were asked to read the evidence pages, discuss them with their laboratory partner, and summarize some of the features of the three example houses on a worksheet. The worksheet had columns for the houses of wood, mud, and straw, and column one (the house of wood) had been filled out. Rows prompted students for the building materials and heat flow properties, color and energy conversion, information on the windows, and other notes on each house. This activity took place in class.

Evidence Search (Internet Search). In the next step, students were asked to search the Internet and find two pieces of evidence (two Web sites) "that will help design a house for the desert: either a type of material that might be good for the desert, or an example of a building in the desert." Students were asked to fill out a worksheet again, listing the keywords they searched on, how useful the search results were, whether they saved the page (using a bookmarking tool integrated with KIE), and why they saved the page if they did. Again, students worked together in pairs in class.

Synthesize Evidence. This step was designed to help hint to students how to reason through the design by supporting them through key design decisions: color and materials. The activity involved completing a worksheet titled "Synthesize Evidence," which is shown in its entirety in Fig. 7.2.

Synthesize Evidence

Name: _____ Period: _____

This worksheet will help you discuss the houses and plan your own house design.

Place these materials (WOOD, STRAW, MUD) on the scale according to how well they insulate or conduct heat.

Put these on
the line: *better*   *better*
WOOD   *insulators*   *conductors*
STRAW   ▶
MUD   ◀————————————————————————

                    1/8 inch   aluminum
                    styrofoam

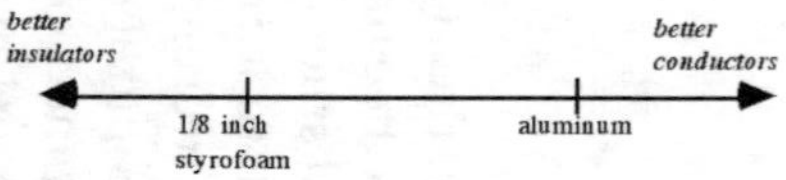

The best **material** for building a desert house to keep it a comfortable temperature is:
_____
_____ Wood
_____ Straw
_____ Mud
_____ Other: _____
The main reason is...

KIE evidence, labs, or everyday experiences to support my claim are...

The best **color** to paint a house in the desert for keeping it a comfortable temperature is:
_____
_____ Black
_____ Brown
_____ White
_____ Other: _____
The main reason is...

KIE evidence, labs, or everyday experiences to support my claim are...

The best **window design** to use on a desert house for keeping it a comfortable temperature is:
_____
_____ No windows
_____ Glass windows
_____ Holes in the walls
_____ Other: _____
The main reason is...

KIE evidence, labs, or everyday experiences to support my claim are...

FIG. 7.2. "Synthesize Evidence" worksheet from "Houses in the Desert" Iteration 1.

Note that the worksheet is targeted toward constructing an argument for a particular set of design choices. We hoped that by focusing on material, windows, and color, students would realize these were the three aspects of the design problem that would be most likely to influence the thermodynamic properties of their house.

Discuss Three Houses (SpeakEasy).   This activity was the only portion of the project that students completed on the computer individually, although we frequently saw students' laboratory partners observing and commenting verbally on the online participation. Each student logged into SpeakEasy, the online discussion tool, where they were presented with a topic and some seed comments comparing the three example houses: the house of wood, the house of straw, and the house of mud. The online discussions encompassed groups of approximately 15 other students in the other sections of the course. Because students were randomly assigned to discussion groups, any given student would only have a few others in their discussion group from the same class period and almost never shared a discussion group with their laboratory partners for the project. Students had time in class to make at least three comments on the topic.

Design Your House (Worksheet).   Finally, after exploring the options through the evidence synthesis and the discussion, students were asked to design their houses on an online worksheet (a ClarisWorks® document) with prompts for certain kinds of description of their house and space for students to use the online drawing tools to sketch their house. Students then saved the pages as HTML and published them.

Iteration 1: Room for Improvement

Although students were engaged by this project, the Houses designers were disappointed with certain outcomes that became the focus of later revisions. In particular, our attempt to lead students to a particular design strategy (insulating the house to isolate it from its thermal environment) failed. We found that students weren't clear on our goals for the project and instead treated it as a purely creative or expressive project. In one particularly telling instance, one student was observed laboriously and miserably drawing individual bricks of his house using the painting tools in ClarisWorks®. When asked why, he replied that he thought his drawing had to look good to get a good grade. He was relieved to hear that it wasn't, but it was illustrative nonetheless that he had misunderstood the point of the assignment until the last step. This overspecificity and overemphasis of surface features was also a problem previously encountered in the Aliens on Tour activity.

Naïve Designs. One disadvantage of our approach was that students made naïve designs. The students' designs were unrealistic, and they knew it. Few took the strategy we had expected of insulating the house by using materials known to be good insulators such as Styrofoam®, which appeared in the chart of *R* values as the most insulating and which the students had tested in experiments on heat conduction.

Close to Examples. One unanticipated consequence of our initial sequence was that students made heavy use of examples in their designs. In our case, this meant using the house of wood, the house of straw, or the house of mud as a model. Unfortunately, many chose the house of wood to emulate because it was the most "normal" looking house, even though the online evidence pages explicitly described how poorly insulated it was, how expensive it was to heat in winter, and so forth. The house of straw had tremendous insulation properties (with an *R* value of 40), but students viewed the house as a novelty. Thus, students tried to generalize from examples but didn't necessarily attend to the features of those examples we thought were most important, a typical educational problem (Anderson, Farrell, et al., 1984; Linn & Clancy, 1992; Lovett & Anderson, 1994).

Little Science Rationale. Related to the students' naïve designs and focus on aesthetics was their lack of scientific justification for their design decisions. Students did not see the relevance of the activities leading up to the house design on their own designs and thus didn't incorporate this information into their project. For instance, students might state that their house would stay warm at night but would not justify this claim with the examples, Internet evidence, or their own laboratories from earlier in the semester.

No Chance to Iterate; Design Fixation. Perhaps the most predictable outcome of the structure of the project was that because students were not forced to iterate their design process, they became victims of design fixation. Students would draft an initial house design (probably without considering the heat flow properties of the house) but would then be unwilling to change the house later when it became apparent that the house had undesirable heat flow properties. The design worksheet reinforced this problem because students who might

spend a great deal of time drawing a house design in ClarisWorks®
would be reluctant to put that effort in all over again.

Iteration 2: Changes

For the second run of Houses, we made five major changes to the
structure of the project to address the prior weaknesses. First, students began the project with an initial design and ended with a final
design, encouraging them to revise their work. Second, we introduced
a new worksheet as part of the project, the Heat Flow Analysis
Worksheet. Here we asked students to (mentally) simulate the heat
flow properties of their design during cold and warm parts of the day.
We considered using Thermal Modeling Kit, simulation software developed previously under the CLP project (see Linn & Hsi, 2000, for more
information), but decided against this, first due to the time it would
take students to simulate a house, and second because the software
emphasized thermal conductivity and did not accurately represent
thermal inertia and heat capacity. Third, we added additional opportunities for students to summarize and synthesize science information
we thought should be relevant to their decision making. These took
the form of formal prompts throughout the project via worksheets,
software, and verbally in class. Fourth, we reduced the importance of
searching for information on the Internet for two reasons. One problem was that we overestimated students' ability to conduct effective
searches—although we found students far more savvy about searching
the Internet in later runs due to the explosion in Internet popularity.
Another problem with searches was that many of the words students
wanted to use as keywords were nearly impossible to search on: *windows* and *adobe* brought up tens of thousands of hits on the trade-
marked software products but few on the building materials, and
searching on *houses* or *housing* nearly always uncovered real estate
listings instead of information about architecture. The fifth major
change we made to the project was to demote the importance of drawings by moving them offline (to paper worksheets) and encouraging
sketching rather than detailed drawing.

Iteration 2: Highly Structured Model

Iteration two of Houses contained seven rather than five separate
steps, although the amount of time on task was roughly the same; the
notable exception to this was adding some homework at the beginning
of the project.

First Design. To combat design fixation and to ensure students had multiple designs to reconcile, we added the first design activity. In class students were introduced to the design problem as before with a minilecture and discussion about the desert climate. However, the introduction was timed to end at the end of the period. In the last few minutes of class, each student was given an initial design worksheet; every student was to individually complete their initial design as homework for the next day. Although some students did not complete their projects individually (either because they disobeyed instructions or because they completed the assignment as make-up work), most teams had at least two designs to start with. We also encouraged students to take an extra, abbreviated design worksheet whenever they made a redesign during the project.

In addition, the initial design worksheet included some analysis; students were asked to use a visual representation of heat flow. Students were prompted to draw two copies of their house, one for day and one for night. Students drew arrows showing the direction and magnitude of heat energy flow on each drawing, following an example provided on the worksheet. This arrow-based representation had been encountered briefly in a simulation activity earlier in the semester using the Thermal Modeling Kit software.

Survey Evidence. Students surveyed a combination of the three house examples and some science information as before.

Synthesize Evidence. As before, students completed a worksheet that encouraged students to make and justify design decisions about materials, color, and windows.

SpeakEasy. As before, students participated in a discussion of which of the three example houses from "Survey Evidence" would be best in the desert.

Synthesize SpeakEasy. This time, partly to collect data on the impact of the SpeakEasy and partly to get students to reflect further on their understanding of the three examples, students individually completed an in-class worksheet. This worksheet repeated one of the three sets of questions from the initial design asking students to choose the best material for the house and to justify their decision. As an embedded comparison, half of the discussion groups had threaded discussion in their SpeakEasy discussions and half had discussions structured around pros and cons of individual houses. Students participated equivalently in both conditions with no obvious differences in comment quality. However, significantly more students using threaded discussions changed their views about what material a house should be built of than students in the control (pro–con) condition (Hoadley, 1999). This is an example of the types of embedded comparisons that allowed us to test some of the theories driving our designs. In this particular case, we were testing our hypotheses about students benefiting from the social representations in SpeakEasy (as opposed to the effect of time on task, self-explanation effects, or the effects of exposure to other students' explanations). The Houses designers and other KIE group members continued research on this topic through other planned comparisons.

Evidence Search.   In this iteration, evidence searching was diminished in importance by making it an optional activity at the end of the project; if students had time, they could search the Internet for additional information. We provided additional scaffolding in the form of hints with search strategies such as using verbs instead of nouns, narrowing searches, widening searches, and so forth. We also added a feature that allowed students to view the results other students had saved from their own searches so items found in one period could be rediscovered by students in a later period.

Design Write-up.   The design write-up was essentially the same, with the difference that graphics were not included in the online description of the design. The ClarisWorks® document stated "If you would like to include graphics in your web page, you need to get permission from the teacher. We will only include pictures if they help explain the science behind your design." Very few students took advantage of this option.

Iteration 2: Room for Improvement

This iteration was successful in helping students focus more on the design decisions and on justifying those decisions. However, the run indicated three lingering problems. First and foremost, students continued to create relatively simple designs that did not use good strategies for maintaining constant temperature. Although the designs were better, they were still closely tied to the examples or to aesthetically motivated inventions. A second problem was that students found the heat flow analysis difficult and often presented incorrect analyses of how heat would flow into and out of their houses in hot and cold weather. We were not entirely surprised by this because the arrow representation was somewhat unfamiliar to the students (it had only been used during the brief Thermal Modeling Kit activity), but their drawings often indicated problem conceptions at a very basic level of the sort described earlier in the CLP project (Linn & Hsi, 2000). A third problem was that students had no shared criteria for what constituted a good solution. This became apparent when students started using the shared search tool to share "good" Web sites with one another; we were often quite surprised with what students found worth saving or sharing, and the students themselves often saw little value in the sites other students had found. We had hoped that the online discussions would help students develop shared criteria for the designs through social scaffolds, but this apparently was not occurring.

Iteration 3: Changes

The design team introduced five changes in Houses to continue to improve the focus on scientific concepts and to help students develop a wider range of design ideas linked to the science. This iteration of Houses introduced a new, explicit focus on problem definition. To improve the science focus and the analysis, we strengthened the initial introduction to the problem (before the individual homework that became the initial designs) by including explicit problem definition activities such as in-class discussion of the day–night heating and cooling cycle in the desert, a discussion of ground and surround interaction (which way heat flows between ground and air in day and night), and a discussion of how light is the major source of heat in the daytime. To improve students' analysis using the heat flow analysis worksheet, we expanded the in-class, out loud support of the arrow representation of heat flow by walking students through an example.

To improve the opportunities for shared criteria, we introduced critique and class discussion of several examples, beginning with the Enertia House Web site, a commercial site on a passively cooled house. There were other opportunities for critique and class discussion (see following).

To increase the effective use of examples and reduce the students' use of examples without effective science criteria, we refined the prompts in our design document template, added a library of preselected examples that students could browse, and used class discussion to focus on science ideas rather than specific examples. This was also reflected in a shift of SpeakEasy topics; students no longer discussed three examples but instead discussed "Does adobe work in the desert? Why or why not?"

We also added a 10 min. video skit to help make design rationale more obvious in examples; this (staged) video featured two graduate students with whom the class was familiar debating the merits of an insulation strategy (such as the straw house) versus the merits of a thermal storage and heat capacity strategy (such as the mud house). We believed that embedding this social representation would help scaffold students to focus on the science issues in the discussion.

Iteration 3: Conceptual Model

I term this iteration the *conceptual model* version of Houses because of the strong focus on science concepts and a reduced focus on generalizing from our three primary examples. We also continued our work on how social representations could support the project by embedding several comparison studies. One study divided the class periods into conditions in which some students spent more time on social critique (pinups of designs, developing alternatives in a whole-class fashion), whereas other class periods had additional time for Internet search and examination of our design library, a "library cart" model that provided preselected examples of student and expert designs.

Define Problem. On the first day, students participated in a whole-class discussion on the problem, including heat properties of the desert, and surveyed a Web site on heat in the desert climate. Students were introduced to the Enertia House example, which the teacher explained. The SpeakEasy discussion was introduced and started at this time (students could participate at any time throughout the project rather than at a designated time in the project). Students took required notes in the KIE system on problem definition with the prompts "Our problem is . . ." "What we need to figure out is . . ." and "Our design needs to. . . ."

Initial Design. As homework, students completed an initial design worksheet for the next day. This worksheet included a pretest survey (new for this iteration) that focused on design goals and criteria in addition to the design decisions and heat flow analysis used in prior semesters.

Survey and Search. The survey and search portion of the project combined what was previously two separate steps. Rather than providing a short list of must-see evidence including the houses of straw, mud, and wood and then sending students to search the Internet, students were provided with a short list of must-see evidence and then given access to a design library that included examples such as the three used in prior iterations, along with more complex ones taken from the Web. As with prior KIE projects, not all of the sites were trustworthy or applicable to the desert problem, therefore students had to be discriminating. In this run, we recycled some examples from the first KIE project students encountered. "Sunlight, SunHEAT!" was a project developed this particular semester by Jim Slotta as an introduction to the KIE software, to asking questions in science, and to the conversion of light energy into other forms of energy (including heat and kinetic energy). As the Web expanded, more examples suitable for this project were available online, and we incorporated several into our project.

Critique and Refine. In this project activity, students critiqued their own designs and came up with a new, combined design for the two-person team. The comparison groups differed in whether this included social critique through sharing designs and discussing them in class or more analytic critique using a worksheet designed to help them self-analyze the design.

Discuss. The discuss phase began by showing the video in class of two people debating an insulation strategy versus a heat storage strategy.

For students who had not yet completed their SpeakEasy discussion obligations (three comments), this step provided a checkpoint; students were instructed to finish their required minimum comments before moving on to later phases. The discussion did remain open for additional contributions and was not graded until the end of the project; therefore, students could contribute more after this time if they wished.

Analyze Your Design. In this stage, students completed a detailed heat flow analysis worksheet for the design they were intending to turn in. For many students this step forced an additional redesign. The heatflow worksheet was supported by an in-class discussion of how to use the arrow representation.

Final Report. In this iteration of the activity, students stopped using an online worksheet and instead used the note-taking features in the Mildred guide to enter their designs. This effectively prohibited students from including pictures in their final design report. The final report represented the students' final design and included prompts

for changes the students had made during the design process (to ensure they had made changes). We encouraged students to support all
design decisions with evidence, which drove a few more groups to redesign or to go back to the design library to justify their decisions. Although these post hoc rationalizations did not always force redesign
when they should have, they did seem successful in getting students to
engage with the science concepts.

Iteration 3: Room for Improvement

The concept-centered approach did recover the focus on science concepts but at the expense of the design problem. The ideas we presented were often too abstract for students to apply or discuss, and
few of the ideas brought up in discussions made it into student designs. Although we had the sense that the self-critique and discussions
helped move the classes toward shared criteria for the designs, they
still had trouble with analysis of the heat flow properties and still did
not arrive at a consensus on criteria that would improve the design
outcomes.

Iteration 4: Changes

Although we as researchers had been experimenting with social scaffolds throughout the development of this project, the fourth iteration
saw the most use of social means to help students with the design
task; the design team for Houses made extensive use of the notion of
shared criteria to help students link science concepts to the design
task. Although the project retained many of the techniques we had
found successful to this point, including the use of a library of examples to help students understand the design space, this version of
Houses represented a shift in focus from supporting individual decision making to fostering group norms and social iteration on the designs. We added more in-class discussion of the problem definition
with an eye toward invoking laboratories and principles the students
had previously encountered to create explicit, shared criteria for what
success would mean in the design problem. The design report was
even more explicitly spread out over multiple steps with instructions
that students should share and respond to each other's designs. We
also introduced an innovative way to help students regroup after the
online discussion and synthesize that discussion's implications for
their own designs. The design library concept was further expanded to
encompass both evidence surveying and evidence search. Finally, par-

alleling our shift in the curriculum as a whole, we emphasized the importance of argumentation and evidence as a means to persuade others. Rather than trying to improve student designs directly in this iteration, we tried to improve students' scientific arguments for or against their designs. This proved to be a powerful change for the better.

Iteration 4: Collaborative Design

This iteration retains the basic steps from the cart iteration but strengthens the collaborative aspects of the project.

Define Problem. As mentioned previously, the define problem phase was introduced to students as a chance to develop class-wide criteria for what constituted a good design; a whiteboard was used by the teacher to brainstorm criteria for success in the desert, and the class discussion included a discussion of the problem definition prompts. Each laboratory group still had to answer these prompts in the project ("Our problem is . . .." "What we need to figure out is . . ." and "Our design needs to . . .").

Initial Design. The initial design task was changed so that even students' initial design assignment included some analysis tasks such as predicting heat flow at noon and midnight. Many of the prompts to help students analyze the heat flow properties of their designs were textual rather than based on placing the heat arrows, giving students a chance to use both verbal and pictorial representations for their ideas.

Survey Evidence. In our design library, we expanded the number and complexity of examples. We also encouraged students to share good sites they had found not only through the shared search interface but also out loud. The teacher, walking around the room, would encourage groups with sites he found important to share verbally with the class. URLs were written on a chalkboard by the teacher in addition to posting in the Web-based interface.

Discuss and Refine. As before, students took a pre- and post-SpeakEasy survey on their current thinking on design decisions. Unlike before, students were asked to read every comment in a heavily seeded discussion on how to best design a house for the desert. Students watched the video as before, and these ideas we also expressed in the SpeakEasy discussion. We embedded another comparison in this particular run. Half the students watched a video with enhanced social features such as coherence of ideas within an individual for the video and the SpeakEasy discussion; in the control condition, the same arguments were made in the same order but neither design strategy was identified with only one of the actors.

Organize Ideas.   This activity represented a new combination of familiar activities for the students. In the past, they had become familiar with presenting arguments in a discussion using SpeakEasy and with organizing evidence to support a point of view using the SenseMaker software. In this iteration, we asked students to take the seed comments from the discussion they had just participated in and, using the SenseMaker, organize the comments by dragging them into claim frames (see Bell, chap. 6, this volume).

Gather Evidence.   The gather evidence activity was a reframing of the search and survey activity; rather than looking for ideas for student designs, the activity was presented as gathering evidence to support the particular student design. The teacher made clear during this phase that the projects would be graded on how well-supported the designs were with evidence rather than solely the quality of the design alone.

Critique and Refine.   As in the prior iteration, this activity was intended to allow students to share designs and critique them. In this iteration, the teacher presented a nonstudent design and helped the students reason through analysis of the design's strengths and weaknesses. Then the teacher selected several student designs and had them put their designs up for everyone to see and the whole class discussed them. Finally, students used a new online tool to post their designs for others to see and contribute feedback on the design. This system, like all of the search utilities we used, was created by Cuthbert (Cuthbert & Hoadley, 1998a). Every team had some feedback on their design, and students were responsible to try to improve their designs based on the feedback, either by making design changes or by better justifying their choices.

Final Report.   The final report, as before, included prompts for student justification of their design decisions with evidence—students could either enter this justification as text or include links directly in their reports because recent changes to the KIE software included the student notes and the URLs from their evidence gathering in the same file. This iteration yielded by far the best student designs, including good arguments linking their design choices to the science principles they had covered earlier in the semester. Because of the social externalization, students often iterated on their designs more than in the past and made marked progress toward the shared criteria the class had developed on what constituted a good design.

Lessons Learned

We set out to explore how design projects could help students learn science and to study the ways collaboration could help support learning. In iterating and refining our tools and activities, we arrived at better and better ways to support student learning and refined our own understanding of our learning goals. We retained many of the same curriculum steps but reorganized and reframed them to develop a more robust curriculum design pattern. Had we initially studied the motivational or learning effects of our earliest interventions, we might not have arrived at our ultimate conclusions based on our best practice application of the technology and curriculum—that helping students develop shared criteria about good scientific argumentation and design and effective processes for self-improvement were the key to advancing understanding in these project-based learning activities. Our lessons learned are summarized (and presented as design principles) in Table 7.1.

Good Design Practice Enhances, Not Detracts, From Good Science. One of the most important lessons learned from this experience was that the trade-off we had perceived between good design and good science was a false one. We had originally thought that we could either emphasize design skills and support students in creating good houses or we could emphasize science and support students in using heat flow concepts. However, through a more authentic approach to the problem and embedding design in social argumentation, we could not only get students to apply and link their existing science understandings but also to learn new science relevant to the problem, yielding much better house designs. It is unclear whether specific training in design methods would have helped, but what is clear is that students benefited from encountering some of the real complexity of the problem and from having their learning grounded in the problem context. By emphasizing a rational process rather than just specific examples, architectural principles, or even scientific principles, the students were able to consolidate and extend their understanding of thermodynamics while designing desert houses.

TABLE 7.1
Lessons Learned

Finding or Experience	Design Principle	Examples
Good design practice enhances, not detracts, from good science.	Link theory and practice in authentic problems by scaffolding rational processes (rather than outcomes).	Houses Iterations 3 to 4 explicitly graded on design rationale, not design quality "Heat Flow Analysis" worksheet forced students to consider effectiveness of their decisions.
Design strategies help kids learn from examples without copying them.	Prevent examples from overconstraining students by engaging students with strategies, not recipes.	"Library cart" model of examples emphasized how several examples might use a similar strategy. Videotaped discussion of design strategies shifted focus to strategies from examples. Students asked to describe and justify changes in final Houses reports. Design iterations built into Houses activity structure.
Collaboration can be used for scaffolding and modeling; peer critique helped motivate students to improve their designs and to better understand what might be refined.	Encourage students to come to consensus on shared criteria for decisions and products.	Class critique of examples like Enertia House Peer critique and design iteration in last iteration of Houses Discussion of design strategies in SpeakEasy

Design Strategies Help Kids Learn From Examples Without Copying From Them. It proved to be difficult to walk the line between providing examples that encouraged copying (without comprehension) and providing examples that allowed students to apply their scientific knowledge without reinventing the wheel. Once our emphasis in the instructions we gave the students shifted from specific design examples to more general design strategies, we could decouple the principles from the examples and help kids step back from the specifics of individual examples. Introducing this distinction between strategies and examples helped students keep them separate in their own classroom discourse. It serves as an important lesson for us as educational designers too; we should perhaps focus our research efforts on creating and communicating design strategies and design principles rather than just artifacts or specific curricular units (see Baumgartner, chap. 11, this volume). We have attempted to take this lesson to heart and step back from instances to discuss broader strategies throughout this volume.

Use Collaboration for Modeling and Scaffolding. A third important lesson was that collaborative tools should be used to help model and scaffold students as they work through difficult problems. Although this is an old lesson (Collins, Brown, & Holum, 1991; Dewey, 1954), it is one that is important to revisit in each curricular or technical design. Whereas specialization (such as in the jigsaw method; Aronson & Yates, 1983) or burden sharing (Johnson, Johnson, et al., 1986) are often primary excuses for collaborative learning activities, the real benefits come from allowing the successes of the classroom to come through in modeling and consensus on criteria for success and to help scaffold students as they do their hard intellectual work. By orienting our design process toward better justification and argumentation, students improved not only their designs but also the connection between those designs and the science principles we were trying to teach. This may be the most important legacy of KIE in that our entire curriculum evolved in this direction of helping students turn information into arguments and thereby into personal knowledge. Far from detracting from the science domain knowledge, the process-oriented approach helped students develop a much better understanding of heat, light, and temperature.

Selected Research Results

What's the bottom line on learning through design? Three findings bear repeating. First, we were able to use design activities successfully to help students learn and integrate their understanding across a range of topics. Even though the entire curriculum was geared to help students develop an integrated understanding, the Houses project succeeded at helping students develop and demonstrate an understanding that spanned disparate topics of heat energy, conduction and insulation, and light energy. Second, although the KIE project's explicit goal was to improve student learning outcomes of science activities by iteratively refining the activity, we achieved not only better learning but better collaboration and better designs. Social supports for learning were required to make this project work. Third, although the challenge of creating a collaborative design activity is imposing, we successfully tapped student enthusiasm in a way that was not possible in our earlier work. This project was rated on surveys one of the most enjoyable of the entire semester, and several students have since mentioned the activity when returning to their middle school for visits. One student even considered a career in architecture after the project; in another case, a student team spent hours at home creating a scale mockup of their house design even though this was not part of the assignment. This type of enthusiasm is presumably less related to the topic than it is to the project type; in designing, students could indulge their creativity as well as participate in collaborative teams while working toward a common, authentic goal.

Multiple Levels of Design in Collaborative Learning Settings

It is instructive that many of our perceived problems with this project were eventually solved by developing the right sort of collaborative context for the students to work in, and this lesson generalizes across the entire range of KIE projects as well. Our initial research and project designs were aimed at improving how individual students cognitively engaged the materials and experiences we could provide with the new medium of the Internet, and this was an important component of their eventual success. However, as noted earlier, the hallmark of KIE eventually became that of a classroom using the Internet as one tool among many in a culture of scientific discourse, debate, argumentation, and inquiry. The CLP project had prepared us to examine the ways we could establish a context for individuals or pairs to engage with data collected in microcomputer based laboratories. With KIE, we opened the door to a much more social inquiry process, one in which claims had to be argued and supported with evidence, one in which information sources had to be critically examined, and one in which students had to come to consensus on shared criteria for the designs that they produced. The Houses project, like the others, got many things right in the early iterations, but we had to evolve the tools, activities, and teacher support to help create a collaborative context in which the thinking we were after could happen. This occurred over the course of our engagement with participants in the setting; in the case of this chapter, with Doug Kirkpatrick's classroom. Extending this process to include other local contexts was an important phase of work of KIE moving toward the WISE era (see Baumgartner, chap. 11; Bell, chap. 10; Shear, Bell, & Linn, chap. 12; and Slotta, chap. 9, this volume).

Saying we need to provide social supports for learning is one thing; actually doing it is another. Collaborative learning is messy. When local context and local culture are a central part of the phenomenon one wishes to study, an intimate relation with the context is paramount. Designing activities and technologies for collaborative learning relies on a number of phenomena at different time scales, from the momentary cognition of students to the development of classroom practices over months or years (Barab & Kirshner, 2001; Lemke, 2001). As designers of collaborative activities that involved technology, we had to work to refine our interventions on a number of levels. Surprisingly central was the way we helped students understand not only what to do but also how to view the social contexts we were creating (such as treating a design project as an extension of the scientific argument making they had been performing all semester). As new sorts of activities arise, they entail new communication genres and may even require new literacies. This is no small, one-off task, but a question of sustained effort within a particular context. As we invent new technologies, it is incumbent on us to develop new visions of practices or curriculum design patterns with those technologies, to be attuned to unintended outcomes, and to shepherd the technologies through changes in a changing world. As educators, we recognize that what we create is more than the sum of some software or worksheets—we create living examples of learning environments that teach us about learning, both as researchers or psychologists and as educators.

ACKNOWLEDGMENT

Portions of this chapter were previously published as "Creating Context: Design-Based Research in Creating and Understanding CSCL" by C. Hoadley. In *Computer Support for Collaborative Learning*, edited by G. Stahl, 2002, Mahwah, NJ: Lawrence Erlbaum Associates. Copyright © 2002 by CSCL. Reprinted with permission.

ENDNOTE

1. This nomenclature is slightly misleading. Generally, all information resources were called *evidence*, whether or not the information was used in supporting or refuting a claim (a more traditional notion of evidence). In particular, when we sent students to Web sites, we called each site *evidence*. We explicitly considered both "good" and "bad" evidence, not only based on how applicable the information was to the argument being made but also based on how trustworthy or comprehensible the information was and whether or not it was based on some empirical data. Thus, a more accurate term might have been *possible evidence* to describe that this was information for consideration in relation to the students' own understanding and in relation to the arguments students were making but that it might or might not actually be evidentiary in the nature of the classroom discourse.

8

Hands-on Investigation in Internet Environments: Teaching Thermal Equilibrium

Douglas Clark
Arizona State University

Helping students see the thinking behind complex topics like thermo-dynamics challenges designers of inquiry instruction. In this chapter I analyze the iterative design and refinement of a 5-day hands-on inquiry project focusing on thermal equilibrium to explore the fourth project genre called an *investigation project*.

Students come to science class with a rich repertoire of ideas about thermodynamics from their personal experiences (Clough & Driver, 1985; Erickson, 1979; Erickson & Tiberghien, 1985; Lewis, 1996; Linn & Hsi, 2000; Wiser, 1988, 1995; Wiser & Carey, 1983). Students often develop multiple, conflicting ideas about thermal equilibrium (D. Clark, 2000, 2001; Davis, 1998; Foley, 1999; Lewis, 1996). Students struggle as they sort through these ideas to create a coherent understanding (D. B. Clark, 2000, 2001; diSessa, 1993, 1994; diSessa & Sherin, 1998; Linn, 1995; Linn & Hsi, 2000). Results from National Assessment of Educational Progress (NAEP), Third International Mathematics and Science Study (TIMSS), and state testing show that students make minimal progress between 4th and 12th grades in the United States on topics such as thermodynamics (Blank et al., 2000; O'Sullivan et al., 1997; Schmidt, McKnight, et al., 1997; Schmidt, Raizen, et al., 1997).

I set out to improve understanding of thermal equilibrium and re-port on iterative refinement of an investigation project called

"Probing Your Surroundings" (or Probing for short) that first appeared in the Computer as Learning Partner (CLP) curriculum (Linn & Hsi, 2000). The current version of Probing uses Web-Based Inquiry Science Environment (WISE) Internet software with custom visualization, electronic peer critique, and laboratory components integrated to support students as they investigate thermal equilibrium. The WISE project is described following (and in more detail in Slotta, chap. 9, this volume). In Probing, students make predictions about the temperatures of everyday objects of various materials, gather temperature data from the objects, devise scientific principles to explain the data, discuss their principles with students who have developed alternative principles, and finally, experiment with the refined principles in a visualization environment. Through iterative design, the project has become effective in supporting student understanding of thermal equilibrium (D. Clark & Jorde, in press).

PROBING IN THE CLP CURRICULUM

The CLP curriculum focuses on student understanding of thermal equilibrium as one of four major curricular foci for thermodynamics. Through design studies, our research group developed the first version of Probing Your Surroundings to address thermal equilibrium using microcomputer-based laboratory equipment and other custom software (Lewis, 1996; Linn & Hsi, 2000; Songer, 1989). Students use the CLP software to design experiments, predict outcomes, collect data in real time, design visualizations, display results, record observations, and prepare analyses.

Longitudinal case studies of students who studied thermal equilibrium in CLP revealed strengths and weaknesses in the instruction. Our research group followed students across their eighth grade CLP semester and into high school (e.g., D. Clark, 2000, 2001). The effectiveness of Probing's existing elements was attested to by the number of times that students refer to Probing as a warrant in their explanations about thermal equilibrium in the case studies. In fact, Probing is the most frequent warrant that students employ in their longitudinal interviews to explain thermal equilibrium (D. Clark, 2000). These studies also showed that students need to generate connections between experientially supported ideas about the relation between how objects feel and their actual temperature to understand thermal equilibrium in everyday contexts (D. Clark, 2000, 2001). We charted students' knowledge integration progress within the curriculum and identified a "reexplanation" strategy to facilitate reflection and knowledge integration. The reexplanation strategy provides students the opportunity to construct specific alternative explanations for their experiential knowledge and allows students to reconnect this experiential knowledge to target normative models in a more productive way through the context of pivotal cases.

With the development of WISE, our research group became interested in harnessing the affordances of an Internet environment to support students in engaging in hands-on inquiry. Specifically, we wanted to make the critical ideas and connections more visible for students engaging in Probing.

PROBING IN WISE

Students encountered the WISE Probing project during the 8th week of a thermodynamics curriculum after studying heat flow, the differentiation of heat and temperature, and insulation and conduction. In the WISE Probing project, students begin by making predictions about the temperature of everyday objects around them in the classroom. Students then use thermal probes to investigate the temperature of these objects and construct principles to describe the patterns encountered (Fig. 8.1). This first portion of the project attempts to cue students' conflicting ideas, including students' sense that objects are different temperatures because "They feel that way" and students'

FIG. 8.1. Probing your surroundings.

sense that objects in the room should be the temperature of the room because "What would make them be a different temperature?"

In the second activity of the project, the Probing software places students in electronic discussion groups with students who have constructed different principles explaining the data. The actual student-constructed principles are seeded as the discussion topics that the groups critique and discuss in the process of working toward consensus (Cuthbert, Clark, et al., 2002). As part of this process, the students are required to support their assertions and claims with evidence from their laboratories and other experiences. This process attempts to elicit self-explanation by helping students focus other students' attention on possible inconsistencies in their explanations and the reasoning, plausibility, completeness, and other attributes of "good explanations." This discussion provides social supports for learning (Linn, 1995; Linn & Hsi, 2000) through the incorporation of our pedagogical principles and builds on the social scaffolding literature (A. L. Brown & Palincsar, 1989; Chi, 1996; Collins, Brown, & Holum, 1991; Vygotsky, 1978).

Finally, following the discussions, the students experiment with the new visualization. Several studies suggest embedding visualizations in a curriculum that focuses students on the connections and ideas within the visualization (e.g., Foley, 1999; Linn & Hsi, 2000; Raghavan & Glaser, 1995; Snir et al., 1993; White, 1993a, 1993b). The visualization is embedded within the context of the Probing project to extend and refine students ideas based on our pedagogical principles surrounding the scaffolded knowledge integration tenet of making thinking visible (see Linn, Davis, & Eylon, chap. 3, this volume). Additionally, we decided to build the visualization around targeted pivotal cases to provide greater embedded support. The Probing visualization moves the focus from an initial pivotal case focusing on objects in a room to a pivotal case focusing on metal and wood objects left in the trunk of a car on a hot summer day. I discuss these pivotal cases in greater detail in the following sections. Most important, the visualization has an integrated tactile model to scaffold students in connecting ideas about sensory perception of heat into their experimentation.

I specifically discuss the iterative refinement process involved in redesigning the curriculum design pattern of this investigation project and identify design principles. This process begins with the project originally developed by the CLP research group that we iteratively enhanced and expanded through Alpha, Beta, and Current versions of the WISE Probing project. This current version of the WISE Probing project is used by students in multiple countries.

RATIONALE FOR VISUALIZATION

The CLP group successfully supported students in integrating accessible models using visualizations in the curriculum (Foley, 1997, 1998, 1999; Lewis, 1991; Lewis, Stern, et al., 1993; Linn & Hsi, 2000). The research of White (1993a, 1993b) also suggests that visualizations are useful for helping students build intermediate causal models explaining phenomena. For these reasons, computer visualizations were chosen as one path to make thinking more visible in Probing.

The CLP project explored the potential of computer visualizations by studying their use in classroom contexts (Foley, 1997, 1998, 1999; Lewis, 1991; Lewis, Stern, et al., 1993; Linn & Hsi, 2000). In particular, Lewis (1991) and Foley (1997, 1998, 1999) investigated the effect of a computer visualization of heat flow on students' understanding of heat and temperature. Lewis (1991) found that the HeatBars software increased students' understanding of heat and temperature by helping them understand the mechanism of heat flow. Foley (1997, 1998) continued this line of investigation, and his findings imply that the dot-density representation cues the use of density models of heat and temperature and that by interpreting the dots as heat and the density of the dots as temperature, the students construct a useful scientific model of heat flow. Foley's (1999) findings also suggest the following:

- Students who see the visualizations as unrelated or unnecessary compared to other types of information (e.g., scientific principles) may fail to cue the scientific model supported by the visualization when needed.
- Students apply the visualizations to their reasoning differently depending on how they interpret them and how they integrate them with the other ideas in their repertoire.
- Activities should be fully integrated into the curriculum to provide opportunities to reflect and reconsider the visualizations in light of new information.
- Students also need to integrate the visualizations with their existing models so they have a lasting impact on their own thinking. Some students do not understand the significance of the visualizations and thus do not apply them in appropriate situations. (pp. 101–107)

In addition to these prior research results, the power and effectiveness of this visualization format also became apparent through pilot longitudinal interview studies in which students warranted explanations about conductivity with this visualization more often than with any other classroom activity (D. Clark, 2000). In designing our visualization, as I discuss later, we took into account these prior research perspectives as well as the longitudinal findings.

Concurrently with our work on Probing, Grillmeyer (2001) worked with visualizations to test a set of design criteria through a series of empirical tests. His four design concerns include the following:

- Providing a clear mapping between objects in the animation and their real-world counterparts.
- Illustrating causal relations.
- Showcasing the most salient aspects of the modeled system.
- Reducing complexity. (pp. 43–48)

Grillmeyer (2001) implemented these concerns using a variety of methods including textual annotations, color, grouping, movement, showing history, and the use of multiple representations. All of the animations incorporated the scaffolded knowledge integration instructional framework. Grillmeyer's visualization studies demonstrated learning gains, but not all of the animations achieved significant increases in student learning, underscoring the difficulty of designing effective animations. Grillmeyer posited that using examples that are true pivotal cases would help. From his perspective, pivotal cases should offer naturally controlled experiments to illustrate both a condition that is consistent with student predictions and one that is not.

Grillmeyer (2001) was not alone. Many researchers have found negative or no gains from the use of visualizations (e.g., Palmiter & Elkerton, 1993; Rieber et al., 1990). Others have found mixed or inconclusive gains (e.g., Byrne, Catrambone, & Stasko, 1999; Carpenter & Just, 1992; Park & Hopkins, 1993; Schnotz & Grzondziel, 1996; Stasko & Lawrence, 1998). Other researchers have found positive gains (e.g., Hansen et al., 1998; Hays, 1996; Hegarty, Carpenter, et al., 1990; Kann et al., 1997; Kehoe et al., 1999; Williamson, 1995). Grillmeyer's review suggests that successful visualizations have certain characteristics including the following:

- Interactive rather than passive presentations as well as dynamic instead of static images to better model the system through clear visualizations of causality.
- Textual annotations to aid in mapping as well as other multiple representations.

- Expression of the salient features and concrete representations to reduce complexity.

Our reviews of the visualization literature suggest that effective visualizations can afford several strengths and advantageous features including the following:

- Identification of causality and causal parsing: Visualizations and animations are more effective than diagrams in supporting students' identification of natural behavior and causal relations (Kaiser, Proffit, et al., 1992; Michotte, 1963). Furthermore, as students work with a visualization, they can begin to depict and parse the causal relation between the objects within the visualization as a mental model (White, 1993a).
- Cognitive offloading: Students may use visualizations as an external cognitive aid to reduce the amount of information that needs to be held in working memory while building connections (Scaife & Rogers, 1996).
- Re-representation: Visualizations may re-represent a problem in a format that facilitates the solution of the problem (Scaife & Rogers, 1996). For example, visualizations may represent numbers in a specific array to highlight patterns.
- Graphical constraining: Visualizations may represent a problem so as to constrain the types of mental models a student could construct based on the visualization (Scaife & Rogers, 1996).
- Context embedded: Visualizations should be embedded in a curriculum that focuses students on the connections and ideas within the visualization (Raghavan & Glaser, 1995; Snir et al., 1993; White, 1993a).
- Conceptual enhancement: A conceptually enhanced visualization promotes knowledge integration by connecting concrete familiar objects with abstract science models and concepts directly (Snir et al., 1993).

Through our research we continue to explore ways to structure effective visualizations incorporating these ideas and findings.

Visualization for Thermal Equilibrium

We integrated a new Probing visualization into the WISE Probing project based on the pivotal cases explored in the foundational longitudinal case studies (D. Clark, 2000, 2001). These pivotal cases are contexts that support conceptual reorganization by providing a context or example highlighting contradictions or shortcomings resulting from the original intuitive idea while promoting an alternative dimension or idea (Linn, in press). Pivotal cases therefore make more visible the problematic aspects of current ideas. Simultaneously, they also make more accessible and comprehensible the utility of the new dimension or idea for the case. From the perspective of the Probing work, pivotal cases have the following characteristics (D. Clark & Jorde, in press):

- The pivotal case is relevant to everyday experience or interesting to the student (e.g., students interact with sensory information about temperature and how things feel normally in their everyday experiences).
- Students' intuitive ideas regarding the pivotal case are supported by their experiences outside of school (e.g., all students have had the experience that some objects feel hotter than others do; students assume that objects that feel hotter are actually hotter, which is an accurate assumption in many cases).
- The pivotal case provides a context or example that these intuitive ideas cannot explain or that motivates reconsideration of these intuitive ideas (e.g., a metal object in the oven feels hotter than a wooden object, but the two objects are the same temperature).
- The pivotal case promotes a new or alternative dimension or idea (e.g., "Objects can feel different but be the same temperature").
- The pivotal case, supported by the curriculum, leads to reorganization of the student's ideas, hopefully toward a more coherent and nuanced view (e.g., "Conductivity as well as temperature determine how an object feels, and so objects can feel different and be the same temperature").

By connecting the targeted scientific principles across multiple everyday contexts, students make significant progress in integrating their scientific understanding because the cases naturally require the integration of the scientific principles with one another in the context of everyday experience (Linn & Hsi, 2000). The pivotal cases in the Probing project involve the prediction and explanation of the temperature and feel of metal and wood objects across different temperature contexts. The pivotal case contexts include (a) metal and wood spoons left in a warm oven; (b) plates, cups of hot chocolate, cans of soda, and other everyday objects left out on a table in a normal room; (c) metal and wood strips left in a car trunk on a hot summer day; and (d) furniture and other objects in a cold winter cabin with the heat turned off.

The Probing Visualization

To set the context for the visualization, students begin the activity by reading a background story for the pivotal case about objects in a hot car trunk (see Fig. 8.2). Beginning with this story, students are prompted to make predictions about the temperature and feel of the objects left in the trunk for several hours. Students then make predictions about the feel and temperature of the objects after the objects have been brought inside the house overnight. After making predictions, the students follow an introductory tour explaining the visualization environment. Following these initial prediction notes and tour, the students then recreate the trunk-into-house story using the main screen of the visualization. In the visualization, the students have wood and metal objects that are both 55 °C to simulate the objects after several hours in the trunk (see Figs. 8.3 and 8.4). By running the visualization the students can observe the rate of heat flow and temperature change of the objects over time.

The visualization is conceptually enhanced (Snir et al., 1993) connecting the abstract model of normally invisible heat flow as visible arrows to the concrete objects and context of metal and wood furniture in a hot car trunk. Temperature is represented by a gray-scale continuum with darker shades denoting higher temperatures. This color scale is visually represented on the left side of the screen. The temperature of objects is also signified numerically directly on their information tags, along with the conductivity of the object. In the visualization, the size of the animated red arrows leaving or entering an object signifies the rate and direction of heat flow into or out of the object. Larger arrows represent a larger rate of heat flow. In the Alpha version, objects showed heat flow as one arrow leaving per side. By the time of the Beta version of the visualization, we had shifted to smaller arrows spaced evenly around the perimeter of the object. In the next section, I discuss the process of data gathering, analysis, and discussion driving iterative refinements such as these.

Students can run the visualization repeatedly while using the tools at the top of the visualization to change environmental attributes. Among other things, students can add new objects, vary the temperature of the room and objects, and vary the conductivities of the objects. Following the visualization, students answer questions regarding their predicted and actual outcomes, as well as write explanations

In this project you have explored what temperature objects become around you. Now you will explore why objects feel hot or cold.

In The Car Trunk: Imagine that on a hot summer day you go to the hardware store and buy a wood chair and a metal table. You load them into the car trunk and leave them there for three hours while you do other errands. The sun has been beating down on the car, and the trunk gets very warm. The wood chair and metal table are both 55 degrees Celsius when you get home.

Inside The House: Once you get home, you then bring the wood chair and metal table into the house where it is 24 degrees Celsius. You leave them inside for 12 hours. After twelve hours you go and feel them and measure their temperature again.

FIG. 8.2. Car trunk and house background story for visualization activity.

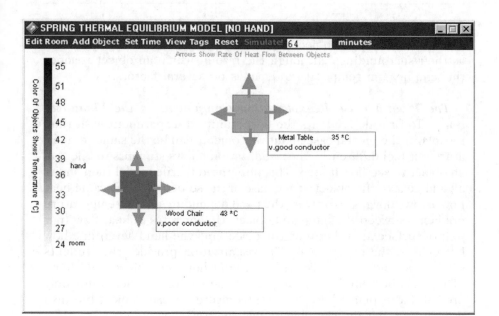

FIG. 8.3.   Core visualization.

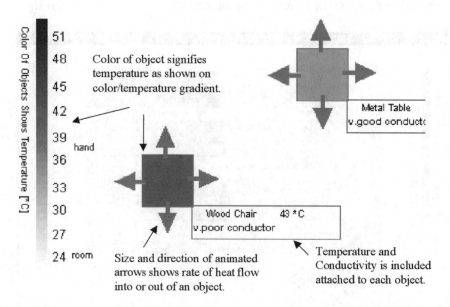

FIG. 8.4.   Close-up of core visualization.

for what they have observed. Watching the visualization allows students to observe that objects eventually reach the same temperature as their surroundings, although the rate at which an object reaches this equilibrium temperature depends on several factors.

The Pivotal Case Reexplanation Component of the Visualization. To provide students the opportunity to experiment with (and reexplain) the pivotal case about why objects can be the same temperature but feel differently, the visualization allows students to click on an object to see how it feels. This integrated tactile model then shows a hand next to the object at the base of the screen with the same heat flow arrows flowing to or from the hand depending on the temperature gradient between the hand and object. Higher rates of heat flow (per unit of surface area) between the object and the hand determine how hot or cold the object feels. The visualization provides the students with audio and text messages describing how the object feels (e.g., "This feels burning hot!"). As part of their notes, students not only predict and explain changes in temperature for each object but also predict and explain why objects feel the way they do.

Starting with the Beta version of the project, students also receive a second screen (see Fig. 8.5) with three cold objects (10 °C) and three hot objects (80 °C) of different conductivities focusing directly on the

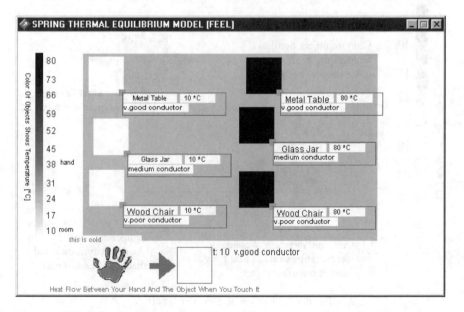

FIG. 8.5.   Supplemental tactile model component of visualization.

pivotal case. This screen is similar to the base thermal equilibrium screen except that students can only feel the objects—this second screen cannot be run as a thermal equilibrium visualization over time. By structuring the screens in this manner we direct student attention specifically toward resolving the pivotal case conundrum of thermal equilibrium, conductivity, and thermal sensation. The goals of this second screen from the perspective of the visualization literature include (a) re-representing (Scaife & Rogers, 1996) the problem in a format that facilitates the connection of conductivity to why objects feel the way they do and (b) graphically constraining (Scaife & Rogers, 1996) the type of mental models a student could construct from the visualization so as to help them build a mental model connecting the target instructed models of thermal equilibrium and insulation and conduction to their experiential knowledge.

RATIONALE FOR PERSONALLY SEEDED DISCUSSIONS

Social supports for learning connect synergistically to other aspects of any project. Our research group first analyzed online discussions and communities through the work of Hoadley (1999) and Hsi (1997), which demonstrated the potential for equity, social relevance, and participation. Our research group's approach resonates with ideas from cognitive apprenticeship and related frameworks for characterizing community practices (Saxe & Guberman, 1998; Tudge & Rogoff, 1989; Vygotsky, 1978). Cognitive apprenticeship (Collins, Brown, & Newman, 1989) calls for innovative participation patterns in communities of practice (see Lave & Wenger, 1992). This synthesis of approaches adds a cognitive dimension to the social learning theories derived from Vygotsky's (1978) social-historical perspective on development.

Our group has made advances in supporting students through online discussions and communities by investigating reflection and knowledge integration through science inquiry (Hoadley, chap. 7, this volume; Hoadley & Linn, 2000; Linn & Hsi, 2000). WISE offers innovative strategies for creating personalized electronic discussions that help elicit self-explanation and clarification from students (Cuthbert, Clark, et al., 2002). As instructional designers and teachers, we have focused on structuring relationships within our online discussions and communities so that the students share resources and help refine each other's ideas.

PERSONALLY SEEDED DISCUSSIONS IN PROBING

We designed the discussion activity in Probing to contrast students' perspectives to help students learn about thermal equilibrium. Contrasting students' perspectives about the same phenomenon can encourage students to clarify their own statements while considering the relevance of other students' opinions (Chi, Lewis, et al., 1989; diSessa & Minstrell, 1998). This perspective taking is important because (a) students have trouble supporting their ideas with evidence, (b) students do not have shared criteria for evaluating explanations, and (c) clarification often involves contrasting perspectives and developing a repertoire of models (both difficult processes; Cuthbert, Clark, et al., 2002). By increasing personal relevance around the process of contrasting student perspectives, we wanted to create relationships eliciting students' conceptual resources to refine the group's ideas.

Following the predictions and data gathering in Probing, students prepare for the discussion by creating principles to describe patterns in their data. Building on work done by Hoadley (chap. 7, this volume) and others on social relevance, we designed the Probing software to place students in electronic discussion groups with students who have constructed different explanatory principles. The student-constructed principles appear as the seed comments in the discussions. The groups critique and discuss these principles, working toward consensus. In these discussions, students and their ideas become critical resources with the common goal of refining the students' ideas. The discussion develops around the different perspectives represented in the seed comments, ideally through a process of comparison, clarification, and justification (part of our learning goals). Jorde and I (Clark & Jorde, in press) studied 300 students who were participants in Probing over the course of one year.

Research on students' initial conceptions about heat and temperature (D. Clark, 2000, 2001; Lewis, 1996; Linn & Hsi, 2000) helped me identify principles students typically used to describe heat flow and thermal equilibrium. I used this conceptual change research and an earlier design from CLP (Lewis, Stern, et al., 1993) to create a new web-based principle builder allowing students to construct their scientific principles from a set of predefined phrases and elements (Fig. 8.6). This principle builder helps students build principles focusing on the core ideas while also providing an interface allowing Probing to compare and sort the students into groups.

The principle builder and personally seeded discussions support the actual practices and daily tasks of the students, which involve con-

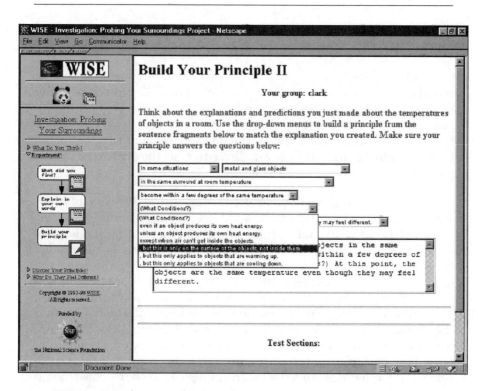

FIG. 8.6.   Students use the principle builder to construct scientific principles that become initial discussion comments.

structing explanations for scientific observations. Students work to
clarify and justify their own scientific principles, comparing and contrasting them with other students' principles. Finally, thinking is
made visible for students as they elaborate on and justify their ideas.

These discussions proved very successful (Cuthbert, Clark, et al.,
2002). Students entered twice as many comments as previous semesters (when they did not comment on their own and other students'
principles). Furthermore, they were much more helpful to one another in the refinement process. By having students explain and defend their own principles, we not only get students to take an interest
in their own ideas but also to take interest in responding to and
critiquing the other ideas in the discussion. The role of the teacher
shifts from presenting alternative views to helping students understand those alternatives, ask for clarification, and refine their own
ideas. We thereby facilitated an online discussion wherein students
were successfully sharing their conceptual resources in the common
task of refining their own ideas.

PRAGMATIC PEDAGOGICAL
PRINCIPLES AND PROBING

Based on the research and ideas discussed previously in terms of the new visualization and personally seed discussions, we created the Alpha version of Probing. In this process we were also heavily informed by the pragmatic pedagogical principles based on the scaffolded knowledge integration framework. In particular, the pragmatic principles were critical.

Making Thinking Visible: Model the Scientific Process of Considering Alternatives. We structured the project to scaffold comparisons by the student and the group through several strategies. We scaffold students personally by prompting them to set out initial hypotheses and ideas and later by prompting them in synthesizing the data. We visually scaffold students in comparing their predictions and data by graphing student results as an overlay of student predictions. Structurally students are supported in considering alternatives within the project by an activity flow that returns students to review and compare their predictions with later findings. Socially students are supported in considering alternatives through a new version of the discussion tool that focuses students on critiquing each other's constructed principles.

Making Thinking Visible: Scaffold Students to Explain Their Ideas. One of our goals involves structuring science activities so that students can devote most of their reasoning power to connecting, linking, and reorganizing their ideas (Linn & Hsi, 2000). Building the activity around the pivotal cases provides a critical component of this scaffolding. Supporting this goal, we structured prompts and notes to elicit thinking and explanation as researched by Davis (chap. 5, this volume). Students don't easily grasp the idea of creating a principle to describe data; therefore, we used the principle builder to help students focus on the critical aspects of the patterns they were seeing. By using students' constructed principles to group the students into online discussion groups and featuring students' principles as seed comments, we employ social supports to prompt self-explanation and critique as well as the consideration of multiple alternatives.

Making Thinking Visible: Use Multiple Visual Representations From Varied Media. Through the CLP research we found that short visualization experiences can have dramatic impact (Linn & Hsi, 2000). Some students may only need a prompt to consider a relation, whereas others will need visual alternatives. The CLP curriculum encouraged students to seek animated depictions along with verbal and symbolic representations. In Probing we focus on this need for multiple visual representations through our inclusion of the visual graphing tools associated with the hands-on components. By allowing students to first make predictions graphically and then to follow by graphing student results overlaying their predictions, we hope to help students get a visual sense of existing patterns in comparison to the patterns they predicted. Additionally, the inclusion of the hands-on components also provides students direct sensation as another "handle" to rely on as they touch the objects to predict temperature. Students also get real-time feedback using the temperature probes to gather temperature data. Additionally, Probing represents predictions and data graphically and numerically. Finally, the visualization not only provides alternative visual cues but also includes numeric, audio, and color-density representations of the data.

PROCESS OF COLLABORATIVE ITERATIVE DESIGN AND REFINEMENT

Driven by these pragmatic principles and research findings, Probing has evolved through several versions of iterative refinement and design. The original CLP version was developed by Lewis, Songer, and Linn through several cycles of refinement (Lewis, 1996; Linn & Hsi, 2000; Songer, 1989). Along with the laboratories, the CLP group developed the initial versions of some of the important pivotal cases. Building on the CLP work, as discussed earlier, we enhanced, revised, and expanded Probing through three more phases including the Alpha, Beta, and Current versions as we evolved the project from CLP to WISE and developed and refined the pivotal cases, visualization, and personally seeded discussions. Earlier in this chapter, I discussed the ideas behind the creation of the Alpha version of WISE Probing. In the next section, I discuss the iterative processes through which we refined the Alpha version into the Beta version and then into the Current version.

Investigating and Refining the Alpha Version of Probing

To determine the effectiveness of the Alpha version, we gathered multiple sources of data about the functionality and effectiveness of the new WISE project. We studied four classes of students (approximately 120 students) under one master teacher (Doug Kirkpatrick) in a California public middle school. Because we wanted a broad spectrum of initial data for this preliminary work, we established four different conditions involving two visualization conditions crossed with two discussion conditions. These data included multiple choice and essay pretest and posttest data, direct observation of students by two researchers and a master teacher, and video observation for extended discussions within the research group. Additionally, we interviewed students before and after the project to determine what the students had learned as well as potential improvements for the project. Based on these data we continued revisions through discussions with expert teachers, technologists, and researchers on our team.

For the Alpha visualization, the data were mixed. Clearly the visualization was very useful for some students but remained inaccessible to others. It was also evident that those students who understood the visualization benefited significantly in terms of their understanding of thermal equilibrium, but even these students often didn't make connections between tactile sensation, thermal equilibrium, and conductivity. We therefore needed to increase the focus within the pivotal case on the tactile components and we needed to increase the overall accessibility of the core pivotal case within the visualization.

Based on these outcomes, our group conducted extensive internal discussions resulting in several improvements. To make the visualization more accessible we shifted from having the students use the visualization to set up the context of the experiment to providing students with the objects and temperatures as presets. Students could still add and modify the components, but the presets ensured that the visualization focused on the pivotal case at the outset of each trial. We also clarified the interface through which students interacted with the visualization by color coding the buttons. Interestingly, based on our discussions with students, we needed to change our representation of heat flow from a simple single arrow on each side of an object to a series of smaller arrows spaced evenly around the object (Fig. 8.7). This finding mirrored similar findings of Foley's (1999) in terms of level of abstraction accessible to students. From those interviews it also became clear that we needed to move the hand icon closer to the object it was touching—we hadn't realized that many students didn't think the hand was close enough to be touching and so missed the connection. Most important, we added the additional tactile screen to the visualization in which students could feel three hot and three cold objects of different materials side by side (Fig. 8.5). As the HeatBars research had demonstrated, simple direct representations were among our most successful (Foley, 1999; Lewis, 1996; Lewis, Stern, et al., 1993). Visually seeing the objects at the same time side by side

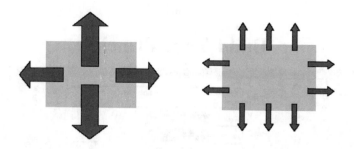

FIG. 8.7. Alpha and Beta heat flow representations.

helps students make connections about what really causes objects to feel differently from one another.

The data on the Alpha personally seeded discussions demonstrated more clear-cut success. Students who worked in personally seeded discussions carried on much more involved discussions than did the students placed in discussion groups in which the initial comments in the discussion consisted of predetermined principles created by past students (Cuthbert, Clark, et al., 2002). These findings supported Hoadley's (1999) findings demonstrating the importance of personal relevance in student discussions. The findings, however, also pointed to further potential improvements for the personally seeded discussions. The instructions for the discussion needed to more clearly specify and scaffold students in effectively critiquing one another's principles. In particular, students struggled with properly warranting their assertions and critiques with evidence from the classroom or personal experience as Bell (chap. 6, this volume) shows. Students often simply dismissed or insulted other students' principles without providing rationale or warrants. Additionally, we needed to clarify the principle-builder interface by removing excess clutter and leaving only the pull-down menu bars (Fig. 8.8). We also needed to clarify and simplify the terms within each pull-down menu because the overwhelming number of permutations confused students. Although we wanted to allow flexibility, we wanted the students to produce principles addressing (normatively or non-normatively) the pivotal case.

In addition to these major changes in the structure and presentation of the visualization and personally seeded discussions, we also significantly revised the hints and notes throughout the project. For instance, in the Alpha visualization students use a paper worksheet with an extended data table to set up experiments and record data. We had thought that a separate physical sheet on which the students could organize their work would be helpful, but it proved to be overly elaborate and confusing for many students given the scope of the project. In place

Alpha

Build Your Principle

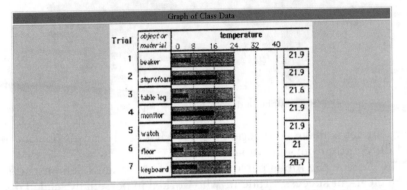

Think about the explanation you created in the last activity. Use the drop-down menus to build a principle from the sentence fragments below to match the explanation you created. When you are finished with your principle, click the "I'm finished..." button at the bottom of the page. (If you don't click the button before you leave this page, you will lose any work you've done so far.)

Category	Principle Pieces To Choose From For Each Pop-Up Menu:			
When Does It Happen?	Immediately	In some situations	Sometimes	Eventually
What Objects?	all objects	most objects except for asbestos and wood	metal objects	Some objects
	metal and glass objects			
Where?	in the same surround at room temperature	in the same surround at room temperature and warmer temperatures	in the same surround at room temperature and colder temperatures	in the same surround at all temperatures
What Do They Do?	remain different temperatures	become close to the same temperature	become the same temperature	
What Conditions?	even if an object produces its own heat energy.	unless an object produces its own heat energy.	except when air can't get inside the objects.	, but this is only on the surface of the objects, not inside them.
	, but this only applies to objects that are warming up.	, but this only applies to objects that are cooling down.		

Your Principle:

Eventually ▼	all objects ▼	in the same surround at room temperature ▼

| Immediately |
| In some situations |
| Sometimes |
| Eventually |

perature ▼	, but this is only on the surface of the objects, not inside them. ▼

Eventually all objects in the same surround at room
temperature become the same temperature , but this is only
on the surface of the objects, not inside them.

If.

Category	Principle Pieces To Choose From For Each Pop-Up Menu:			
How Do They Feel?	At this point, the objects are different temperatures and they feel different.	At this point, the objects are different temperatures even though they feel the same.	At this point, the objects are within a few degrees even though they may feel different.	
	At this point, the objects are within a few degrees even though they may feel the same.	At this point, the objects are the same temperature even though they may feel different.	At this point, the objects are the same temperature and they feel the same.	

At this point, the objects are different temperatures even though they may feel the same. ▼

FIG. 8.8.   *(Continued)*

Beta

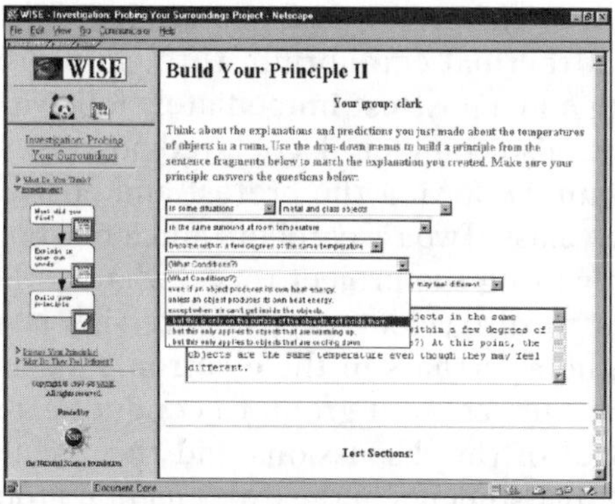

FIG. 8.8.   (This page and facing) Comparison of Alpha and Beta principle builders. See Fig. 8.6 for enlarged view of the Beta version.

of the worksheet we created a series of online notes with suitable
prompts to help students focus on the critical issues. Similarly, we revised the prompts within the notes throughout the project significantly
to make them more accessible to students. By including parsimonious
generic prompts, we helped students begin to focus on the critical connections and ideas Davis (chap. 5, this volume) demonstrates.

Testing and Refining the Beta Version of Probing

We focused our experimentation with the Beta version on the effectiveness of the visualization because the Alpha results had already
demonstrated the effectiveness of the personally seeded discussions.
The Alpha visualizations, although showing promise, had demonstrated a need for significant revision.

We gathered multiple sources of data about the functionality and
effectiveness of the Beta project. One hundred and twenty students in
four classes of eighth-grade students completed this project during
one semester under the supervision of the same experienced teacher.
Experimental groups for the study included (a) 60 students in two
classes in an intervention condition implementing the reexplanation
tactile model and (b) 60 students in two classes in a control condition
(D. Clark & Jorde, in press). Both conditions involved the laboratory,
discussion and core thermal equilibrium visualization, but the visualizations in the reexplanation condition included the integrated tactile
model (hand) and tactile screen to better represent the pivotal case as
well. This intervention added only 15 min to the 5-day project. The

control group used this additional 15 min for additional reflection on the project and the online discussions.

Clark and Jorde (in press) assessed students' knowledge integration in terms of thermal equilibrium through a pretest immediately prior to Probing and a posttest immediately following. Six weeks after Probing students also completed a delayed posttest as part of their semester final exam. Following the pretest and posttest we interviewed students in each class. Two researchers and a master teacher observed students directly using the project to see what worked or didn't. During the projects, we also videotaped the interview students as they participated with their partners in the electronic discussions and visualizations to allow our research group to conduct extended discussions about the impact of the discussions and the visualizations.

Results show that students in the experimental group provided significantly more sophisticated answers on posttests and delayed posttests than did their counterparts in the control group (Fig. 8.9; D. Clark & Jorde, in press). Interview transcripts of experimental and control group students corroborate these findings. Students in the experimental group demonstrated a higher mean ability to explain why objects feel the way they do and to connect this explanation to normative predictions about the temperatures of objects in different surroundings.

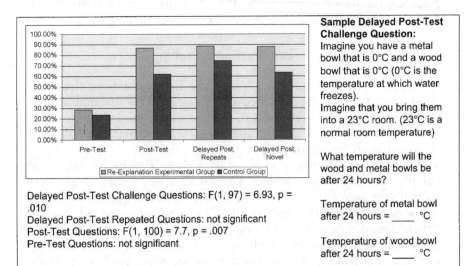

Sample Delayed Post-Test Challenge Question:
Imagine you have a metal bowl that is 0°C and a wood bowl that is 0°C (0°C is the temperature at which water freezes).
Imagine that you bring them into a 23°C room. (23°C is a normal room temperature)

What temperature will the wood and metal bowls be after 24 hours?

Temperature of metal bowl after 24 hours = _____ °C

Temperature of wood bowl after 24 hours = _____ °C

What is the main reason for the temperatures you predicted for the wood and metal bowls?

Delayed Post-Test Challenge Questions: $F(1, 97) = 6.93$, $p = .010$
Delayed Post-Test Repeated Questions: not significant
Post-Test Questions: $F(1, 100) = 7.7$, $p = .007$
Pre-Test Questions: not significant

FIG. 8.9. Beta pretest and posttest results.

Based on the data and discussions with expert teachers, technologists, and researchers we continued the iterative revision process. We continued to streamline the principle builder. We also further specified discussion instructions to scaffold students in critiquing each other's principles using warrants and evidence from classroom and personal experiences. Most significantly for the discussions, we found that the improved instructions and scaffolding allowed students to interact with one another more effectively using evidence and warrants. As a result, students wanted and required more time as they made more productive comments. Based on this finding, we extended the curricular time devoted to the discussion from one 50-min block to two 50-min blocks.

The revisions to the visualization involved more sweeping changes. Even though the results achieved using a Beta version of the visualization and pivotal case had been significant and impressive, our observations and interviews with students, discussions with experts, and videotaped analyses suggested that further significant modifications might achieve even more dramatic results (see Fig. 8.10). Similar to

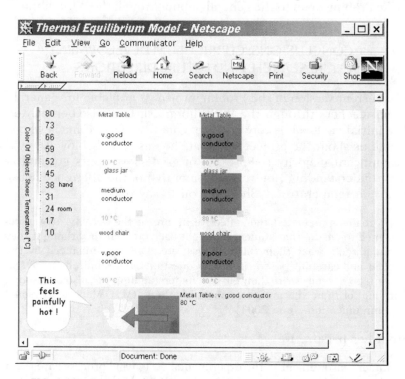

FIG. 8.10. Revision of the Beta visualization based on student interviews, videotaped analyses, and expert discussions.

Foley's (1999) findings about color choices in representations, we changed the color scale from a gray scale to a red scale because interviews suggested that students could more easily connect a red scale to temperature. The color and temperature key is now represented as a thermometer to make this connection even more accessible. The delivery and format of the messages about how an object feels have been enhanced. We clarified the audio portion and embedded the textual announcements in cartoon bubbles that the students more easily associated with personal experience. We also clarified the connection of heat flow from hot objects to cold objects with regard to the hand by including the hand's temperature as text as well as color so that the structure paralleled the structure for other objects on the screen. Codification of these design principles is displayed in Table 8.1.

In addition to further revising the visualization and discussion, we also continued to refine the prompts and notes throughout the project. Through all of these revisions we continued to focus on helping make the concepts within the pivotal case more visible and accessible to the students. On completion of this process, we felt prepared to make Probing open to the general public through the WISE library.

CONCLUSIONS: CURRICULUM DEVELOPMENT, RESEARCH, AND FUTURE DIRECTIONS

The current version of the Probing project is available for general use by all teachers through the WISE library (http://wise.berkeley.edu). The initial feedback is very positive. One teacher in Canada who contacted us about the project said that she was "totally blown away that a significant majority (~85–90%) of grade 7 students got and kept their understanding (for at least 3 months) of the difference between heat and temperature." She went on to say that

> [I] really appreciated the reflective nature of the activity. It was designed to ensure that students thought back on what they thought they understood, what their thinking was, etc. This was enhanced by the clear and carefully posed situations/questions, the requirement of students to not only write their current understandings but also to respond to and critique the understandings of others. (M. O'Mahony, personal communication, June 2001)

From her perspective

> Student involvement in the experimental design and process gave them a better understanding of the problem. It made them internalize the scientific problem. For example . . . they knew, intellectually, that all

TABLE 8.1
Design Principles for Visualizations

Design Principle	Examples
Use representations connected to students' everyday experiences.	Incorporation of cartoon bubbles for voice, redscale vs. grayscale for temperature, and depiction of temperature scale as a thermometer
Structure visualization to focus on simultaneous or side-by-side comparison of pivotal cases.	Both HeatBars and the second tactile visualization facilitate specific comparisons in a side-by-side layout to help students make the connections by highlighting differences between the conditions. Students may miss connections if they can only see one case at a time.
Reduce complexity by removing functionality and variables not critical to highlighting the central targeted concept.	The second tactile visualization has the thermal equilibrium functionality removed to focus students on the connection between sensation, temperature, and conductivity. The functionality only allows students to compare how objects of different materials feel in terms of heat flow, temperature, and conductivity. Students could also make these comparisons in the full-functioned thermal equilibrium visualization, but many students apparently didn't make the connections because they are too engaged with the other possible functions of the visualization.
Ground the visualization in the broader curriculum as well as in the context of other hands-on activities.	As suggested by Foley and other theorists, grounding the visualization in the context of the broader curriculum and hands-on activities seems to help students accept the visualization as plausible and to connect it to other ideas from class and personal experience.
Don't overly abstract the representations.	Initially we used only one arrow on each side of an object. This abstraction required nonessential decoding by students to unpack. The size of the arrow represented amount of heat flowing out of the object. Longer sides of an object therefore had a larger arrow. Students were much more receptive to multiple arrows of equal size spaced equally around the object.

the objects in the room should be the same temperature . . . which was verified by their lab data. However, the fact that different objects felt warmer or cooler really created a personal cognitive dissonance within them. Not only did this discrepant situation disturb any lassitude present but it was intriguing enough to make them want to want to be able to explain it. Again, the context and the way the problem was developed and introduced made this part so successful. (M. O'Mahony, personal communication, June 2001)

In addition to anecdotal testimony to the effectiveness of the current version of Probing, we are currently working to continue the process of analysis and refinement by instituting automatic pretest and posttest measures. Through WISE, every student worldwide engaging in a Probing project will begin the project with a randomly assigned pretest question from a bank of our knowledge integration assessments. The student will complete this same question again at the end of the project. Over time, the quantitative data we collect from students around the world will help us continue to target aspects of the project for further refinement.

Meanwhile, we continue the iterative refinement process by investigating the potential impact of enhancing the pivotal case. Students in the Beta re-explanation experimental group tended to make the connection that conductivity affects rate of heat flow as well as how an object feels, but many students would seemingly benefit from more biological depth. Emphasizing biological aspects such as the fact that students are producers of heat or focusing on how humans sense coldness in their fingers as a result of this heat flow might facilitate even stronger connections between the physics, biology, and the students' experiential knowledge. This might entail expanding the tactile model and enhancing it in terms of the actual biological mechanisms for why objects feel hot or cold.

We will continue to refine the Probing project, but the existing template has already provided a design pattern for other investigation projects. These results suggest that the Current version is a powerful and successful approach open to future customization. These results also underscore the critical nature of longitudinal case-study work curriculum development. These results also contribute to the literature on visualization design (D. Clark & Jorde, in press), online discussions (Cuthbert, Clark, et al., 2002), and conceptual change (D. Clark, 2000). At the heart of all of these accomplishments, the pragmatic pedagogical principles and our iterative design process have demonstrated the potential to develop powerful curriculum projects to better serve the needs of all our students.

III

NEW PARTNERSHIPS

9

The Web-Based Inquiry Science Environment (WISE): Scaffolding Knowledge Integration in the Science Classroom

James D. Slotta
University of California, Berkeley

The Web-Based Inquiry Science Environment (WISE) project seeks to extend the Knowledge Integration Environment (KIE) approaches to a wider audience of teachers in a broad range of school settings. Internet technology has developed greatly over the past 5 years with improvements in personal computers, Web browser software, and network access. Building on the foundation of KIE (see Davis, chap. 5, this volume; Bell, chap. 6, this volume; and Hoadley, chap. 7, this volume), WISE has capitalized on these developments to create a second-generation learning environment with improved usability and accessibility for classrooms. New features include a browser-based interface and powerful Web server functionality. Because it is completely Web based, WISE does not require the installation of any software on school computers or servers. In addition, WISE has continued to expand the library of inquiry projects that are available to teachers, supporting an increasing range of science topics and student age groups.

WISE investigates (a) effective designs for inquiry activities and assessments, (b) technology supports for students and teachers, (c) authoring partnerships to create a library of inquiry projects, and (d) professional development programs to enable a wide audience of teachers to succeed with inquiry and technology. In this chapter I describe the WISE learning environment and curriculum partnerships and discuss a research program aimed at helping all teachers adopt inquiry and technology methods.

THE WISE LEARNING ENVIRONMENT

WISE provides an Internet-based platform for middle school and high school science activities in which students work collaboratively on inquiry projects, making use of "evidence" from the Web. WISE projects range in duration from 2 days to 4 weeks, providing inquiry topics for teachers in Grades 4 to 14. Typical projects engage students in designing solutions to problems (e.g., design a desert house that stays warm at night and cool during the day), debating contemporary science controversies (e.g., the causes of declining amphibian populations), critiquing scientific claims found in Web sites (e.g., arguments for life on Mars), and investigating scientific phenomena (e.g., thermal equilibrium). Figure 9.1 displays the WISE student interface, including the pop-up windows for reflection notes and cognitive hints. Students navigate through activity steps in the left-hand frame of their Web browser called the "Inquiry Map." Each step in the project can result in the display of Web pages (to be used in support of student designs or debates), in the appearance of the WISE notes window, an online discussion, or any one of numerous inquiry tools (e.g., Java applets for data visualization, simulations, and causal maps). As the students work through the sequence of activities that comprise the project, the teacher circulates within the classroom, interacting with one small group of students at a time, helping them interpret Web materials, reflect on the topic, and interact with their peers.

The use of Internet materials is fundamental to WISE, and all projects make use of some content from the World Wide Web as well as additional Web pages authored for purposes of the project. In WISE activities, students learn to use the Internet productively for inquiring, critiquing Web sites, designing approaches, or comparing arguments. Each project includes a lessons plan, preassessments and postassessments, links to the National Science Education Standards, a description of the learning goals, and ideas that students will likely bring with them to the project. All student work is saved on central project servers that enable student accounts and teacher accounts to be coordinated. Technology features for teachers include classroom management tools, grading environment, and the capability to make comments that students receive the next time they log into WISE. All of these materials can be seen and activities explored at the project Web site: http://wise.berkeley.edu.

All WISE curriculum and assessments are authored collaboratively using Web-based authoring tools designed as an integral part of WISE. Authors use the curriculum design patterns that have been tested in other projects (Linn, Clark, et al., 2003). Authors develop

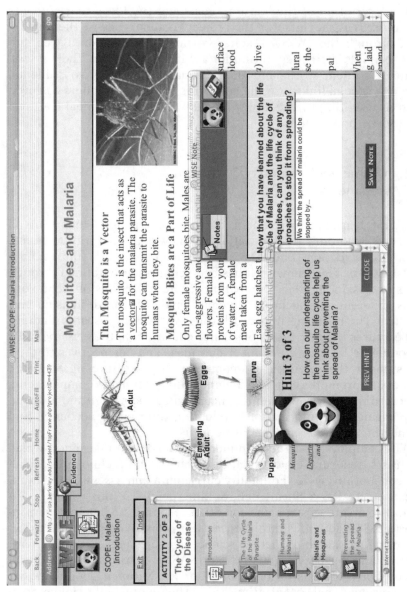

FIG. 9.1. Web-Based Inquiry Science Environment (WISE) student interface showing pop-up notes and hints windows.

support materials for each project, including a detailed lesson plan, preassessments and postassessments, links to the science standards, and a description of the learning goals and the ideas that students may possess at the outset of the project. Teachers access these materials through the "WISE Teacher Portal," a user-tailored Web site that scaffolds their preparation for a WISE project run, their assessment of student work, and their formative feedback to students. Through special links into the authoring software, teachers can even customize WISE projects toward local issues, geographical features, or student populations.

Design Framework for Inquiry Curriculum and Assessments

The WISE learning environment, curriculum, and assessments are all designed according to the scaffolded knowledge integration framework for instruction (Linn, Davis, & Eylon, chap. 3, this volume; Linn & Hsi, 2000). This framework has been continuously refined through years of classroom trials, comparing different versions of technology tools, different approaches to guidance, and different designs for curriculum. The resulting framework thus synthesizes research findings and captures the intricacies of science education in the classroom. By encouraging learners to connect new ideas and perspectives to their ideas about the scientific phenomenon they are investigating, the framework promotes cohesive understanding. Students compare, contrast, critique, sort out, and reconceptualize their scientific ideas incorporating new information, evaluating alternative accounts, and connecting everyday and scientific ideas.

WISE employs a partnership model of curriculum design in which scientists, teachers, educational researchers, and technology specialists collaboratively design inquiry curriculum and assessments (Linn, Shear, et al., 1999; Shear, Bell, & Linn, chap. 12, this volume). Authors also create lesson plans and other resources to help teachers integrate WISE activities into their existing classroom practices. WISE authoring partnerships include science agencies (e.g., National Aeronautics and Space Administration [NASA], National Oceanic and Atmospheric Administration [NOAA], or The National Geographic Society), professional organizations (e.g., The American Physiology Society), and museums (e.g., the Monterey Bay Aquarium) that are committed to developing educational materials related to their scientific expertise. Partners are attracted by the WISE technology, which can deliver the curriculum to a global audience of teachers and students

while providing innovative user supports and professional development programs to enable teachers to adopt WISE successfully. The
authoring partners work together to design a pilot project, observe its
use in science classrooms, and refine the project based on their observations. Additionally, WISE allows teachers and schools to make their
own connections to instruction, incorporate personally relevant problems, link to local science museums or environmental issues, and create custom prompts, hints, assessments, or online discussions.

Science agencies and organizations benefit from the technology
features of WISE, which delivers content and functionality to a global
audience of teachers and students. More importantly, the scaffolded
knowledge integration framework provides a resource for the design
of activities and assessments as well as for review criteria to help authors continuously improve their materials. Table 9.1 illustrates how
the WISE team has used the tenets of scaffolded knowledge integration to articulate guidelines for the design of inquiry activities. To support and facilitate partnerships, we are currently incorporating such
guidelines into our online authoring and review environment.

THE WISE CURRICULUM LIBRARY

WISE partnerships have designed, authored and refined a small library
of more than 50 curriculum projects that are currently available in the
WISE library. For example, we have formed partnerships with NASA
scientists and contractors to design numerous projects including the
following: "Rats in Space," in which high school biology students critique the use of rats as models for humans in NASA bone loss studies
(Slotta, Dodson, et al., 1999); "Sprouting Space Plants," in which
fourth and fifth graders design a terrarium for use on the Space Sta-
tion Freedom, comparing the growth of NASA space plants with regular earth plants; and "Life in the Universe," in which middle school
students evaluate the habitat that might exist on the known planets
that have been discovered in other solar systems. In another effort,
marine researchers from NOAA and The National Geographic Society
have worked in close partnership with teachers and WISE project researchers to create an environmental science project for WISE called
"Ocean Stewards," in which high school students design a research ex-
pedition to the Marine National Sanctuary that is nearest to their local
watershed.

Still other partnerships have been formed with educational research projects that benefit from the existing strengths of WISE,
incorporating their own research questions in the design of new

TABLE 9.1
WISE Instruction Framework: Scaffolded Knowledge Integration

Major Tenets	Design Guidelines	Inquiry Activities
Making science accessible	Project builds on student ideas. Project builds scientific knowledge framework. Students can connect project to personally relevant questions. Project connects to standards-based curricula. Project models the inquiry process. Project ideas are accessible to diverse learners.	Investigating a driving question or inquiry task Eliciting student ideas Connecting to personally relevant problems
Making thinking visible	Students create and use personal representations. Students express their ideas. Students are scaffolded to explore new representations. Students encounter multiple representations. Representations are incorporated into assessments. Activity promotes learning through representations. Activity illustrates the process of inquiry.	Modeling, simulating, animating Graphing, representing data Representing arguments Questioning/explaining Drawing
Helping students learn from others	Activity incorporates different kinds of social activity structures. Students listen and learn from each other. Peers have productive interactions to develop understanding. Students develop shared criteria for scientific discourse. Students have the opportunity to share their findings after generating their own ideas.	Developing criteria Discussing with peers online Discussing with peers in the classroom Reflecting on discussion Conducting a debate Critiquing peers
Promoting autonomy and lifelong learning	Project engages students in meaningful reflection. Project engages students as critics of diverse scientific information. Project engages students in multiple approaches to science inquiry. Project helps students understand and generalize the inquiry process to diverse science projects. Project provides opportunities for learning and applying context-embedded content knowledge.	Writing reflection notes Conducting a project Preparing for a debate Describing an inquiry Critiquing own performance Designing an inquiry Revisiting ideas outside of class

projects. One important partnership involves researchers from the University of Washington and The American Association for the Advancement of Science who seek to develop curriculum based on science controversy. This project, called Science Controversies Online Partnerships for Education (SCOPE; see Bell, chap. 10, this volume), has developed many controversy-based projects including "Deformed Frogs," in which students evaluate competing hypotheses about malformations in North American amphibians (see Shear et al., chap. 12, this volume), or "Cycles of Malaria," in which they critique different strategies for controlling malaria worldwide. These materials offer diverse perspectives that can help students learn to critique materials and appreciate viewpoints.

The WISE curriculum library continues to grow as these partnerships develop new projects and assessments for all age levels and science domains. Additionally, teachers themselves can improve on the curriculum, customizing WISE projects to meet their personal goals and classroom settings. Teachers can use the WISE customization tools to make their own connections to instruction, incorporate personally relevant problems, link to local science museums or environmental issues, and bring current science controversies to life. We made it easy to add relevant Web pages to a WISE project, and create custom prompts, hints, assessments, or online discussions. We have also developed several new online supports for teachers who can share their customizations and annotate projects to share their successful approaches.

TEACHING WITH INQUIRY AND TECHNOLOGY

Even with the support of a learning environment like WISE, the challenges of teaching with inquiry and technology are substantial (see Linn, Davis, & Bell, chap. 1, this volume). For many science teachers, WISE represents a departure from traditional methods such as lectures, textbook assignments, and hands-on experiments.

WISE professional development research is exploring how teachers adopt inquiry and technology methods, how to support them in the difficult first trials, and how their students benefit along the way informed by the scaffolded knowledge integration perspective on instruction. Ultimately, the goal of WISE is to help teachers interact deeply with their students concerning their ideas about science, helping all students develop a personal understanding and a rich experience of inquiry. WISE project researchers investigate the pedagogical ideas that teachers bring to the table as they adopt an innovation like

WISE, including their attitudes about technology and inquiry. Based on observations and interviews of teachers as they implement WISE, we are developing a program that includes workshops, interactions with mentors, and online supports. This program helps teachers customize their science course so that it complements the use of WISE. By helping teachers develop a sense of ownership and control over their use of WISE, we hope to enable them to develop a comprehensive understanding of the pedagogical ideas underlying our innovations.

Teaching With WISE

WISE projects require teachers to interact closely with students as they work in pairs or small groups, supporting autonomous investigations while making complex decisions about allocation of instructional time. Teachers must set up a WISE project run, help students register for WISE, manage their passwords and user accounts, and get them started on the first day with WISE. This includes motivating the inquiry topic as well as explaining the WISE interface and promoting success with the learning environment. Teachers are also challenged to grade student work online as well as to make comments and interact with students during the course of a project. Finally, one of the most difficult challenges in adopting WISE or other inquiry projects concerns the adjustments that a teacher must make for the inquiry project to fit well within his or her existing course. The teachers who have had the best success with WISE have made substantial changes to their course content immediately preceding and immediately following the actual WISE run. Preliminary activities help students develop important ideas that they will draw on in the course of the WISE inquiry unit. Follow-up discussions or activities help them make connections between the WISE unit and the rest of the course. Such adjustments are also more commonly observed in the practice of teachers who have used WISE for several semesters as they exhibit an increasing level of "ownership" of the curriculum (Levey, 1998).

Features of WISE, such as the Teacher Portal, supplemental resources (e.g., lesson plans and preassessments and postassessments), customized comments for students, and online support from the WISE project staff make inquiry teaching more accessible to teachers. The learning environment itself can also help support teachers by making inquiry visible. Teachers can observe students performing the inquiry curriculum and follow students' progress within the project. However, these supports are often insufficient, and most first-time WISE teachers are preoccupied with implementing the technology and simply surviving the day. The opportunities offered by WISE for interacting with students concerning their ideas about science are often lost amidst the flurry of new challenges in simply getting WISE to run successfully with their class.

Ideally, professional development must help teachers interpret new inquiry practices in terms of their prior instructional methods. For example, in contrast to prior textbook-based methods that completely excluded science controversy and source credibility, WISE critique activities may expose students to biased, incomplete, or erroneous information. Other new practices will be concerned with student collaborations such as learning to focus on those students who are experiencing difficulties whereas enabling the others to remain on task.

We have designed a model of mentored professional development that incorporates the knowledge integration perspective on learning about inquiry instruction (Linn, Eylon, & Davis, chap. 2, this volume). Professional development can address the interpretive nature of science instruction by helping teachers identify some of their own ideas about inquiry and seek pivotal cases to understand how inquiry could fit into their practice. We address the deliberate nature of science teaching by helping teachers customize WISE curriculum and adopt a tailored lesson plan for their own science course. We address the cultural aspect of science teaching by connecting teachers in collaborative activities and by including a WISE mentor who helps model new practices and provides careful feedback throughout the process.

The WISE Mentor Model

WISE mentor model of professional development helps teachers develop a cohesive understanding about inquiry instruction by building on their existing ideas about student learning, technology, and the role of the instructor. Following the four principles of the scaffolded knowledge integration framework for instruction, we make inquiry visible through visits to a mentor's classroom where WISE is being run and through workshops where videotape of WISE master teachers is discussed. We make ideas about inquiry accessible by helping teachers compare their own practice with that of the mentor who models the use of WISE in the teacher's own classroom. Additionally, our workshops focus on helping teachers reflect on the challenges of adopting WISE and creating a lesson plan for the successful incorporation of a WISE unit into their overall curriculum. We provide social supports for teachers using WISE with peer networks and mentor relationships. Finally, we encourage autonomy by engaging teachers in customizing WISE lessons based on their experiences, scoring student work according to WISE scoring standards, engaging in iterative refinement of their instruction, and reflecting on the reasons for any customizations.

Ultimately, when teachers feel a sense of ownership of the curriculum and confidence in how it is meeting their goals for student learning, they will be more successful and more likely to customize and improve on the innovations (Songer, 2000). A WISE mentor facilitates this process, scaffolding new teachers as they (a) explore the WISE technology and choose an appropriate project and (b) plan how that project will fit into their existing course curriculum or how they might alter or rearrange their syllabus to help make the WISE project a better fit. After this planning stage, the mentor helps the teacher succeed in his or her first WISE run. Even though WISE is technologically straightforward and easy to use, many teachers benefit from reassurance, support, and demonstrations. The mentor demonstrates how to help students register in WISE, how to conduct an initial discussion of the WISE project with their students, and how to lead the class through the project, balancing in-depth interactions with individual students and whole-class discussions. In subsequent stages of the model, the mentor continues to be involved, helping the teacher learn to use the online assessment and feedback tools and eventually to customize a WISE project using the authoring environment. In subsequent semesters or school years, the mentor helps the teacher plan his or her curriculum more deliberately to build around the use of WISE, ultimately leading to a smooth integration of the WISE technology and inquiry curriculum. Finally, the mentor tries to enable the development of a community of peers within the teacher's school who are all involved with WISE, with the goal of establishing an ongoing professional development network concerned with science inquiry and technology.

We have investigated this model in diverse settings including whole-school studies and district-wide scaling initiatives. Teachers often are bound by logistical constraints (e.g., time within their syllabus and access to technology resources) and are motivated by a wide range of factors (e.g., the ideal technology innovation for some teaches is one that can stand alone without their involvement). WISE curriculum, which focuses on depth coverage of specific topics, presents a challenge to school districts that are striving to meet a breadth of content standards (Krajcik, Marx, et al., 2000). These districts often evaluate programs based on their impact on students' achievement on standardized tests. Whereas the most effective way to improve student performance on such tests is to directly target the test topics in short term regurgitation of facts, WISE is focused on establishing lifelong learning skills and promoting autonomous understanding. The success of WISE within a school and district setting depends on a variety of factors concerned with the teacher, the school science department, technology resources, and the school district science curriculum policies. Our goal is to develop a successful model of mentoring that is somewhat tolerant to these factors, enabling a wide audience of teachers to succeed with WISE and helping promote forward progress in how schools and districts incorporate technology and inquiry into their science curriculum.

A WHOLE-SCHOOL STUDY
OF THE WISE MENTOR MODEL

We began a whole-school study in a middle school where none of the six science teachers had any experience with WISE nor with computer-based instruction. This study included a mentor who worked closely with each teacher as they worked through the various stages of running a WISE project: preparations, use of WISE in the classroom, and assessment of student work. The mentor helped the teachers customize their course curriculum to make the WISE project a better fit. During a teacher's initial use of the project, the mentor modeled effective inquiry instruction during the first period of each day, allowing the teacher to take over in subsequent periods. This allowed teachers to observe the mentor's approach and also freed them to interact with students right from the start. On completion of the first WISE project (usually lasting between 5 and 10 school days) the mentor facilitated assessments and helped the teacher use the online grading system (a feature of the WISE teacher portal). The mentor also tried to raise the level of student–teacher interactions from procedural guidance to a deeper level of integrated understanding about student inquiry. After all six teachers had cycled through the computer laboratory in this way, they prepared for their second WISE project. During this second WISE project run, interactions between mentor and teachers were greatly reduced as the role of the mentor shifted to one of careful observations and feedback.

By the end of this 2-year study, the mentor's presence had completely faded with no further interactions required by the teachers. One measure of teacher success was the pretests and posttests of student understanding as well as embedded assessments of student project work (e.g., their WISE notes and arguments). Another was the teacher's ability to continue running WISE autonomously and their interview reflections over the course of this study. Differences in teaching style were examined, and student outcomes were compared in terms of their sensitivity to the depth of teacher–student interactions and the coherence of the curriculum plan. We also explored how different teachers interacted with the mentor to determine what kinds of feedback were helpful to teachers who held various ideas about technology, inquiry, and science learning.

Teacher–Mentor Interactions

The mentor was heavily involved in each teachers' first classroom trial of WISE but gradually faded his involvement as the first year progressed. Initially, the mentor helped by modeling WISE instruction for teachers. As there were six periods in each school day, the mentor could demonstrate in the first period how to introduce WISE to students, how to help them register, and so on. By the end of that day, however, the teacher was leading each period and the mentor was observing and offering feedback between periods. When the first WISE project was complete, usually lasting between 5 and 10 school days, the mentor assisted in the postassessments and then helped the teacher learn to use the WISE online grading system. At this time, the mentor also provided feedback to the teacher concerning his or her interactions with the students and with the class as a whole. For example, one teacher was advised to stop the class more frequently and focus all of the students on a short verbal question or discussion. Occasional pauses or interruptions like this can be quite helpful, as they enable the teacher to provide a broadcast feedback to the class based on observations and interactions with students. As one teacher neared the completion of his or her first WISE project run, the next would begin preparations with the mentor, then begin using WISE once the previous teacher was finished with the computer laboratory.

After all six teachers had cycled through the computer laboratory in this way, they prepared for their second WISE project. Once again, the mentor conferred with each teacher to help select an appropriate project for their course and to help adjust the curriculum activities immediately preceding and following the WISE run for purposes of continuity. During the WISE run itself, however, interactions between mentor and teachers were greatly reduced, in some cases to "on demand" only. The role of the mentor shifted to one of careful observations of the individual teachers who felt that they were really demonstrating their new skills in this second WISE run. After each day of the run, the mentor conferred with the teacher to give feedback on the nature of questions asked to students, the flow of whole-class and small-group interactions, and the ideas that students were exhibiting in the project. In this way, the mentor tried to raise the level of interactions from procedural guidance to a deeper level of integrated understanding about student inquiry.

As the first year came to a close, only one of the teachers felt unable to continue using WISE in his curriculum primarily because he could not find a project that fit his particular course syllabus to his satisfaction. At this point in the study, it was clear that teachers differed in their abilities to use WISE autonomously, in their level of comfort in working with students, and in their commitment to integrating inquiry and technology within their course. I discuss these differences in the next section. In general, we were encouraged by the progress exhibited by all six teachers in the school and by their growing level of autonomy. As the second year of the study began, all five returning teachers were well prepared to run WISE. They had thought in advance about the topics they would teach and how the WISE units would fit within their syllabus. In addition, they had begun to interact with one another regarding issues of scheduling the laboratory, and at times they even discussed issues of student learning and their own teaching practice. During this year, the mentor was not present in the school for most of the time. He met with each teacher briefly at the beginning of the semester to help plan their use of WISE then met with them once again just before their WISE project run began. At least once during the first semester the mentor observed the teacher and gave feedback on their student interactions at the end of that session. Midway through the second year, the mentor completely removed himself from the setting and kept in touch with the teachers only as necessary. At this point in the study, the five teachers were truly autonomous and were using WISE enthusiastically as a department. Even the sixth teacher who had excused himself returned at the end of the year to inquire about authoring or customizing a WISE project that better matched his curriculum.

Differences Between Teachers

Although the discussion following focuses on the differences between two 7th-grade teachers, the six teachers were all seen to vary in the nature of their interactions with students as well as their flow of activities within a class period. Several of the teachers struggled with the misinterpretation of WISE as a "teacher-proof" computerized activity that students guided themselves through. Quite to the contrary, the classroom teacher is an essential part of the equation in fostering student inquiry. However, one teacher was even heard to utter, "This is great! I can just sit here and grade papers." Helping teachers revise such early conceptions of WISE was one of the more difficult matters for the mentor to address. Several of the teachers persisted in the belief that if the students are quiet and engaged, they do not need to be bothered, and the teacher can just make sure nobody is having any problems. The mentor responded to these ideas by trying to express the value of teachers playing an active role in student inquiry and how WISE offers teachers the opportunity to do so by scaffolding the class as a whole.

Teachers varied in the depth of their interactions with students as well as in the frequency of their whole-class interactions. Some teachers engaged deeply with individual students for several minutes at a time, whereas others cycled quickly through the class, stopping at each computer for just a second or two to check in on students' progress. One teacher interacted with students at such a deep level that she literally ignored the class as a whole, trusting that WISE was occupying them but never addressing the whole class. Another teacher addressed the whole class so frequently that students could never become truly focused on their project work. In general, such interactions are quite difficult to balance, and the majority of the mentor's feedback to teachers was in this area of expertise. Overall, it was found that teachers did not observably change their styles—those who were highly. interactive remained so, and those who were hands off remained hands off. Given feedback from the mentor, however, each individual teacher was able to adjust within their own style to improve their interactions with students.

SANDRA AND GILBERT: COMPARING SEVENTH GRADE LIFE SCIENCE TEACHERS

Two teachers in particular make an interesting case study for comparison because they teach in the same grade level (seventh), the same area (life science), and because they chose the same WISE projects to use in their courses. These teachers, pseudo-named Sandra and Gilbert, are also interesting because they differ quite dramatically in their inquiry practices. Our earliest interviews revealed that they approached their classes with different teaching styles and had different ideas about teaching with inquiry and technology. Although both are mature teachers with at least 5 years' experience in their school, neither proved exceptionally successful in using WISE on the first day, and we observed dramatic differences in their interactions with students. Interactions with the mentor also differed, leading to differential improvements in their professional development with WISE during the first and second years of the study. We chose these two teachers for the comparison study detailed following because they exhibited ideas about teaching and learning that are common to many teachers and because they both ultimately succeeded with WISE, drawing on different aspects of the mentoring and technology supports provided within this study.

Sandra is a veteran teacher with more than 10 years experience who prefers hands-on laboratories and loves to work closely with her students in small groups. Her life science course focuses on topics of animal and plant biology in close connection with the California state standards and a textbook chosen by her school district. She has traditionally made use of many hands-on laboratories in which students work individually or in small groups dissecting worms, examining cells under microscopes, and weighing plant material before and after different procedures. Many of her curriculum laboratories have been discovered at meetings of science teachers or through professional magazines. Sandra can be described as technology shy in the sense that she never used computers in her class curriculum and was unfamiliar even with her own classroom computer. Critiquing WISE, she commented on how it is difficult for her to read things from the computer screen and likes to have printed materials to grade. She was enthusiastic, however, about the connections that WISE projects make to current topics (e.g., the deformed frogs issue) and to materials on the Web. She was also excited about the use of science controversy as a source of curriculum and chose the Cycles of Malaria project and the Deformed Frogs projects partly for this reason.[1] Sandra insisted that she could never adopt WISE without the close assistance of a mentor and was highly receptive to feedback from the mentor, often soliciting advice.

Gilbert has less teaching experience than Sandra, although as chair of the science department was more involved in the details of this whole-school study and saw himself as a leader. His teaching style can be described as traditional with a focus on controlling the class and an authoritative role with his students. His syllabus was quite similar to that used by Sandra, as the two plan their curriculum together each year. Although Gilbert uses many of the same laboratory activities, and his classroom is filled with animals in cages and science toys, he devotes more time to lecture in his curriculum than Sandra, and his hands-on activities are characterized by a higher level of orderliness and control. Gilbert is slightly more technology savvy than Sandra, although he had never used technology in his instruction and rarely used his classroom computer except for a computerized grade book. He was enthusiastic about WISE because of its promise to bring an innovation to his department that would help to integrate technology into science instruction—a district-wide goal that was far from achieved within this particular school. Although Gilbert appreciated the achievements of the WISE mentor (who was a retired master teacher) and spoke to the importance of mentoring and professional development, he seldom interacted with the mentor and never sought advice on teaching with WISE.

To begin the year, all six teachers completed the WISE workshop, as well as a short 2-day WISE project called "Life on Mars" in which students explored evidence on both sides of a claim about a recently discovered meteorite from Mars. This short preliminary project served to introduce WISE to the students, helped get teachers and students registered, and allowed the mentor to model effective inquiry instruction. After all six teachers had run through the workshop and Life on Mars, they each ran a more substantial WISE project guided by the mentor as described previously. Both Sandra and Gilbert chose Cycles of Malaria for their first WISE project because it corresponded topically with their treatment of disease vectors. In the second (spring) semester, they both ran the WISE Deformed Frogs project because of its focus on science controversy and topical relevance. In the second year, they ran the same two projects again, which enabled us to contrast their practices as well as their student achievements. Because Cycles of Malaria was the first WISE project that was led by these two teachers (Life on Mars was quite short and led predominantly by the mentor), it provides a good lens into their inquiry teaching practices and the results as measured by their students' success on WISE assessments. We observed Sandra and Gilbert as they taught the WISE Cycles of Malaria project, carefully coding interactions with students and mentors and interviewing them before and after the project run. We analyzed student work in this project, using both preassessments, postassessments and embedded assessments that focus on knowledge integration measures. Because these two teachers ran the project again in the second year, we were able to look for indications of progress, particularly as reflected in student assessments. We can address any differences between the two teachers initially and then compare their progress. In the next section, I detail the Cycles of Malaria project and how students are assessed.

The Cycles of Malaria Project

In the Cycles of Malaria project, students debate three different approaches for controlling malaria worldwide: (a) developing of an effective pesticide that targets the anopheles mosquito, (b) developing a

vaccine against this disease, and (c) creating social programs that reduce exposure to mosquitoes (e.g., through distribution of bed nets or
community clean ups). Students explore evidence relating to each
control method and debate alternative approaches. Teachers in middle and high school biology and advanced placement biology have used
the project. To make thinking visible, the project includes animations
and video of the mosquito and parasite lifecycles as well as maps showing the worldwide incidence of malaria. To make the science debate
accessible to students, we included the story of Kofi, an African child
suffering from malaria, and teachers often made connections to more
personally relevant diseases in North America (e.g., HIV or sickle-cell
anemia). The project promotes autonomy and lifelong learning by encouraging students to compare scientific viewpoints, evaluate conflicting recommendations, and reflect on personal travel decisions. To
learn from others, students discuss their ideas with peers and engage
in class debates. Pivotal cases that help students learn about malaria
include comparisons between countries choosing to control use of
DDT with those discontinuing use. In these pivotal cases students look
at both infant mortality rates and data on the size of bird populations.
They use this pivotal case to interpret arguments in legislation calling
for a global ban of DDT.

To customize Cycles of Malaria, middle school biology teachers included field trips to local ponds or puddles to collect mosquito larvae.
More important, teachers were observed to practice various methods
of integrating the WISE curriculum with their existing materials and
syllabus. For example, a high school chemistry teacher elected to focus on the chemical compounds within the DDT pesticide and how
they impact the environment. In this way, teachers in diverse settings
and topic areas can provide their students with a meaningful implementation of the Cycles of Malaria project.

WISE Assessments: The Cycles of Malaria Project

WISE preassessments and postassessments challenge students to reflect and respond to complex problems. For example, before and after
Cycles of Malaria students are asked to apply concepts of vaccines, life
cycles, and disease vectors to novel situations and to solve problems
relating to travel and medical research. Students also evaluate applications to personally relevant situations (e.g., traveling to a foreign
country) and transfer of ideas to novel situations (e.g., advising a
small country on a pending law to clean up standing water around all
rural villages). Two example items are presented following with sam-

ple student responses. These responses are coded and scored in terms
of the number of connections made by students to other ideas and experiences as well as for any causal explanation that is contained within
the response. Such coding allows for a wide range of student achievement on each item:

> Preassessment and postassessment Item 1:
> A country is planning a law that would fine people for letting pud-
> dles or buckets of water stand around their property. Would this law
> slow down the spread of malaria? What is the main reason for your
> answer?
>
> Example student reflections:
> Yes this would slow the spread of malaria because it would keep
> mosquitoes away from the towns and make people clean up their
> mess [student with limited connection and missing or incorrect
> causal account].
>
> Yes, this would be a good law, because mosquitoes lay their eggs in
> puddles and buckets, so banning those would mean fewer mosquito
> larvae [student with substantial connections and accurate causal
> explanation].
>
> Preassessment and postassessment Item 2.
> What advice would you give to a friend who is planning a trip to a
> country where malaria is common?
>
> Example student reflections.
> I would tell him to keep away from people with malaria, always wear
> a face mask, and take a vaccine before he goes [student with lim-
> ited connections and erroneous causal account].
>
> I would say, always wear bug spray and keep inside at dusk when all
> the mosquitoes are coming out. Also, sleep under a bed net at night
> [student with accurate causal account and substantial connections].

Preassessment and postassessment items are coded for connections, correctness, and coherence of explanations and arguments.
Wearing a face mask (the first student) might be a connection to a
health-related idea, but it is an incorrectly held idea (face masks do
not prevent malaria) and is incoherent, as it is not causally connected
to the explanation.

Embedded assessments used within WISE projects include reflection notes, online discussions, drawings, causal maps, and graphically
outlined scientific arguments, among others. These assessments provide a measure of the project's impact on student understanding, providing helpful feedback to partnerships concerning their designs, to

our research studies, and to teachers concerning the ideas held by students throughout the activity. Reflection notes can be coded by researchers in terms of the connections students make to ideas within the project, the course, the news, or everyday experiences. In Fig. 9.2 following, students reflect on the dilemma of using the "Miracle Insecticide" DDT and whether it should be banned globally.

> We think DDT is a dilemma because it kills the mosquitoes but also harms the environment. So nobody can decide whether DDT should get used or not [student reflection with few connections].

> DDT was on the verge of wiping malaria off the Earth until Rachel Carlson published her famous novel *Silent Spring*. Then it was discovered that birds' egg shells were becoming too thin, as well as other environmental problems. So countries stopped spraying DDT and the environment began to recover, but so did the mosquitoes that carry malaria [student reflection with substantial connections].

These two examples illustrate how student reflections contain varying levels of connection to other ideas, concepts, and experiences. These reflections are coded to obtain a connections score for each student reflection note, which can then be used in analyses of student or teacher progress as described in the following sections.

Sandra and Gilbert: Inquiry Practices

We contrasted the adaptations of Cycles of Malaria made by Gilbert and Sandra in their first run of this project, focusing on curriculum adjustments, classroom presentation, and student interactions. The mentor had facilitated in their preparation for this project, although their unfamiliarity with WISE and with the specific content of Cycles of Malaria made it difficult for the teachers to adjust their overall curriculum effectively. Thus, the overall impression reported by both teachers during interviews was that the project did not fit well within their syllabus, and it was a stretch to make connections to the disease topics covered prior to the project. Neither teacher implemented any curriculum topics following WISE that would lead to further connections by their students. In general, the teachers both expressed some frustration at their inability to integrate WISE within their curriculum.

In their classroom presentation of WISE, the teachers made great efforts to emulate the model that had been demonstrated by the mentor. The mentor's style, developed over several years of efforts with WISE and previously with KIE and Computer as Learning Partner, in-

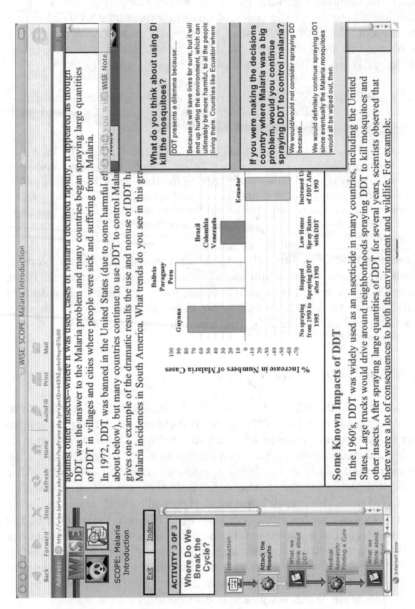

FIG. 9.2. Students' reflection.

222

volves a somewhat delicate blend of whole-class lecture, elicitation of student ideas, question and answer, and demonstration. Although Sandra and Gilbert made efforts to achieve a similar style, the results of their efforts were at times quite disparate from the model. In essence, both teachers added their existing style to the equation, knowing no other way to teach. This resulted in a fairly strong lecture component from Gilbert and a more interactive style from Sandra. The two styles differed markedly from that of the mentor, and observers frequently worried that students were not getting some of the important messages. For example, in introducing WISE, the mentor often coordinates a class discussion concerning the nature of scientific versus courtroom evidence and how the World Wide Web can be used as a source of evidence for one's arguments and designs. This leads to a discussion of critical evaluation in terms of source authority implicit motivations by Web authors. Such discussions were missing from Sandra and Gilbert, who struggled through the basic process of just getting their students logged on and working within WISE. Apparently, the challenges of implementing a new technology and curriculum innovation required some level of triage by teachers in terms of meeting the bottom line of getting students engaged with the program.

We carefully observed teacher interactions with the students, counting the number of separate occasions when a teacher stopped to discuss the WISE content with a pair of students. Many of these teacher–student interactions were focused on the science content, which was an area in which the teachers felt they had some strength. Some interactions were concerned with the WISE technology or with the nature of the inquiry task (comparing three different control strategies for Malaria). Generally, the length of a student–teacher interaction correlated with its depth. When a teacher paused only briefly at a pair of students' computer, the interaction was typically meant to just check in on them, see what they are doing, or let them know they are being watched. In contrast, more protracted interactions were generally focused on the inquiry topic. To even the casual observer, it was obvious that Gilbert preferred more cursory interactions, whereas Sandra engaged in lengthy discussions that could go on for several minutes. Indeed, a qualitative difference between the two teachers became quickly apparent, as Gilbert was usually seen constantly circulating among his students, making sure that everyone was on task, and Sandra was usually seen interacting deeply with one pair of students or another. This difference, illustrated by Fig. 9.3 following, led to separate concerns about the progress of students in each teacher's class. For Gilbert the concern was that students would miss out on the important aspects of teacher as a learning partner. For Sandra's class the concern was that she was spending too much time in personal interac-

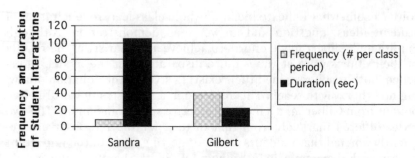

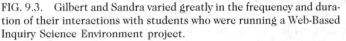

FIG. 9.3.   Gilbert and Sandra varied greatly in the frequency and duration of their interactions with students who were running a Web-Based
Inquiry Science Environment project.

tions with the students and never pulling back to summarize or synthesize her impressions.

Sandra and Gilbert: Student Learning

We explored the impact of the observed differences in teacher–student interactions by examining student work in the project. It seemed
likely that such noticeable differences in teacher practice would be reflected in student work on the projects. To our surprise, however,
there were no significant differences in students' scored responses to
these pretest and posttest items, as shown in Fig. 9.4. Apparently,
WISE Cycles of Malaria was fairly tolerant of differences in teaching
styles, as students in both classes made significant pretest and posttest gains, $F(1, 162) = 182.9$, $p = .0001$.

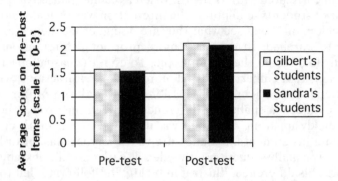

FIG. 9.4.   Students of Gilbert and Sandra showed nearly identical pretest and posttest score gains, suggesting that Web-Based Inquiry Science Environment "Cycles of Malaria" project is somewhat robust to
teacher differences.

In further investigating the possible impact of teacher differences on student achievement in WISE, we performed a more detailed analysis on the individual pretest and posttest items to look for possible differences between students in the two classes. Within the six-item test, three of the items were more focused on content-specific details. For example, Item 1 asks students, "How can I catch malaria?—a) by kissing, b) by mosquitos c) through shared needles d) by coughing." In contrast, the other three items were focused on knowledge integration, designed to challenge students as they apply the ideas within the project and extend their understanding. For example, Item 4 asks students what advice they would give to their friend who was planning a trip to a country where malaria is widespread.

The six test items are shown in Fig. 9.5 (collapsed across pretest and posttest scores), with Items 1 through 3 as the three content-focused items and Items 4 through 6 as the three knowledge integration items. Apparently, WISE assessments were sensitive to variations in teacher practice, as Sandra's students are seen to have an advantage over Gilbert's in the three knowledge integration items. Interestingly, Gilbert's students illustrated a greater attention to detail with a slightly better performance on the more factual items. In a repeated measures analysis of variance, this interaction of test items with teacher is significant, $F(5, 810) = 11.5$, $p < .0001$.

Another measure of the impact of teacher differences on student understanding is found in students' performance within the WISE project itself—particularly in the reflection notes taken by students during their WISE project work. These notes can be analyzed as de-

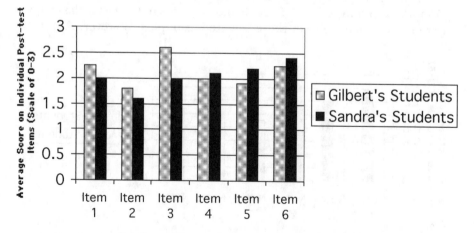

FIG. 9.5.   Comparison of scores on "Cycles of Malaria" project posttest show Sandra's students significantly outperform Gilbert's students on most conceptually challenging items.

scribed previously, coding each note in terms of the connections made by students to other ideas or content within the project. For example, when asked to reflect on the merits of developing a vaccine, a pair of students working together in Sandra's class observed the following (with connections underlined):

> We think that developing a vaccine is a good idea because it could create for the body an immunity in which people would not be infected by the parasites, even if they were bitten by an already infected mosquito. Also, it would be easy to make, easy to transport, and does not effect the environment. The overall price of the vaccines would also make the poorest countries be able to afford them. However, some of the problems with this solution are that scientists have not yet been able to create a really effective vaccine, although there was a vaccine in England that used DNA to prevent from getting infections such as malaria, it wasn't as effective as it needs to be. Scientists also are afraid that introducing new DNA may cause cancer for some people.

When such reflections were coded for a set of WISE notes, it was found that the two teachers' students differed dramatically in terms of the number and the coherence of connections they made within their reflections. For example, one pair of students working in Gilbert's class responded to the same prompt for reflection in the following way, with connections underlined: "We think that developing a vaccine is a good idea because it could protect everyone from the disease. However, some of the problems with this solution are it would take a long time and it would be very expensive." There were certainly students in Sandra's class who were less reflective and students in Gilbert's class who were more reflective than these selected examples. However, Fig. 9.6

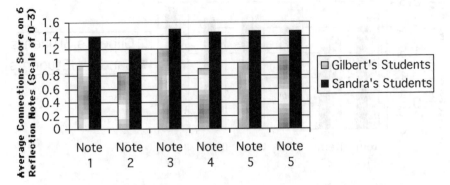

FIG. 9.6. Sandra's students are seen to reflect more deeply, making more connections to ideas within their embedded assessments than Gilbert's students.

shows dramatic overall differences between the students who worked on WISE in these two teachers' classes. Apparently, Sandra's depth of student interactions resulted in far more substantial reflection by her students than the relatively superficial interactions that Gilbert preferred.

Sandra and Gilbert: Comparing Progress from Year 1 to Year 2

In the second year of this study, both Sandra and Gilbert ran the Cycles of Malaria project again, allowing us to compare their efforts in the first and second years. From the start it was clear that the two teachers had made notable improvements in their use of WISE within the classroom. The benefit of having run this project before and the resulting comfort with WISE allowed the teachers to focus more on communicating with students about the science and inquiry processes. Additionally, both teachers were able to make substantial adjustments to their curriculum in this second year, adding a new focus on tropical disease that allowed them to foreshadow the Malaria project and provide greater context for their students. In interviews, both teachers said that one of the most important differences between Year 1 and Year 2 was the opportunity to tailor their curriculum so that it would complement the WISE materials. However, there remained observable differences in the style of interactions with students. Not surprisingly, both teachers retained their basic styles from one year to the next, with Sandra still preferring to spend most of her time working closely with one pair of students at a time and Gilbert preferring short, procedurally focused exchanges with students. Both teachers made some improvements, however, with Gilbert making greater efforts to communicate with his students about their science understanding and Sandra making an effort to pull back from one-on-one interactions and address the whole class.

Figure 9.7 shows the connections scores on student reflection notes in the teachers' first and second run of the WISE Cycles of Malaria project. Although differences between Sandra and Gilbert remained significant in Year 2, $F(1, 117) = 32.22$, $p < .0001$, both teachers made significant gains in this measure. In interviews following this second run, both Sandra and Gilbert described a much greater sense of ownership of the curriculum, a much higher comfort level with the technology, and a greater integration of WISE within their curriculum. Although some differences in classroom practice remained between these two teachers, the pattern of data shown in Fig.

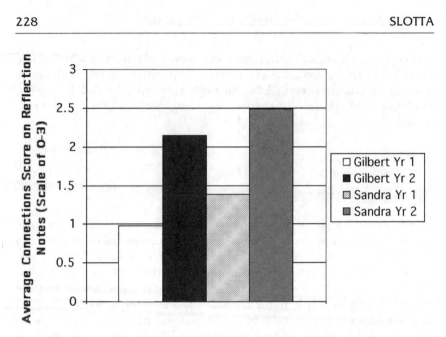

FIG. 9.7. Both teachers improved markedly from Year 1 to Year 2 in terms of their students' connections in the embedded assessments. The difference between the teachers is still present but diminished.

9.7 suggests that the WISE technology and mentoring process was able to scaffold their interactions with students, leading to a much richer set of student reflections. This result is satisfying given the fact that the WISE mentor had faded from the classroom completely during the second year of this study.

Conclusions From the Study of Sandra and Gilbert

This study has helped illustrate how diverse teaching approaches influence student learning outcomes and how curriculum designs can meet the needs of diverse teachers. It also demonstrated that WISE embedded assessments are sensitive to teaching style, as classes from the two teachers differed in their patterns of learning gains. The WISE Cycles of Malaria project was adopted successfully by Sandra and Gilbert, who had similar seventh grade life science curricula but quite different teaching styles. In the first WISE project run, the mentor was quite important to both teachers' success, and WISE proved to be robust in the sense that students in both classes showed evidence of knowledge integration as measured by preassessments and postassessments as well as embedded assessments. WISE professional development was also seen to be successful, as both teachers improved in their use of WISE from one year to the next, even with the fading of the mentor. This improvement was measured by the embedded assessment of coded reflection notes.

As a result of this study, we have gained important insight about the need for mentor participation, the role of WISE technology in the classroom, and the progress of teachers from one year to the next. We have continued to improve our support technologies for teachers in the classroom, our methods of dialoging with districts and school science departments, and the kinds of interactions we encourage between the mentor and the teacher. Additionally, we are continuously improving our WISE planning guides for teachers to create a customized lesson plan around a WISE project, including activities to precede and follow on the WISE unit itself. Through such research, we are also able to implement and observe the WISE curriculum and assessments in a much wider range of contexts, allowing us to improve our materials, support more diverse customizations, and document student learning gains.

FUTURE DIRECTIONS

WISE has proven to be an effective framework for inquiry curriculum in a broad range of science topics and student age groups. The study reported here suggests that WISE can accommodate teachers with diverse perspectives and styles while still preserving the desired inquiry experience for students. Our professional development model is well suited to implement in school district partnerships. Moreover, our authoring partnership model can support a wealth of different curriculum collaborations. This flexible foundation has given rise to several promising projects that I review in this section. In the SCOPE project, WISE provides the student learning environment technology platform and the pedagogical framework for partnerships of scientists to develop curriculum projects relating to current science controversies (see Bell, chap. 10, this volume). Another collaboration has been with the Synergy Communities For the Aggregation of Learning about Education project whose investigators are exploring how diverse educational research efforts can share their findings, materials, and technologies (see Baumgartner, chap. 11, this volume). WISE researchers are currently partnering with several other research groups who are developing new tools for water quality curriculum that run on the Web and hand-held devices (Slotta, Clark, et al., 2002).

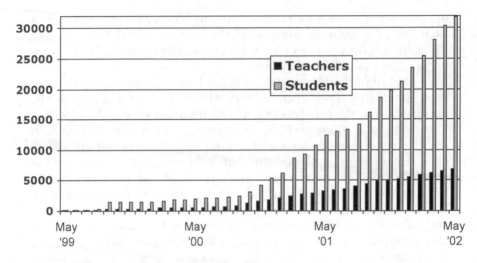

FIG. 9.8.   The number of Web-Based Inquiry Science Environment teachers and students over the past 3 years.

The number of teachers and students who have performed WISE projects has grown dramatically over the past 3 years (see Fig. 9.8). Although this growth demonstrates the ease with which motivated teachers can implement WISE, many of these teachers deserve mentoring to help them use WISE to its fullest advantage, and typically they lack support from their school or district. We must research the necessary professional development for scaling beyond these "maverick" teachers (Songer, 2000) to establish WISE as a scalable innovation for science instruction in whole schools and districts.

Building on the study described in this chapter, WISE has formed partnerships with several school districts to research the adoption of technology and inquiry innovations within a systemic context. These partnerships began with commitments from senior school district administrators to adopt WISE for inquiry science instruction. These districts have agreed to form a network of teachers supported with paid release time and mentored by a master teacher who is released from regular teaching duties to facilitate the adoption of WISE within the district. We will work closely with administrators from each district to align WISE projects to the relevant state science standards and district curriculum frameworks. Although the districts vary in their technology capacity, each is committed to supporting WISE with Internet connected computers for all participating teachers. These are typical, diverse districts, providing typical supports for the WISE program. Our ongoing research program will investigate the elements necessary for WISE to succeed in these districts.

ENDNOTE

1. These two WISE activities were both developed in partnerships by the SCOPE project, also funded by the National Science Foundation. SCOPE is investigating the role of controversy in science education and is described in detail in Bell (chap. 10, this volume).

10

The Educational Opportunities of Contemporary Controversies in Science

Philip Bell
University of Washington

In this chapter, I explore why teachers and students might wish to learn about current controversies in the natural sciences and how controversy fits into the goal of combining inquiry and technology to improve science learning. To this end, I provide an overview of the Science Controversies Online Partnerships for Education (SCOPE) project and focus specific attention on what the SCOPE research group has been learning through our research efforts about fostering virtual communities and developing controversy-focused learning opportunities.

The SCOPE project was a logical extension of the light debate research conducted as part of the Knowledge Integration Environment (KIE; see Bell, chap. 6, this volume, for details). The SCOPE research group sought to generalize the findings and curriculum design patterns for argumentation and debate. The project set out to connect directly and deeply into scientific communities. I detail the motivation for our approach and highlight design knowledge relevant to bringing scientific controversy into the classroom.

SCOPE is a National Science Foundation funded research collaboration among educational researchers at the University of California, Berkeley, and University of Washington, and editors from the journal *Science*. The SCOPE project effort is also directly coupled to its sister research project, the Web-Based Inquiry Science Environment (WISE; described by Slotta, chap. 9, this volume). Both WISE and SCOPE spun off of the parent KIE research effort. Whereas SCOPE continues to explore the educational possibilities associated with scientific controversy, we make use of and contribute to the development of the more general WISE approach to science inquiry instruction derived from the KIE learning environment and curriculum research.

RATIONALE FOR INQUIRY AND CONTROVERSY IN SCIENCE CLASSROOM

The United States successfully prepares large numbers of world leaders in scientific research, but international comparisons place our best 12th graders at or near the bottom in achievement (Schmidt, Raizen, et al., 1997). Citizens need better understanding of the science relevant to their lives, and science controversies offer great promise. In schools, the current curriculum in science is more decreed than designed, and these decreed curriculum materials rarely if ever discuss current or historical controversies in science. Most scientists spend their time working at the forefront of knowledge in which controversy in all of its forms is more the rule than the exception (Latour, 1998), but students rarely glimpse these aspects of science (Driver, Leach, et al., 1996). Instead, well-meaning individuals create goals, texts, and assessments that neglect controversies and are never subjected to the process of principled design.

High-level decisions about what should be included in school curricula often involve complicated trade-offs. Although we still have much to learn about the educational opportunities associated with contemporary scientific controversies, the benefits for inquiry learning are clear. First, a controversy focus makes the dynamic process of scientific advancement visible and provides contextualized windows on the intersection of science, technology, and society. This brings us to the second educational benefit. During scientific controversies, the contending parties frequently scrutinize each other's arguments and assumptions with extreme care (Brante, 1993). A focus on controversy aligns well with an instructional focus on student argumentation, debate, and active negotiation of meaning—educational forms that actively engage learners in knowledge integration while also having epistemic fidelity with science (see Bell, chap. 6, this volume). Third, learning about current scientific controversies can often be justified from the perspective of promoting more significant democratic participation in society because they frequently have noteworthy social and political relevance (see Martin & Richards, 1995, for a theoretical basis for this connection; see Cross & Price, 1996, for a description of educational issues). Fourth, framing instruction around current controversies allows students to develop an integrated understanding of scientific issues across the numerous contexts in which they experience them—in the classroom, on television and radio, in print media, on the Web, and in conversation (see Bell & Linn, 2001, for a more substantial discussion of this issue).

Of course, there are also potential drawbacks to a controversy approach. First, students might come to believe that all scientific progress occurs on a platform of contention or that work in the natural sciences is only about contention. Students should encounter a rich variety of epistemological influences on scientific advance. We should be astutely concerned about the image of science that becomes reified in curricula—although as educational designers we must make choices and basically essentialize some set of images. Second, the contentious demeanor of some controversies—especially those that are political in nature and have significant affective or ethical dimensions—might spill over into the social context of the classroom. We must guard against voices being marginalized in public and private contexts and from other assaults on fostering an equitable learning environment in the classroom while at the same time not ducking these topics in the curriculum. Third, given an even-handed educational treatment to complex controversies with multiple stakeholders and its coupling to an equitable classroom culture, we need to concern ourselves with the possibility that students might develop a radical relativistic epistemological stance to the issues—that all perspectives are equally valid. Fourth, current scientific controversies often hinge on nuanced theoretical and methodological points in the relevant disciplines, and they often make more sense embedded within the social and historical contexts of the work. There are significant challenges in helping students develop a generative understanding of these dimensions within the constraints associated with science education in formal public schooling.

This chapter explores these tradeoffs. It provides an overview of the progress made to date within the SCOPE research project on exploring the incorporation of a controversy approach in science instruction.

EDUCATIONAL ENCOUNTERS WITH IMAGES OF SCIENCE

In the information rich world, knowledge is a rare commodity. In most disciplines the creation of knowledge is a highly time- and resource-intensive endeavor. Most disciplines require its practitioners to train for years before they can reliably produce knowledge about the world that is relevant to the discipline. The research itself may also need to be conducted over long periods of time and involve substantial technological infrastructure and expertise. Needless to say, disciplinary knowledge is one of the most precious possessions of humankind.

The educational question becomes, How is it possible for students to develop an understanding of scientific knowledge? From the vantage point of a knowledge-transmission pedagogy, the educational endeavor would become one of clearly communicating the knowledge (and its applications) to each pupil, perhaps at increasing levels of complexity over the course of instruction. From this perspective, if we culturally value the periodic table of elements, we are obligated to carefully describe it and demonstrate its implications to learners. Straightforward presentation of the settled knowledge of a discipline serves as the dominant educational mode in our society. Many textbooks readily prove this point.

When I was in the seventh grade, I learned about the chemical elements for the first time (that I can recall). Over the course of a couple weeks, the science teacher instructed us to memorize the descriptive information for dozens of the elements—its name, abbreviation, atomic number, number of protons and neutrons, and even the approximated atomic weight. To be fair, there was also a fair amount of discussion about the characteristics of elements as well. However, the ultimate test of our understanding of this acquired knowledge (or information)—what counted from the perspective of students—was being able to quickly inscribe all of the data from memory onto a blank page in a 30-min test period. Now what view of the chemistry discipline did this lesson provide to students? It is not a very high fidelity one, for sure, even though the settled knowledge of the discipline had been carefully presented. I have often wondered how many students decided during this particular lesson that they did not want to intellectually pursue science (or chemistry in particular) because the nature of the work did not interest them.

Of course, this lesson actually had very little to do with inquiry in chemistry. I would later learn that teaching methods are rarely, if ever, neutral with regard to the structure and practices of the discipline involved (Schwab, 1978). That is, the methods of teaching subject matter—through lessons, assessments, the framing of driving questions, and so forth—need to bear some congruence with the nature of work in the parent discipline.

The now familiar call for inquiry approaches emphasize that students need to construct their own understanding of the world.[1] From these knowledge construction perspectives on instruction, students should be engaged directly in inquiry to conjecture, test, and refine their own knowledge about the world. Often this translates into having students construct the same settled knowledge of the discipline for themselves. Of course, this is often implemented as a series of inquiry projects in which students are presented with materials that appropriately constrain their activities to see the settled knowledge unfold before their eyes. Does scientific knowledge unfold in this manner? These approaches can make knowledge construction look deceptively straightforward and unproblematic, almost recipe-like. This is troublesome if we concern ourselves with the image of the discipline students develop through their engagement in inquiry. Of course we want students to realize that experiments can be used to confirm specific scientific knowledge, but such experiences do not typically represent the varied, uncertain, personality filled, passionate, circuitous, and contentious routes often associated with the initial construction of knowledge in science. Surely students do not have the time to recreate all of the important knowledge of a discipline (cf. Driver, Leach, et al., 1996)—let alone have time to explore all of the debates, side trips, and blind alleys associated with the history of a particular line of disciplinary inquiry—even those that were ultimately successful. However, I believe that it is a problem that students never see any of this broader context for inquiry or learn about its prevalence in day-to-day workings of scientific practice. What we are arguing for with the SCOPE project is that students can benefit from having more frequent encounters with how scientific understanding actually unfolds over time and how it intersects with the interests of society.

Various images of science epistemology have been posited for students in the research literature. Kuhn (1991) proposed a theoretical account for domain-general metacognitive development that shapes individual reasoning and the ability to construct and critique arguments. Koslowski (1996) described a science-specific manner by which individuals bootstrap their personal knowledge through experimentation and refinement of their thinking. Driver, Leach, et al. (1996) proposed an ideal model-based epistemology that depicts scientific knowledge construction as disciplinary, highly social, and focused on inquiry into tentative and conjectural knowledge. Bell and Linn (2001) argued that students' epistemologies are disciplinary specific in significant measure, often fragmented (rather than uniform, coherent, or stage-like), and shaped by the ecology of their numerous interactions with science throughout their lives (in both formal and informal learning contexts). From the knowledge integration perspective, a student's ability to understand scientific advancement and any associated controversy hinges both on knowledge of the particulars at hand and about the epistemic practices of the discipline.

Realistically, do students ever get to see depictions of science that allow them to develop an integrated understanding of inquiry in science? On average, only 1 page out of 100 in the typical science textbook even alludes to scientific understanding having changed over time (Champagne, 1998)—let alone that it was perhaps a controversial or convoluted process. Such a conservative and overly static depiction of the nature of science in formal instruction must surely confuse students and other nonscientists who regularly view the controversial dimensions of science in other parts of their lives (cf. Collins & Shapin, 1986). In stark contrast to the "settled knowledge" pedagogical approach, students see knowledge from research being reported, frequently debated, and regularly overturned in the mainstream press. In addition, they are likely to come across diverse and contradictory information on the Web on science topics. They might read rich, historical accounts of scientific pursuits that describe the social, technological, and historical context of scientific discovery. Perhaps some of them even talk to professional scientists who relay stories about the exciting, competitive, and dynamic nature of science. We seek to help students develop an understanding of science in the making (cf. Latour, 1987) in corresponding intellectual, cultural, and historical contexts—as understanding unfolds and intersects with the interests of society.

IMAGES OF SCIENTIFIC CONTROVERSY

It is important to realize that the nature of controversy in the natural sciences is by no means uniform. There are many sources for and manifestations of scientific controversy. The term *controversy* (derived from the Greek *controversus*) literally means "the clash of opposing opinions; debate; disputation" (Brante, 1993, p. 181). We can expect there to be generative as well as debilitating entailments of these controversial dimensions of science. Enduring disputes can find periods of consensual understanding. Numerous stakeholders can be given public voice to detail different perspectives. Disparate communities can be brought together in multidisciplinary collaboration to make progress on complex problems. Temporary solutions might be adopted while additional analysis takes place. Conjectural insights might have to be wrestled out of data sets that are necessarily imperfect due to ethical overrides. Complex, systemic solutions might be designed and put in place for multifaceted, real-world problems. Moral oversight of scientific work might be mandated. Discrete policy decisions might have to be enacted based an exploration of known trade-offs. New technologies might be applied to the enduring or emergent problems of society. Regulatory differences for science and technology across nation states might be investigated and better understood. New lines of research with profound ethical implications might have to be pursued before the beneficial possibilities for such work are understood.

A guiding assumption for our research is that students should be provided with educational opportunities to learn about these various forms of scientific controversy. Without a sophisticated epistemological understanding of controversy, the public manifestations of these disputes are likely to look perverse and arbitrary.

As a global society, people also lack sources of information about complex scientific controversies and opportunities to interact with controversial issues. Mainstream press science articles often neglect detail or leave out evidential bases. Relevant educational experiences are more the exception than the rule. Balanced journalism can lead to overly dichotomized depictions of a muddled issue.

Even practicing scientists need a better understanding of current scientific controversies, as they are prominent stakeholders in such issues. We can frame learning opportunities as occurring both inside and outside of a controversy. As an insider to a controversial endeavor, scientists can develop new approaches for accomplishing their work or for communicating it to external audiences. When scientists are outsiders of a particular controversy, there are educational opportunities associated with understanding the nature and basis of contention. Scientists can also play unique roles in interpreting controversial issues for nonscientific audiences. In SCOPE, we have frequently called on scientists in this way to serve as "controversy docents" in our educational design efforts.

How might we approach educating students about such complex issues? Internet technologies that allow for sustained information pooling and organization, social interaction, and knowledge networking can theoretically augment traditional print communication in productive and novel ways. To some degree, this has been happening in online spaces for several years. The SCOPE project has been exploring such approaches as will become clear later in the chapter.

PROVIDING CONTROVERSIAL IMAGES OF SCIENCE TO STUDENTS

In a recent volume about the pressing issues of educational research, Bruner (1999) framed the central mission of the field:

The master question from which the mission of education research is derived: What should be taught to whom, and with what pedagogical object in mind? That master question is threefold: what, to whom, and how? Education research, under such a dispensation, becomes an adjunct of educational planning and design. It becomes design research in the sense that it explores possible ways in which educational objectives can be formulated and carried out in the light of cultural objectives and values in the broad. (p. 408)

This framing of the educational research enterprise can help us question the lurking epistemological forces and the underlying assumptions found in traditional science instruction. The argument I advance focuses on how citizens of the world can develop a powerful integrated understanding of science from being taught about the controversial nature of work in the natural sciences. We focus not on controversy for its own sake, but rather we wish to bring some clarity to the issues surrounding scientific knowledge generation and application. To that end, we seek to engineer approaches that allow for a heightened representation of science controversy in the science curriculum for that purpose.

Joseph Schwab was one of the earliest proponents of inquiry-focused science instruction. Schwab (1962) stated that science was too commonly taught as

... a nearly unmitigated rhetoric of conclusions in which the current and temporary constructions of scientific knowledge are conveyed as empirical, literal, and irrevocable truths (in which students are asked) to accept the tentative as certain, the doubtful as undoubted, by making no mention of reasons or evidence for what it asserts. (p. 24)

Focusing on controversies is one way to make the "temporary constructions" (Schwab, 1962, p. 24) of science visible and meaningful to students. At a high level, the view of science controversy we are building on includes two separate strands of epistemic action: (a) how scientific inquiry and understanding unfold over time amongst researchers and provide insight into the workings of our natural world and (b) how science and technology interface with the venues of the broader society. Brante (1993, p. 181) referred to these two forms as *scientific controversy* and *science-based controversy*, respectively. Part of our research focus is to push further on our understanding of the nature of scientific controversy itself (e.g., Hines, 2001). As our SCOPE research program continues to unfold, this further refines our view of what we seek to teach.

The specific educational audience should influence how a controversy gets framed or presented instructionally. The cultural values and priorities of one community might be significantly different than those of another around a specific controversy; this should inform what aspects of the controversy we bring to those communities. Considering an example might help make this point. Consider the controversial aspects of using DNA forensic technologies for the illumination and possible remediation of human rights abuses. Even more specifically, consider how such technologies could shed light onto acts of genocide in war-torn countries. The educational focus one might imagine for the residents and, in particular, the victims in that country (e.g., what might be learned through the application of DNA technologies; how do we balance the information to be gained versus the inherent risks to privacy as genetic information is surrendered) are quite different than what might be the focus for students outside of that country (e.g., what the DNA analysis tells us about what transgressions took place). As described in chapter 4 (Bell, Hoadley, & Linn, this volume), our view is that innovations are culturally embodied within specific communities and that we need design methods that address this complexity.

Selecting Images of Science

Inquiry in the natural sciences offers many, although partial, images of science. The history and philosophy of science generate accounts of science epistemologies, norms, and processes that have been used to inform science instruction (as is the case with the instruction studied in Hatano & Inagaki, 1991). These perspectives have frequently been rationalist philosophical accounts of scientific progress, resembling the straightforward and unproblematic approaches described earlier. Over the last 2 decades, social studies of science have provided detailed, relatively systematic, and nonpartisan accounts of scientific practice along with depictions of scientific cultures and subcultures (cf. Biagioli, 1999; Jasanoff et al., 1995). This research has explored the nature of science frequently from a social constructivist epistemology of everyday practice. These various lines of inquiry document a plurality of scientific practice and epistemic action. A uniform depiction of the nature of science seems increasingly wrong-headed and indefensible in light of these empirical studies. This pluralist perspective on the nature of science has far-reaching implications for science education. In particular, it becomes increasingly suspect to be presenting students with monolithic depictions of a scientific method or other aspects of science—all specific forms should be situated in the broader context of the diversity of scientific inquiry.

This realization leaves us with a number of unresolved issues. First, images of science should take precedence for a broad audience of young science learners (if one takes them as a reasonable audience to start with). Which images of science are the most generative for citizens who may or may not elect to pursue a career in science? As part of our continuing quest to identify appropriate priorities for science education, we need to develop a mapping between the unfolding images of science and the specific manner in which they might be useful to the citizens at large—in terms of individualistic as well as collective outcomes. This educational dimension has not typically been part of the program of research of the scholars who study the natural sciences.

Second, once we identify coherent images of science to bring to students, what are the appropriate educational approaches for doing so? Science learners are not scientists. It is counterproductive to unfurl all of the complexities of the frontiers of science to students as any kind of default educational approach. We need to find intermediate or iterative approaches that help students increase their understanding of the plurality of science and continue to build on their prior understandings (cf. Smith et al., 1994). In a related manner, how do we help students develop a coherent view of what inquiry in the natural sciences is about over the course of a student's educational experience? How many different forms of inquiry should they experience and learn about in depth?

Not only have analytical endeavors that document the nature of science become more common, but also the nature of scientific inquiry is radically changing in and of itself (e.g., Keller, 2002). New forms of computational inquiry are becoming increasingly common in science disciplines (e.g., Chong & Ray, 2002; Kitano, 2002). Interdisciplinary research—in such fields as astro-biology or bioengineering—are successfully providing novel insights about the natural world and technological advances. In addition, there is evidence that science is continuing to become increasingly connected to the commercial and political sectors. All of these changes to the nature and purposes of science need to be contemplated from the perspective of identifying educational priorities for science instruction.

DESIGNING INQUIRY PROJECTS ABOUT CONTROVERSY—THE SCOPE PROJECT

As we were conducting the KIE research focused on getting students to engage in argumentation and debate about the nature of light (Bell, chap. 6, this volume), we realized that the instructional approach would work more generally with educational treatments of controversies in science. We established a research collaboration with the editors at *Science* magazine (at the American Association for the Advancement of Science) and focused on exploring the educational possibilities associated with current controversies using Internet technologies.

In a nutshell, we wanted to explore how science and education communities could be bridged to support improved understanding of complex, multidisciplinary, contemporary controversies in science. To this end, SCOPE has been building educational initiatives involving diverse groups of stakeholders and science educators interested in specific controversies including the global decline in amphibian populations (with most of this work being focused on deformed frogs in North America), approaches to the treatment and control of malaria, and the risks and benefits of genetically modified food (GMF). Engagement with each of these topics has allowed us to implement and study a range of approaches with emerging network-based software environments and educational approaches that support collective knowledge networking and individual knowledge integration. In the sections that follow, I briefly describe the three main controversies, the approaches we have explored, and some of what we have been learning about helping students learn about these controversies.

Another strand of SCOPE research, beyond the focus of this chapter, is analyzing what we have learned about providing network-based interaction and information pooling technologies to professional scientists, other stakeholders, and classroom teachers (Fischer-Fortier & Bell, 2003). This research complements the controversy learning research in that it significantly informs the educational approach taken in our curriculum projects and classroom instruction.

The three controversy contexts SCOPE has explored thus far have many unique epistemological dimensions and educational features. For each topic, I summarize the controversy, the educational opportunities and the approach that has been explored, and the design knowledge that has been identified through our research. I begin the exploration by revisiting the mysterious increase in frog deformities found across the United States.

Deformed Frogs in North America

Over the past 10 years there has been a dramatic increase in the relative frequency of malformations in frog populations in certain locations in North America. The underlying basis for this increase is still being investigated. Leading hypotheses focus on a parasite that might be becoming more prevalent, environmental pollutants, an increase in ultraviolet radiation, or a combination of these causes. In terms of scientific controversies, the deformed frog mystery represents a relatively bounded scientific controversy in Brante's (1993) sense of the term. There is a surprising phenomenon and scientists are pursuing competing theoretical accounts that might explain the situation. The deformed frog issue is one small, relatively coherent facet of the more complex issue surrounding the largely unexplained decline of amphibian populations around the world.

Deformed frogs is a generative topic for students to investigate because it is a pressing environmental and wildlife stewardship issue they find compelling, and the scientific concepts and topics implicated in the issues and evidence are central to understanding biology more generally—animal development, hormones and hormone mimics, ecosystems, parasitic relationships, and life cycles. At the penultimate point in our design and research activities associated with KIE, we focused our attention on helping kids understand the deformed frog controversy (as described in detail in Shear, Bell, & Linn, chap. 12, this volume). This effort would become the pilot work for the SCOPE project. The topic fit our selection criteria at the time in that it focused on a timely debate in science that was at the same time manageable in size; it aligned with the classroom learning goals of our collaborating teachers; it leveraged the expertise of the natural scientists involved in the partnership; and perhaps most important, it was a topic that was genuinely compelling to our middle school students as well as the adults (see Fig. 10.1).

Inquiry into the deformed frog issue has been a multidisciplinary pursuit in that scientists are investigating issues of organism development (at the cellular and macrocellular levels), environmental system dynamics, and chemical resemblance and transformation. This multidisciplinarity allows the deformed frog topic to serve as a viable focus for multiple courses in the kindergarten through 12th grade science curriculum (life sciences, environmental science, chemistry, and general science). It also poses a challenge in terms of needing students to coordinate multiple disciplinary views to more holistically understand the fabric of the controversy.

As detailed in chapter 12, we convened a partnership of educational researchers, classroom science teachers, natural scientists, and technologists that worked to render KIE curriculum that would bring students into an investigation of the evidence and claims being made about the deformed frog situation. The result was a 4-week curriculum sequence involving observations of tadpoles developing into frogs, analysis of a popular newscast about the topic, web-based curriculum projects in which students investigated the evidence scientists were

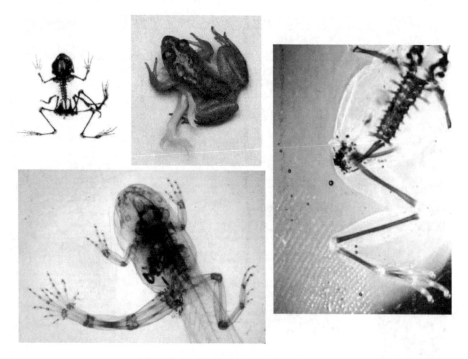

FIG. 10.1. Typical frog deformities.

working with, a frog dissection that highlighted aspects of frog anatomy and development, and a field investigation in which students learned about the habitat of frogs. The curriculum projects focused on the nature of the controversy and each of the two leading hypotheses being explored by scientists (about parasites called *trematodes* and about the risks of environmental chemicals—shown in Fig. 12.1 in Shear et al., chap. 12, this volume). The partnership also authored interview protocols and written assessments to better understand how students were thinking about the topic and the underlying science. Such information provided valuable feedback for further refining the curriculum materials.

The deformed frogs curriculum projects, originally developed in KIE, have been translated and kept up to date as part of the SCOPE curriculum library (made available in the WISE format). SCOPE has also launched an online forum about the declining amphibian controversy. The forum is a self-moderating collection of information about the declining amphibian problem (see Fig. 10.2). This controversy forum houses the latest versions of the deformed frog curriculum sequence and collects together references and news items related to the topic.

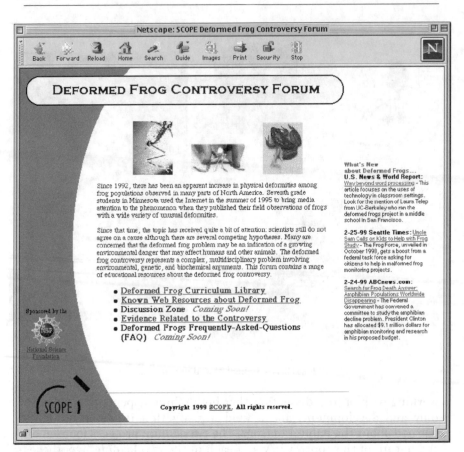

FIG. 10.2.   The Science Controversies Online Partnerships for Education
(SCOPE) declining amphibian forum.

Design Principles Emerging From
the Deformed Frogs Project

Three primary design principles resulted from our initial work in
the deformed frogs topic.

***Highlight the Evidentiary Basis of Contemporary Scientific Con-
troversies.***   The deformed frog topic allowed students to learn about
a science issue that was an active area of scientific publication. The research was also receiving significant coverage in the popular press,
also increasing its relevance to students. The original KIE approach of
engaging students with the evidence of science was brought to focus
here on a contemporary debate in science—a focus that has been
maintained by subsequent SCOPE efforts. We seek to make the evi-

dentiary basis of science approachable and informative to nonscientists. This does require specific scaffolding to help students understand issues of experimental method, the underlying conceptual basis, and the relevance to the controversy. Beyond that, we develop evidence that depicts the data associated with scientific inquiry and ask students to construct a critical understanding of it.

Paint an Overview and Then Curricularly Isolate the Hypotheses Associated With the Controversy. SCOPE has pursued a curricular model for the Internet investigations that started with this early deformed frog work. We begin by establishing the context of the controversy. We then invite students to explore each of the significant hypotheses associated with the controversy and its associated evidence. This curriculum design pattern for a controversy project provides students with a way to wed the context of the controversy to a more detailed understanding of the scientific perspectives within the topic.

Create Coherent Curriculum Design Patterns That Conjoin First-Hand Scientific Investigations With Internet Inquiry of Relevant Scientific Evidence and Data. The practices of natural scientists are more diverse than what is typically included in the science curriculum. At the risk of essentializing the nature of science, we want students to recognize that scientists frequently engage in: empirical experimentation, significant interaction with their colleagues, reading and critique of the primary (and secondary) literatures, and formal and informal professional activities. With SCOPE, we are exploring the educational opportunities associated with a more ecologically grounded and multifaceted depiction of inquiry in science. The 4-week deformed frog sequence included a blend of first-hand inquiry, engagement with rich depictions of the scientific literature, and social activity structures focused on the construction and debate of meaning. Such sequences allow for students to develop a more holistic view of complex controversies while allowing them to develop an understanding of specific dimensions of the relevant topics.

Treatment and Control of Malaria

A second SCOPE controversy focuses on malaria. There is evidence to suggest that malaria has been plaguing humankind over the span of recorded history. Between 300 and 500 million individuals become infected with the disease each year, and between 2 and 3 million people die from malaria each year—most of whom are children under 5 years of age. Why is it that we have not yet been able to eradicate this disease (as we have others)? What is known about the complex lifecycle of the parasite and the transmission vector for the disease, or how resistance develops to antimalarial medications? What preventive strategies are viable, effective, and affordable for nations and communities around the globe? How can some of the poorest nations control the spread of this ravaging disease within their populations largely without the help of the richest nations in the world? These issues frame some of the terrain associated with this disease.

As the SCOPE project was working on the malaria topic, a controversial decision to globally ban DDT was being explored by the United Nations Environmental Program. Spraying DDT is one of the primary malaria prevention strategies in 22 developing nations, and yet there are numerous environmental and human health risks associated with DDT.

Because malaria represents a compelling global crisis with multidisciplinary research, prevention, and treatment efforts always underway, there are a multitude of dimensions related to the disease that might become an educational focus. We started in SCOPE by launching an online forum for researchers and field practitioners whose work focuses on malaria (see Fig. 10.3). The malaria forum provided a venue for scientists to communicate and learn about various aspects of work being conducted related to malaria.

The SCOPE malaria forum provided a mechanism by which the SCOPE team could author web-based curriculum projects about various dimensions of work currently taking place about the disease. The SCOPE "Cycles of Malaria" project provides students with an overview of the nature and impact of the disease along with a range of prevention methods being pursued. This project serves as an entry point for further exploration of the issue through other curriculum projects (see Fig. 10.4). The spread of malaria in local sites is modulated by a number of interrelated factors. An educational computer simulation was developed by Margaret Corbit to help students understand the salience of particular factors and the systems dynamics associated with malaria transmission. Research is focused on how students can learn from complex, dynamic simulations of realistic scenarios.

There are two versions of the SCOPE "Global Ban of DDT" project that we have developed and studied—one has a human physiology focus and is for students in life sciences courses and the other highlights aspects of chemistry associated with the issues and is intended for use in high school chemistry classrooms. In the DDT projects, students explore evidence about what is known about the negative impacts of DDT on the environment and human health. They also learn how DDT is being used and can be used more efficiently to pre-

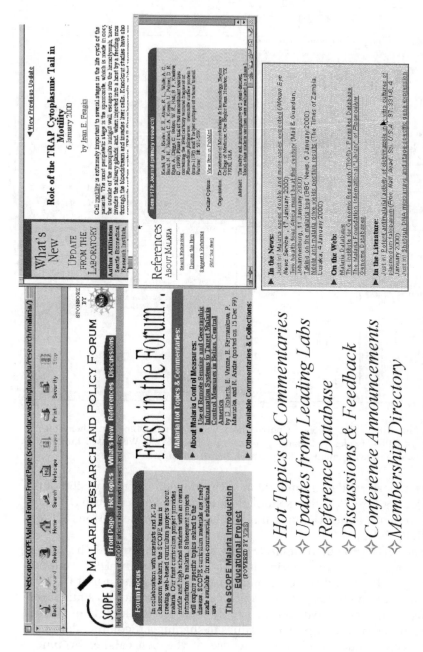

FIG. 10.3.   The Science Controversies Online Partnerships for Education (SCOPE) malaria research and policy forum.

249

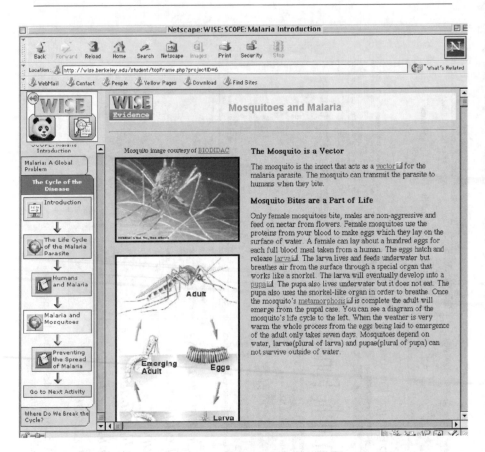

FIG. 10.4. The Science Controversies Online Partnerships for Education (SCOPE) "Cycles of Malaria" project (developed in the Web-Based Inquiry Science Environment [WISE] learning environment).

vent malaria while minimizing negative impacts. In the version of the project tailored for high school chemistry, students use the DDT context to learn about the meaning of chemical representations (Owens & Bell, 2002).

The DDT project ultimately asks students to explore the ethical trade-offs between protecting human life (by spraying DDT) and protecting wildlife and the environment (by banning the use of DDT). It represents a complex political and scientific issue with no simple solutions. Students are called on to apply their understanding of the science along with their personal values in shaping a recommendation on this policy issue. Students make use of the SenseMaker argument mapping tool to support them in framing out an argument about the DDT ban controversy (see Fig. 10.5).

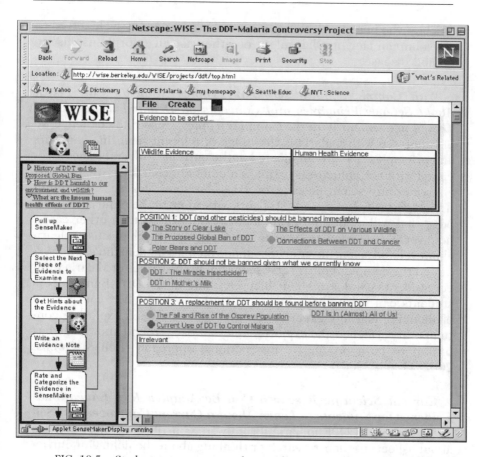

FIG. 10.5.   Student argument created using the SenseMaker tool about the proposed ban of DDT.

Design Principles Emerging From the Malaria Project

Five primary design principles resulted from our research on the malaria topic.

Case Studies That Highlight the Human Face of a Controversy Can Promote the Salience and Relevance of the Topic to Students.   One of the challenges about asking many science students to learn about malaria is that it is a disease that they are relatively unlikely to encounter in their everyday experience (with notable exceptions). This presented us with a problem of how to make the malaria topic compelling and salient to the broad distribution of students we wanted to learn about the disease. We decided to start the introductory Cycles of Malaria project with a compelling case study of a boy who becomes inflicted with malaria. It productively served to put a human face on what might be otherwise an amorphous, disembodied disease.

With Complex, Multidisciplinary Topics Students Can Learn About Science Principles and Concepts on Demand in Service of Their Engagement With the Complex Topic. A second challenge we encountered with malaria is the range of relevant scientific concepts and principles that are implicated in the current work and issues associated with the controversy. This is a common characteristic of many contemporary scientific controversies. To some degree, curriculum design patterns can provide students with some of the requisite knowledge that will come up during a curriculum project. In other cases, however, we decided to provide students with mechanisms to learn about related scientific concepts and principles on demand as they explored the complex controversy scenario. In the Cycles of Malaria project students can learn about lifecycles, and in the DDT Ban projects students can learn about biomagnification. Although it can lead to challenging learning experiences, this dance between exploring contemporary evidence and exploring relevant background knowledge has proven to be a productive instructional approach (Bell & Owens, 2002; Owens, 2001).

Current Scientific Research Can Be Adapted Into Educational Evidence for Students to Learn About a Current Controversy. Scientists in the SCOPE malaria forum were contributing short articles about aspects of their research or thinking about the field. Our curriculum design approach was to adapt these scientific articles into pieces of evidence used in curriculum projects. In this way, students were learning about more recent developments in science than what is typical. We are also able to conceptually scaffold their engagement with the scientific research so they can develop a better understanding of it. This coordination of educational depictions of scientific research is a process that could be employed more broadly to help students learn about new developments in science.

Curriculum Projects in a Sequence Should Be Topically Segmented to Promote Disciplinary Engagement in Aspects of a Controversy. With multidisciplinary topics, our first impulse was to try and attend to multiple disciplinary strands within a single curriculum project (e.g., environmental science, chemistry, and social behavior). However, what often happened is that students would idiosyncratically focus on particular disciplinary issues and not others. Granted that in some educational contexts, this would be a desirable outcome, but in other contexts (e.g., a high school chemistry class), the desire is for students to learn about one discipline even though they are exploring a multidisciplinary topic. We have found that we can better promote disciplinary engagement in issues in such a context by segmenting curriculum projects around a disciplinary perspective rather than having multiple disciplinary strands running through all of the projects. For example, if students are learning about the proposed DDT ban in a chemistry class, it is helpful to focus their engagement on chemistry issues in one or more of the curriculum projects. Other projects in the sequence can focus on the other disciplinary perspectives.

Multidisciplinary Inquiry Into a Complex Controversy Can Promote Student Perspective Taking. There are competing theoretical understandings of the proposed DDT ban controversy. By having students develop an understanding of various disciplinary perspectives, they can come to understand the perspectives of various stakeholders associated with a contemporary scientific controversy. Still, this is a nontrivial educational undertaking in that many perspectives require significant grounding and invoke complex aspects of expertise.

GMF

A third SCOPE controversy centers on GMF. Recombinant DNA (rDNA) technologies now allow for crops to be precisely designed in an unprecedented manner. Genes from one species that are associated with specific, desirable traits can be inserted into the DNA of existing crop species (see McHughen, 2000, for an introductory overview of issues). Rather than having available crop varieties rest on the random crossing procedures associated with traditional plant hybridization processes, plants can be more systematically engineered. Many farmers applaud the new crop varieties that can actively resist the negative influences of disease, environment, and insects. However, these technological possibilities are not without substantive resistance, critique, and concern. Some individuals invoke a moral imperative that humans should not be "playing God" by creating transgenic species that would never have come about in nature. Others argue that humans do not yet know if we can control the spread of genes once the new crops are introduced into the highly interconnected ecosystem (Rifkin, 1998). Some believe that the anti-GMF sentiments in North America and Europe might impede the use of transgenic crops and end up most strongly impacting the populations of the developing nations who have the most to gain from these advancements. Consumers and environmentalists have urged for labeling of food products containing GMF, whereas others have stated that it would be too costly a practice. Scientists righteously argue that drought resistant and nutritionally enhanced plants can be designed for use in developing nations where the needs are paramount; social scientists have observed that such technological advancements are unlikely to substantially impact the entrenched conditions that reinforce starvation and poverty in these parts of the world.

The development of a new transgenic crop variety is a painstakingly arduous process and the companies engaged in this work argue that their intellectual property needs to be protected for them to protect their substantial investment and to promote further innovation. Critics of these global multinational companies worry that farmers will become financially "addicted" to the new varieties, ending an age-old agricultural tradition of planting the seeds collected from one's last crop—which could become an illegal practice in many situations with the GMF seeds. At a pragmatic level, many wonder if the products of rDNA technologies are healthy and safe to consume. Are they going to increase the risks to individuals who have specific food allergies? Are current regulatory processes at the Food and Drug Administration and Department of Agriculture sufficient to provide oversight to the impacts on our food production system? In short, the technology is surrounded with controversy and with possibility.

What should students (and the public at large) know about genetically modified foods? Unless people take extraordinary care with their food selection, they are regularly consuming transgenic crops that have been engineered as part of their daily diet. For example, 60% of all soya crops grown are GMF varieties; soya is an ingredient found in many daily products (e.g., flour, oil). How do we help students come to understand the social and scientific issues associated with GMF? How do we help them wade through the entrenched pro and con positions that typically appear as ideologically driven soundbites and rhetoric? How can we help them make informed decisions about this new technology when there can be no absolute guarantees as to its safety?

Students and teachers find the GMF topic to be personally compelling and relevant. As with the malaria topic, with GMF we are presented with a highly multidimensional and complex collection of topics and issues. We launched an online forum focused on crucial aspects of the GMF controversy intended to serve as an educational home for GMF on the Web (see Fig. 10.6). Our curricular approach has been to develop and study a palette of curriculum projects that fo-

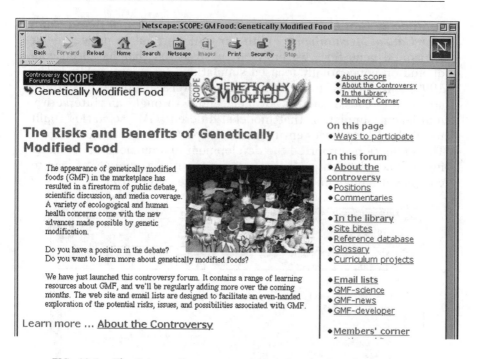

FIG. 10.6. The Science Controversies Online Partnerships for Education (SCOPE) forum on genetically modified foods.

cus on different dimensions of the controversy. Students can learn about the new possibilities associated with the application of rDNA technologies to agriculture (Seethaler, 2002). They can explore the causal factors and possible implications associated with the horizontal flow of genes from transgenic crops to their wild species once GMF crops are introduced into the fields, or they can explore how nutritionally enhanced crops can be used to prevent disease and other results of malnutrition. SCOPE research has focused on core aspects of these issues related to GMF: how students understand the distinctions between agricultural practices and the meaning of the term *natural* (Seethaler, 2002) and how students marshal evidence during classroom debates in ways that demonstrate an understanding of the issues (Havelock & Bell, 2001).

Design Principles From the GMF Topic

At this time two primary principles resulted from our research on the genetically modified food topic.

Students Can Use Interactive Simulations to Learn About Complex Causal Mechanisms.   With our GMF curriculum project about horizontal gene flow, we built on the research that has been conducted on conceptually focused simulations (or microworlds; Foley, 1999; Snir, Smith, et al., 1993). Students were supported in learning about the causal factors of gene flow through an interactive, multiagent simulation that modeled different GMF scenarios (built using the AgentSheets environment, http://www.agentsheets.com/). The simulation supported the development of a nuanced understanding of how selection pressures associated with specific genes lead to complex dynamics in aggregate systems (see Fig. 10.7).

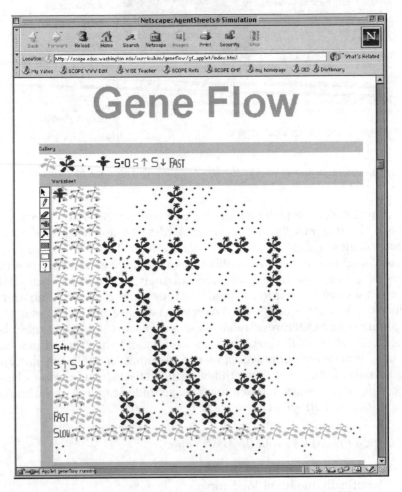

FIG. 10.7.   The Science Controversies Online Partnerships for Education (SCOPE) gene flow multiagent simulation.

Debate Activities Associated With Complex, Multidisciplinary Issues Can Productively Identify Areas for Further Learning and Intellectual Inquiry. In our controversy projects, we have often used collaborative, whole-class debate activities as a culminating activity by which students exchange and discuss their varying interpretations of the evidence and the substantive issues of the controversy. Our work with the GMF topic led to the curricular implication that debate activities involving such complex, multidisciplinary and multistakeholder topics can be used to have students bring up a range of new educational topics and learning opportunities.

The debate becomes a means of identifying subsequent topics for learning and intellectual inquiry. It is difficult to predict the range of topics that students might bring up given the possible range associated with the GMF controversy. This leads to an educational implication that can be difficult to come to terms with on the fly: How can we support students' emergent interests in a pedagogically appropriate way and in an intellectually honest manner? This is an educational tension that we continue to explore in our research. This design principle provides an excellent example of the localized nature of educational design knowledge. That is, the collaborative debate activity structure works well as a culminating activity when there is a solitary disciplinary issue at hand (Bell, 1998), but it doesn't do the same educational work, as it were, when used with a multidisciplinary, multistakeholder topic.

IMPLICATIONS FOR TEACHING ABOUT SCIENTIFIC CONTROVERSY

I identify three elements of teaching about controversy. First, because science knows no national boundaries and most modern scientific problems span disciplinary boundaries, scientists need to engage in international collaboration. The solution of global environmental problems as well as the complexity of problems at the frontiers of knowledge increasingly require international and multidisciplinary collaboration. SCOPE has been developing tools and mechanisms to foster effective global communication about current scientific controversies.

Practical problems and technological opportunities rarely fit in specific scientific disciplines. An interdisciplinary approach is needed to address environmental problems, explore the implications of new scientific advances (e.g., in genomics), incorporate technological breakthroughs into diverse contexts, and design educational programs.

Most current modes of communication (professional meetings, campus colloquia, journals) support established disciplinary interaction. SCOPE has been designing tools intended to open the community to multiple disciplines without compromising existing channels of communication.

New Digital Resources for Scientists and Science Learners Can Enhance Curriculum Design

The second implication for teaching about controversy is that the SCOPE projects build community by enhancing digital resources, specifically in the area of "social interoperability"—defined by Fox and Marchionini (1998) as "the need for individuals and groups with vested interests to attempt to understand all points of view" (p. 30). These issues offer great promise for digital libraries (Borgman, 1996; Scherlis, 1996; Shneiderman et al., 1998) and lend themselves to our knowledge integration perspective (Linn, Eylon, & Davis, chap. 2, this volume; Linn, 1996; Linn, diSessa, et al., 1994). The inclusion of *Science* magazine in the SCOPE team allows us to research these issues in an authentic professional context (Treloar, 1998).

As we seek to link more and more collections and media types, we need at the same time to build an understanding of how these materials can promote consideration of alternative views (Paepke et al., 1998). Progress among these lines is just beginning (Hemmje et al., 1994; Koenemann & Belkin, 1996; Rao et al., 1995). Users of large connected collections may actually explore fewer threats to the validity of their views precisely because they can locate more supporting information. Our research has been exploring whether our design approaches are increasing social operability in interpreting scientific controversies.

And finally, the SCOPE research is answering central questions about science learning by determining the views of controversy citizens and students develop and by contrasting these with the views of scientists and stakeholders. We are exploring how these views of controversy serve students as they interpret public information about science. We analyze how the neglect of controversy in the curriculum compels citizens. We are developing learning experiences that promote understanding of controversy in science while at the same time capturing the criteria that scientists use to resolve disputes. We seek ways to help learners connect their understanding of scientific controversy to an interpretation of empirical findings, issues of statistical variation, and more general issues of method, as well as the coherence of explanatory mechanisms. We are exploring how teachers come to teach about scientific controversy (see Slotta, chap. 9, this volume). We look at pedagogical practice associated with teaching about scientific controversy and examine the knowledge and skills teachers draw on as they adopt and customize controversy curriculum. Havelock (2002) explored teacher use of controversy in conjunction with an online community for teachers.

CONCLUSIONS

The salience and purview of the natural sciences greatly expanded over the course of the 20th century, and the initial indications from the 21st century show only further expansion. Science is attempting to understand natural phenomena across the expanse of time, across the profound diversity of the planet, and across the breadth of the universe. The educational issues that surround this intellectual terrain are immense and are far from being theoretically well understood. This chapter has characterized the research efforts associated with the SCOPE project that are seeking to explore these educational issues. This is happening at a time when network technologies have interconnected individuals and information sources in ways that are historically unprecedented. We need to bring clarity to how these new technological resources can be employed for knowledge networking and learning about science.

Science educators need to be mindful of the diverse forms of inquiry associated with expert scientific practice. We must look at the diversity of practice without losing sight of the appropriate educational objectives for our children and our citizenry. With the widespread call for greater emphasis on inquiry-based instruction (National Research Council, 1996), there is an undesirable prospect that this could be translated into a solitary focus on hands-on activity. Scientific inquiry takes many forms and this includes first-hand experimentation as well as critical examination of the scientific literature. With SCOPE, we are supporting students in making sense of the emerging scientific literature in hopes of offering an alternative to what might be construed of as an overly simplistic doctrine or ideology of hands-on activity. We argue that the characterization of scientific inquiry in the curriculum should echo the diverse forms of inquiry as it has come to be understood in professional scientific practice.

Although the primary research questions of the SCOPE project focus on the educational opportunities associated with contemporary scientific controversies, our work also brings features of the scientific enterprise into focus—and available for empirical study. We have been drawing on psychological, anthropological, and sociological methods for studying communities of natural scientists including both self-report and more subtle observational approaches (Baker & Dunbar, 1996; Hall & Stevens, 1996; Latour, 1987, 1995, 1996). This allows us to study why scientists hold alternative views, how their disputes are resolved, how they critique the work of others, and how they make use of each other's research and thinking. Such research will contribute to the growing literature that has been documenting the everyday practices and epistemics of science.

ENDNOTE

1. This is apart from the argument that all learning involves knowledge construction. Here we are focused on knowledge construction teaching approaches.

11

Synergy Research and Knowledge Integration: Customizing Activities Around Stream Ecology

Eric Baumgartner
Inquirium

How can designers and researchers share tools and ideas that build on one another? How can designers and researchers create flexibly adaptive curricula that teachers can shape to fit their particular classroom context while retaining the core design elements that distinguish innovative learning environments? The research described in this volume has demonstrated the value of scaffolded knowledge integration (SKI) as a means to engage students in scientific inquiry and science learning. This work has also shown how specific approaches to the design of instructional materials—principled, collaborative, and iterative design—each contributed to student learning within a specific instructional context.

This chapter explores the challenges of leveraging the SKI framework and the design principles from the Knowledge Integration Environment (KIE). The discussion is rooted in a research partnership effort called the "Synergy Project" that designed a new Web-Based Inquiry Science Environment (WISE) project about water quality and subsequently refined this unit, along with related technological scaffolds, over time. I discuss the role that SKI played in this process and describe the ways in which synergy research attempts to draw on existing intellectual, curricular, and technological resources to inform design.

SYNERGY RESEARCH

The Synergy Project is a collaboration among researchers at the Center for Innovative Learning Technologies (CILT). Synergy research explores how to create and support widespread collaboration around topics of common interest to address specific learning goals. The members of a synergy project work together to rapidly design curriculum for new learning settings. This goal requires rethinking how to best reuse and repurpose prior research and technology supports and when to design new innovations to address unmet needs for student learning.

Synergy research that refines knowledge of the interaction between contexts and theory is particularly important in light of recent developments within science education. In addition to work around KIE and WISE, the past several years have seen the development of a rich range of innovative science education curricula that have been refined through small, intensive classroom studies (Edelson, Gordin, et al., 1999; Krajcik, Blumenfeld, Marx, & Soloway, 1999; Reiser, Tabak, et al., 2001; Songer, 1996; Vye et al., 1998). These materials have built on emerging pedagogical and sociocognitive theories of learning, as well as advances in technology, to develop and refine curricula that engage students in the act of doing science.

The designers of many of these learning environments have now begun to move beyond the demonstration or "hothouse" classrooms in which the innovations were first studied. Researchers are working closely with schools and districts to encourage the use of these environments in many classrooms and in so doing are exploring different approaches to dealing with the obstacles to widespread adoption of innovative, research-based curricula.

Successful adoption of innovation on a broad scale—adoption that preserves the core elements of curricular innovation—is extremely challenging, and to date, evidence of successful adoptions is not particularly strong. Many past efforts to effect reform through curriculum have proven unsuccessful (Cohen, 1988; Cuban, 1993). Others have shown that as innovations travel farther and farther from their origins, they become diffuse, often losing the key instructional elements that made them innovative in the first place. Worse, in some cases these elements are unintentionally subverted in ways that completely undermine the designer's original pedagogical intent. These so-called lethal mutations symbolize the challenge facing the designer: How can we encourage the wide-spread use of research-based curricula in ways that will remain true to the core teaching and learning principles that comprise the innovation?

These challenges to curricular adoption echo a broader concern voiced over the years by many researchers about the lack of cumulative, influential research in education (Hilgard, 1996; Huberman, 1989; Kennedy, 1997; Peterson, 1998; Suppes, 1978). Several issues arise again and again in these reflections on the state of research in education. These include ongoing disputes among stakeholders and the complex, systemic nature of education.

The multiple stakeholders in science education have historically fought to control the agenda—and the resources—rather than collaborating to promote lifelong science learning (Lagemann, 1997; Linn, Songer, et al., 1996; Welch, 1979). This struggle for control is reflected in distinctions between theory and practice and sustained by frequent attempts to discredit teachers, curriculum materials, educational research, student achievement, or school administration. Often stakeholder groups succeed in independently establishing curriculum standards, setting promotion policies, or determining what can be taught.

The complex nature of educational practice also works to limit the perceived utility of specific curricular innovations. Practitioners often view their settings as significantly different from that of the researcher and subsequently marginalize the research as not relevant to their own needs (Kennedy, 1997; Richardson, 1994; Robinson, 1998). The fact that research is often strongly contextually bound places the burden on the practitioner to interpret its significance. One consequence of this fact is a growing trend to fund research that is deemed more scientific in that it attempts to remove the effect of context from the intervention being studied. These efforts to improve credibility have had, as Lagemann (1997) stated, "corrosive effects" on educational research (p. 13). The complexity of educational practice, together with the history of past broad-based reform movements, would suggest that context does matter, and what is important is helping researchers and practitioners to better account for its role.

Synergy Through Curricular Design

Kennedy (1997) pointed to differences in context—perceived and real—as an important reason why practitioners often view reform-based curriculum as not appropriate for their own classroom needs. Teachers may view the original hothouse classrooms as too different from their own in terms of resources, student experience and knowledge, administrative support, and structure, for the curriculum to work in their case. Given the challenges facing curriculum adoption, one might well ask: Why modify curriculum in the first place?

Rather than viewing research to practice as a process of applying refined research-based interventions to multiple diverse settings, I have adopted a view of educational practice as a design-based enterprise in which educational practitioners actively construct a learning environment to satisfy a particular set of contextual goals and constraints.

A design-based approach to educational research is not a new idea. Many educators have called for the reformulation of science education as a design science (A. Brown, 1992; diSessa, 2000; Gardner, Greeno, et al., 1990; Linn & Hsi, 2000). Design as an enterprise attempts to generate solutions that meet a specific set of criteria, often through a process of iterative refinement (see Bell, Hoadley, & Linn, chap. 4, this volume). Within educational research, this approach acknowledges the context of the learning setting as an important constraint on the design process. Design is also a more multidisciplinary, inclusive paradigm for marrying research and practice. Rather than framing the role of practitioners as that of implementing a predefined agenda, design-based approaches recruit practitioners and researchers to work together to design solutions that meet the needs of both parties. In this respect, the partnership process described in this volume is a powerful example of the role collaboration plays in the design process (see, e.g., Slotta, chap. 9, this volume; Bell, chap. 10, this volume; and Shear, Bell, & Linn, chap. 12, this volume).

Synergy research builds on this approach and draws on varying intellectual, curricular, and technological resources to design an effective learning environment. Instead of trying to design curricula to be context proof, synergy research explores productive adaptations of curriculum to align with the demands of local classroom context. We term this process of modifying curriculum to meet local needs the process of *customization*. Such an approach is ambitious in that it seeks to preserve the key instructional innovations of a curriculum while allowing other aspects of the curriculum to be adapted to a teacher's own instructional practice. It suggests that curriculum designers need to look closely at the elements of curriculum that contribute to effective teaching and learning while also developing an understanding for the aspects of curriculum that are most likely to be modified. Such research is useful in that it helps us to better understand how innovation can be communicated, productively adapted, and improved.

Synergy and Water Quality

The CILT Synergy water quality project sought to leverage the key research from CILT, KIE, and WISE to support instructional design in a new topic area. In pursuing this focus, the project addressed two research goals.

First, the project investigated the process of applying principles of SKI (see Linn, Davis, & Eylon, chap. 3, this volume) to the design of a new science curriculum in a new classroom context. This afforded the research team the opportunity to examine how designing for knowledge integration using the specific principles of SKI would contribute to instructional design. Understanding the value of SKI to the design process is important because it explores the generative nature of the framework. Instructional theories and frameworks can be viewed through both explanatory and generative lenses (Baumgartner & Bell, 2002). Explanatory theories offer post hoc analyses of empirical data and often provide powerful means for explaining results across multiple settings. Generative theories do their work up front, during the design process, by offering guidance for the designer, informing specific design decisions, and providing a means to assess whether a given design is consistent with the theory behind it.

A second focus of synergy research is to understand how changes in curricular context interact with instructional theory in ways not anticipated by the original research group. For example, much of the research that led to SKI is based on studies of middle school students learning about heat and temperature within a particular teacher's classroom (Linn & Hsi, 2000). How well do the principles of SKI speak to the design of curriculum for learners in other settings? In our case, by exploring the design of a water quality unit for use in a different school, we began to push on the existing contextual boundaries that defined SKI. In this respect, synergy research serves to refine instructional theory by exploring its generative power in broader and broader settings.

Framing Synergy Research

In this chapter, I examine synergy research with the goal of understanding how intellectual, curricular, and technological elements from KIE, WISE, and CILT research can be successfully used to customize a new water quality curriculum. In particular, I examine the following:

- How can SKI inform the design of new technological scaffolds for knowledge integration?
- How can key elements of the KIE be customized for use in new contexts, and what is gained or lost in this process?
- How can researchers and curriculum developers design innovative science curricula that anticipate customization by others? What are the trade-offs of designing for customization?

These questions reflect the central focus of synergy research on the process of design and the generative nature of science education research. Because of synergy's design focus, I discuss the role that multiple kinds of resources—intellectual, curricular, and technological—can play in contributing to our central goal of curriculum design. Framing customization around these forms of resources emphasizes the mix of theoretical and pragmatic factors that come into play in designing curriculum for specific settings and goals.

CURRICULAR DESIGN CONTEXT

Our research group's approach to curriculum design is based on the partnership inquiry process (Linn, Shear, et al., 1999). This approach invites researchers, educators, and scientists to iterate over the design (and redesign) of curricular goals, instruction, technology, and assessment. A major challenge, but also a major strength, of this approach lies in the constant negotiation of goals and methods from participants with diverse perspectives and experience. In our group's case, in addition to classroom teachers, technologists, researchers, and educators, we were fortunate to have an environmental scientist actively participating in the design and development of specific activities and curricular materials.

This research reported here is based on two significant partnership projects involving researchers, teachers, and scientists. The first, called "Strawberry Creek," was a high school level WISE project that our group developed using the WISE partnership model. The following year, we customized Strawberry Creek to design a new project, called "Pine Creek," for a sixth-grade science class.

Strawberry Creek Partnership

The Strawberry Creek project began as a collaboration among researchers from WISE and CILT and two local high school teachers. In previous years, the teachers had taken students on field trips to collect data at Strawberry Creek, a local stream that empties into San Francisco Bay. They sought to expand this experience into a short project with the goal of documenting the health of the creek and viewed WISE as a means to design instruction around the core activity of visiting the creek and collecting data.

The primary learning goals for the Strawberry Creek design partnership were for students to successfully engage in an investigation of creek water quality, to make a judgment of the health of the creek, and to understand and reason about the effects of various water quality factors such as dissolved oxygen, pH, and temperature.

The participating teachers intended to use the project simultaneously in three different science classes: one chemistry class, two biology classes, and two physics classes. This led to a curricular design goal of producing three tightly coupled projects that would be customized for students in the different disciplines. Students in each class would focus on water quality factors that were appropriate to their discipline. For example, chemistry students would test the chemical properties of the creek, including phosphate and ammonia levels. All students would have access to the water quality data collected by all classes.

The researchers entered the project with the intent of designing a creek unit that would meet the partner teachers' goals but also be customizable for use by other teachers at other schools (and with other creeks or rivers). The need to support the customization of water quality projects internally as well as externally meant that we spent several design meetings discussing issues related to flexibly adaptive design.

The project was designed using WISE, a World Wide Web browser-based application for collaboratively authoring cognitively scaffolded science curricula (see Slotta, chap. 9, this volume, for further description of WISE). The three projects that were developed (Strawberry Creek/Biology, Strawberry Creek/Chemistry, and Strawberry Creek/Physics) each involved approximately 10 hr of class instruction. Students worked in pairs to review online information about water quality factors and construct a causal map of water quality that graphically depicted the relations among the factors. Students then went on a field trip to Strawberry Creek to collect data from nine different sites along the stream. Once students returned to the laboratory and finished analyzing the water samples, they entered their data into an online water quality database, which allowed them to browse and analyze data from all five classrooms. Using this data, students made their own evaluations and recommendations about the state of the creek in final written reports.

The initial curricular resource that we drew on was Kegley and Andrew's (1997) *The Chemistry of Water* text. This text was the primary resource Kegley used to teach a field-based, undergraduate-level environmental chemistry course. Both collaborating teachers had taken this course and based their own water quality activities on these experiences. Kegley also met with members of our group to discuss issues specific to Strawberry Creek and provide suggestions for curricular activities.

We reviewed a wide set of water quality curricula during the design process including materials from Project GREEN, Science Learning in Context, the Center for Highly Interactive Computing in Education at the University of Michigan, Global Lab, and Vanderbilt's Scientists in Action series (Krajcik, Blumenfeld, Marx, Bass, et al., 1998; Stapp, 1997; Tinker, 1997; Vye et al., 1998). These materials informed our selection of a core set of water quality factors on which to focus as well as specific staging activities that would familiarize students with the water quality testing equipment.

Pine Creek Partnership

The following year, we established a partnership with two middle school science teachers who had engaged students in investigations of a local creek for several years. The two teachers had access to 5 years worth of water quality data for the stream and wanted to create a WISE project that would help students to make sense of this data.

Pine Creek provided the research team with the opportunity to explore the process of customization across two major dimensions. First, the project needed to be contextualized around a different watershed with its own set of ecological concerns. Second, the 6th-grade students who would interact with the Pine Creek project were significantly younger than the 10th to 12th graders who used Strawberry Creek material. However, the 6th graders were familiar with the creek and the issues surrounding it, as their teachers had incorporated the creek into science lessons throughout the year.

For this project, we used Strawberry Creek as a model and adapted the curricular materials to address the particular environmental concern facing Pine Creek (primarily the threat of eutrophication due to fertilizer runoff) and to be age appropriate. The project covered 8 days of instruction time and incorporated 5 years of evidence collected by students including test data and site photographs.

Data Collection

To inform the redesign of the curricula, we conducted classroom observations and collected student artifacts from the classroom trials. Students completed pretest and posttests assessing their understanding of water quality factors, and we interviewed a subset of students following the unit to further explore their understanding. In addition, all of students' work within the WISE environment was stored on university servers and was available for analysis.

To enable us to reflect on the partnership process itself, we archived notes from design meetings and interviewed teachers to document their goals for the project. We conducted and taped formal debriefing meetings after the curriculum was piloted; these meetings brought together teachers and researchers to candidly discuss the project and share their perspectives about what worked, what did not work, what should be changed, and why.

ASPECTS OF SYNERGY RESEARCH: DESIGN, CUSTOMIZATION, AND GENERALITY

I focus here on three examples of synergy research within the water quality design effort. These examples illustrate the affordances of specific intellectual, curricular, and technological resources for the partnership design process and cover three broad aspects of the customization process:

- Creating a new design: Here I describe the contributions of SKI or other research to the design of a new tool for SKI: the causal mapping tool (CMT). I discuss how this tool itself supports flexibly adaptive design and explain why we felt it necessary to create a new tool ourselves rather than customizing already existing technology.
- Customizing an existing design: I describe the process of adapting an important component of the KIE system—evidence pages—to serve a different purpose in Strawberry Creek. I discuss the motivation for adapting existing curricular resources and the challenges of doing so in ways that stay true to their original design principles.
- Designing for future customization: I describe our efforts to create a generic creek project that could be customized for use in new watersheds and new classrooms. I explain the tension between creating a general-purpose curriculum and tailoring a unit for a specific context and describe a curricular framework that addresses this tension.

These examples are not meant to suggest a single best approach to design. Rather, they highlight particularly important elements of the partnership design process and show how synergy research can draw

on existing intellectual, curricular, and technological resources to
meet a specific set of design goals.

Design: SKI and the CMT

A key goal for the design of Strawberry Creek was to provide a means
to allow students to make sense of the complex system of causal relations that comprise water quality. These relations include biological
and chemical indicators like pH, macroinvertebrate counts, dissolved
oxygen levels, and nitrate levels; water quality is commonly viewed as a
aggregate of these indicator levels, rather than a single value (e.g.,
Kegley & Andrews, 1997).

The principles of SKI provided a framework for the design of a tool
to support student reasoning about water quality as a causal system.
We needed to do two things: identify a useful representation that
would help students make visible their reasoning about causal systems
and figure out how to structure student activity around the use of this
tool in ways that were consistent with SKI's emphasis on accessible
science, autonomous learning, and social supports.

Causal maps—node and link graphs in which nodes represent
causal factors and links represent causal relations between factors—
offered an explicit means to make causal thinking visible. Several existing resources helped us to identify node and link representations as
a productive means to represent systems of causal relations. Science
textbooks often use a stylized form of these graphs to show the relations within systems such as the carbon cycle and the water cycle.
Concept mapping offers a similar representation as learners map out
causal factors and identify the relations between them (Novak, 1990).
Experts also use these representations in their own work: "Stella," a
powerful dynamic modeling program, uses nodes and links to represent measurable elements within a system and the relations among
those elements (Steed, 1992).

Within science education, researchers have also adopted these representations. In addition to studies in which researchers brought
Stella—and all the power and complexity that it represents—into the
classroom (Mandinach & Cline, 1994), researchers have designed new
learning tools that leverage this representation to allow learners to
create their own causal systems. Of particular interest is the software
program "Model-It," a qualitative modeling environment designed to
allow students to generate node and link graphs for causal behavior
and test their causal models by observing the performance of their
model over time (Jackson et al., 1994). Model-It has been successfully

used by middle school students to model environmental phenomena including water and air quality (Spitulnik, 1998).

We also had specific pedagogical and technological needs that shaped the ultimate design of the CMT. Pedagogically, we wanted something that offered the strong ontological typing of a dynamic modeling environment. However, we did not need the ability to actually run models over time. Although building and testing dynamic models can be a powerful learning experience (Spitulnik, 1998; White & Schwarz, 1998), we lacked the time in the curriculum to adequately support it. Additionally, by designing our own tool, we were able to build on ideas for formative assessment that were suggested by colleagues, including the ability to store snapshots of student work over time to study students' understanding of water quality over the course of the project.

Technologically, we had to build something ourselves. Deciding to design within the WISE environment allowed us to take advantage of the many supports for knowledge integration built in to WISE, which provided an infrastructure for developing online curricula, storing and retrieving student work, and supporting collaboration among the project development team. WISE is also designed to provide cognitive supports for SKI including reflective prompts, timely guidance, and activity maps.

However, this decision also limited us to software that could run within a web browser and store student data on WISE's central servers, ruling out traditional desktop applications that store student files to the local computer. This led us to design a Java applet that would allow students to build causal maps and could save their maps with the rest of their WISE work.

The CMT

We built on our knowledge of important features of existing modeling applications to develop our own CMT. The CMT allowed students to create factors (boxes) and define causal relations (arrows) between them, as shown in Fig. 11.1. Student causal maps are saved automatically and stored on WISE servers, allowing the tool to be seamlessly integrated within any WISE project.

The CMT supports knowledge integration in several ways. First and foremost, it provides an explicit, manipulable representation for causal relations, affording students that opportunity to represent their understanding in an explicit way. We intended the CMT to provide a means for helping students to reason about the effect of long causal chains. Students could use the representation to think about the effects of specific environmental actions (e.g., increasing fertilizer

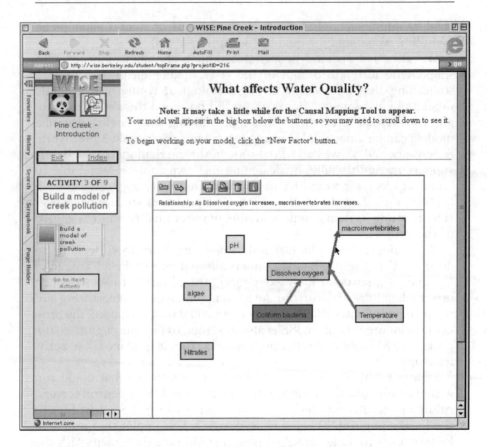

FIG. 11.1.   Causal mapping in the Web-Based Inquiry Science Environment
(WISE) Pine Creek project.

use) in terms of the entire system rather than focusing solely on the
factors that were directly impacted by the action.

Second, because students work in pairs during WISE projects, the
causal map became a shared social artifact. Students had to agree on
what to represent in the same way that they had to agree on what to
write down when they took a WISE note. In this way, the CMT became
another social support for prompting students to articulate their understanding and integrating into existing pedagogical practices by
providing another object of reflection for the student group.

Refinement of the CMT.   We assessed the role of the CMT within
Strawberry Creek in several ways. Because the software recorded
changes to students' causal maps over time, we were able to study how
these maps developed over the course of the project. We examined the

changes as students represented their initial ideas about water quality and then gradually refined their maps to account for specific water quality factors that they learned about during the project. We also observed students' use of the CMT during the classroom trial and interviewed a subset of students about the project and their causal maps once the project had ended. We were interested in understanding how students constructed, refined, and used causal maps to reason about water quality. Our expectation was that students would use the CMT to create a normative model for water quality, one that would best represent their current understanding at any given time.

To examine change over time, we examined first and final models from each group. The first represented the students' model as it existed at the end of the first day of instruction. We believed that this model would best represent students' initial ideas about water quality. The final model represented the last model that students worked on during the project. This model was revised at least once following student review of online evidence about water quality. Students also had a chance to revise their model following the field test and analysis of field data, but not all students chose to revise their models at that point in the project.

What we learned from the Strawberry Creek trial did not lead us to redesign the CMT itself but rather to try to recast the way in which the causal mapping task was represented within the creek project. Students were fairly successful in learning to use the CMT to build relations between factors, and students actively refined their models over the course of the project. Three trends surprised us and suggested that we needed to provide explicit criteria to the students for assessing their own causal maps.

First, students tended not to remove their initial factors. We had expected that part of the refinement process would be the deletion of outdated ideas. On average, students deleted less than one old factor per group. For example, the initial model shown in Fig. 11.2 has two factors, wind and number of factories, that are not addressed in the Strawberry Creek project. Both factors remain on the group's final model, shown in Fig. 11.3.

Second, many students included Strawberry Creek or Creek Health as a single factor. Because we considered the overall health of the creek to be represented by the entire model and not a single factor, we were surprised to find students doing this. This often led to causal maps that looked much like spokes of a wheel. Such causal maps may fail to represent the relations between specific factors in favor of direct indications of how the student thinks the factors affect overall water quality. For example, in Fig. 11.3, students have connected facto-

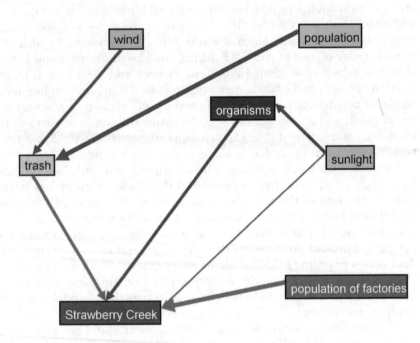

FIG. 11.2. Group C15's initial model.

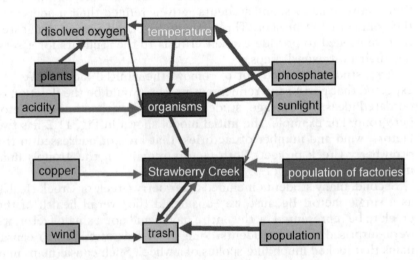

FIG. 11.3. Group C15's final model.

ries directly to Strawberry Creek rather than tying the number of factories to changes in the levels of what the factories produce. This approach makes the nature of the relation implicit instead of explicit: What about factories negatively impacts creek health and how? In contrast, the students' representation of the role of temperature reflects the approach we had intended: Changes in temperature are tied to changes in specific water quality factors (dissolved oxygen levels or organism population) rather than to a generic Creek Health factor.

Third, in interviews with students following the unit, it became clear that students themselves did not view their causal maps as representations of their own understanding. For example, Pat, when prompted to explain his causal map from Strawberry Creek to an interviewer, explained that "My model is the model I made for you. My model for me was something I made to remind myself of the relationships." These responses indicate that students may generate different models for different purposes. In Pat's case, it appears that in addition to the online version the group constructed, he used a different, implicit model to reason about the causal relations behind water quality.

Taken together, these trends suggest two things. First, causal maps do not serve as valid representations of student understanding. This conclusion is consistent with research on concept maps that has raised questions about the validity of these representations as measures of what students know (Mandinach & Cline, 1994; Novak, 1990; Rice et al., 1998; Ruiz-Primo & Shavelson, 1996). Second, better scaffolding is needed to help students develop criteria for evaluating their own causal maps that could help them determine when to add or remove factors and relations.

These results both reinforce and inform our design of the project to support knowledge integration. The design principles that led us to create the CMT were not predicated on causal maps being valid representations of student knowledge; rather, they focused on providing an explicit way for students to express causal relations, creating a social artifact that could spur discussion among students and teachers. In this sense the CMT succeeded.

Our later redesign of the curriculum focused on modeling the use of causal maps in a way consistent with SKI's goal of helping students to critique their own ideas. In this respect, the initial use of the CMT was not as successful, and in the later Pine Creek project, the partnership team developed an introductory activity to help students identify criteria for assessing their causal maps. In this activity the teacher modeled a phenomenon well known to the students—her own irritability level—and used student suggestions for causal factors and relations to build a causal map on the whiteboard. This activity follows the principles of knowledge integration, encouraging students to become autonomous learners who develop their own criteria for monitoring their own progress.

Customization: Toward a New Genre of WISE Project

Much has been made about the risk of lethal mutations to innovative educational practice. The trouble with this phrase is that it may incorrectly imply that any sort of change to established practice is a negative one. To the contrary, we view change—mutation—to be an expected action taken to adapt innovation to particular contexts. Productive mutations can result in successful customizations of innovative practice to meet new goals.

Customization can also serve to test or extend our understanding of specific instructional ideas. We can explore very different contexts from the original research and discover whether specific innovations continue to be successful in those settings and what modifications would lead to success. For example, one design issue within the Strawberry Creek partnership led to a deeper understanding of KIE and the nature of evidence within WISE projects. This issue emerged during the early design process for the Strawberry Creek project and centered on how the creek project was appropriating WISE evidence pages to provide background information about water quality factors.

In KIE and WISE projects, designers create or select Internet evidence pages for students to critique. In these cases, students are expected to consider the source of the information, the web page's author, and the context in which the evidence claims were being made. Viewing evidence and reflecting on it formed the bulk of student work in many KIE and WISE projects.

In the Strawberry Creek project, the goal was to integrate knowledge around water quality. As a capstone activity, we expected students to draw on instruction about many of these concepts. The project provided a means to synthesize some of those ideas into an integrated whole. However, we sought to add ideas about the normative water quality factors so students could review the role that these factors played within stream ecology.

We wanted students to review evidence about factors that affected water quality not because the connections among these ideas were suspect but to develop a rich understanding of the dynamic system that affects water quality. We wanted students to spend more time on knowledge integration activities and less time critiquing online evidence.

Evidence pages were the most convenient mechanism for providing such normative content. Some pages were authored by project members, and some were based on materials available online. This use of evidence pages generated internal debate within the partnership about the overall framework of the Strawberry Creek project and whether we had compromised the principles of KIE by encouraging students to read evidence pages with an uncritical eye.

The partnership's appropriation of WISE evidence pages led to the realization that we were customizing WISE to support a new genre of project. We were designing a WISE project around an ongoing scientific investigation that did not easily fit within the existing genres of critique, debate, and design projects described by Davis (see chap. 5, this volume), Bell (chap. 6, this volume), and Hoadley (chap. 7, this volume).

This new genre of project has come to be called an *investigation project* and includes the "Probing Your Surroundings" project discussed by D. Clark (see chap. 8, this volume). In Strawberry Creek, students were collecting their own data from the creek itself and entering that evidence into the project via web forms. Most WISE projects asked students to critically assess evidence but did not place them in the position of gathering their own data.

Investigation projects also enable students to critically analyze evidence, but students must also develop their own interpretations of the data rather than assessing the strength of preexisting claims. The Strawberry Creek project emphasizes students' ability to generate and interpret their own water quality data and reconcile their evidence with the causal maps that they generate. In effect, we were customizing WISE to support a new kind of project that shared a common intellectual foundation in SKI.

Making Design Explicit

As educators customize intellectual, curricular, and technological resources from a variety of sources, they need to ensure that the final design reflects a consistent instructional framework. Often, curricular and technological resources presume a particular theoretical perspective but do not make this assumption explicit. Frequently designers fail to anticipate how resources could be used by others less familiar with their theoretical stance on teaching and learning. The debate that led to adding an investigation genre to WISE echoes this need to make design rationale explicit. Our familiarity with SKI meant that we were aware of the implications of our decision to repurpose evidence pages for our needs. Other designers with less opportunity to work directly with the WISE research group may not have this awareness.

This decoupling of theory from instructional resources reflects the effort required to make these connections explicit. In addition, because the original design partnership has internalized these connections, the designers may not anticipate customizations of their curricular and technological resources, making it difficult to predict which elements of their work need to be annotated.

For example, although WISE provides introductory materials that explain the principles of SKI, once a designer begins to build a project in WISE there is little intellectual guidance built into the project authoring environment. The physical structure of an evidence page—a page of HTML text that identifies the author of the page and points to another web page somewhere on the Internet—does not constrain its use. Rather, it is the use of evidence pages within specific genres of WISE projects, such as critique projects, that leverages knowledge integration. Similarly, WISE provides support for authoring prompts that can guide students thinking. The role of prompts has been extensively researched within the KIE project (Davis, chap. 5, this volume; 2003a). However, the prompt editing interface itself does not provide guidance for how the curriculum designer might compose prompts to best support knowledge integration.

Ultimately, these examples underscore the need to design new approaches to integrating research findings with the elements of instructional practice, including curricular materials that represent the most tangible elements of successful innovation. The idea of flexibly adaptive design addresses this need by calling for the embedding of key elements of an instructional framework within curricular materials. For example, STAR-Legacy embeds the structure of an inquiry cycle within the software that students use, providing an explicit representation of the designers' intent (Schwartz et al., 1999). This idea may be extended by anticipating how specific aspects of a designed curriculum could be customized and providing scaffolds to guide this customization in a productive manner.

Generality: SKI and the Generic Creek Debate

Strawberry Creek was the first of several iterations of water quality projects developed by our group that relate to local environmental conditions. Shortly after Strawberry Creek ran, the project was adapted for use in another San Francisco Bay Area high school. The following year, a major revision of the project has focused on use in a middle school setting. In addition, a customized version of the original Strawberry Creek project was used to teach about the Salton Sea, a large, manmade lake near the Colorado River in southeastern California.

The need to support not only Strawberry Creek, a high school unit about a particular creek in the Bay Area, but also other sites and schools ranging from middle school through high school meant that we needed to support components of the creek curriculum in ways that would allow them to be modified to work in local contexts. We approached this task with both theoretical and pragmatic concerns. Theoretically, we wanted to ensure that the customized projects reflected the SKI framework. Pragmatically, we wanted to design curricular and technological elements that could be easily reused in the context of these new water quality projects.

The debate over what we referred to as the generic creek project began with the claim that a water quality project had to target local watershed issues. This position grew out of the SKI principle of making science accessible. Investigating a local stream or river contextualized the activity within the student's life and community and allowed students to integrate their knowledge of the community and the potential threats to the watershed's health, with a growing understanding of what impacts water quality. This approach implied that every creek project would be a distinct entity and require significant customization.

At the other extreme was our interest in providing teachers interested in using WISE with a general purpose water quality project that they could use without customization. The motivation for this approach was to encourage biology and life sciences teachers to try running a WISE project for the first time. Research with teachers using technology shows that in general, customization comes only after teachers become familiar with an existing project (Linn, Clark, et al., 2003). If a project needs significant customization before it can be run, novice teachers are less inclined to use WISE.

The teachers in our design partnership wanted a project built around the issues at Strawberry Creek. One alternative, a generic project that would investigate a well-known or fictitious body of water, was rejected because it was not accessible to local students, an aspect of learning established in prior research (e.g., Linn & Hsi, 2000).

After ruling out this alternative, we were faced with the challenge of finding ways to reuse material in multiple water quality projects and to help future designers think about how such projects should be structured. We explored the notion of a project pattern in which the activities and steps of the project were predefined, but teachers could customize these steps to reflect local questions and local concerns. Ultimately, we found this model ineffective for many of the same reasons that had limited our use of outside resources. Chief among these were barriers of grade level and time. Our partner teachers each had different amounts of time to allocate to the project, which meant that we needed to both subtract and add activities based on how much time they had. We also found that the set of water quality factors a teacher wanted to focus on varied depending on the targeted learning goals, the available testing equipment, and the current hypotheses about the condition of the local stream. (For example, at Pine Creek nitrate levels were suspected to be high, and safety precautions precluded testing for fecal coliform bacteria. At Strawberry Creek, fecal coliform bacteria were present, and tests revealed this.)

Supporting Flexibly Adaptive Design

To support flexibly adaptive design, we needed to define a suitable grain size for what constitutes customization. For example, one might customize a project at the project level by changing the nature of the overall investigation that students pursue. Individual activities within the project may also be added, rearranged, or removed to adapt the project to fit within a specific time frame or to provide students with additional opportunities to learn. Specific aspects of activities may be modified to target learners of different ages, backgrounds, and expectations. Finally, the watershed under study will vary to reflect local environmental interests.

We addressed the grain size issue through a two-tier model for customization that emphasizes adaptability at both the activity and content level. This approach reflects our interest in defining a central activity sequence that aligns with SKI while remaining flexible enough to allow teachers and designers to adapt these activities to their own context and goals.

We identified a basic set of five core activities that make up a water quality project (see Table 11.1). This activity sequence may be customized in two ways. First, designers can adapt the overall length of the unit by omitting an entire activity or inserting a new activity into the sequence. Second, customization can occur within each activity driven by the nature of the local site and the set of factors and mechanisms that the teacher chooses to include. The advantage to this approach is that we can provide a set of generic resources that can be reused within each activity while also leaving room for teachers or developers to tailor the materials for their own context.

The Drink or Swim Project.
To explore the viability of this approach to customization, we designed a small demonstration project called "Drink or Swim" that investigates the water quality of a fictitious stream called Rocky Creek. Our goals for this project were to create a generic project that a teacher new to WISE could use without

TABLE 11.1
Summary of Core Activity Sequence for Water Quality Projects

Core Activity	Description
Introduction	The initial framing of the project and introduction of the watershed and local watershed issues. Specific watershed and issues vary by project.
Indicator factors	Students review a set of water quality indicator factors. Specific factors vary by project.
Mechanisms that affect water quality	Students review the causal mechanisms such as thermal pollution or eutrophication that affect water quality indicators. Specific mechanisms vary by project.
Data collection and analysis	Students review and assess water quality data for the watershed. Specific data sets vary by project.
Summary and reflection	Students marshal evidence to argue about the health of the watershed. The specific nature of the culminating activity—debate, written or oral presentation, and so forth—varies by project.

any customization. The project was intended to be fairly short, about 3 hr of instruction, and focused on understanding how pH, dissolved oxygen, and coliform bacteria serve as indicators of water quality.

To reduce instruction time, the project eliminated one major activity, choosing not to focus on more complex causal mechanisms that might have led to changes in the levels of these three factors. The remaining activities were customized to reflect an investigation of Rocky Creek, and a canned data set was created to allow students to analyze water quality data within this setting.

The resulting project has been added to the WISE project library and has been used by several teachers. Because we have defined a central activity sequence, we can make sense of the customizations that led to Drink or Swim—removal of the mechanisms activity, a restricted set of indicator factors, and adaptation to the Rocky Creek watershed—as a discrete set of changes that preserve a knowledge integration focus.

The nature of water quality projects and environmental science activities in general may lend themselves to greater customization for local settings than do curricula in other science domains. Many WISE projects do not require this degree of customization, including other life sciences projects that focus on malaria. However, the fundamentally local character of water quality projects makes them a particularly personally relevant domain for pursuing synergy research.

DISCUSSION

These three examples from the water quality design process exemplify the challenges of incorporating a range of intellectual, curricular, and technological resources into the design of new curriculum for new settings. Although SKI provided a general framework for the design process, we found that elements of SKI, as well as other resources we sought to leverage, did not always align with the goals of the customization process. Because of our familiarity with SKI and the participation of researchers from KIE, we were able to negotiate these tensions while preserving a knowledge integration focus.

However, as we focus on future customization, it is likely that practitioners without such close ties to the original designers will seek to adapt these materials. In this case, we need to explore new ways to connect curricular materials with the research frameworks that guided their design.

SKI and the Design Process

The SKI framework contributed at multiple stages of the design process. SKI served both as a framework for collaboration as well as an intellectual resource that guided our design decisions.

The partnership design process provided us with a framework for negotiating a shared set of learning goals and contextual constraints across researchers, teachers, technologists, and scientists. These goals provided the grounding we needed to decide whether we could integrate curricular resources from various sources. Ongoing collaboration has led to pervasive improvements to our research as well. For example, work to allow WISE to support causal mapping has led to a generic tool kit that allows WISE to integrate virtually any interactive technology that runs in a web browser. The nature of the creek projects, which support student generation of data and the use of online evidence within the creek projects, has led to a new genre of WISE projects.

As an intellectual resource, SKI principles guided the design of the CMT and provided a useful lens through which we could assess the value of potential curricular resources. SKI also helped to shape the overall activity structure that we used in all the creek projects, placing particular emphasis on the importance of investigating a local watershed and providing students with opportunities to integrate their understanding of the various factors that contribute to water quality.

Examining curricula developed using other intellectual frameworks, such as project-based science (PBS) (Krajcik, Blumenfeld, Marx, Bass, et al., 1998; Krajcik, Blumenfeld, Marx, & Soloway, 1999) or anchored instruction (Vye et al., 1998), also shed light on some of the pragmatic differences among these approaches to instruction. These distinctions become apparent when we reviewed curriculum not solely to assess these frameworks but with an eye toward incorporating curricular materials into our own designs. For example, although KIE and PBS share many of the same goals with respect to engaging students in scientific inquiry, KIE has focused on shorter term, 1- to 2-week capstone activities that emphasize the integration of ideas and principles. The PBS group, on the other hand, focuses on projects that allow students to guide their own inquiry and frequently last 6 to 8 weeks. The difference in expectations for available instruction time alone make it difficult for curricular resources to migrate between these groups.

Customization as a process provides an important mechanism for synthesizing key intellectual ideas within the field. By engaging in curricular design, researchers must develop a deep, practical understanding of the work of others. Such knowledge helps us to adopt tangible curricular resources in an informed way. We have begun to call this approach "walking in each others' shoes" in that it advocates engaging in the design process from a different perspective to come to a better understanding of the theoretical principles that underlie other groups' design efforts. This approach offers potential benefits for both parties: It allows the customizing researcher to explore the principles and implications of a new theoretical context and provides the original researchers with information about whether their existing resources are flexible enough to support customization by others.

Challenges for Customization

To design for effective customization, we need to reflect on the challenges facing adoption of curricular resources. Surprisingly, our research group found it very hard to adopt others' curricular materials for use within our own context. There were a variety of reasons for this difficulty. These barriers, many of which are quite pragmatic, reflect how our target learning context differs from that of the materials' original designers:

• Access: Often research-based materials were not available in print or could only be acquired through preexisting social networks. For example, one researcher's close ties to researchers at the Concord Consortium allowed her to gather material related to Science Learning in Context (Tinker, 1997) and Global Lab (Berenfeld, 1994) that would have been very difficult to track down otherwise.

• Age level: Many of the materials we reviewed were targeted at middle school students. In the Strawberry Creek project, we were designing for high school students. We were concerned about issues surrounding the reading level of the material and whether older students would engage with material that might come across as too simple or too childish. (Conversely, once we began to work on the Pine Creek project, we were faced with this challenge in reverse; we needed to adapt the Strawberry Creek materials for use with middle school students.)

• Mismatched learning goals: Materials that did not align well with our stated learning goals were not good candidates for adoption or customization.

• Evidence of success: Some curricula, although interesting to read, lacked published assessments or data about the effectiveness of the material in promoting student learning. Much of the work of the KIE and WISE research groups has been on the iterative codesign of curriculum and assessment; we place high value in materials that include cognitive assessment measures and provide us with a means to inquire about student learning.

• Time: Many materials involved longer units that ranged from 2 to 8 weeks. We were designing a unit that would run only 1 to 2 weeks. This ruled out direct adoption of many of the sustained inquiry curricula.

The technological barriers to reuse are more pragmatic than those described previously but important to address nonetheless. It is important to note that many of the technology supports we reviewed were subject to curricular barriers such as available time or access. Other barriers included the following:

• Mismatched hardware or software requirements: Our decision to build curricula within WISE gained us substantial leverage in design but also limited adoption of existing technology. WISE uses a centralized server to store and retrieve student work. This allows students to log on from any modern web browser anywhere in the world and continue working exactly where they left off. However, it also means that software that expects to run in a stand-alone manner and save work to files on a local hard disk will need to be modified to support a client–server model.

• Misleading claims about cross-platform software solutions: Given that WISE operates in a browser-based environment, a natural direction to look for compatible technological resources is Java. Java is touted as an efficient, cross-platform programming language that allows a designer to write a program once and have it run anywhere. In practice, this rarely happens. In our case, teachers ran WISE projects on Windows and Macintosh computers using either Netscape or Microsoft Internet Explorer. We had to support these users in at least four possible configurations of operating system and browser. Unfortunately, most available Java resources were based on a standard (Java Development Kit 1.1) that excluded Macintosh users who used Netscape. One reason we chose to design our own Java-based tools was so that we could address cross-platform issues from the ground up.

Some of these barriers, particularly the technical ones, may be addressed through future design efforts. Yet fundamentally, the customization process involves repurposing existing ideas and materials in ways that extend beyond the vision or expectations of the original designers. Many of these barriers will continue to exist; despite clever design, mismatches in grade level and available instruction time will undoubtedly occur. However, by addressing these issues during the initial design process, researchers and designers may be able to identify known constraints on the use of their innovations. This explicit connection of curricular elements to contextual constraints is an important aspect of flexibly adaptive design and argues for continued exploration of new ways to represent the intersection between research on how people learn and curricular materials designed to support learning.

Pursuing Flexibly Adaptive Design

Once we adopt a design-based view of research and practice, customization becomes a central activity for researchers and practitioners. We have seen how this can lead to disconnects between theories of instruction and the curricular artifacts that tacitly embody these theories. How can we address this disconnect? To understand how to create resources that can support flexibly adaptive design, we have identified two significant challenges.

First, we need to identify key dimensions along which we expect customization to occur. These dimensions are driven by practitioners' own goals as well as specific differences in context that exist from one teacher's classroom to the next. Often these dimensions must be discovered empirically through partnership projects or classroom study. It is also possible that future synergy research may develop a generative theory of context: that is, an integrated view of the nature of customization that can predict particularly important dimensions of contextual variation that flexibly adaptive designs must address.

Second, we need to represent flexible design at an appropriate level of abstraction that allows designers to adapt the innovation in ways that retain the key intellectual contributions of the work. Such a representation must afford productive customization and provide explicit connections between the tangible elements of the curriculum and their theoretical basis.

In the case of our water quality work, we have generated several curricular materials that are designed for reuse but that do not yet provide the explicit connections we would like. In addition to the curriculum itself, which is available through the WISE Web site, several smaller components or "packets" emerged that offer value to the learning technologies community. For example, the assessment items that we used are available for use by others in new settings. Core evidence pages about specific causal factors such as pH or dissolved oxygen could be reused in new WISE projects or by designers working in a completely different context. Two core technologies, the CMT and the visualization tool used to analyze water quality data, are both being redesigned to remove WISE-specific dependencies and so allow their use by other curriculum developers in other settings. It is perhaps unsurprising that software modules offer the best initial example of the kind of packets that could emerge from synergy research because efforts in software engineering have long sought to reuse programming code. A more important research issue will be to determine what other kinds of packets exist and what kinds of knowledge must be included to truly make these packets portable.

SUMMARY: TOWARD SYNERGY COMMUNITIES

The CILT Synergy Project has focused on exploring the issues facing customization within a familiar research collaboration using established partnership models. For synergy research to inform the refinement of what Lagemann (2002) called "usable knowledge," we need to develop approaches that extend beyond these bounds and embrace collaboration on a larger scale.

One effort that is addressing these challenges is the National Science Foundation funded SCALE grant. This effort is expanding the CILT synergy work to synthesize research on water quality among education researchers on a national level. The SCALE project provides a venue for discussion and synthesis of methods across research traditions with an eye toward constructing common frameworks that support assessments of student achievement and customization within the subject domain. The project studies how designers, researchers, and practitioners can work together to effectively customize curricular materials for use in different schools, regions, and partnerships, drawing heavily on our partnership model to convene a diverse group of experts who share an interest in the subject domain. SCALE communities will design materials for widespread use, test them in diverse settings, and identify features of curriculum materials that make them flexible. These materials—along with information about how they can be used and examples from varied classrooms—will be made available on the project Web site: http://scale.soe.berkeley.edu/.

SKI represents an important theoretical idea that has emerged from years of research. Synergy research has also led to collaboration and a synthesis within the broader learning technologies community. Our initial work galvanized our own research group and led to new insights for the WISE and CILT communities. Other designers of water quality curricula have also sought to understand each others' work, negotiate points of common interest, and create collaborations. The challenge going forward is to understand how the lessons of SKI can be successfully applied to design innovative, effective science education practice across a wide range of settings. As a field, we need research that explores how to synthesize curricular innovation across contexts, how to document variations in practice, and how to engage in flexibly adaptive design that anticipates and adapts to the complexities of classroom practice. Recent efforts, including the CILT Synergy Project described here and the ongoing SCALE project, suggest that researchers have begun to attend to these issues.

12

Partnership Models:
The Case of the Deformed Frogs

Linda Shear
SRI International

Philip Bell
University of Michigan

Marcia C. Linn
University of California, Berkeley

This chapter describes how a partnership designed, tested, and refined the integration of an innovative learning environment and curricula into the life of an urban middle school. Using a Knowledge Integration Environment (KIE) project about a current scientific controversy related to frog deformities, the partnership sought to expand teachers' pedagogical strategies, to bring new models for technology use to the school, and ultimately to improve students' knowledge, skills, and appreciation of science.

As discussed in chapter 1 (Linn, Davis, & Bell, this volume), bringing research-based innovations into the classroom is challenging because education is a complex enterprise. The successful implementation of new classroom innovations simultaneously requires modifying teacher roles and practices, integrating new programs into existing curricula, responding to classroom management requirements and available resources, and offering appropriate supports for student development of new skills, among many other dimensions of challenge—all within an organizational context that some contend is often designed for promoting stability rather than facilitating instructional improvement (e.g., Elmore, 2000). In the case of KIE, the innovation itself is also multidimensional, requiring the integration of new pedagogical strategies, new science content, and new models for the role of technology in the classroom (Linn, Bell, et al., 1998). For these and other reasons, implementation is a complex process that must be examined in its own right (Fullan & Pomfret, 1977; McLaughlin, 1987) and cannot be viewed as a simple adoption of the goals and products of the designer.

KIE approaches this complexity through the use of partnerships. This strategy leverages a wide range of expertise while it offers significant benefit to each participant, fostering widespread commitment to the common goal. This chapter describes one such partnership and discusses the elements that made it successful and the dimensions on which success is measured.

Partnerships have been a foundation of KIE work throughout the project's 20-year history (Linn, 1987; Linn & Hsi, 2000). The trajectory of partnership approaches began with one teacher in one classroom, a testbed with a successful history from earlier work (see Linn & Hsi, 2000) that has enabled extensive research on design principles and learning outcomes. Once the KIE was established and tested, the program began to expand into new settings with new teachers.

The partnership is a mechanism to leverage diverse expertise, provide extensive professional development opportunities both in vitro and in vivo, and evolve the learning environment to be effective in a wide variety of settings. The preceding chapters in this section described partnership strategies designed to support KIE implementation on a larger scale: professional development partnerships that offer knowledge integration mechanisms consistent with local needs (Slotta, chap. 9, this volume), electronic activity structures to build community (Bell, chap. 10, this volume), and research partnerships that expand our repertoire of models (Baumgartner, chap. 11, this volume).

The terms *partnership* and *collaboration* have been variously defined in research and in practice. In traditional models of joint work between research and schools, researchers—including natural scientists—function as the experts, whereas teachers function as the recipients of the innovation (e.g., Linn, Songer, et al., 1996). By contrast, KIE uses a model of mutual-benefit partnerships, respecting the expertise of each partner and viewing each as having something to contribute and something to gain.

KIE science education partnerships typically focus on collaborative design and implementation of curriculum in keeping with several other current models for school reform (e.g., Blumenfeld et al., 2000; Reiser, Spillane, et al., 2000). Just as design experiments (A. Brown, 1992) are an important mechanism for linking theory and practice, partnerships are an important mechanism for establishing common ground between researchers and practitioners. Partnerships ease the transition between the designed curriculum and that which is actually enacted in the classroom (Cohen, Raudenbush, et al., 2001) by sharing the tasks of design and enactment, rooting both in the same common goal. They also promote the learning of both practitioners and reformers in a process of coconstructing the curriculum and practices that will be implemented in the classroom (McLaughlin & Mitra, 2001).

This chapter describes the Deformed Frogs partnership, the activity structures used to support the design partnerships vision of KIE, and the outcomes that the partnership was able to achieve.

THE DEFORMED FROGS PARTNERSHIP

Partnership and School Context

The KIE Deformed Frogs partnership was a year-long university–school collaboration between the University of California at Berkeley (UC Berkeley) and Franklin Middle School,[1] an inner-city school in Northern California. The partners on this project included Franklin teachers, KIE researchers, and graduate students from the Integrative Biology department at UC Berkeley, all of whom came together to design and implement new KIE curriculum at Franklin. The partnership was initiated through a UC Berkeley outreach program called Interactive University whose goal was to foster connections between the university and urban students, particularly those who are typically underrepresented in higher education.

The six Franklin teachers on the team represented a wide range of classroom contexts and student needs. Franklin serves a highly diverse community, with two thirds of its 860 students qualifying for free or assisted lunch programs and 25% designated English as a second language. KIE classes included seventh-grade honors biology (two classes, $n = 66$), "regular" seventh-grade biology (two classes, $n = 62$), a Russian bilingual class with Grades 6, 7, and 8 in one classroom ($n = 25$), and a small class of students designated gifted, learning disabled, with four of these students participating on KIE projects as members of the other classes. The diversity of these classes helped to expand the range of student abilities and language levels that KIE hoped to reach. In addition, a sixth-grade science teacher participated in the design process. The school's technology coordinator both participated in design and managed the computer laboratory where the online portions of project activity took place.

Partnership Activities

The partnership ultimately designed and conducted two new KIE curriculum units: a brief introductory unit on twins and a 3-week debate project about deformed frogs. Initially, the partnership held monthly, day-long team meetings. Meetings were briefer and more frequent during implementation. The activities of the year-long partnership included the following:

- Initial team building and goal setting: The diverse members of the team all discussed objectives, articulated their personal goals, and came to consensus on project topics to pursue.
- Design, development, and implementation of the KIE twins project: This was a brief activity to introduce students and teachers to the KIE instructional environment. This effort helped establish a collaborative design process and fostered respect for the diverse skills and contributions of the various members of the team.
- Design and development of the KIE project on deformed frogs: This design process took into account lessons learned from the twins project.
- Implementation of the "Deformed Frogs!" project: This was done first with the seventh-grade science classes and then with the Russian bilingual class.
- Group reflection on partnership activities: Reflection resulted in redesign of the KIE activities for the following year and also informed the everyday practice of the teachers, researchers, and scientists on the team.
- Ongoing professional development activities: These were based on the partnership and took a different shape for each member of the team but included presentations (individual or collaborative) to teachers in the district or to researchers, as well as career paths that evolved based on experience on this project.

Research activities were also embedded into the partnership. Although this aspect of the project was carried out mainly by KIE researchers, its process and results were reflected on jointly, informing the group's understanding of student learning and making the research process visible to all project participants. Research methods entailed inquiry into student learning outcomes as well as study of the partnership itself. Student learning was measured by a science posttest and conceptual survey, a science beliefs quiz completed before and after the project, coded data from the work that students did online in KIE, performance on the final project debate, and student interviews before and after the project. The partnership audiotaped project meetings to capture important components of project process and the learning that resulted for participants, conducted interviews with participants after the project was over, and maintained contacts in the following year to promote and track ongoing project outcomes.

The Deformed Frogs! Project

The Deformed Frogs! project asks students to don a scientist hat to explore a current unsolved mystery: the apparent increase in physical deformities among frog populations throughout North America. Seventh-grade students in Minnesota used the Internet in the summer of 1995 to bring media attention to the phenomenon when they published their field observations of frogs with a wide variety of unusual deformities. Since that time the topic has received quite a bit of attention among scientists, who still do not agree on a cause, and the press, with the concern that the deformed frog problem may be an indication of a growing environmental danger that may affect humans and other animals.

The topic was selected for a number of reasons. It represents a complex, multidisciplinary problem involving environmental, genetic, and biochemical arguments, yet it fit well with Franklin's seventh-grade science curriculum focus on genetics and simple organisms. Because it is a current scientific issue, the topic legitimately engages students in scientific inquiry and debate and connects to real-world environmental issues they could read about in the newspaper. Finally, it was a compelling topic for the participants, and teachers correctly predicted that students would find deformed frogs sufficiently "gross" and "cool" to want to learn more.

In the Deformed Frogs! project, students evaluate the available evidence on the Internet and conduct an in-class debate about the causes of the problem. Activities begin with a *Nightline* video that introduces the controversy and classroom discussion of initial student ideas about possible causes. Students work in pairs to look at and critique background information in KIE about the controversy. They then select one of two leading hypotheses on which to focus their research: parasites that might be interfering physically with the natural development of frog limbs or pesticides that may, after exposure to sunlight, block the hormonal signals that control limb development. Students survey the evidence in KIE (Fig. 12.1), taking analytic notes on each piece of evidence with the help of Mildred the Cow (Davis, chap. 5, this

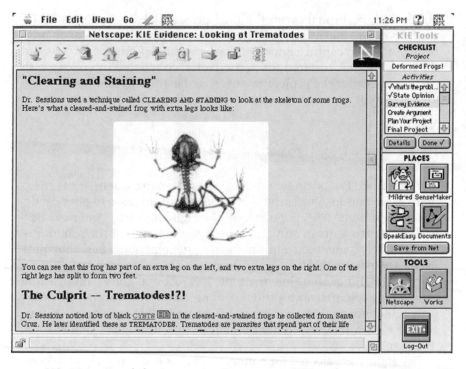

FIG. 12.1.   Knowledge Integration Environment (KIE) evidence to support
the parasite hypothesis.

volume), who is available for hints about productive avenues of analysis. The project culminates in an in-class debate between supporters of
each hypothesis based on evidence-based presentations developed
with the help of SenseMaker (Bell, chap. 6, this volume).

The project anchored the science curriculum by providing activities
on a frog theme interspersed throughout the year. As they became familiar with the curriculum, the teachers were able to make more and
more connections between frogs and other topics. One of the scientists in the partnership led students on a field trip to assess a local
pond as a possible frog habitat and to explore amphibian ecology. Students learned about frog anatomy through hands-on frog dissections
and a tank of developing tadpoles in the classroom. For inner-city children, many of whom had never seen a tadpole, these activities provided important links between life experience and the science they
study in class. These links were strengthened by the use of the
Internet to explore a current scientific controversy; the online evidence was reflected in articles students read in the newspaper about
newly published research results on the effect of pesticides on frog de-

formities, allowing students to participate in science as a dynamic enterprise in a way that is impossible to portray through a static textbook. The activity also helps students to experience the Internet as an authentic tool for scientific research.

Partnership Activity Structures

Throughout the year, the project was guided by activities of the partnership, designed to support the knowledge integration both of students and of adult team members.

As described earlier, members of the deformed frogs partnership included a diverse set of teachers, biology graduate students, researchers, and developers from the KIE team. Each of these disciplines—educational research, science, and educational practice—would be likely to promote different perspectives on the task of curriculum development and implementation. Although these different perspectives are each critical to a successful project, working together productively with different goals can be a challenge.

In early getting-to-know-you activities, we learned that the team included significant depth of expertise in the domains of biology, pedagogy, classroom management, seventh-grade science, and learning environment development. We learned that participants differed in explicit project goals: For example, the seventh-grade biology teacher was looking for textbook alternatives to inspire students who tended to be disengaged from science class, whereas the bilingual teacher sought a compelling project that would give her students access to the same challenging science content as other classes while providing authentic motivation for building skills in academic English. Team members also varied widely in their beliefs about and experience with curriculum, instructional methods, and the role of technology in the classroom: For example, technology at Franklin was taught through stand-alone computer or typing classes in a laboratory setting, and integration with subject-matter courses was generally limited to typing in papers on the computers. We also learned that in many ways we lacked a common language about teaching, learning, and science that we would need to negotiate designs: The "education speak" of the researchers on the team was as foreign to other participants as was "Duncan speak"—the name the teachers coined after Duncan, one of the team scientists—for communication patterns of the scientists.

A wide range of activity structures, consistent with our scaffolded knowledge integration instructional framework, were used throughout the project to build common goals and common vocabulary, to develop an appreciation of the expertise that each member brought to the team, and to structure the work in ways that leveraged that expertise effectively in the design and enactment of curriculum for the classroom. In addition to these components of getting the work done, the activity structures were designed to promote knowledge integration for each participant, particularly on the topic of pedagogical practices and tools.

In the enactment of theory-based change, implementers must understand not only the surface features of the innovation; they must understand the "first principles" on which the innovation is based (McLaughlin & Mitra, 2001). Activity structures for this partnership were designed to make visible the ways that KIE enacts elements of the scaffolded knowledge integration framework (Linn, Eylon, & Davis, chap. 2, this volume) and other founding pedagogical principles and to foster group discussion on how they might play a role in the particular learning environment of Franklin. Through these discussions, all project participants—teachers, scientists, and researchers—integrated their knowledge of teaching, learning, seventh graders, and deformed frogs. The following are activity structures that were included.

Regular, Extended Project Team Meetings.   One day of teacher release time per month was provided by the joint support of the Interactive University project and the district. Through this support we were able to hold monthly, day-long, off-site team meetings. Extended team meetings were essential in allowing time not only for immediate planning but also for codevelopment, deep exploration of student learning, and joint reflection. At the beginning of the project, for example, these meetings offered an opportunity to learn about individual goals, negotiate joint goals, and unpack what was meant by inquiry using some of the activities described next.

Walking in Each Other's Shoes.   Early in the project we took the time to visit the contexts where members of the partnership worked to get a better appreciation for the perspectives and expertise of each team member and to build a foundation of mutual respect. This included visits by researchers and scientists to each of the classrooms, which allowed us to observe the varied classroom contexts and teaching strategies of each of the teachers. For example, we watched groups of students in the regular science class counting purple and white kernels on ears of corn to research dominant and recessive traits, with frequent teacher interjections to manage issues of respect in the classroom. In the Russian bilingual classroom, the teacher gave an assignment to write a story and helped the students through their discomfort about coming up with a topic on their own; this, she told us, stems from the fact that education in their home country is very traditional and very focused on right and wrong answers. "You can't be wrong if you write a story," she told them. During these classroom visits the team's scientists had an opportunity to lead discussions with the students about deformed frogs. Scientist and educational research participants on the team hosted similar visits to the laboratories in which we worked. As in the school, each visit promoted discussion not only of the tasks of the work but of the contexts—both physical and intellectual—that shaped our approaches.

Shared Design of Curriculum Materials. One of the core functions of our extended meeting time was to design and review curriculum. These sessions gave us the opportunity to grapple with issues of pedagogy, science content, scientific language, technology, and other important issues on which a shared perspective was crucial. For example, we worked together to write the questions that Mildred, KIE's cognitive cow guide, would ask the students to promote critique of internet materials based on discussions within the partnership of goals for student learning about the Internet as an information resource. As team roles and processes became clearer over the course of the project, we distributed the development process by assigning primary responsibility for development of each aspect of the system to one subgroup with review by the full team in the next meeting. Generally, for example, scientists took the first pass at writing KIE evidence based on scientific content, the researchers had initial responsibility for overall pedagogical design, and teachers developed rubrics for assessments and other components related to classroom implementation. Scientists were also instrumental in forging contacts with the research scientists who were generating new evidence in this current controversy even as the project was being developed. These roles took advantage of the primary expertise of each participant group and structured the collaboration so that everyone contributed and everyone learned from the others.

Shared design was also an opportunity to share expertise among all participants as it related to the various pedagogical, practical, and scientific components of the project. For example, as we considered the model of scientific inquiry that we wanted to present to the students through this project, a discussion with the scientists about the complexity of the scientific method in action prompted teachers to change their introduction of scientific method in the classroom to emphasize the plurality of approaches that scientists actually use.

Shared Reflection on Artifacts.   To make thinking visible within the design meetings, members frequently brought in samples of their own work and of student work. For example, the KIE team showed types of assessments used in the past that measured student conceptual learning, and discussed how similar approaches might be useful in Franklin classrooms.

These artifacts played a significant role in keeping the project team focused on student learning and pedagogy as primary criteria for design. For example, one of the challenges faced by this diverse team was agreement on the level at which scientific content should be presented. The scientists on the team were concerned with accuracy. The depictions of biological mechanisms they generated tended to be at a detailed and sophisticated level—such as an illustration of the role of gradients in hormonal processing—to avoid the student misconceptions they feared would ensue from simplified models. Teachers, by contrast, were concerned with accessibility. They often raised issues of student developmental levels and curriculum paths: For example, their students had not yet studied basic chemistry, so the idea of chemical gradients was likely to be far beyond their grasp. To help resolve this difference in perspective, the partnership gave students a pretest before their first KIE unit to better understand their current scientific thinking and brought in the results as artifacts for shared reflection. Making student thinking visible to the team facilitated discussions of student knowledge integration and the need for intermediate models of scientific processes to build on their current understanding, supporting the collaborative design of project materials based on those shared criteria.

Modeling of Pedagogical Approaches.   Another way to make visible the pedagogical foundations of the KIE environment was through modeling. In an early design meeting, for example, the group watched a video of Mr. K (the classroom teacher with whom the KIE team has a longtime association) leading technology-supported student inquiry. The team then discussed the video, with teachers commenting on what strategies Mr. K had used that were similar or different from their own and the issues of the Franklin environment that might require adapting his approaches (e.g., the students in Franklin's urban environment tended to behave differently than the students in the video, leading to discussions of classroom management approaches that might be necessary for successful facilitation of student knowledge integration). This is an example of one way that the activity structures on this project facilitated participant knowledge integration—with explicit discussion of current teaching practices and specific ways in which new practices might be embedded—and supported the common research-based call for professional development activities to be integrally tied to classroom application (e.g., Elmore, 2002; Loucks-Horsley et al., 1998).

Modeling was also used in the classroom itself: Mr. K came in to facilitate an early KIE class with Franklin students, the project scientists introduced initial science concepts, and the researchers on the team led early classes in which students were learning to work and think with KIE, demonstrating specific discussions that are useful for introducing new ideas of critiquing evidence or techniques that encourage productive peer-to-peer dialogue in debates. Initially, the teachers were most active in facilitating classroom activities, but these models helped them to become increasingly comfortable with facilitating learning through KIE as the project progressed.

Grading Party. Case studies of teachers implementing visions of reform into their classroom practices show varied degrees of integration with existing techniques: In some cases, surface features of the innovation are "grafted" onto more traditional approaches (Knapp, 1997). To promote more thorough integration, collaborative development of curricula for us also meant collaborative development of some of the classroom practices that are often particularly entrenched: for example, how grades are assigned. In KIE, posttests attempt to assess not just the right or wrong answer but the degree of knowledge integration exhibited in student explanations of their answer (D. Clark, 2000). For teachers accustomed to more traditional testing mechanisms, this strategy raised concerns about how they would be able to make fair judgments about the learning exhibited in student work and how they would find the time. The team set aside a day of group work as a grading party in which teachers, scientists, and researchers all grappled together with how to apply the grading rubrics they had designed earlier. The team sought to identify student knowledge integration when they saw it. The collaborative process had several benefits: It helped to get the work done and provided a forum for discussing the merit of particular student responses, removing some of the subjectivity of the process and allowing the participants to gain more general insights into student thinking.

Postproject Reflection. The team also set aside time late in the project to reflect as a group on the learning that students exhibited, both in written materials and through performance on the final project debate. The group watched excerpts of videotapes of debates in each class and used them to compare and contrast approaches that teachers had taken to structuring this activity (e.g., in one classroom students were presenting their scientific arguments to their peers, and in another, the debate was judged by a panel that included other Franklin teachers and the school principal). This meeting was a time to celebrate students' successes and also to deepen each participant's understanding of what had happened this year and plan improvements for the following year.

Joint Professional Development Activities. After the project was over, the group continued to walk in each other's shoes by sharing professional development opportunities in various career contexts. For example, researchers joined the teachers in an invited presentation about the Deformed Frogs! project at a district-wide teacher meeting, and one of the teachers joined one of the researchers to present project results at a meeting of the National Association for Research on Science Teaching. A year after the partnership officially ended, the group collaborated on a presentation to the Governors' Conference in San Francisco that featured students who had participated in the Deformed Frogs! project in its second year at Franklin. Each of these opportunities promoted further reflection on the potential impact of the team and on potential growth paths for the individuals on the team.

RESULTS

Results of partnership activities are discussed here from two perspectives: outcomes as reflected in student achievement and outcomes as reflected in the professional development of project participants. Student learning is the ultimate goal of science education partnerships and is therefore an important reflection of whether the distributed expertise of the team was successfully brought to bear on educational challenges. Professional development outcomes are no less important. For the teachers, these outcomes included their comfort and ability to use new approaches and tools in the classroom: critical components of the staying power of the innovation and its ability to sustain benefit for student achievement beyond the life of the partnership.

Deformed Frogs! and Student Achievement

On the project overall, student cognitive outcomes were assessed through analysis of pretests and posttests of science understanding, language, and scientific beliefs; student debate performance; student interviews; and notes taken in KIE. Brief excerpts of results are presented here; for more detailed analysis, see Shear (1998).

Compared to most of the seventh-grade curriculum at Franklin, the causal mechanisms that were the focus of the Deformed Frogs! project are extremely complex, requiring students to understand fairly detailed concepts related to limb growth in tadpoles and hormonal processing. Project materials had been developed to allow students to build scientific ideas on a number of levels, from the simple phenomenological ("Sunlight changes things") to more complex causal relations ("Because the chemical methoprene changes structure when it reacts with sunlight, methoprene in a natural environment may be more dangerous to amphibians than lab-tested methoprene"). The deepest level reflected in the design goals was that of the causal mechanism behind the two hypotheses: according to researchers, how do parasites or pesticides cause frog deformities?

The teachers in the partnership were impressed that many of their students were able to offer coherent descriptions of these mechanisms in the final debate and on the written posttest. Across the wide range of students with whom the team worked—ranging from honors students, to low-performing students, to some with very limited skills in English—different levels of knowledge integration based on similar instruction are to be expected. The goal was to support each student as he or she built new skills in scientific understanding and scientific thinking rather than to expect a particular threshold of performance from all students. This range of performance is illustrated in the following results from the bilingual class: Student responses to a posttest question asking them to describe the parasite hypothesis were coded by a team of teachers and researchers on a scale that reflected depth of understanding and appropriate use of evidence. The coding key used is shown in Table 12.1, and results for the bilingual class are shown in Fig. 12.2.

Figure 12.2 shows that over 50% of the students were able to articulate the mechanism of the parasite hypothesis to some degree, and nearly 25% were able to provide a complete instructed explanation, indicating that trematode parasites embed themselves into the tissue of a tadpole where limbs will grow and block normal leg growth during metamorphosis. Because student familiarity with these issues prior to instruction was extremely unlikely, no pretest questions on mechanisms were given, and these responses are taken to represent new learning.

In interpreting these results, it is important to keep in mind the diversity of students in this single class: Students were in three different

TABLE 12.1
Coding Key for Mechanism Questions

Code	Definition	Example
1	No response	
2	Unclear, random	My answer is based on the pestice theory and I support it all the way.
3	Descriptive	I think that this frog became deformed because it has some chemicals in the lake.
4	Other causal	Trematodes jump on a frog and limbud to life in there and eat their vitamins.
5	Partial instructed mechanism	When the frog is still tadpole the trematode go in its limbbuds, and then it makes a lot of legs.
6	Full instructed mechanism	Trematode get into tadpoles limb bud and when the legs grow the trematode blocks the way.

grades, had very different experiences with schooling in their various home provinces in the Soviet Republic—ranging from very rigorous schooling to no school at all for up to 3 years—and had a broad range of English language skills ranging from preproduction to conversational fluency.[2] Bilingual classes frequently postpone access to challenging content in favor of direct language instruction (Cummins, 1989; Garcia, 1994; Wong Fillmore, 1989); it is therefore significant that many of the students in this class, as demonstrated on the posttest and in debate performances, were able to integrate knowledge of both science and language simultaneously (see Shear, 1998, for extended discussion of these issues).

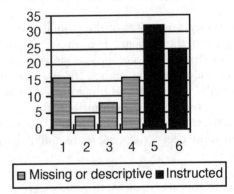

FIG. 12.2. Results for parasite mechanism in the bilingual class.

In each of the classes with which we worked, teachers were struck by the changed patterns of success achieved on this project. One indicator was simply task completion: Based on teacher estimate, roughly 65% of the students in regular seventh-grade science generally turned in assignments. By contrast, engagement on the Deformed Frogs! project was so high that all students but one turned in their work. To the teacher, this was significant not only because students were learning more, but because she was able to see—and give them credit for—the learning that was taking place:

> This project . . . gave me another way to measure non-productive students: [I know more about those who are] the first to raise their hands in class discussion, but never turn in work.

Increased engagement with schoolwork was made evident in other ways during the project, including taking the parasites versus pesticides debate outside into recess or even a weekend basketball game or tracking the progress of this current science controversy in the newspaper after the project ended. Again, teachers cited this as surprising behavior from students who typically showed little interest in science.

In fact, a number of the most striking student performances came from students who were traditionally disengaged in science class. The sidebar tells the story of Janice, one previously failing student whose debate performance was so unprecedented for her that the partnership repeatedly reflected on what they could learn from her success on this project that might allow them to support others in the future. Janice became a pivotal case for the partnership, as her performance clearly illustrated that the instructional approaches the team was exploring had the capability to support students that teachers had tried, and failed, to reach in the past. Her story was also used in discussions among the teaching staff at Franklin as—based on this experience—they began to explore the broader use of alternative assessments to support students who are capable of learning but do not show evidence of it through traditional assessment techniques.

For some students, newfound success on the Deformed Frogs! project inspired them to perform at higher academic levels in subsequent class activities. One student, for example, appeared distracted through most of the computer work and delivered a showy presentation that demonstrated little learning but received the highest grade in his class on the posttest, which demanded both subject matter knowledge and application of that knowledge in new ways and was scored jointly by the team of teachers, researchers, and scientists. His

Janice is a seventh-grade student who was observed in non-KIE activities to be completely disengaged from classroom work, often sitting by herself with her head down on her desk. According to her teacher, she typically turned in tests without reading them, writing "I DON'T KNOW!!!" in response to each question. In an interview she indicated that she wants to be a hair dresser when she grows up, and therefore science is irrelevant to her life.

By contrast, on the Deformed Frogs! project this student was observed to be focused and working most of the time, even asking on occasion for help with the correct spelling of a word she was typing and otherwise asking not to be interrupted so that she could focus on the evidence, which was difficult for her to read. Nevertheless, she continued to protest that frogs are "boring" and that her partner would be making the presentation because she herself was not interested.

When the debate day came, however, Janice stepped up to the microphone and delivered a presentation that clearly cited five pieces of evidence drawn from a wide range of sources encountered in the project and made thoughtful arguments about the significance of each, even critiquing claims that students had made earlier in the debate in support of the other hypothesis. Her argument indicates that she had engaged in the analysis of a great deal of evidence and was able to link these separate ideas to construct a coherent overall model of the frog deformity problem.

Her teacher summarized her performance this way:

I have this student who the first day said, "I hate frogs. Why do we study about frogs—what difference does it make anyway? I will NEVER get up in front of the class and talk about frogs." She ... absolutely knocked me off my feet—I wanted to cry. This student was able to express herself, she was able to present ... her side of the argument and use evidence to back it up.

Although Janice's success on this project was not seen to translate to success in more traditional academic formats such as written tests, the Deformed Frogs! debate did enable her to prove to classmates, to teachers, and to herself that she is capable of learning and performing, particularly when she feels comfortable with the social context in which learning is situated and when she is allowed to express her opinion rather than being expected to memorize the right answers.

teacher considers this to be a turning point for this student who had previously been labeled a *failure*:

So I have one student who does nothing, and got the highest grade in the class [on the Frogs posttest]. . . . He's now begun to think ahead, and to excel and turn some work in, because he says, well, I can do this and a lot of people thought I could.

Interestingly, patterns of success changed for some high-achieving students as well. The honors science teacher, for example, described a "star student" who excels in traditional school situations. She learns quickly, is academically motivated, and takes success for granted, appearing somewhat aloof from most class activities: Like many of the honors students, she would "do well on Jeopardy." According to the teacher, this student did not take work in the computer laboratory seriously; after all, this type of activity is not real science. The student got a low *B* on the posttest: an unusually low score for her. Summarized by the teacher, "If I give her a routine math problem she'll get it right away. This required her to *apply* it."

The Deformed Frogs! project, then, represented a new type of learning environment with new opportunities for engagement and for assessment. Some students who were traditionally unsuccessful learned that they could succeed; others who were traditionally successful with a cognitive minimalist approach to school requirements learned that other approaches might be more productive.

Additional outcomes for these students related to their approaches and views about science. Teachers told the team that debates over parasites and pesticides continued into the rest of the school year, refueled by frequent newspaper articles reporting new discoveries of evidence. One teacher remarked that the students have a new appreciation of science as an evolving field without a single right answer. They also learned to use the Internet in authentic ways to support scientific research and to use it intelligently. A primary focus of KIE work was the skill of critiquing what they read on the Web—Who wrote it and with what possible agenda? One student reported in a postproject interview that he had learned not to believe everything he sees on the Internet because not all of it is true. This is in contrast to the increasingly dangerous assumption most students have that everything they see in print, or particularly everything they see on a computer, is factual and credible. The partnership made this important type of student learning a priority rather than establishing the model of the Internet as an online textbook.

Professional Development Outcomes

Another important measure of partnership success is the professional development of project participants. The goal of professional development is to enable the knowledge integration of each participant, building on existing expertise to enhance their own practice by learning from others.

For the teachers in the partnership, knowledge integration took the form of expanded repertoires of teaching strategies. They all gained experience with integrating technology into their teaching as well as learning a number of other new techniques that they subsequently embedded into their everyday teaching. For example, teachers reported applying the KIE concept of supporting conjectures with evidence when they teach mathematics, thinking hard about alternative means of assessment for everything they teach and using the debate activity structure in other classroom contexts. They benefited from the project's face-to-face meetings as an opportunity for genuine collaboration among their peers. The teachers shared tips and perspectives and helped each other with pedagogical or practical challenges, opportunities often lacking in day-to-day teaching. They also reported growing more reflective about their own practice: One teacher, for example, learned about the value of focusing on students' learning of language in science class from the bilingual teacher involved, and another reported that she took steps to rethink her teaching of science in general.

For the scientists on the team, two primary outcomes were the strengthening of ties within the scientific community (as evidenced by several conference presentations) and the integration of educational understanding with their science expertise. Both scientist participants have a professional interest in teaching, and this was an outstanding opportunity for them to engage in curriculum development, spend time in classrooms, and learn what works and what does not. The scientists report that within the scientific community there are numerous examples of scientists who try, and fail, to take their work into schools. Part of the problem is the available time required, but much of the problem is the disconnect between the way scientists view their research and which issues motivate and excite them with the perspectives and motivations of middle school students. This partnership went a long way toward bridging the gap, in part through its active negotiation of age-appropriate issues and scientific models on which materials should focus. As a result, the scientists we worked with have since been able to represent a successful approach to the scientific community and to others who are still trying to figure out how to make it work.

For KIE project participants, knowledge integration on this project extended the models for this learning environment to new contexts and new populations of teachers. It was an outstanding opportunity to work closely with teachers who were new to using technology and to explore the important challenges of working in an urban environment. The partnership was able to broaden its understanding of technology-supported learning to new populations of students, including bilingual children. The established practices of the teachers, for example, informed designs of glossaries and argument construction tools in ways that have improved the learning environment for students beyond Franklin.

All team members also participated in more traditional professional development opportunities through this project: for example, presenting at conferences both within their own disciplines (e.g., research and scientific conferences) and presenting jointly across disciplines (e.g., a collaborative teacher and researcher presentation at a research conference).

These experiences demonstrated the power of a partnership to support the professional development of each participant. The classroom teachers presented results at academic meetings; the scientists taught complex science to students, their parents, and their teachers; and the technologists designed tools that offered support to a wider range of students.

DISCUSSION: GUIDING PRINCIPLES OF SCIENCE EDUCATION PARTNERSHIPS

The project described in this chapter suggests that KIE science education partnerships are guided by the following four principles:

1. *Design partnership activities to foster knowledge integration for all participants*. Just like students, adults come to learning situations with a repertoire of existing ideas. In many cases they bring a strong expertise in a particular domain or context. For example, the partnership described in this chapter was comprised of accomplished educators who were well versed in teaching and classroom management, scientists with deep knowledge of biological processes and scientific thinking, and a research team with significant experience in student learning and technology-supported learning environments. The group designed partnership activities to leverage and make visible the contributions and perspectives of each participant, as well as to promote the willingness of participants to see themselves as a learner as well as an expert. As a result, each member of the team expanded their repertoire of ideas about learning approaches and environments, science content, and the scientific thinking of seventh graders.

2. *Create compelling, shared tasks to support the professional development of the group*. Collaboration has become a buzzword in educational circles. In some educational improvement efforts collaboration is seen as an end in itself rather than a venue to support purposeful activity (Warren-Little, 1990), leaving teachers with little felt incentive to participate. By contrast, KIE science education partnerships select a compelling project of immediate utility around which to focus the

collaboration. Tasks such as selecting the level of abstraction at which to present scientific models, designing assessments, or scoring student work involve participants from all areas of expertise and require negotiation to achieve outcomes.

3. *Ensure that partners respect both shared and individual goals.* Although curriculum design and implementation is a shared task, the diversity of the team means that each participant has a role. The teachers on this project, for example, were looking for new and better projects with which to reach their students, as well as opportunities to further their own professional development or to reinject excitement into their practice. Scientists, by contrast, were looking for connections to possible careers related to education and to bring their selected topic of study to a wider audience. Researchers wanted to enhance their tool set and to hear outcomes of their work in the voices of children. KIE partnerships negotiate tasks and approaches to promote the achievement of individual as well as shared goals.

4. *Make student learning the centerpiece of activities.* One risk of working with a diverse team necessarily characterized by diverse individual goals and perspectives is that forward progress may be hampered by poor planning. In KIE partnerships, the common goal of supporting student learning offers a way to focus activities, schedule work, negotiate agreements, and measure success. Repeatedly, differences of opinion about the level at which scientific content should be presented were resolved with pretests or other student artifacts that provided evidence of student learning needs. For example, a pretest on twins showed that very few students had a genetic understanding of twinning (over 50% of the students in one class believed that two people are twins if they simply dress alike), suggesting ways to tailor course content for age appropriateness and resolving design differences that had earlier focused on the science and not the student.

CONCLUSIONS

Partnerships bring to education the broad, rich variety of expertise necessary for design, testing, implementation, and improvement of innovations. Creating activity structures and goals for partnerships to ensure their success has been an important prong of the KIE research program. The design of partnership activities and goals reflects the knowledge integration perspective embodied in all the educational activities of the research project.

Promoting the knowledge integration of a research partnership means ensuring that all the partners engage in knowledge integration themselves and, in addition, that the partners support the knowledge integration of their collaborators. The activities described in this chapter enable partnerships to support each other's knowledge integration.

To succeed, partnerships need a shared view of learning goals and buy in to the knowledge integration process. One reason that partnerships characteristic of science education in the 1950s and 1960s were less successful is that they often embraced a hierarchical structure as well as assuming far more compartmentalization of knowledge than do knowledge integration partnerships like the one described in this chapter. In particular, early collaborative science education reform efforts relied on natural scientists to determine the subject matter, educators to design the assessments, and teachers to perform the instruction. Often, individual participants blamed others for failing to bring these projects to fruition rather than recognizing the necessity of negotiating goals and designing activities that ensured mutual respect.

Today's partnerships take a much more interactive approach to science education reform. They also bring individuals and resources, often including technology-based tools, that make these efforts more feasible. In particular, a learning environment that hosts both the curriculum and student artifacts not only delivers activities more consistently but keeps a more effective record of modifications. In addition, technology-enhanced learning environments such as the Web-Based Inquiry Science Environment (WISE) document student and teacher interactions in ways that improve the ability of the whole partnership to inspect successful and unsuccessful aspects of instruction, enabling each partner to test ideas concerning potentially beneficial student–instructor interactions.

Many obstacles to the success of partnerships have emerged in this work. Often, finding time for meetings and discussions as well as locations to hold such events stands in the way of partnership interactions. In the work described here, both the Interactive University project and the school district contributed to freeing participants from day-to-day responsibilities to participate in collaborative design activities. Often this luxury is difficult or impossible to arrange.

Participants in partnerships, even when they have the opportunity to meet and share common goals and common perceptions of the nature of learning, often fail to collaborate and integrate their understanding because of the myth of a common vocabulary, the difficulty in agreeing on interpretations of observations, or the lack of shared

norms for success. The Deformed Frogs partnerships and other partnerships organized by KIE, WISE, and the Computer as Learning Partner all have tested and refined a set of activity structures to promote
collaborative knowledge integration. These activity structures fit the
scaffolded knowledge integration framework and enable partnerships
to (a) make the group's ideas accessible, (b) make the partnership's
thinking visible, (c) help partnership participants learn from each
other, and (d) promote an autonomous and self-regulating partnership process.

Making Ideas Accessible. For the Deformed Frogs partnership, a
focus on the controversy about causes of declining amphibian populations made the science and associated instructional challenges accessible to everyone. All of the partners learned something about either
the nature of controversy, the nature of student learning and instruction, or the scientific ideas associated with declining amphibian populations. Shared enthusiasm for the topics of discussion contributed to
the excitement and animation that tended to characterize meetings
of this group.

In addition, frequent presentations before other groups captured
the spirit of these meetings. Often, discussions initiated at meetings
continued when the partnership made presentations. At one memora-
ble seminar at UC Berkeley when the Deformed Frogs partnership presented its designs as a work in progress, a classroom teacher impressed both the entire audience and the other members of the
partnership with an eloquent account of the nature of knowledge integration and the reason that elements of the software work so well for
students in her class. Publicity surrounding the project eventually resulted in an invitation to discuss the project and the science on which
it is based at the Governors' Conference in San Francisco, as mentioned earlier. The partnership participants, and especially the students who guided the governors through an analysis of the available
evidence, enjoyed contrasting this form of science learning with that
recalled by the governors about their own experiences.

Making Thinking Visible. The partnership engages in a number of
structured activities to make both the process of instruction and the
nature of student learning visible. The grading party has proven extremely successful because it is a joint effort at assessing student
work. It typically takes three or four iterations for the group to agree
on common norms for student work, and often these discussions include analyses of the science topic as well as discussions about the
epistemological underpinning of student beliefs.

Learning From Each Other. Activity structures that helped the group to learn from each other include, of course, group meetings and email exchanges but also feature visits to the classroom. Each member of the partnership when visiting the classroom brings a broad range of expectations that often collide with their experience in school. These visits often result in powerful discussions among partnership members. For example, a teacher may feel that a particular lesson was unsuccessful until a visiting scientist points out—to the teacher and to the students—that some of the dead ends being pursued by the students actually mimicked lines of reasoning that the scientists themselves had pursued.

Promoting Partnership Autonomy. Ideally, partnerships will develop a sustainable mode of interaction in which the varied participants remain available but interact less frequently. During the course of the year in which the partnership was most active, activities like regular analyses of student progress and scaffolding of classroom interactions helped to position the teachers to use the activities independently in subsequent years. Ongoing partnership interactions have included as-needed technical support, updates to web pages based on scientific advances related to the controversy, and group presentations in subsequent years.

Many classroom-based innovations fade after their initial implementation, as funding becomes less available to continue active outside support. Activities designed to promote knowledge integration, the autonomy of partnership participants, and strong ties among team members are key to the persistent success of innovations, offering a mechanism to contribute to the ongoing learning of students and professionals alike.

ENDNOTES

1. In this chapter, the names of the school and its inhabitants have been changed.
2. In keeping with the teacher's normal practices, the test was given in English, but students were allowed to ask for help with any vocabulary that had not been a particular target of instruction (e.g., they were allowed to ask for a translation of *currently* but not *parasite*).

IV

NEXT STEPS

IV

NEXT STEPS

13

Specific Design Principles: Elaborating the Scaffolded Knowledge Integration Framework

Marcia C. Linn
University of California, Berkeley

Philip Bell
University of Washington

Elizabeth A. Davis
University of Michigan

The series of design-based research studies of inquiry projects yield specific design principles to help designers and teachers transform science students into lifelong learners one inquiry project at a time. Here we connect these principles to the metaprinciples and pragmatic pedagogical principles introduced in chapter 3 (Linn, Davis, & Eylon, this volume). We discuss how these principles can help design partnerships (see Shear, Bell, & Linn, chap. 12, this volume), create new projects, or help individual teachers improve their practice.

By synthesizing findings from design-based research studies (see chap. 4, Bell, Hoadley, & Linn, this volume) in specific design principles we elaborate on our metaprinciples and pragmatic principles to make these efforts available to a broad range of researchers, designers, and teachers. The design narratives reported in earlier chapters show the potential of technology-enhanced learning environments along with the challenges of using these opportunities successfully.

The specific principles emerge from iterative refinement of inquiry projects in complex classroom contexts. These specific principles capture the lessons learned from the testing and refinement that has occurred.

Specific principles rest on empirical results from design-based research studies. As such, the specific principles apply primarily to the context and the inquiry project used in the research but offer starting points for new design partnerships and individual teachers. Because the specific principles emerged from separate design narratives, they have some overlap with each other.

For design partnerships creating new projects, specific principles offer ideas for activity structures and features. A specific principle such as "Encourage students to come to consensus on shared criteria for decisions and products" elaborates the pedagogical principle that says, "Scaffold groups to consider cultural values and to design criteria and standards." The specific principle also points to a curriculum design pattern, in this case a collaborative discussion in which students critique principles written by their peers. The principle articulates the pedagogical goal of the design pattern. The research that led to the specific principle (see Clark, chap. 8, this volume) gives design partnerships further clues about how to design a new project.

For individual teachers who are refining a project, specific principles offer suggestions. For example, the specific principle, "Create opportunities for learners to explain their ideas and provide justifications," may motivate those reviewing a project to analyze embedded prompts to see if they are eliciting explanations or justifications and to change the prompts if they are not succeeding.

Typically projects need customization to succeed with new students, teachers, or curriculum. Specific principles capture the design refinements from successful iterations of projects in a particular setting. The specific principles can inform the customization process, suggesting specific ways to improve a project. For example, the specific principle, "With complex, multidisciplinary topics, enable students to learn about science principles and concepts on demand by offering enrichment in areas where few are prepared," suggests analyzing the prior knowledge of the anticipated student population and designing customized, on-demand resources to meet their needs.

Specific design principles showcase a feature of a learning environment such as a software tool (see examples in Linn, Davis, & Bell, chap. 1, this volume) or a curriculum design pattern. For example, Web-Based Inquiry Science Environment (WISE) projects often implement the "read evidence, critique, reflect, and seek new information" pattern (Linn, Clark, et al., 2003).

METACOGNITIVE, PRAGMATIC PEDAGOGICAL, AND SPECIFIC PRINCIPLES

The following sections articulate how the metaprinciples and pragmatic pedagogical principles from *Computers, Teachers, Peers: Science Learning Partners* (Linn & Hsi, 2000) connect to the specific principles introduced in earlier chapters. We have placed the specific principles under the most appropriate pragmatic principle, but some specific principles could also substantiate another pragmatic principle. Our Web site offers a hyperlinked version of the relations and indicates when specific principles might illustrate more than one metaprinciple or pedagogical principle.

Research evidence to support each specific principle comes from studies reported in this book. Illustrative features taken from contemporary learning environments contextualize the specific principles. Often additional evidence and other relevant features appear in the chapter where the specific principle was introduced. Readers can elaborate and annotate these representations at the Web site.

Metaprinciple: Make Science Accessible

The first metaprinciple described in chapter 3 (Linn, et al., this volume) calls for making science accessible so students can recognize new ideas and generate connections between the new ideas and existing ideas. Design of material to add to the mix of ideas held by students demands careful analysis of the ideas students bring to science class. Well-designed examples—including *pivotal cases*—can stimulate extensive knowledge integration and start students on the path of regularly reconsidering their scientific ideas (Linn, in press). Some examples have built-in feedback mechanisms that help students monitor their progress in understanding science. Examples can have unintended consequences and lead students to generate unproductive connections, lull students into complacency, or reinforce non-normative models.

In chapter 3, Linn et al. (this volume, Table 3.2) described the pragmatic pedagogical principles associated with the metaprinciple that says to make science accessible. This section links specific principles with each pragmatic principle.

Build on Student Ideas. To make science accessible, the first pragmatic principle calls for designing instruction that encourages students to build on their ideas rather than isolate new information from existing knowledge. Specific principles depict the challenge of reducing complexity while maintaining desirable difficulties. These specific principles also reiterate the value of pivotal cases as discussed in chapter 3 (Linn et al., this volume). Pivotal cases can encourage students to build cohesive understanding by specifically linking disparate contexts such as hot and cold environments to bring connections among normative ideas to life. At present, however, researchers cannot predict which examples will pivot student views in normative directions and which will lead students down wrong paths. Tests in the context of classroom learning can help refine the initial designs suggested by specific principles.

To encourage students to build on their scientific ideas as they develop more and more powerful and useful pragmatic scientific principles, specific examples include the following:

- Reduce complexity of examples, visualizations, or models by eliminating functionality and details that distract from the main concept.

  Example evidence: When researchers iteratively streamline models and examples they can improve student learning (Clark, chap. 8, this volume).

  Example feature: The equilibrium model (Clark, chap. 8, this volume) and the heat flow model (Linn et al., chap. 3, this volume) showcase essential elements of complex concepts.

- Match the level of abstraction to the level of sophistication of student knowledge.

  Example evidence: When students encounter examples that are too abstract, they memorize and forget (Linn & Hsi, 2000). When examples are overly concrete, they can distract learners from the main point (Clark, chap. 8, this volume).

  Example feature: Iterative design of the arrows that represent the rate of heat flow in the equilibrium simulation demonstrated that multiple arrows of equal size spaced equally around the object worked best (Clark, chap. 8, this volume).

- With complex, multidisciplinary topics, enable students to learn about science principles and concepts on demand by offering enrichment in areas in which few are prepared.

  Example evidence: Students can build on their knowledge when curriculum materials provide mechanisms for learning about related scientific concepts and principles on demand (Bell, chap. 10, this volume).

  Example feature: WISE and Science Controversies Online Partnerships for Education (SCOPE) provide hints on demand. The inquiry map enables designers to use hinges to give students choices among topics.

- Provide an overview and pointers that direct students to related science topics.

  Example evidence: By creating activities that challenge students to generate connections across contexts and topics, designers add desirable difficulties (Bell, chap. 10, this volume; Bjork, 1999; Kintsch, 1998).

Example feature: The WISE inquiry map allows designers to create, test, and revise activity sequences and to reuse promising patterns.

Connect to Personally Relevant Problems. To make science accessible, another pragmatic principle says to design "instruction that features personally relevant problems." Implementing this principle involves seeking examples that resonate with student experiences and interests. For some students science is personally relevant when it connects to knowledge they envision needing in a scientific career. For others, science is only relevant when it applies to an immediate problem or concern such as keeping a lunch cool or protecting the environment. Often instructors need to customize examples to their students and courses.

Specific principles that encourage learners to investigate personally relevant problems and revisit their science ideas regularly include the following:

- Connect representations to students' everyday experiences.

  Example evidence: When students encounter everyday representations such as thermometers, they can connect familiar ideas to complex science (Clark, chap. 8, this volume).

  Example feature: The thermal equilibrium activity uses cartoon bubbles to depict the connections between the thermometer, temperature scale, and hand.
- Link theory and practice in authentic problems by scaffolding rational processes (rather than outcomes).

  Example evidence: When students were graded on the justifications of their design practices, they gained better understanding of the scientific principles than when graded on the product (Hoadley, chap. 7, this volume).

  Example feature: WISE permits designers to decide when to provide student feedback.
- Represent thinking with argument representations to depict: (a) students theorizing about the controversial topic and (b) other perspectives associated with the controversy.

  Example evidence: To support students in making connections to their prior knowledge, scaffold the expression of ideas in the knowledge representation (Bell, chap. 6, this volume). Include ideas in an argument map to bridge from student understanding to the other perspectives on the debate topic.

Example feature: The SenseMaker argument mapping tool allows students to express their ideas. Curriculum designers can seed the representation with items representing different controversy perspectives.

- Introduce complex contemporary controversies in science.

Example evidence: Contemporary controversies motivate students to connect ideas from the media and enable students to revisit ideas (Bell, chap. 10, this volume).

Example feature: Designers can use the inquiry map to implement the tested design pattern of reviewing evidence—using SenseMaker to represent arguments—and debating peers.

- Enable teachers to repeatedly and gradually integrate inquiry and technology into their practice.

Example evidence: Trial and refinement enables teachers to test ideas and refine them in the context of use (Slotta, chap. 9, this volume).

Example feature: The WISE teacher interface makes it easy for teachers to modify the order of activities, content of notes, nature of hints, and topics of discussion.

- Make student learning the centerpiece of design activities so all participants have an accessible and personally relevant goal.

Example evidence: By focusing on student learning, designers can resolve conflicts with evidence from classroom pretests, embedded notes, or classroom observations (Shear et al., chap. 12, this volume).

Example feature: The WISE software offers a way to focus activities, schedule work, negotiate agreements, and measure success to support student learning.

- Case studies that highlight the human face of a controversy can promote the salience and relevance of the topic to students.

Example evidence: When students recognize that events can connect to people like them, they become more motivated to understand the problem (Bell, chap. 10, this volume).

Example feature: The "Cycles of Malaria" project features a case study of a boy who becomes infected with malaria to put a human face on an unfamiliar disease; teachers connect malaria and AIDS.

Communicate the Diversity of Inquiry.   The third pragmatic principle associated with making science accessible says "to communicate the rich diversity of the inquiry process." Far too often students leave science class with an image of inquiry as dogmatic and inflexible.

Specific principles that scaffold science activities so learners participate in diverse inquiry processes include the following:

- Balance curriculum sequences to conjoin first-hand scientific investigations with Internet inquiry about relevant scientific evidence and data.

  Example evidence: Blending first-hand inquiry, engagement with rich depictions of the scientific literature, and social activity structures focuses students on construction and debate of meaning (Bell, chap. 10, this volume).

  Example feature: Using the inquiry map instructors can sequence first-hand inquiry, rich depictions of the literature, and social interactions to support debate and interpretation of complex science.

- Develop a repertoire of patterns of inquiry.

  Example evidence: A variety of inquiry patterns have proven successful in learning environment designs (Linn, Clark, et al., 2003).

  Example feature: The inquiry map captures customized patterns to help designers vary inquiry activities.

- Design examples that encourage use of knowledge integration strategies and not recipes.

  Example evidence: Iterative design of the desert houses examples revealed ways to create a suite of examples that promote inquiry (Hoadley, chap. 7, this volume).

  Example feature: WISE supports a "library cart" of examples for students to consider and guides students to develop strategies for selecting among examples.

- Connect the examples in visualizations to the inquiry goals of the project and to personal experiences.

  Example evidence: Visualizations and examples succeed when they engage students in using personal experience or insights to explain complex science (Clark, chap. 8, this volume).

  Example feature: The thermal equilibrium simulation uses a depiction of a human hand (Clark, chap. 8, this volume); the earthquake project incorporates a prediction activity using earthquake-prone areas (Linn, in press).

Metaprinciple: Make Thinking Visible

The second metaprinciple described in chapter 3 (Linn et al., this volume) calls for making thinking visible so students can learn about the ideas of others and communicate their ideas to teachers and peers.

Making thinking visible includes designing models or visualizations to communicate complex concepts. Table 3.2 in chapter 3 (Linn et al., this volume) illustrates the pragmatic principles associated with this metaprinciple. This section links specific principles with each pragmatic principle.

Model the Inquiry Process.   The first pragmatic principle for making thinking visible says to "model the scientific inquiry process of considering alternatives and distinguishing among them." Often students think that scientists can envision an entire research program without worrying about conflicting perspectives or compelling alternatives. Students have reported that scientists disagree because they are perverse rather than recognizing the evidentiary basis for disputes. Media depictions of science often reinforce this view by telling a coherent discovery story filled with insight about what to investigate next rather than angst about competing views.

Showcasing the controversy in science is itself controversial. Some scientists call for courses in science appreciation that emphasize breakthroughs rather than the more mundane exploration of unrewarding conjectures. Others question accounts of scientific progress such as those of Latour (1999) that emphasize the social context of discovery.

This principle, combined with the principle that calls for showcasing diverse inquiry processes, jointly capture the complexity of inquiry. They suggest curriculum design patterns that vary inquiry processes.

Specific principles to model the scientific process of considering alternative explanations and explaining mistakes include the following:

- Scaffold use of knowledge representation tools to promote interpretation and theorizing about evidence.

  Example evidence: Knowledge representation tools help students articulate their ideas about scientific evidence. Students create more elaborate arguments when they use a knowledge representation as they interpret evidence than when they create the knowledge representation after exploring the evidence (Bell, chap. 6, this volume).

  Example feature: The SenseMaker knowledge representation tool supports students in constructing scientific arguments.
- Require coordination between theory and evidence in knowledge representations.

  Example evidence: Argument representations can focus students on elaborating theory–evidence coordinations and increase the frequency of arguments that include causal explorations of how evidence relates to the debate topic (Bell, chap. 6, this volume; Bell & Linn, 2002).

Example feature: The SenseMaker argument map interface promotes consideration and coordination of scientific evidence (as dots) and claims (as frames).

- Create case studies and other narrative accounts of the process of solving scientific problems.

    Example evidence: Case studies provide a narrative about science learning that helps students understand the process of selecting alternatives and connects to the process of monitoring progress (Linn & Clancy, 1992).

    Example feature: Learning environments can scaffold case study exploration, ask for predictions, provide feedback, and engage learners in interactions with mentors.

- Adapt current scientific research to create educational evidence so students can learn about a current controversy.

    Example evidence: Depictions of scientists' explanations of contemporary research findings models new developments in science (Bell, chap. 10, this volume).

    Example feature: SCOPE has devised patterns for adapting scientific articles about recent developments in science so they communicate to broad audiences of learners.

- Support multidisciplinary inquiry about complex controversy to promote student perspective taking.

    Example evidence: When students have grounding in each perspective they can compare issues effectively (Bell, chap. 10, this volume).

    Example feature: Evidence pages can showcase perspectives of various stakeholders associated with a contemporary scientific controversy.

- Mentor users of new curriculum and technology to make inquiry practices visible.

    Example evidence: When mentors join teachers on the first day of using a new technology-enhanced curriculum, they enable more flexible use of the innovations (Slotta, chap. 9, this volume).

    Example feature: Learning environments enable teachers to test alternative inquiry practices easily, to inspect student work immediately, and to record modifications for easy subsequent use.

- Segment topics to promote disciplinary engagement in all aspects of a controversy.

    Example evidence: When learners explore the full scope of an argument, interleaving varied foci, they gain a more robust understanding than when they select particular disciplinary issues to focus on and avoid others. (Bell, chap. 10, this volume).

Example feature: Learning environments can interleave topics and issues so that students connect their ideas broadly. In exploring the proposed ban on DDT, students can explore issues in chemistry and biology.

Scaffold the Process of Generating Explanations. The second pragmatic principle associated with making thinking visible says to "scaffold learners to explain their ideas to others." In a sense, explaining advances, raising conjectures, and asking questions is the essence of science. Yet, in science classes, often the main communication of scientific ideas comes from the text and the main rhetorical task involves clarification. Specific principles suggest ways to scaffold or support learners so that they explain their views by using evidence and developing sound arguments. Scaffolds can enrich the explanations considered by learners and help classes develop some shared criteria and standards for their explanations. Consistent with principles articulated for making science accessible, these principles call for introducing a full range of alternatives rather than artificially constraining the topic. Striking a balance between breadth of connections and streamlining of scientific topics to ensure targeted exploration remains a task for customization in the instructional setting.

The principles in this section have close connections to the principles associated with orchestrating social supports as described in the next section. Here we focus on the scaffolds that elicit ideas and explanations. We seek ways to get all the views held by learners into the discussion. In the section on social supports, we focus more on the design of the interactions among those in the social context.

Specific principles to scaffold learners to explain their ideas to teachers, peers, experts, and themselves include the following:

- Highlight the evidentiary basis of contemporary controversies in science.
  Example evidence: When science activities reveal how the experimental methods become entwined in the controversy, students get a window on science in the making (Bell, chap. 10, this volume).
  Example feature: Learning environments can scaffold the pattern of exploring data, connecting the data to scientific evidence, critiquing methods, and evaluating the claims in light of the methods.

- Scaffold students to produce arguments that make connections between empirical evidence and theoretical conclusions.

  Example evidence: Debates encourage students to connect evidence to the debate topic rather than giving descriptions or vague interpretations (Bell, chap. 6, this volume; Bell & Linn, 2002).

  Example feature: The Knowledge Integration Environment (KIE) and WISE learning environments allow for curriculum designers to prompt students to make causal connections between evidence and the debate topic.

- Create compelling, shared tasks to engage professional development partnerships in explaining their views and considering the views of others.

  Example evidence: Rather than making collaboration an end in itself, support purposeful activity (Warren-Little, 1990), giving teachers an incentive to explain their views (Shear et al., chap. 12, this volume).

  Example feature: Science education partnerships select tasks such as designing assessments or scoring student work to make design accessible to all participants.

- Create opportunities for learners to explain their ideas and provide justifications.

  Example evidence: When students respond to prompts that ask for explanations or when they spontaneously explain their ideas they learn more (Davis, chap. 5, this volume).

  Example feature: WISE and SCOPE as well as other learning environments support embedded prompts for explanations.

- Use historical debates between scientists to showcase scientific argumentation.

  Example evidence: Comparisons of several approaches for introducing students to argument mapping showed that historical debate is a powerful way to elicit core fluencies associated with use of the argument map representation (Bell, chap. 6, this volume).

  Example feature: The SenseMaker argument mapping tool allows for the modeling of the arguments of experts.

- Require students to put forth their own ideas before viewing the ideas of others.

  Example evidence: When students develop an argument for their principle or perspective, they more regularly use evidence to respond to questions and critiques (Clark, chap. 8, this volume).

Example feature: WISE supports discussions in which students must first post their principle or ideas before viewing the ideas of other learners.

Use Multiple Visual Representations From Varied Media. The third pragmatic principle associated with making thinking visible says to "provide multiple visual representations from varied media." Modern technologies have stimulated the development of a vast array of visualizations that have yet to help learners. Often visualizations come from tools used by experts in the course of their research such as molecular modeling environments, computer assisted design environments, or geographical information systems. Experts spend long periods of time learning these tools and typically use them to test new ideas or implement complex solutions. The tools often take too long to learn and, when learned, lack the sort of feedback that would help learners with more basic understanding. Creating visualizations that meet the needs of learners remains a high priority for science education.

To make visualizations helpful for science learners, we need to find ways to design materials that build on what students know and address common conundrums. Specific principles associated with providing multiple varied representations resonate with the discussion of pivotal cases in chapter 3 (Linn et al., this volume). They highlight the need to balance breadth and depth in design of inquiry instruction. They show ways that we are developing instructional patterns to manage complexity and introduce visualizations and suggest directions for further research.

Specific principles for providing multiple visual representations from varied media include the following:

- Design representations of scientific evidence to highlight key ideas.
  Example evidence: A media effect was documented in student's interpretation of pairs of evidence that were conceptually isomorphic, indicating that the media format and surface details of the items significantly shaped student thinking about the items (Bell, chap. 6, this volume).
  Example feature: Multimedia web pages allow students to explore rich depictions of scientific evidence and data.
- Structure visualizations so learners can compare cases—simultaneously or side by side.
  Example evidence: When visualizations illustrate the compelling comparison in a pivotal case they are more effective; stu-

dents often miss connections when they see one case at a time (Clark, chap. 8, this volume).

Example feature: Both "HeatBars" and the thermal equilibrium simulation use a side-by-side layout to highlight differences between conditions.

- Support student initiated modeling of complex science with powerful, easy to learn environments.

    Example evidence: When students can create their own models of phenomena they explore first hand—such as motion—they learn complex concepts (diSessa, Hammer, et al., 1991).

    Example feature: Programming environments and modeling tools can support student design of representations.

- Provide interactive simulations to allow learners to explore complex causal mechanisms.

    Example evidence: When students can change parameters and evaluate the results, they learn more than when the model just shows the process (Bell, chap. 10, this volume; Foley, 1999; Snir et al., 1993).

    Example feature: Applications such as AgentSheets to create opportunities for learners to explore causal factors through an interactive, multiagent simulation (Reppening et al., 2001).

- Design visualization environments to help learners recognize salient information.

    Example evidence: Visualizations can distract learners rather than encouraging understanding. Students benefit from practice in dealing with visual material to become proficient in recognizing the salient information (Kali, Orion, et al., 2003).

    Example feature: Models of earthquakes, the rock cycle, and related topics to help learners identify salient aspects of geological phenomena.

In summary, recent research offers many directions for making the thinking of learners, experts, and teachers visible. In addition, research illustrates the challenges of using visualization tools to make complex scientific phenomena visible. Technology offers unique avenues for creating visualizations, but realizing the benefit remains an important research program.

Metaprinciple: Help Students Learn From Others

Our third metaprinciple described in chapter 3 (Linn et al., this volume) calls for helping students benefit from the ideas of others. Researchers have demonstrated advantages for distributed cognition, communities of learners, and collaborative groups. In chapter 3, Linn et al. (this volume, Table 3.4) described the pragmatic pedagogical principles associated with the metaprinciple that says to orchestrate social supports.

Encourage Learners to Listen to Others. The first pragmatic principle associated with helping students learn from others calls for encouraging learners to listen to others. When students explain their ideas to other students, they may clarify their own thinking by making it visible to themselves as discussed earlier. They can also help their peers understand an idea by articulating concepts using familiar vocabulary and relevant examples. In addition, when students can take on the role of teacher or tutor, they often delve more deeply into a topic and discover gaps in their own understanding. These opportunities also enable teachers to learn from each other. Learning environments support teachers in analyzing the impact of inquiry by allowing others to inspect the work of students. Focusing discussion on student learning enables all teachers and developers to participate equally, whereas focus on teacher behavior can reduce the effectiveness of social interactions (e.g., Shear et al., chap. 12, this volume; Slotta, chap. 9, this volume).

Specific principles that encourage students to listen to each other include the following:

- Help teachers using classroom debates to moderate equitable interactions, to model appropriate question asking, to probe theoretical positions of the debate in equal measure, and to serve as a translator between students—all in the fewest turns of talk possible.

    Example evidence: During a whole-class debate, teachers play a number of different roles that set the stage for allowing students to share their thinking and learn from each other (Bell, chap. 6, this volume).

    Example feature: Using student work in the learning environment, whole-class debates can promote further learning and refinement in thinking.

- Design debates so students can safely share, explore, test, refine, and integrate their scientific ideas.

    Example evidence: During collaborative debates, students regularly probe each other's arguments and interpretations of evidence. Students report that debates expand the range of ideas and evidence they consider and that they are significant learning opportunities (Bell, chap. 6, this volume; Bell, 2002; Bell & Linn, 2002).

Example feature: Collaborative debates focus on the deep exploration of ideas and arguments by the group and downplay partisan tactics and posturing.

- Engage classes of students with a common corpus of evidence so teachers can develop effective instructional strategies, and students can establish common ground during classroom discussions.

Example evidence: A shared corpus of evidence focuses students on an exploration of the same materials, helping to establish a common ground for discussion (Bell, chap. 6, this volume).

Example feature: A Web tool allows for a collection of evidence to be represented all at once in a "helicopter" view. The learning environment can also provide a listing of evidence related to a project.

- Carry out debates about complex, multidisciplinary topics to help students productively identify issues and open questions.

Example evidence: Whole-class collaborative debate about a well-specified topic in which students can exchange ideas and revisit interpretations reveals substantive issues and counterarguments (Bell, chap. 10, this volume).

Example feature: Learning environments with features such as the inquiry map and SenseMaker enable participants in a debate to record their arguments visibly and readily analyze the arguments of their peers.

- Design partnership activities to foster knowledge integration for all participants.

Example evidence: Partnership design of precollege curriculum expanded the repertoire of ideas about learning, science, and students (Shear et al., chap. 12, this volume).

Example feature: Group activities can leverage individual contributions and engage each person as both a learner and an expert.

- Enable teachers to observe and discuss their inquiry practices with peers to encourage creative adaptation of innovations.

Example evidence: When teachers regularly discuss their inquiry practices, focusing on student reactions, they can support each other (Slotta, chap. 9, this volume).

Example feature: Discussion tools and scheduling tools help teachers exchange ideas. Records of student work in learning environments promote analysis of practice.

- Design collaborations among heterogeneous groups to encourage consideration of multiple alternatives.

    Example evidence: Heterogeneous groups, as long as each group is of roughly equal size, can generate more ideas than homogeneous groups (Hoadley, chap. 7, this volume).

    Example feature: Learning environments allow teachers to assign groups and monitor their progress by looking at embedded work.

- Design peer critique of student work and encourage students to develop criteria for these critiques.

    Example evidence: Peer critique helps motivate students to improve their designs and to better understand what might be refined (Hoadley, chap. 7, this volume).

    Example feature: Learning environments can support peer critique of any electronically represented work.

Promote Productive Interactions.   The second pragmatic principle associated with helping students learn from others says to "design technology-enhanced activities to promote productive and respectful interactions." Starting discussions with opportunities for individuals to learn about each other and develop appreciation of the expertise of the participants can help. This also means that the discussion needs to allow participants time to contribute and return to the discussion multiple times. Selecting topics for discussion that direct the attention of the group to a common goal helps keep the discussion focused on the issue rather than on personalities. Hoadley (chap. 7, this volume) explored the role of varied seed comments. Clark (chap. 8, this volume) showcased discussions in which each participant or small group proposes a principle for group consideration.

Specific principles to help design technology-enhanced activities to promote productive and respectful interactions include the following:

- Ensure that partners respect both shared and individual goals.

    Example evidence: KIE partnerships negotiate tasks and approaches to promote the achievement of individual as well as shared goals (Shear et al., chap. 12, this volume).

    Example feature: Online discussion can support both individual and joint design of assessment tools.

- Create online discussions among individuals with diverse background in groups of about 15 and sustain the discussion for about 3 weeks.

Example evidence: Research shows that groups of 15 typically have a good range of ideas and participate enough to interact several times a week for about 3 weeks (Hsi, 1997).

Example feature: Online discussion tools allow designers to assign groups, monitor progress, require comments, and enter seed comments.

- Provide resources that enable the participants to warrant their contributions with evidence.

  Example evidence: Online discussions succeed more often with well-designed evidence and materials (Hoadley, chap. 7, this volume).

  Example feature: Learning environments can reveal contributions of others and provide seed comments (Hoadley, chap. 7, this volume).

- Choose the focus of discussion to ensure that everyone has a similar stake in the outcome.

  Example evidence: Discussions of controversies, student work, and persuasive messages engage everyone in the same task.

  Example feature: Learning environments make discussions inspectable and enable designers to improve future discussions by adding resources or reframing the question.

Scaffold the Development of Classroom Norms. The third pragmatic principle associated with helping students learn from others says to "scaffold groups to consider cultural values and to design criteria and standards." Often students infer school-based standards such as forming complete sentences or using standard grammar rather than considering ways to develop group norms. Furthermore, groups may subtly or even blatantly base their behavior on social norms that have more to do with status than with evidence. Instead, designers can focus attention on negotiating group standards and criteria and enable each participant to contribute to the process.

Specific principles that scaffold groups to consider cultural values and to design criteria and standards include the following:

- Focus students' attention on criteria of science, methods, credibility, and usefulness so they can identify strengths in evidence.

  Example evidence: Provide criteria students can use to evaluate scientific evidence (Davis, chap. 5, this volume).

  Example feature: Learning environments can embed prompts in complex activities and also create repositories of criteria for critique of arguments.

- Use argument map representations comparatively during whole-class debate presentations to promote accountability to the body of evidence under consideration.

  Example evidence: Conversation analysis of student discourse showed that web casting argument maps during a debate promoted questioning and discussion about the entire corpus of evidence, not just the items initially mentioned by students in their presentations (Bell, chap. 6, this volume).

  Example feature: Students' SenseMaker representations can be broadcast throughout the classroom, allowing for comparison and interrogation of their argument maps.

- Encourage students to come to consensus on shared criteria for decisions and products.

  Example evidence: Collaboration activities such as responding to each others' principles and voting on options can help students reach consensus (Clark, chap. 8, this volume).

  Example feature: Specialized discussion formats that require students to contribute before critiquing ideas of others can support consensus building.

- Provide opportunities for critique and refinement of ideas.

  Example evidence: Critique activities can motivate students to improve their designs and to recognize aspects they can refine (Hoadley, chap. 7, this volume).

  Example feature: Learning environment features that enable exchange of designs and revisions increase the cycles of design and refinement (Hoadley, chap. 7, this volume).

- Seed discussions with examples that highlight potentially complex applications of norms.

  Example evidence: Design seed comments that place views in social context so students can connect to the authors (Hoadley, chap. 7, this volume).

  Example feature: Learning environments enable designers to create seed comments in multiple formats and test their effectiveness.

Employ Multiple Social Activity Structures. The fourth pragmatic principle associated with learning from others says to "employ multiple social activity structures." By offering multiple discussion formats, designers increase the ways into the discussion for individuals. These include offline work in small groups as well as online work in small and large groups. Formats that ask for opinions prior to discussion, or that require evidence in contributions, or that stimulate discussion with seed comments from fictitious peers all invite some participants to contribute. Offering opportunities to participate anonymously engages some learners and seems to reduce the anxiety of all participants—even those who never take advantage of the feature (Hsi, 1997).

In the Computer as Learning Partner research, we found that students were most successful when they collaborated with one peer on a complex project. This stemmed from the comfort individuals felt in one-on-one discussions as well as from the logistic difficulties of working with large groups and a small computer screen. However, larger groups also offer students opportunities. In larger groups, students need to justify their opinions more coherently to get them heard and to negotiate tasks more carefully than they do when working with one partner.

Multiple formats for online discussions also increase the likelihood that all the participants will find an effective format for their ideas. Often students lurk behind the scenes rather than contributing in a large online discussion. However, when students must express an opinion prior to reading comments from others, they often discover their voice. Sometimes students who initially contribute a group idea become motivated to contribute on their own later.

Specific principles to employ multiple social activity structures include the following:

- Interleave group, individual, and pair interactions.
  Example evidence: Students vary in the forms of interactions that engage them (Linn & Slotta, in press).
  Example feature: Learning environments can provide for variation in social interactions—allowing critiques, examples, questions, and illustrations.
- Offer alternative methods for participants to identify themselves in online discussion.
  Example evidence: When students can remain anonymous or take credit for ideas later, they feel more welcome in a discussion (Hsi, 1997).
  Example feature: Learning environments can have multiple layers of information—allowing teachers but not students to know the author of messages.
- Encourage participants to try new formats for contributing.
  Example evidence: When students are required to make regular comments, they typically comply and often continue to participate once they start (Hsi, 1997).

Example feature: Learning environments can keep track of participants and remind individuals of assignments. Teachers can inspect student comments and encourage shy individuals.

- Devise new structures and activities to stimulate creativity.

    Example evidence: Individuals may be motivated to rethink their ideas when they encounter a new format for contributing such as the construct-a-principle format tested by Clark (chap. 8, this volume).

    Example feature: Designers can use social activity structures for individuals to post data, compare diagrams, and negotiate experimental designs, as well as for discussions of controversial topics (Williams & Linn, 2002).

Metaprinciple: Promote Autonomy and Lifelong Learning

Our fourth metaprinciple described in chapter 3 (Linn et al., this volume) calls for promoting autonomy so students can become lifelong learners. In chapter 3 Linn et al. (this volume, Table 3.5) described the pragmatic pedagogical principles associated with the metaprinciple that says to promote autonomy and lifelong learning.

Encourage Reflection. The first pragmatic principle associated with promoting autonomy and lifelong learning says to "engage learners in reflection to promote autonomy and lifelong learning." When learners reflect, they make their thinking visible to themselves, monitor their progress, and reach new insights (Davis, chap. 5, this volume). The pattern of conducting an exploration and then reflecting improves inquiry projects. Integrating reflection with action comes up repeatedly in inquiry projects. In many cases prompts that intend to elicit reflection instead motivate learners to move on to the next step or to conclude that they were successful. Our research shows that curriculum design patterns that combine an experiment, investigation, or research endeavor with reflection can improve both activities. This pattern requires testing in the context of use to ensure that learners engage in productive reflection.

Specific principles that engage learners in reflecting on their own scientific ideas and on monitoring their own progress in understanding science include the following:

- Design prompts for planning and monitoring to promote generation of sophisticated explanations.

Example evidence: The students responding to general prompts for reflection used more evidence and generated more principles than those responding to specific prompts (Davis, chap. 5, this volume).

Example feature: Learning environments support patterns that include self-monitoring prompts.

- Design prompts to remind students of the pieces of the project to promote completion of the project.

  Example evidence: Students reminded to complete aspects of a project generally did so (Davis, chap. 5, this volume).

  Example feature: Learning environments support patterns that include activity prompts.

- Design prompts for planning and monitoring to promote principled knowledge integration.

  Example evidence: General prompts were better than specific prompts for eliciting knowledge integration (Davis, chap. 5, this volume).

  Example feature: Learning environments support patterns that include general prompts.

- Combine prompts that ask for self-monitoring with other activity structures so students get feedback on their progress.

  Example evidence: Some students who responded to directed or self-monitoring prompts displayed an illusion of comprehension (Davis, chap. 5, this volume).

  Example feature: Learning environments support patterns that include generic prompts for reflection along with feedback.

- Use activities to structure student work with argument maps and evidence explanations.

  Example evidence: Students engaged in the perspective-taking activity structure learned more than students who were asked to simply bolster their initial position (Bell, chap. 6, this volume; Bell, 1998). Students engaged in perspective taking also theorized more in their SenseMaker arguments. Students with less initial knowledge about the subject matter were helped to a greater degree.

  Example feature: SenseMaker argument maps help students to theorize about evidence and the debate topic.

- Engage curriculum designers in reflecting on their designs and using results to customize instruction.

  Example evidence: Inquiry projects benefit from continuous improvement based on the success of students and the evaluation of technologies (Slotta, chap. 9, this volume).

Example feature: Learning environments provide extensive information about student progress and support regular revision of activities.

Engage Learners as Critics.   The second pragmatic principle associated with promoting autonomy and lifelong learning says to "engage learners as critics of diverse information." Critique activities are often neglected in science courses (Bell, chap. 10, this volume). Students have difficulty learning to identify flaws in their own work—programmers often cannot enumerate a good set of tests for their designs (Linn & Clancy, 1992). Debugging solutions can stump even experts. Curriculum design patterns that introduce critique need to also help learners develop criteria for evaluating information.

Specific principles that engage learners as critics of diverse scientific information include the following:

- Scaffold learners in identifying when and how to critique persuasive Internet messages.

  Example evidence: Without prompting, students accepted Internet evidence at face value (Davis, chap. 5, this volume).

  Example feature: Learning environments support patterns that include Internet search and prompts for critique.
- Encourage elaboration of ideas and conjectures when asking for critiques.

  Example evidence: Students who write long, elaborative critiques also identify more compelling issues in the materials they evaluate (Davis, chap. 5, this volume).

  Example feature: Learning environments support patterns that include prompts for elaboration.
- Make evidence collections visible using argument representations so students consider a corpus of evidence.

  Example evidence: In early versions of the debate activity, students focused on a small number of evidence items during discussion. By representing the entire collection of evidence in an argument map, students were found to keep more of the entire corpus of evidence in mind (Bell, chap. 6, this volume).

  Example feature: Learning environments can make the entire corpus of evidence visible to students as they construct their own interpretation of the evidence and theorize about the debate topic.

- Ask students to critique experiments done by experts, students, and stakeholders.

  Example evidence: By comparing and critiquing alternative designs students can develop more coherent and generative criteria (Slotta & Linn, 2000).

  Example feature: Learning environments support the pattern of evaluating sources and comparing experiments.

- Encourage students to apply the criteria they use for others to their own investigations.

  Example evidence: Students can generate explanations more easily than they can critique, but eventually they need to develop valid criteria for their own work (Linn & Clancy, 1992).

  Example feature: Learning environments can support the pattern of developing criteria for products of others and then applying the criteria to personal projects.

- Enable designers to critique their designs and those of their peers.

  Example evidence: When students, teachers, or software designers engage in mutual critique and refinement, the community can create improved products (Hoadley, chap. 7, this volume; Shear et al., chap. 12, this volume).

  Example feature: Electronic supports for exchange of projects, student work, and commentary enables communities to develop more viable products.

Engage Learners in Varied, Sustained Projects. The third pragmatic principle associated with promoting autonomy and lifelong learning says to "engage learners in varied, sustained science projects." When learners engage in sustained reasoning, they have the opportunity to use the full range of inquiry skills (e.g., Linn & Hsi, 2000). Getting started on inquiry requires a major change in practice for many students and their teachers.

Specific principles that engage students in varied, sustained science project experiences include the following:

- Encourage students to revise their ideas and products over time.

  Example evidence: Design fixation inhibits students from linking theory and practice (Hoadley, chap. 7, this volume).

  Example feature: Students can be asked to describe and justify changes in designs.

- Provide short, medium, and long projects so teachers and students can experiment with alternative durations of inquiry projects.

    Example evidence: Most teachers prefer to start with a short inquiry project to introduce the ideas and develop their own practice (Slotta, chap. 9, this volume).

    Example feature: Learning environments can offer inquiry projects in sequences so teachers can interleave them with other work.
- Vary the initiative required of students to complete projects to meet the needs of students in diverse schools and courses.

    Example evidence: Most teachers and students prefer highly scaffolded inquiry projects so they can learn to deal with more complex projects using established patterns of interaction.

    Example feature: Learning environments can emphasize promising patterns and encourage students to use them more and more independently over time (Linn, Clark, et al., 2003).
- Design projects that require the full range of inquiry skills including planning, experimenting, communicating, debugging, assessing progress, presenting results, and negotiating understanding.

    Example evidence: Students gain a coherent view of the nature of science when they experience inquiry projects that include controversy and require resolution of conflict (Bell, chap. 10, this volume).

    Example feature: Learning environments can scaffold all the aspects of inquiry, from planning, to experimentation, to analysis of results, to communicating findings, to debating alternatives, to compiling a portfolio.

Establish a Generalized Inquiry Process. The fourth pragmatic principle associated with promoting autonomy and lifelong learning says to "establish a generalized inquiry process suitable for diverse science projects so students can revisit ideas." If students can revisit their ideas and their inquiry skills, they can continue to apply them in new contexts and settings.

Specific principles that help designers establish a generalizable inquiry process suitable for diverse science projects so students can revisit ideas include the following:

- Design inquiry environments so students can appreciate both the variety of inquiry patterns and the similarities in inquiry across contexts.

Example evidence: Students often separate personal inquiry from scientific inquiry rather than seeking overlaps and consistencies (Linn & Hsi, 2000).

Example feature: Learning environments enable students to compare inquiry maps from multiple projects to explore the varied inquiry practices in science.

- Design prompts and other activities to allow learners to identify their weaknesses.

Example evidence: Students need to monitor their inquiry activities to develop sustainable skills (Davis, chap. 5, this volume)

Example feature: Learning environments can make the inquiry process visible and ask students to reflect on their use of the skills.

- Connect scaffolded inquiry activities to self-initiated inquiry.

Example evidence: Make explicit the use of inquiry in science, personal life, and policymaking and encourage students to connect these contexts (Bell, chap. 10, this volume).

Example feature: Create activities that highlight inquiry patterns in new settings such as consumer's reports or policy debates.

CONCLUSIONS

The design principles compiled here illustrate ways to synthesize research and reveal common findings. The online database links similar principles, evidence, and features. It also includes features and principles from other groups. We invite critiques, contributions, and elaborations of the design principles proposed here. Please join us at our Web site to participate in this endeavor.

Design-based research studies inform the knowledge integration perspective on instruction and the scaffolded knowledge framework for instruction. Design principles can guide those designing curriculum and in turn lead to refinements of views of learning and instruction.

14

Closing Thoughts:
Internet Environments
for Science Education

Marcia C. Linn
University of California, Berkeley

Elizabeth A. Davis
University of Michigan

Philip Bell
University of Washington

Bat-Sheva Eylon
The Weizmann Institute of Science

The effort to change science courses one inquiry project at a time started with the knowledge integration perspective on learning and with extensive research on technology in the classroom (Linn & Hsi, 2000). This prior work as well as the current research involved a collaborative partnership with expertise in all the relevant aspects of education. This research provides a head start on designing inquiry projects that could convert students into lifelong science learners.

The partnership used the metaprinciples and the pragmatic pedagogical principles from the Computer as Learning Partner (CLP) to design a series of technology-enhanced learning environments. These studies yielded four distinct curriculum design patterns for critique, debate, design, and investigation projects.

The learning environments incorporate all the results of the CLP work. The partnership designed inquiry projects and tested and refined these projects in varied settings using *design-based research studies*, also referred to as *design studies*. The findings are summarized in design narratives (see Part II).

In addition, the partnership found that the pragmatic pedagogical principles that guided the initial designs could be elaborated into specific principles that capture the insights from local settings and might nudge future designers in new, potentially promising directions. These new specific principles are articulated in Linn, Bell, and Davis (chap. 13, this volume).

Tests of these inquiry projects using design-based research studies led to important questions about scaling the findings beyond the few schools and settings where the research took place. These are discussed in Part III. The curriculum design patterns and their associated pragmatic pedagogical principles enabled rapid design of new projects and more comprehensive research. Designers could create clones of tested projects and determine the effect of specific customizations. Studies revealed effective practices for design teams both as they created new projects and as they tested and refined existing projects (see Shear, Bell, & Linn, chap. 12, this volume). As summarized in Table 14.1, students in many varied classrooms have made gains in knowledge integration as a result of using these projects.

To understand how new teachers in diverse settings could build on their prior experiences to incorporate successful inquiry projects, the partnership developed a mentored professional development model and tested it in a whole school (see Slotta, chap. 9, this volume; Williams & Linn, 2002). In addition, the partnership studied how those implementing existing inquiry projects customize the instruction to their own environment, students, curriculum, and scientific phenomena such as local bodies of water (see Baumgartner, chap. 11, this volume).

The design studies also led to refinements of the perspective on learning and the framework for instruction. The studies revealed insights into the complexity of knowledge integration and into the factors that influence instruction designed to promote knowledge integration (see Linn, Eylon, & Davis, chap. 2, this volume; Linn, Davis, & Eylon, chap. 3, this volume). For example, the beliefs about the nature of science that students bring to science class often constrain their inquiry processes (see Bell & Linn, 2002). Promising aspects of the instructional studies led to the Web-Based Inquiry Science Environment (WISE), a technology-enhanced learning environment so they could be studied more widely. The partnership also built a user friendly authoring environment so leaders of educational programs could create partnerships to design new projects easily.

Experience conducting design studies and summarizing the results in design narratives led to improvements in the research methods. To contribute to the knowledge integration of those concerned with im-

TABLE 14.1
Progress in Knowledge Integration in Studies of WISE Projects Conducted by Graduate Students, Postdoctoral Scholars, and Other Colleagues in Varied Classroom Contexts With Diverse Students Using Any of 40 Projects

Project Name (Earth, Life, Physical Science)	WISE Assessments (Content, Inquiry/Investigation)	N Students	Context	Grade	Pre-Post Effect Size	% Gain
Earth science: The Next Shake	Content: Soil and structure, plate tectonics Inquiry: Evidence, predictions, investigation	151	Suburban	8	1.57**	38.4
Earth science: Ocean Stewards	Content: Biodiversity, marine health, and preservation Inquiry: Investigations, design, and experience	29	Urban	10–12	1.45**	280
Earth science: Plate Tectonics	Content: Plate tectonics, continental motion Inquiry: Evidence, simulation, argument	362	Urban	9–11	1.3*	70
Earth science: Rainforest Interactions	Content: Food webs, endangered species, rainforests Inquiry: Causal mapping, evidence, data	22	Urban	6	0.45**	37
Life science: GMF	Content: GMF, crosses, genetic engineering Inquiry: Evidence, argument	173	Suburban Urban	8 8	1.09** 1.32**	47 98
Life science: Pine Creek	Content: Pollution, microorganisms eutrophication Inquiry: Investigation, probe ware, causal maps, data	183	Suburban	6	0.42*	36
Life science: Plants in Space	Content: Plant growth, nutrients, light, photosynthesis Inquiry: Prediction, explanation, graphing	23 21	Urban Urban	5 5	2.72** 5.11**	138 182

(Continued)

343

TABLE 14.1
(Continued)

Project Name (Earth, Life, Physical Science)	WISE Assessments (Content, Inquiry/Investigation)	N Students	Context	Grade	Pre-Post Effect Size	% Gain
Life science: Dinosaur Extinction Debate	Content: Debate over cause of extinction Inquiry: Evidence, investigation, argument	300	Urban	9–10	1.65**	242
Life science: Cycles of Malaria	Content: Disease vector, parasites, vaccines, epidemic Inquiry: Evidence, argument, competitive methodology	356	Suburban	7	0.63**	35.4
Life science: DDT Controversy	Content: Pesticides, pollution, biomagnification Inquiry: Evidence, investigation, argument	67	Urban	10	0.34*	98
Physical science: Houses In The Desert	Content: Passive solar, insulation, heat capacity Inquiry: Design strategy, investigations, comparisons	167	Suburban	8	0.90*	320
Physical science: Light and Color	Content: Optics, light, vision, and color Inquiry: Investigations, perception, prediction	180	Suburban	8	0.42*	36
Physical science: How Far Does Light Go?	Content: Nature of light, telescopes, infrared Inquiry: Evidence, investigation, simulation, argument	172	Suburban	10	0.78*	78
Physical science: Probing Your Surroundings	Content: Thermal equilibrium, insulation, and conduction Inquiry: Investigations, data, perception, prediction	101	Suburban	8	2.59**	188

Note. WISE = Web-Based Inquiry Science Environment; GMF = genetically modified foods.
$*p < .001. **p < .0001.$

344

proving science education, including policymakers, curriculum framework committees, and school reformers, the partnership developed *compelling comparison studies* to meet the needs of decision makers (see Bell, Hoadley, & Linn, chap. 4, this volume).

In response to user needs, new partnerships added projects in specific areas. The WISE project library currently includes over 25 projects in English and a growing number of projects in other languages including Norwegian, German, French, and Dutch. More and more spontaneous users find WISE projects on the Internet. Many teachers participate in local WISE professional development programs.

In summary, evidence for the success of inquiry instruction and the desire to change students into lifelong learners one inquiry project at a time has led to many questions, dilemmas, and obstacles as well as a bit of progress.

ISSUES AND CONCERNS

The challenges of knowledge integration and the resulting repertoire of views that students develop resonates with the poor performance of American students in traditional science courses that many have identified. Students do not connect their views, they fail to generalize their ideas to new problems, and they often cannot recognize problems that closely resemble those they have studied.

The process of knowledge integration remains abstract. It is not readily refutable but can guide the refinement of instruction. Knowledge integration as a process of learning has face validity, aligns with most theories of learning, and explains learning at the cognitive level while valuing the role of social interactions. It raises questions yet needs more precision.

A view of learning as knowledge integration along with assessments of student progress raises issues about instruction. Courses do not motivate students to revisit and refine their ideas as often as desired. Moreover, students tend to forget material because courses isolate rather than connect ideas.

Too often assessments reinforce piecemeal science learning. We need greater consensus on what constitute valid indicators of lifelong learning. Teachers report that those who excel in inquiry projects by developing arguments or explaining trade-offs often differ from those who succeed on textbook-designed tests.

Learning environments can play a crucial role in assessment and redesign of instruction. They can track iterative improvements to instruction using embedded assessments. These assessments could become the de facto standard for science learning, but they require far more effort to use than do current standardized tests.

Designers need to learn more about how to redesign instruction that fails to promote inquiry. Results from knowledge integration assessments reveal weaknesses. Can the pedagogical principles help diagnose weaknesses in instruction and design remedies? As the design narratives attest, these redesigns of instruction rely on many complex forces, only some of them represented in principles. Redesigns often lead to improvements in knowledge integration that may or may not stem from principled refinement. Also, when remedies fail to improve learning, the results can help improve the principles, but the new principles still need testing.

Knowledge integration as a process involves iterative refinement of ideas. This view applies to individual learners, to groups of learners, and to those developing the knowledge integration perspective themselves. Methods for refining this knowledge remain in flux as well.

Role of Inquiry in Lifelong Learning

The results reported here suggest the benefit of inquiry projects for improving the knowledge integration of students about specific science topics. Inquiry projects provide students with a sense of how knowledge integration plays out in lifelong learning. These projects benefit most learners but also raise crucial questions.

Teachers report that students return to their classes years later to discuss news articles about deformed frogs, insights into home insulation, or analyses of current movies that make non-normative claims about an inquiry topic they studied in middle school. Anecdotes, however, cannot make up for longitudinal studies. Do students abstract more general inquiry processes from their specific experiences? Longitudinal studies would help determine whether inquiry projects can convert students into lifelong learners.

We advocate that students engage in inquiry projects every semester, but we wonder when to start with inquiry, how to match inquiry projects to the curriculum, and what sequence of inquiry activity makes sense. We need studies that illustrate the benefit of multiple inquiry projects conducted year after year. We need to understand how dense to make the inquiry treatment and how to combine inquiry with other forms of science learning such as memorizing details and learning from textbooks.

Learning environments bring to life the trade-off between explicit orchestration of inquiry and open-ended investigation. WISE can direct almost every student action or leave the inquiry process to the student. Much of science inquiry fits the model of normal science as characterized by Kuhn (1970). Although normal science has many trade-offs and opportunities for creativity, it also has established patterns and practices not entirely unlike the explicit steps and patterns in WISE projects.

Learning environments can provide a remedy for what many teachers and observers refer to as hands-on but not minds-on science. Environments like the Knowledge Integration Environment and WISE can encourage systematic critiquing of results, regular reflection, and evidence-based argumentation. This role clearly moves science instruction closer to normative inquiry.

Giving students a task resembling revolutionary science must also be a part of science instruction. Some programs empower students to achieve major insights, but often these programs require resources beyond typical schools (e.g., diSessa, 2000). Science projects for science fairs or other organized competitions can provide these experiences, but participation rates are low. We need to better understand how students might go from relatively directed inquiry in science class to more open-ended, wide-ranging inquiry associated with major breakthroughs in science.

Equity and Literacy

Leveraging inquiry and technology raises important questions about equity. Although access to technology is rapidly increasing, schools with large proportions of students in poverty are still at a disadvantage (Linn, 2003). Creating instructional materials that challenge all learners and enable everyone to engage in a serious, nuanced knowledge integration process requires attention to the cultural differences in classrooms and deep understanding of the entering ideas of students. Most instruction connects poorly to student ideas. Some students, however, have gained the ability to deal with these poor connections far better than others. To increase equitable outcomes from science instruction requires both materials that connect more widely to the ideas of students and opportunities for everyone involved in the enterprise to engage in a more intentional process of customization. Instead, today's curriculum policymakers seem intent on reducing the degrees of freedom in schools and imposing untested mandates on well-intentioned students, teachers, and administrators.

Equity in science education must align strongly with technology literacy and language literacy. To become an educated scientist today means learning to use the tools of science, and those tools include technology. Denying students access to technology innovations as part of science instruction limits their preparation for future scientific careers. Virtually all learners will need some technology knowledge for the careers that they choose. Ensuring that technology is responsibly integrated into the curriculum will enhance the possibility that students develop both science and technology literacy and are set on a path toward continued intellectual success. Many technologies fit easily into science courses, but others distract or demand too much time. Continued research can provide technologies that promote technology literacy while enhancing science learning.

Success in science also involves communicating effectively about scientific material and phenomena, an important component of language literacy. Students studying science need opportunities to communicate ideas to their peers, to their teachers, and to experts. Students need to learn how to interpret persuasive messages and to read science materials for the purpose of learning science. They also need to develop the capability of making their points in debates and personal activities. Critical appraisal of scientific material characterizes successful scientists yet rarely becomes a component of science instruction. To ensure equitable opportunities in science, teachers need to provide students with opportunities to develop both language and technology literacy as well as science literacy.

TECHNOLOGY-ENABLED RESEARCH OPPORTUNITIES

New technologies enable us to capture knowledge integration in the making and study this process in greater detail. Until recently, we generally studied science learning that occurred as the result of weeks or months of instruction. New technologies enable us to track learning over minutes or seconds as learners experiment with models or explore examples and explain their thinking. We can also connect these experiences to make sense of the ways that students sustain their thinking and conduct inquiry.

A number of representation tools and cognitive supports appear to have substantial benefit for encouraging and studying knowledge integration. For example, SenseMaker, AgentSheets, and embedded prompts enable students to make explicit the links and connections among their ideas so that these connections are inspectable not only by peers and teachers but also by learners themselves (see Bell, chap.

6, this volume). Both the metacognitive and the cognitive aspects of this inspectability shed light on how student learning progresses.

Embedded assessments help explain why transfer of information from one domain to another perplexes students. Often students describe the salient feature of materials presented in a learning environment in ways that differ substantially from those utilized by experts. Students find systems thinking incredibly difficult—as do most adults. For example, in the study of malaria, students had difficulty with the concept of biomagnification—wanting to conclude that reducing the use of DDT would equally reduce impact on all species instead of considering how DDT interacts with the food web.

Detailed records of student learning help explain why approaches that help some students with knowledge integration are less successful for others. Some students disparage most comments from peers and experts, whereas others rely on these extensively. Some students find representations involving modeling and simulation more compelling than those involving text. As a result, an important aspect of science instruction involves helping students learn to take advantage of a broader range of resources in reasoning. Students benefit when they can learn from their peers, from experts, from texts, from models, and from animations.

Embedded assessments reveal the multiple views of scientific phenomena that students hold. Harvesting a broad range of student views can improve professional development, help teachers gain more deep pedagogical content knowledge about scientific phenomena, and also engage collaborations of designers and classroom teachers in identifying appropriate responses to these views.

Understanding of the trajectories of students as they conduct inquiry projects reveals the benefit of projects. When students grapple with complex materials rather than flounder, they learn the benefit of sustained reasoning. Diverse learners need varied supports. Technology-enhanced learning environments can help, as can teachers prepared to engage in just-in-time tutoring. Considerable research reported in this volume and elsewhere supports the advantage of challenging students with complex questions frequently ignored in texts and bypassed in an effort to cover too many topics in the curriculum. Simplification may be, in fact, the enemy of good science instruction.

New Research Directions

Technology-enhanced learning environments enable new research directions. The technology, for example, makes it easy to compare a prior version of a curriculum to a new one and to gather embedded assessment information that sheds light on the effectiveness of the innovation.

For example, to test whether revisiting ideas motivates learning even when the original information has been forgotten, researchers might study how students who report forgetting scientific information attempt to retrieve it. Researchers can study whether students become better at revisiting topics by creating opportunities to revisit ideas and looking for progress. Researchers could create situations that might stimulate revisiting and determine whether they succeed.

To study advantageous ways to shape knowledge integration, we need better understanding of how activities contribute to knowledge integration. We need to find the best balance of reflection and explanation because these activities take instructional time. To optimize learning, we want to space reflection activities so that most students succeed with some scaffolding. Ideally, we also want to connect reflection to monitoring of progress so that students begin to appreciate the value of reflecting. We want to identify practices that enable learners to abstract inquiry processes and use them in new settings.

To support learners, we need more detailed understanding of how representations, especially spatial representations, contribute to knowledge integration. We would like representations to prompt students to test their existing ideas against the implications of the representation and to highlight essential information. For the "Heatbars" simulation, for example, students typically evaluated the rate of heat flow results against their expectations—which were often that heat would flow at the same rate in different materials (Linn & Hsi, 2000). In other representations such as the concept maps described by Baumgartner (chap. 11, this volume), such testing was less likely as students simply added more and more information to the map.

To study the role and design of self-monitoring activities, researchers need more detailed understanding of how current opportunities work. They can vary feedback on argument maps and concept maps and determine student responses. A learning environment can embed this information. Using embedded responses to self-monitoring opportunities, researchers can distinguish spontaneous and prompted monitoring and determine when students monitor their own progress as well as whether more monitoring is helpful.

We need to study how design knowledge finds its way into design practice. For example, when principles become embedded in artifacts that are reused either as intact elements or as metaphors for further innovation, do they continue to have similar impacts?

NEXT STEPS

These chapters firmly establish the complex systemic nature of education as well as the rapid changes occurring along a vast array of dimensions. New research methodologies to capture this complexity and offer insight into improvements are emerging. These include the use of case studies, comparison studies, and representations of findings in the studies reported here.

Research synthesis techniques include many social activities such as small workshops or serious collaborations in which groups represent their emerging understanding in artifacts, designs, embedded assessment techniques, and other novel formats. Design principles, learning environments, and inquiry projects can serve as objects for investigation. We invite readers to join us at our Web site to participate in this research synthesis.

Bibliography

Alberts, B. (2001, March). *Science education and the science of education: A view from the National Academy of Sciences*. Presidential Address to the National Academy of Sciences, Clark University.

Alexander, C., S. Ishikawa, et al. (1977). *A pattern language: Towns, buildings, construction*. New York, Oxford University Press.

American Association for the Advancement of Science (AAAS). (1993). *Benchmarks for science literacy*. New York, Oxford University Press.

American Association of University Women (AAUW). (2000). *Tech-Savvy: Educating girls in the new computer age*. Washington, DC, AAUW Educational Foundation.

American Institutes for Research. (1998). *Gender gaps: Where schools still fail our children*. Washington, DC, American Association of University Women Educational Foundation.

Anderson, J. R. (1982). "Acquisition of cognitive skill." *Psychological Review, 89*: 369–406.

Anderson, J. R. (1983). *The architecture of cognition*. Cambridge, MA, Harvard University Press.

Anderson, J. R., A. T. Corbett, et al. (1995). "Cognitive tutors: Lessons learned." *The Journal of the Learning Sciences, 4*: 167–207.

Anderson, J. R., R. Farrell, et al. (1984). "Learning to program in LISP." *Cognitive Science, 8*: 87–129.

Anderson, J. R., & C. D. Schunn. (2000). Implications of the ACT-R learning theory: No magic bullets. *Advances in instructional psychology: Educational design and cognitive science*. R. Glaser (Ed.). Mahwah, NJ, Lawrence Erlbaum Associates. Vol. 5: 1–34.

Aronson, E. (1978). *The jigsaw classroom*. Beverly Hills, CA, Sage.

Aronson, E., & S. Yates. (1983). Cooperation in the classroom: The impact of the jigsaw method on inter-ethnic relations, classroom performance, and self-esteem. *Small groups and social interactions*. H. Blumberg, P. Hare, V. Kent, & M. Davies (Eds.). London, Wiley: 119–130.

Atkinson, R. C., & R. M. Shiffrin. (1968). Human memory: A proposed system and its control processes. *The psychology of learning and motivation: Advances in research and theory*. K. W. Spence & J. T. Spence (Eds.). New York, Academic. Vol. 2: 89–195.

Baddeley, A. D., & D. J. A. Longman. (1978). "The influence of length and frequency of training session on the rate of learning to type." *Ergonomics, 21*: 627–635.

Bagno, E., & B.-S. Eylon. (1997). "From problem-solving to a knowledge structure: An example from the domain of electromagnetism." *The American Journal of Physics, 65*: 726–736.

Bagno, E., B. Eylon, et al. (2000). "From fragmented knowledge to a knowledge structure: Linking the domains of mechanics and electromagnetism." *The American Journal of Physics, 68*(7): S16–S26.

Baker, L. M., & K. Dunbar. (1996, July). *Problem spaces in real-world science: What are they and how do scientists search them?* Paper presented at the Cognitive Science '96 Annual Meeting, San Diego, CA.

Barab, S. A., & D. Kirshner. (2001). "Rethinking methodology in the learning sciences" [Special issue]. *Journal of the Learning Sciences, 10*(1/2).

Barab, S., & A. Luehmann. (2003). "Building sustainable science curriculum: Acknowledging and accommodating local adaptation." *Science Education, 87*: 454–467.

Bargh, J. A. (1997). The automaticity of everyday life. *Advances in social cognition: The automaticity of everyday life*. R. S. Wyer (Ed.). Mahwah, NJ, Lawrence Erlbaum Associates. Vol. 10: 1–61.

Baumgartner, E. (2000). *Science by design: How teachers support scientific inquiry through design projects*. Unpublished doctoral dissertation, Northwestern University, Evanston, IL.

Baumgartner, E., & P. Bell. (2002, April). *What will we do with design principles? Design principles and principled design practice*. Paper presented at the annual meeting of the American Educational Research Association, New Orleans, LA. Retrieved from http://scale.soe.berkeley.edu/papers/

Baumgartner, E., & B. J. Reiser. (1998, April). *Merging engineering and scientific reasoning: High school students' use of scientific evidence in design projects*. Paper presented at the annual meeting of the National Association for Research in Science Training, San Diego, CA. Available from http://www.InternetScienceEducation.org/

Becker, H. J. (1999). *Internet use by teachers: Conditions of professional use and teacher-directed student use*. Unpublished manuscript, Center for Research on Information Technology and Organizations, University of California, Irvine, and the University of Minnesota.

Becker, H., J. Ravitz, et al. (1999). *Teacher and teacher-directed student use of computers and software*. Unpublished manuscript, University of California at Irvine, Center for Research in Information Technology in Organization.

Bell, P. (1997). Using argument representations to make thinking visible. *Proceedings of CSCL '97: The Second International Conference on Computer Support for Collaborative Learning*. R. Hall, N. Miyake, & N. Enyedy (Eds.). Toronto, Ontario, Canada, University of Toronto Press: 10–19.

Bell, P. (1998). *Designing for students' science learning using argumentation and classroom debate*. Unpublished doctoral dissertation, University of California, Berkeley.

Bell, P. (2002). Using argument representations to make thinking visible for individuals and groups. *CSCL II: Carrying forward the conversation*. T. Koschmann, R. Hall, & N. Miyake (Eds.). Mahwah, NJ, Lawrence Erlbaum Associates: 449–485.

Bell, P., & E. A. Davis. (2000). Designing Mildred: Scaffolding students' reflection and argumentation using a cognitive software guide. *International Conference for the Learning Sciences*. B. Fishman & S. F. O'Connor-Divelbiss (Eds.). Mahwah, NJ, Lawrence Erlbaum Associates: 142–149.

Bell, P., E. A. Davis, et al. (1995). The Knowledge Integration Environment: Theory and design. *CSCL '95: Proceedings of the Computer Supported Collaborative Learning Conference*. J. L. Schnase & E. L. Cunnius (Eds.). Mahwah, NJ, Lawrence Erlbaum Associates: 14–21.

Bell, P., & M. C. Linn. (2000). "Scientific arguments as learning artifacts: Designing for learning from the Web with KIE." *International Journal of Science Education, 22*: 797–817.

Bell, P., & M. C. Linn. (2002). Beliefs about science: How does science instruction contribute? *Personal epistemology: The psychology of beliefs about knowledge and knowing*. B. K. Hofer & P. R. Pintrich (Eds.). Mahwah, NJ, Lawrence Erlbaum Associates: 321–346.

Bell, P., & K. S. Owens. (2002). "Promoting the contextualized learning of science through the study of controversy." Manuscript in preparation.

Ben-Zvi, R., B. Eylon, et al. (1986). "Is an atom of copper malleable?" *Journal of Chemical Education, 63*: 64–66.

Bereiter, C. (1994). "Constructivism, socioculturalism and Popper's World 3." *Educational Researcher, 23*(7): 21–23.

Bereiter, C., & M. Scardamalia. (1993). *Surpassing ourselves: An inquiry into the nature and implications of expertise*. Chicago, Open Court.

Berenfeld, B. (1994). "Technology and the new model of science education: The Global Lab experience." *Machine-Mediated Learning, 4*(2–3): 203–227.

Biagioli, M. (1999). *The science studies reader*. New York, Routledge.

Bielaczyc, K., P. L. Pirolli, et al. (1995). "Training in self-explanation and self-regulation strategies: Investigating the effects of knowledge acquisition activities on problem solving." *Cognition and Instruction, 13*: 221–252.

Bjork, R. A. (1994). Memory and metamemory considerations in the training of human beings. *Metacognition: Knowing about knowing*. J. Metcalfe & A. P. Shimamura (Eds.). Cambridge, MA, MIT Press: 185–205.

Bjork, R. A. (1999). Assessing our own competence: Heuristics and illusions. *Attention and performance XVII. Cognitive regulation of performance: Interaction of theory and application*. D. Gopher & A. Koriat (Eds.). Cambridge, MA, MIT Press: 435–459.

Blank, R., J. Kim, et al. (2000). *Survey results of urban school classroom practices in mathematics and science: 1999 Report: Using the survey of enacted curriculum conducted during four USI site visits*. Norwood, MA, Systemic Research, Inc.

Bloom, B. S. (1956). *Taxonomy of educational objectives: The classification of educational goals*. New York, McKay.

Blumenfeld, P. C., B. J. Fishman, et al. (2000). "Creating usable innovations in systemic reform: Scaling up technology-embedded project-based science in urban schools." *Educational Psychologist, 35*: 149–164.

Borgman, C. (Ed.). (1996). *Social aspects of digital libraries: A report on the UCLA-NSF Social Aspects of Digital Libraries workshop* (Los Angeles, Feb 15–17). Los Angeles, CA, Department of Library and Information Science. Retrieved from http://dlis.gseis.ucla.edu/DL/

Boud, D., & G. Feletti (Eds.). (1991). *The challenge of problem-based learning*. London, Kogan Page.

Bransford, J. D. (1979). *Human cognition: Learning, understanding, and remembering*. Belmont, CA, Wadsworth.

Bransford, J. D., A. L. Brown, et al. (Eds.). (1999). *How people learn: Brain, mind, experience, and school*. Washington, DC, National Research Council.

Bransford, J. D., R. D. Sherwood, et al. (1990). Anchored instruction: Why we need it and how technology can help. *Cognition, education, and multimedia: Exploring ideas in high technology*. D. Nix & R. Spiro (Eds.). Hillsdale, NJ, Lawrence Erlbaum Associates: 115–141.

Brante, T. (1993). Reasons for studying scientific and science-based controversies. *Controversial science: From content to contention*. T. Brante, S. Fuller, & W. Lynch (Eds.). Albany, State University of New York Press.

Brown, A. (1992). "Design experiments: Theoretical and methodological challenges in creating complex interventions in classroom settings." *The Journal of Learning Sciences, 2*(2): 141–178.

Brown, A. L., D. Ash, et al. (1995). Distributed expertise in the classroom. *Distributed cognitions: Psychological and educational considerations*. G. Salomon (Ed.). Cambridge, England, Cambridge University Press: 188–228.

Brown, A. L., J. D. Bransford, et al. (1983). Learning, remembering, and understanding. *Handbook of child psychology: Cognitive development*. P. H. Mussen (Ed.). New York, Wiley.

Brown, A. L., & J. C. Campione. (1994). Guided discovery in a community of learners. *Classroom lessons: Integrating cognitive theory and classroom practice*. K. McGilly (Ed.). Cambridge, MA, MIT Press: 229–270.

Brown, A. L., & A. S. Palincsar. (1989). Guided, cooperative learning and individual knowledge acquisition. *Knowing, learning, and instruction: Essays in honor of Robert Glaser*. L. B. Resnick (Ed.). Hillsdale, NJ, Lawrence Erlbaum Associates: 393–451.

Brown, J. S., A. Collins, et al. (1989). "Situated cognition and the culture of learning." *Educational Researcher, 18*(1): 32–41.

Bruer, J. T. (1993). *Schools for thought: A science of learning in the classroom*. Cambridge, MA, MIT Press.

Bruner, J. S. (1979). *On knowing: Essays for the left hand*. Cambridge, MA, Belknap Press of Harvard University Press.

Bruner, J. (1999). Postscript: Some reflections on education research. *Issues in education research: Problems and possibilities*. E. C. Lagemann & L. S. Shulman (Eds.). San Francisco, Jossey-Bass: 399–409.

Byrne, M. D., R. Catrambone, et al. (1999). "Evaluating animations as student aids in learning computer algorithms." *Computers & Education, 33*: 253–278.

Card, S., T. Moran, et al. (1983). *The psychology of human–computer interaction*. Hillsdale, NJ, Lawrence Erlbaum Associates.

Card, S. K., G. G. Robertson, et al. (1996). The WebBook and the Web Forager: An information workspace for the World-Wide Web. *Conference proceedings on Human Factors in Computing Systems* (CHI96). New York, Association for Computing Machinery Press: 111–117. Retrieved from http://www.acm.org/sigchi/chi96/proceedings/index.htm

Carey, S. (1985). *Conceptual change in childhood*. Cambridge, MA, MIT Press.

Carpenter, P. A., & M. A. Just. (1992). *Understanding mechanical systems through computer animation and kinematic imagery. Final Report*. Unpublished manuscript, Department of Psychology, Carnegie-Mellon University, Pittsburgh, PA.

Carter Ching, C. (2000). *Apprenticeship, education, and technology: Children as oldtimers and newcomers to the culture of learning through design.* Unpublished doctoral dissertation, University of California, Los Angeles.

Case, R. (1985). *Intellectual development: Birth to adulthood.* Orlando, FL, Academic.

Case, R. S., S. Griffin, et al. (1999). Socioeconomic gradients in mathematical ability and their responsiveness to intervention during early childhood. *Developmental health and the wealth of nations: Social, biological, and educational dynamics.* D. P. Keating & C. Hertzman (Eds.). New York, Guilford.

Chambers, D. W. (1983). "Stereotypic images of the scientist: The Draw-A-Scientist test." *Science Education, 67*: 255–256.

Chamot, A. U., & J. M. O'Malley. (1986). *A cognitive academic language learning approach: An ESL content-based curriculum.* Washington, DC, National Clearinghouse for Bilingual Education.

Champagne, A. (1998, February). *Attributes of debates among the science literate.* Paper presented at the American Association for the Advancement of Science (AAAS) Annual Meeting, Philadelphia, PA.

Champagne, A. B., L. E. Klopfer, et al. (1980). "Factors influencing the learning of classical mechanics." *American Journal of Physics, 48*: 1074–1079.

Chase, W. G., & H. A. Simon. (1973). "Perception in chess." *Cognitive Psychology, 1*: 33–81.

Chi, M. T. H. (1996). "Constructing self-explanations and scaffolded explanations in tutoring." *Applied Cognitive Psychology, 10*: S33–S49.

Chi, M. T. H. (2000). Self-explaining: The dual processes of generating inferences and repairing mental models. *Advances in instructional psychology.* R. Glaser (Ed.). Mahwah, NJ, Lawrence Erlbaum Associates: 161–238.

Chi, M. T. H., M. Bassok, et al. (1989). "Self-explanations: How students study and use examples in learning to solve problems." *Cognitive Science, 13*: 145–182.

Chi, M. T. H., N. de Leeuw, et al. (1994). "Eliciting self-explanations improves understanding." *Cognitive Science, 18*: 439–477.

Chi, M. T. H., P. Feltovich, et al. (1981). "Categorization and representation of physics problems by experts and novices." *Cognitive Science, 5*: 121–152.

Chi, M. T. H., M. W. Lewis, et al. (1989). "Self-explanations: How to use examples in learning to solve problems." *Cognitive Science, 13*: 145–182.

Chi, M. T. H., & J. D. Slotta. (1993). "The ontological coherence of intuitive physics. Commentary on A. diSessa's 'Toward an epistemology of physics.' " *Cognition and Instruction, 10*: 249–260.

Chong, L., & L. B. Ray. (2002). "Whole-istic biology." *Science, 295*(5560): 1661.

Clancy, M. J., & M. C. Ling. (1992). *Designing Pascal solutions: A case study approach* (1st ed.). New York, W. H. Freeman and Company.

Clark, C. T., P. A. Moss, et al. (1996). "Collaboration as dialogue: Teachers and researchers engaged in conversation and professional development." *American Educational Research Journal, 33*: 193–231.

Clark, D. (2000). *Scaffolding knowledge integration through curricular depth.* Unpublished doctoral dissertation, University of California, Berkeley.

Clark, D. B. (2003). Analyzing student knowledge integration: Theories or pieces? *Proceedings of the National Association of Research in Science Teaching Conference.* Philadelphia. Retrieved from http://courses.ed.asu.edu/clark/

Clark, D., & D. Jorde. (in press). "Computer visualizations and tactile models: Helping students revise disruptive experientially-supported ideas about thermodynamics." *Journal of Research in Science Teaching.*

Clark, D., & M. C. Linn. (in press). "Scaffolding knowledge integration through curricular depth." *The Journal of Learning Sciences.*

Clark, D., & J. D. Slotta. (2000). "Interpreting evidence on the Internet: Sex, lies, and multimedia." *International Journal of Science Education, 22*: 859–871.

Clark, H. C. (1996, April). *Cyber-coaching in Computer as Learning Partner.* Paper presented at the 1996 Annual Meeting of the American Education Research Association, New York.

Clement, J. (1988). "Observed methods for generating analogies in scientific problem solving." *Cognitive Science, 12*: 563–586.

Clement, J. (1991). Nonformal reasoning in experts and in science students: The use of analogies, extreme cases, and physical intuition. *Informal reasoning and education.* J. F. Voss, D. N. Perkins, & J. Siegel (Eds.). Hillsdale, NJ, Lawrence Erlbaum Associates: 344–362.

Clement, J. (1993). "Using bridging analogies and anchoring intuitions to deal with students' preconceptions in physics." *Journal of Research in Science Teaching, 30*: 1241–1257.

Clough, E. E., & R. Driver. (1985). "Secondary students' conceptions of the conduction of heat: Bringing together scientific and personal views." *The Physical Educator, 20*: 176–182.

Cobb, P. (2001). Supporting the improvement of learning and teaching in social and institutional context. *Cognition and instruction: 25 years of progress.* S. M. Carver & D. Klahr (Eds.). Mahwah, NJ, Lawrence Erlbaum Associates: 455–478.

Cobb, P., & J. Bowers. (1999). "Cognitive and situated learning perspectives in theory and practice." *Educational Researcher, 28*(2): 4–15.

Cognition and Technology Group at Vanderbilt (CTGV). (1997). *The Jasper project: Lessons in curriculum, instruction, assessment, and professional development.* Mahwah, NJ, Lawrence Erlbaum Associates.

Cohen, D. K. (1988). Teaching practice: Plus ça change. . . . *Contributing to educational change: Perspectives on research and practice.* P. Jackson (Ed.). Berkeley, CA, McCutchan.

Cohen, D. K., S. W. Raudenbush, et al. (2002). Resources, instruction, and research. *Evidence matters: Randomized trials in education research.* R. Boruch & F. Mosteller (Eds.). Washington, DC, Brookings Institute: 30–119.

Cohen, E. G. (1984). Talking and working together: Status, interaction, and learning. *The social context of instruction: Group organization and group processes.* P. L. Peterson, L. C. Wilkinson, & M. Hallinan (Eds.). New York, Academic: 171–187.

Cohen, R., B. S. Eylon, et al. (1983). "Potential difference and current in simple electric circuits: A study of students' concepts." *American Journal of Physics, 51*: 407–412.

Cole, M. (1996). *Cultural psychology: A once and future discipline.* Cambridge, MA, Belknap Press of Harvard University Press.

Coleman, E. B. (1998). "Using explanatory knowledge during collaborative problem solving in science." *The Journal of the Learning Sciences, 7*(3 & 4): 387–427.

Collins, A. (1992). Toward a design science of education. *New directions in educational technology.* E. Scanlon & T. O'Shea (Eds.). New York, Springer-Verlag.

Collins, A., J. S. Brown, & A. Holum. (1991). "Cognitive apprenticeship: Making thinking visible." *American Educator, 15*(3): 6–11, 38–39.

Collins, A., J. S. Brown, & S. Newman. (1989). Cognitive apprenticeship: Teaching the crafts of reading, writing, and mathematics. *Knowing, learning and instruction: Es-*

says in honor of Robert Glaser. L. B. Resnick (Ed.). Hillsdale, NJ, Lawrence Erlbaum Associates: 453–494.

Collins, A., & W. Ferguson. (1993). "Epistemic forms and epistemic games: Structures and strategies to guide inquiry." *Educational Psychologist, 28*: 25–42.

Collins, H. M., & S. Shapin. (1986). Uncovering the nature of science. *Science in schools*. J. Brown, A. Cooper, T. Horton, F. Toates, & D. Zeldin (Eds.). Milton Keynes, England, Open University Press: 71–79.

Confrey, J., K. Bell, et al. (2001, April). *Systemic crossfire: What implementation research reveals about urban reform in mathematics*. Paper presented at the Annual Meeting of the American Educational Research Association, Seattle, WA.

Cronbach, L. J. (1975). "Beyond the two disciplines of scientific psychology." *American Psychologist, 30*(2): 116–127.

Cross, R. T., & R. F. Price. (1996). "Science teachers' social conscience and the role of controversial issues in the teaching of science." *Journal of Research in Science Teaching, 33*: 319–333.

Crouch, C. H., & E. Mazur. (2001). "Peer instruction: Ten years of experience and results." *American Journal of Physics, 69*: 970–977.

Cuban, L. (1986). *Teachers and machines: The classroom use of technology since 1920*. New York, Teachers College Press.

Cuban, L. (1990). "Reforming again, again, and again." *Educational Researcher, 19*(1): 3–13.

Cuban, L. (1993). "The lure of curricular reform and its pitiful history." *Phi Delta Kappan, 75*: 182–185.

Cummins, J. (1989). *Empowering minority students*. Sacramento, California Association for Bilingual Education.

Cuthbert, A. (2002). *Learning science through the design of passive solar dwellings: Can specialization contribute to improved learning outcomes and design methods*. Unpublished doctoral dissertation, University of California, Berkeley.

Cuthbert, A. J., D. B. Clark, et al. (2002). WISE learning communities: Design considerations. *Building virtual communities: Learning and change in cyberspace*. K. A. Renninger & W. Shumar (Eds.). New York, Cambridge University Press: 215–246.

Cuthbert, A., & C. Hoadley. (1998a, April). *Designing desert houses in the Knowledge Integration Environment*. Paper presented at the Annual Meeting of the American Educational Research Association, San Diego, CA. (ERIC Document Reproduction Service No. ED 423 299)

Cuthbert, A., & C. Hoadley. (1998b, April). *Using KIE to help students develop shared criteria for house designs*. Paper presented at the Annual Meeting of the American Educational Research Association, San Diego, CA. (ERIC Document Reproduction Service No. ED 423 300)

Davis, E. A. (1998). *Scaffolding students' reflection for science learning*. Unpublished doctoral dissertation, University of California, Berkeley.

Davis, E. A. (2003a). "Prompting middle school science students for productive reflection: Generic and directed prompts." *The Journal of the Learning Sciences, 12*(1): 91–142.

Davis, E. A. (2003b). "Untangling dimensions of students' beliefs about scientific knowledge and science learning." *International Journal of Science Education*.

Davis, E. A., & P. Bell. (2001, April). *Design principles for scaffolding students' reflection and argumentation in science*. Paper presented at the annual meeting of the

American Educational Research Association, Seattle. Retrieved from http://www-personal.umich.edu/~betsyd/scaffolding.htm

Davis, E. A., & D. Kirkpatrick. (2002). "It's all the news: Critiquing evidence and claims." *Science Scope, 25*(5): 32–37.

Davis, E. A., & M. C. Linn. (2000). "Scaffolding students' knowledge integration: Prompts for reflection in KIE." *International Journal of Science Education, 22*: 819–837.

Davis, E. A., M. C. Linn, et al. (1995). "Students' off-line and on-line experiences." *Journal of Educational Computing Research, 12*(2): 109–134.

Davis, E. A., & D. Petish. (2001, April). *Developing expertise in science teaching—and in science teacher education.* Paper presented at the annual meeting of the American Educational Research Association, Seattle. Retrieved from http://www-personal.umich.edu/~betsyd/DavisPetishAERA01.pdf

Design-Based Research Collective. (2003). "Design-based research: An emerging paradigm for educational inquiry." *Educational Researcher, 32*(1): 5–8.

Dewey, J. (1896). Original letter to the Trustees of the University of Chicago arguing for the creation of a Laboratory School.

Dewey, J. (1900). "Psychology and social practice." *The Psychological Review, 7*: 105–124.

Dewey, J. (1901). *Psychology and social practice.* Chicago, University of Chicago Press.

Dewey, J. (1929). *The sources of a science of education.* New York, H. Liveright.

Dewey, J. (1954). My pedagogic creed. *Three thousand years of educational wisdom.* R. Ulich (Ed.). Cambridge, MA, Harvard University Press: 629–638.

diSessa, A. (1988). Knowledge in pieces. *Constructivism in the computer age.* G. Forman & P. Pufall (Eds.). Hillsdale, NJ, Lawrence Erlbaum Associates: 49–70.

diSessa, A. (1991). Local sciences: Viewing the design of human–computer systems as cognitive science. *Designing interaction: Psychology at the human–computer interface.* J. M. Carroll (Ed.). Cambridge, England, Cambridge University Press: 162–202.

diSessa, A. A. (1992). Images of learning. *Computer-based learning environments and problem solving.* E. De Corte, M. C. Linn, H. Mandl, & L. Verschaffel (Eds.). Berlin, Springer-Verlag.

diSessa, A. (1993). "Toward an epistemology of physics." *Cognition and Instruction, 10*: 105–225.

diSessa, A. A. (1996). What do "just plain folks" know about physics? *Handbook of education and human development: New models of learning, teaching, and schooling.* D. R. Olson & N. Torrance (Eds.). Oxford, UK, Blackwell: 709–730.

diSessa, A. A. (2000). *Changing minds: Computers, learning and literacy.* Cambridge, MA, MIT Press.

diSessa, A. A., D. Hammer, et al. (1991). "Inventing graphing: Metarepresentational expertise in children." *Journal of Mathematical Behavior, 10*: 117–160.

diSessa, A. A., & J. Minstrell. (1998). Cultivating conceptual change with benchmark lessons. *Thinking practices.* J. G. Greeno & S. Goldman (Eds.). Mahwah, NJ, Lawrence Erlbaum Associates: 155–187.

diSessa, A. A., & B. L. Sherin. (1998). "What changes in conceptual change?" *International Journal of Science Education, 20*: 1155–1191.

Driver, R., E. Guesne, et al. (Eds.). (1985). *Children's ideas in science.* Philadelphia, Open University Press.

Driver, R., J. Leach, et al. (1996). *Young people's images of science.* Buckinghamshire, England, Open University Press.

Edelson, D., D. Gordin, et al. (1999). "Addressing the challenges of inquiry-based learning through technology and curriculum design." *Journal of the Learning Sciences, 8*: 391–450.

Edwards, D., & N. Mercer. (1987). *Common knowledge: The development of understanding in the classroom.* London, Methuen.

Elmore, R. F. (2000). *Building a new structure for school leadership.* Washington, DC, The Albert Shanker Institute.

Elmore, R. F. (2002). *Bridging the gap between standards and achievement.* Washington, DC, The Albert Shanker Institute.

Erickson, G. L. (1979). "Children's conceptions of heat and temperature." *Science Education, 63*: 221–230.

Erickson, G., & A. Tiberghien. (1985). Heat and temperature. *Children's ideas in science.* R. Driver, E. Guesne, & A. Tiberghien (Eds.). Philadelphia, Open University Press: 52–83.

Eylon, B. S., & U. G. Ganiel. (1990). "Macro–micro relationships: The missing link between electrostatics and electrodynamics in students' reasoning." *International Journal of Science Education, 12*: 79–94.

Eylon, B., & J. Helfman. (1984). Analogical problem-solving processes in physics. *Science teaching in Israel: Origins, development and achievements.* A. M. Mayer & P. Tamir (Eds.). Jerusalem, Israel Science Teaching Center: 259–271.

Eylon, B. S., & M. C. Linn. (1988). "Learning and instruction: An examination of four research perspectives in science education." *Review of Educational Research, 58*: 251–301.

Eylon, B. S., & F. Reif. (1984). "Effects of knowledge organization on task performance." *Cognition and Instruction, 1*: 5–44.

Feldman, A., C. Konold, et al. (2000). *Network science, a decade later: The Internet and classroom learning.* Mahwah, NJ, Lawrence Erlbaum Associates.

Findeli, A. (2001). "Rethinking design education for the 21st century: Theoretical, methodological, and ethical discussion." *Design Issues, 17*: 5–17.

Fischer-Fortier, D., & P. Bell. (2003). *Mediating online knowledge networking within an interdisciplinary scientific community.* Manuscript under review.

Fishman, B., S. Best, et al. (2000, April). *Fostering professional development in systemic reform: A design proposal for developing professional development.* Paper presented at the annual meeting of the American Educational Research Association, New Orleans. Retrieved from http://www-personal.umich.edu/~fishman/papers/FishmanNARST2000.pdf

Fishman, B., & R. W. Marx. (2001, April). *Design research on professional development in a systemic reform context.* Paper presented at the annual meeting of the American Educational Research Association, Seattle.

Flower, L. S., & J. R. Hayes. (1980). The dynamics of composing: Making plans and juggling constraints. *Cognitive processes in writing.* L. W. Gregg & E. R. Steinberg (Eds.). Hillsdale, NJ, Lawrence Erlbaum Associates.

Foley, B. (1997, March). *How computer simulations help students construct models in science.* Paper presented at the annual meeting of the American Educational Research Association, Chicago. Available from http://www.InternetScienceEducation.org/

Foley, B. (1998, April). *Designing computer visualization tools for learning.* Paper presented at the annual meeting of the American Educational Research Association, San Diego. Available from http://www.InternetScienceEducation.org/

Foley, B. (1999). *Visualization tools: Models, representations, and knowledge integration*. Unpublished doctoral dissertation, University of California, Berkeley.

Forum on Education and the Economy. (1986). *A nation prepared: Teachers for the 21st century. The Report of the Task Force on Teaching as a Profession*. Washington, DC, Carnegie Corporation.

Fox, E. A., & G. Marchionini. (1998). "Toward a worldwide digital library." *Communications of the ACM, 41*(4): 29–31.

Fullan, M., & A. Pomfret. (1977). "Research on curriculum and instruction implementation." *Review of Educational Research, 47*: 335–397.

Gagne, R. M. (1965). *The conditions of learning*. New York, Holt, Rinehart & Winston.

Garcia, E. (1994). *Understanding and meeting the challenge of student cultural diversity*. Boston, Houghton Mifflin.

Gardner, H. (1985). *The mind's new science: A history of the cognitive revolution*. New York, Basic Books.

Gardner, M., J. G. Greeno, et al. (Eds.). (1990). *Toward a scientific practice of science education*. Hillsdale, NJ, Lawrence Erlbaum Associates.

Gick, M. L., & K. J. Holyoak. (1980). "Analogical problem solving." *Cognitive Psychology, 12*: 306–355.

Glaser, R. (1976). Cognitive psychology and instructional design. *Cognition and instruction*. D. Klahr (Ed.). Hillsdale, NJ, Lawrence Erlbaum Associates: 303–316.

Glenburg, A. M., & W. Epstein. (1987). "Inexpert calibration of comprehension." *Memory and Cognition, 15*: 84–93.

Gordin, D. N., J. L. Polman, et al. (1994). "The climate visualizer: Sense-making through scientific visualization." *Journal of Science Education and Technology, 3*(4): 203–226.

Gray, B. T. (1997, January). *Controversies regarding the nature of score validity: Still crazy after all these years*. Paper presented at the annual meeting of the Southwest Educational Research Association, Austin, TX. Retrieved from http://ericae.net/ft/tamu/valid.htm

Greeno, J., & H. A. Simon. (1988). Problem solving and reasoning. *Stevens' handbook of experimental psychology*. R. C. Atkinson, R. Herrnstein, G. Lindzey, & R. D. Luce (Eds.). New York, Wiley: 589–672.

Grillmeyer, O. (2001). *Designing effective animations for computer science instruction*. Unpublished doctoral dissertation, University of California, Berkeley.

Gunstone, R., C. Gray, et al. (1992). "Some long-term effects of uninformed conceptual change." *Science Education, 76*: 175–197.

Guzdial, M., & J. Turns. (2000). "Effective discussion through a computer-mediated anchored forum." *The Journal of the Learning Sciences, 9*: 437–470.

Hall, R., & R. Stevens. (1996, July). *Teaching/learning events in a workplace: A comparative analysis of their organizational and interactional structure*. Paper presented at the Cognitive Science '96 Annual Meeting, San Diego, CA.

Halloun, I., & D. Hestenes. (1985). "The initial knowledge state of college physics students." *American Journal of Physics, 53*: 1043–1055.

Hansen, S., D. Scrimpsher, et al. (1998). *From algorithm animations to animation-embedded hypermedia visualizations* (Tech. Rep. No. CSE98–05). Department of Computer Science and Engineering, Auburn University, Auburn, Alabama.

Hart, C., P. Mulhall, et al. (2000). "What is the purpose of this experiment? Or can students learn from doing experiments?" *Journal of Research in Science Teaching, 37*: 655–675.

Hatano, G., & K. Inagaki. (1991). Sharing cognition through collective comprehension activity. *Perspectives on socially-shared cognition*. L. Resnick, J. M. Levine, & S. D. Teasley (Eds.). Washington, DC, American Psychological Association.

Havelock, B. (2002). *Using the Internet to support teacher learning: Technology, collaboration, and science in teacher practice*. Unpublished doctoral dissertation, University of Washington, Seattle.

Havelock, B., & P. Bell. (2001, November). *Using scientific controversy to support student reasoning in science classrooms*. Paper presented at the Sixth International History, Philosophy, and Science Teaching Conference (IPHPST 2001), Denver, CO.

Hawkins, J. (1991). Technology-mediated communities for learning: Designs and consequences. *Electronic links for learning: The annals of the American Academy of Political and Social Science*. V. M. Horner & L. G. Roberts (Eds.). Newbury Park, CA, Sage. Vol. 514: 159–174.

Hawkins, J., & R. D. Pea. (1987). "Tools for bridging the cultures of everyday and scientific thinking." *Journal for Research in Science Teaching, 24*: 291–307.

Hays, T. (1996). "Spatial abilities and the effects of computer animation on short-term and long-term comprehension." *Journal of Educational Computing Research, 14*(2): 139–155.

Heath, S. B. (1983). *Ways with words: Language, life, and work in communities and classrooms*. Cambridge, England, Cambridge University Press.

Hegarty, M., P. A. Carpenter, et al. (1990). Diagrams in the comprehension of scientific texts. *Handbook of reading research*. R. Barr, M. L. Kamil, P. Mosenthal, & P. D. Pearson (Eds.). New York, Longman. Vol. II: 641–668.

Hegarty, M., J. Quilici, et al. (1999). "Multimedia instruction: Lessons from evaluation of a theory-based design." *Journal of Educational Multimedia and Hypermedia, 8*(2): 119–150.

Heller, K., K. Heller, & P. Heller. (2001). *Cooperative group problem solving in introductory physics*. New York, Brooks/Cole.

Heller, P., & M. Hollabaugh. (1992). "Teaching problem solving through cooperative grouping. Part 2: Designing problems and structuring groups." *American Journal of Physics, 60*: 637–644.

Heller, P., R. Keith, et al. (1992). "Teaching problem solving through cooperative grouping. Part 1: Group versus individual problem solving." *American Journal of Physics, 60*: 627–636.

Hemmje, M., C. Kunkel, et al. (1994). LyberWorld—A visualization user interface supporting full-text retrieval. *Proceedings of the 17th Annual International Conference on Research and Development in Information Retrieval*. W. Croft & C. van Rijsbergen (Eds.). London, Springer-Verlag: 249–257.

Hickey, D., & S. Zuiker. (2003). "A new perspective for evaluating innovative science programs." *Science Education, 87*: 539–563.

Hilgard, E. (1996). History of educational psychology. *Handbook of educational psychology*. D. C. Berliner & R. C. Calfee (Eds.). New York, Simon & Schuster Macmillan: 990–1004.

Hines, P. J. (2001). "Why controversy belongs in the science classroom." *Harvard Education Letter, 17*(5): 7–8.

Hoadley, C. (1999). *Scaffolding scientific discussion using socially relevant representations in networked multimedia*. Unpublished doctoral dissertation, University of California, Berkeley.

Hoadley, C. (2002). Creating context: Design-based research in creating and understanding CSCL. *Computer Support for Collaborative Learning 2002.* G. Stahl (Ed.). Mahwah, NJ, Lawrence Erlbaum Associates: 453–462.

Hoadley, C., B. P. Berman, et al. (1995). SpeakEasy Networked Communication Tool (Version 1.0) [Computer program]. Berkeley, University of California.

Hoadley, C., & N. Enyedy. (1999). Between information and collaboration: Middle spaces in computer media for learning. *CSCL '99: Proceedings of Computer Supported Collaborative Learning 1999.* C. M. Hoadley & J. Roschelle (Eds.). Mahwah, NJ, Lawrence Erlbaum Associates: 242–250.

Hoadley, C., & S. Hsi. (1992). The Multimedia Forum Kiosk (Version 1.0) [Computer program]. University of California, Berkeley.

Hoadley, C., & S. Hsi. (1994). "Multimedia: A chance for change." *Computer Professionals for Social Responsibility, 12*(2): 10, 12–13.

Hoadley, C. M., S. Hsi, et al. (1995). The Multimedia Forum Kiosk and SpeakEasy. *Proceedings of the third ACM international conference on multimedia.* P. Zellweger (Ed.). San Francisco, CA, ACM Press.

Hoadley, C. M., & M. C. Linn. (2000). "Teaching science through on-line peer discussions: SpeakEasy in the Knowledge Integration Environment." *International Journal of Science Education, 22*: 839–857.

Hofer, B., & P. Pintrich. (1997). "The development of epistemological theories: Beliefs about knowledge and knowing and their relation to learning." *Review of Educational Research, 67*: 88–140.

Hofer, B. K., & P. R. Pintrich (Eds.). (2002). *Personal epistemology: The psychology of beliefs about knowledge and knowing.* Mahwah, NJ, Lawrence Erlbaum Associates.

Hogan, K. (1999). "Thinking aloud together: A test of an intervention to foster students' collaborative scientific reasoning." *Journal of Research in Science Teaching, 36*: 1085–1109.

Holyoak, K. J. (1985). "The pragmatics of analogical transfer." *The Psychology of Learning and Motivation, 19*: 59–87.

Hsi, S. (1997). *Facilitating knowledge integration in science through electronic discussion: The Multimedia Forum Kiosk.* Unpublished doctoral dissertation, University of California, Berkeley.

Hsi, S., & C. M. Hoadley. (1997). "Productive discussion in science: Gender equity through electronic discourse." *Journal of Science Education and Technology, 6*(1): 23–36.

Hsi, S., C. Hoadley, et al. (1995). "Lessons for the future of electronic collaboration from the Multimedia Forum Kiosk." *Speculations in Science and Technology, 18*(4): 265–277.

Huberman, A. M. (1989). *Research on teachers' professional lives.* New York, Pergamon.

Hutchins, E. (1995). *Cognition in the wild.* Cambridge, MA, MIT Press.

Inagaki, K. (1981). "Facilitation of knowledge integration through classroom discussion." *The Quarterly Newsletter of the Laboratory of Comparative Human Cognition, 3*(2): 22–28.

Inhelder, B., & J. Piaget. (1970). *The early growth of logic in the child; classification and seriation.* New York, Humanities Press.

Inhelder, B., & J. Piaget. (1972). *The growth of logical thinking from childhood to adolescence.* New York, Basic Books. (Original work published 1958)

Jackson, S. L., S. J. Stratford, et al. (1994). "Making system dynamics modeling accessible to pre-college science students." *Interactive Learning Environments, 4*: 233–257.

Jacoby, L. L., & M. Dallas. (1981). "On the relationship between autobiographical memory and perceptual learning." *Journal of Experimental Psychology: General, 110*: 300–340.

Jansson, D. G., & S. M. Smith. (1991). "Design fixation." *Design Studies, 12*(1): 3–11.

Jasanoff, S., G. E. Markle, et al. (1995). *Handbook of science and technology studies.* Newbury Park, CA, Sage.

Johnson, R. T., D. W. Johnson, et al. (1986). "Comparison of computer-assisted cooperative, competitive, and individualistic learning." *American Educational Research Journal, 23*: 382–392.

Kafai, Y. B. (1995). *Minds in play: Computer game design as a context for children's learning.* Hillsdale, NJ, Lawrence Erlbaum Associates.

Kafai, Y. B., & M. Resnick. (Eds.). (1996). *Constructionism in practice: Designing, thinking, and learning in a digital world.* Mahwah, NJ, Lawrence Erlbaum Associates.

Kaiser, M. K., D. R. Proffitt, et al. (1992). "Influence of animation on dynamical judgments." *Journal of Experimental Psychology: Human Perception and Performance, 18*: 669–689.

Kali, Y. (2002). "CILT 2000: Visualization and modeling." *Journal of Science Education and Technology, 11*(3): 305–310.

Kali, Y., N. Orion, et al. (2003). "Effect of knowledge integration activities on students' perceptions of the earth's crust as a cyclic system." *Journal of Research in Science Teaching, 40*: 545–565.

Kann, C., R. W. Linderman, et al. (1997). "Integrating algorithm animation into a learning environment." *Computers & Education, 28*: 223–228.

Kegley, S. E., & J. Andrews. (1997). *The chemistry of water.* Sausalito, CA, University Science Books.

Kehoe, C., J. T. Stasko, et al. (1999). *Rethinking the evaluation of algorithm animations as learning aids: An observational study* (Tech. Rep. No. GIT-GVU-99-10). Atlanta, Graphics, Visualization, and Usability Center, Georgia Institute of Technology.

Keller, E. F. (2002). *Making sense of life: Explaining biological development with models, metaphors, and machines.* Cambridge, MA, Harvard University Press.

Kennedy, M. (1997). "The connection between research and practice." *Educational Researcher, 26*(7): 4–12.

King, A., & B. Rosenshine. (1993). "Effects of guided cooperative questioning on children's knowledge construction." *Journal of Experimental Education, 61*(2): 127–148.

Kintsch, W. (1998). *Comprehension: A paradigm for cognition.* Cambridge, MA, MIT Press.

Kitano, H. (2002, March). "Systems biology: A brief overview." *Science, 295*(5560): 1662–1664.

Knapp, M. S. (1997). *Between systemic reforms and the mathematics and science classroom: The dynamics of innovation, implementation, and professional learning.* Madison, WI, National Institute for Science Education.

Koedinger, K. R., & J. R. Anderson. (1998). "Illustrating principled design: The early evolution of a cognitive tutor for algebra symbolization." *Interactive Learning Environments, 5*: 161–180.

Koenemann, J., & N. Belkin. (1996). A case for interaction: A study of interactive information retrieval behavior and effectiveness. *Proceedings of CHI'96, Human Factors in Computer Systems*. New York, Association for Computing Machinery Press: 205–212.

Kolodner, J. (1993). *Case-based reasoning*. San Mateo, CA, Kaufmann.

Kolodner, J. L., D. Crismond, et al. (1998). Learning by design from theory to practice. *Proceedings of the Third International Conference of the Learning Sciences*. A. Bruckman, M. Guzdial, J. L. Kolodner, & A. Ram (Eds.). Atlanta, Edutech Institute, Georgia Institute of Technology.

Koslowski, B. (1996). *Theory and evidence: The development of scientific reasoning*. Cambridge, MA, The MIT Press.

Kozma, R. B., J. Russell, et al. (1996). The use of multiple, linked representations to facilitate science understanding. *International perspective on the psychological foundations of technology-based learning environments*. S. Vosniadou, E. DeCorte, & H. Mandel (Eds.). Hillsdale, NJ, Lawrence Erlbaum Associates: 41–60.

Krajcik, J. S., P. C. Blumenfeld, R. W. Marx, K. Bass, et al. (1998). "Inquiry in project-based science classrooms." *Journal of the Learning Sciences, 7*: 313–351.

Krajcik, J. S., P. C. Blumenfeld, R. W. Marx, & E. Soloway. (1994). "A collaborative model for helping middle grade science teachers learn project-based instruction." *The Elementary School Journal, 94*: 483–497.

Krajcik, J., P. Blumenfeld, R. W. Marx, & E. Soloway. (1999). Instructional, curricular, and technological supports for inquiry in science classrooms. *Inquiry into inquiry: Science learning and teaching*. J. Minstrell & E. V. Zee (Eds.). Washington, DC, American Association for the Advancement of Science Press: 283–315.

Krajcik, J., R. W. Marx, et al. (2000, April). *Inquiry based science supported by technology: Inquiry and motivation among urban middle school students*. Paper presented at the annual meeting of the American Educational Research Association, New Orleans. Retrieved from http://www-personal.umich.edu/~krajcik/AERA.outcomes.pdf

Kuhn, D. (1991). *The skills of argument*. Cambridge, England, Cambridge University Press.

Kuhn, D. (1993). "Science as argument: Implications for teaching and learning scientific thinking." *Science Education, 77*: 319–337.

Kuhn, T. S. (1970). *The structure of scientific revolutions*. Chicago, University of Chicago Press.

Lagemann, E. C. (1997). "Contested terrain: A history of education research in the United States, 1980–1990." *Educational Researcher, 26*(9): 5–15.

Lagemann, E. C. (2002, January 24). Usable knowledge in education: A memorandum for the Spencer Foundation board of directors [Memorandum]. Chicago, Spencer Foundation. Retrieved from http://www.spencer.org/publications/usable_knowledge_report_ecl_a.htm

Lampert, M., & M. L. Blunk. (1998). *Talking mathematics in school: Studies of teaching and learning*. Cambridge, England, Cambridge University Press.

Lan, W. (1996). "The effects of self-monitoring on students' course performance, use of learning strategies, attitude, self-judgment ability, and knowledge representation." *Journal of Experimental Education, 64*(2): 101–115.

Larkin, J. H., & F. Reif. (1979). "Understanding and teaching problem solving in physics." *European Journal of Science Education, 1*: 191–203.

Latour, B. (1987). *Science in action: How to follow scientists and engineers through society.* Cambridge, MA, Harvard University Press.

Latour, B. (1995). "The 'pedofil' of Boa Vista: A photo-philosophical montage." *Common Knowledge, 3*: 147–187.

Latour, B. (1996). *Aramis, or, the love of technology.* Cambridge, MA, Harvard University Press.

Latour, B. (1998, April 10). "From the world of science to the world of research." *Science, 280*: 208–209.

Latour, B. (1999). *Pandora's hope: Essays on the reality of science studies.* Cambridge, MA, Harvard University Press.

Latour, B., & S. Woolgar. (1986). *Laboratory life: The construction of scientific facts.* Princeton, NJ, Princeton University Press.

Lave, J. (1987). *Cognition in practice.* New York, Cambridge University Press.

Lave, J., & E. Wenger. (1991). Situated learning: Legitimate peripheral participation. *Learning in doing: Social, cognitive, and computational perspectives.* R. Pea & J. S. Brown (Eds.). Cambridge, MA, Cambridge University Press: 29–129.

Lave, J., & E. Wenger. (1992). *Situated learning: Legitimate peripheral participation.* Cambridge, England, Cambridge University Press.

Lehrer, R., S. Carpenter, et al. (2000). Designing classrooms that support inquiry. *Inquiring into inquiry learning and teaching in science.* J. Minstrell & E. Van Zee (Eds.). Washington, DC, American Association for the Advancement of Science Press: 80–99.

Leinhardt, G., K. M. Young, et al. (1995). "Integrating professional knowledge: The theory of practice and the practice of theory." *Learning and Instruction, 5*: 401–408.

Lemke, J. L. (1990). *Talking science: Language, learning, and values.* Norwood, NJ, Ablex.

Lemke, J. L. (2001). "The long and short of it: Comments on multiple timescale studies of human activity." *Journal of the Learning Sciences, 10*: 17–26.

Lenhart, A., L. Rainie, et al. (2001). *Teenage life online: The rise of the instant-message generation and the Internet's impact on friendships and family relationships.* Washington, DC, Pew Internet & American Life Project.

Lesgold, A., S. Lajoie, et al. (1992). SHERLOCK: A coached practice environment for an electronics troubleshooting job. *Computer assisted instruction and intelligent tutoring systems: Shared goals and complementary approaches.* J. H. Larkin & R. W. Chabay (Eds.). Hillsdale, NJ, Lawrence Erlbaum Associates: 201–238.

Levey, B. (1998). *Designing instruction for teachers using technology in their science classes.* Unpublished master's thesis, University of California, Berkeley.

Lewis, E. L. (1991). *The process of scientific knowledge acquisition among middle school students learning thermodynamics.* Unpublished doctoral dissertation, University of California, Berkeley.

Lewis, E. (1996). "Conceptual change among middle school students studying elementary thermodynamics." *Journal of Science Education and Technology, 5*(1): 3–31.

Lewis, E. L., & M. C. Linn. (1994). "Heat energy and temperature concepts of adolescents, adults, and experts: Implications for curricular improvements." *Journal of Research in Science Teaching, 31*: 657–677.

Lewis, E. L., J. Stern, et al. (1993). "The effect of computer simulations on introductory thermodynamics understanding." *Educational Technology, 33*(1): 45–58.

Linn, M. C. (1985). "The cognitive consequences of programming instruction in classrooms." *Educational Researcher, 14*(5): 14–16, 25–29.

Linn, M. C. (1986). Science. *Cognition and instruction*. R. Dillon & R. J. Sternberg (Eds.). New York, Academic: 155–204.

Linn, M. C. (1987). "Establishing a research base for science education: Challenges, trends, and recommendations." *Journal of Research in Science Teaching, 24*(3): 191–216.

Linn, M. C. (1990). Establishing a science and engineering base for science education. *Toward a scientific practice of science education*. M. Gardner, J. G. Greeno, F. Reif, A. H. Schoenfeld, A. diSessa, & E. Stage (Eds.). Hillsdale, NJ, Lawrence Erlbaum Associates: 323–341.

Linn, M. C. (1992a). The computer as learning partner: Can computer tools teach science? *This year in school science 1991: Technology for teaching and learning*. K. Sheingold, L. G. Roberts, & S. M. Malcolm (Eds.). Washington, DC, American Association for the Advancement of Science Press.

Linn, M. C. (1992b). "How can hypermedia tools help teach programming?" *Learning and Instruction, 2*: 119–139.

Linn, M. C. (1994a). Gender and school science. *The international encyclopedia of education*. T. Husén & T. N. Postlethwaite (Eds.). New York, Pergamon. Vol. 4: 2436–2440.

Linn, M. C. (1994b). "The tyranny of the mean: Gender and expectations." *Notices of the American Mathematical Society, 41*(7): 766–769.

Linn, M. C. (1995). "Designing computer learning environments for engineering and computer science: The Scaffolded Knowledge Integration framework." *Journal of Science Education and Technology, 4*(2): 103–126.

Linn, M. C. (1996). "Cognition and distance learning." *Journal for the American Society for Information Science, 47*: 826–842.

Linn, M. C. (2000a). "Designing the knowledge integration environment: The partnership inquiry process." *International Journal of Science Education, 22*: 781–796.

Linn, M. C. (2000b). Technology and educational opportunity. *Log on or lose out: Technology in 21st century teacher education*. Washington, DC, AACTE Publications: 9–12.

Linn, M. C. (2001). Science education: Preparing lifelong learners. *The international encyclopedia of the social and behavioral sciences*. N. J. Smelser & P. B. Baltes (Eds.). New York, Pergamon. Vol. 3: 13668–13673.

Linn, M. C. (2003). Technology and gender equity: What works? *Women in science and technology*. N. F. Russo, C. Chan, M. B. Kenkel, C. B. Travis, & M. Vasquez (Eds.). New York, American Psychological Association.

Linn, M. C. (in press). WISE design for lifelong learning–Pivotal cases. *Cognition, education and communication technology*. P. Gärdenfors & P. Johannsson (Eds.). Mahwah, NJ, Lawrence Erlbaum Associates.

Linn, M., P. Bell, et al. (1998). "Using the Internet to enhance student understanding of science: The Knowledge Integration Environment." *Interactive Learning Environments, 6*(1–2): 4–38.

Linn, M. C., & N. C. Burbules. (1993). Construction of knowledge and group learning. *The practice of constructivism in science education*. K. Tobin (Ed.). Washington, DC, American Association for the Advancement of Science Press: 91–119.

Linn, M. C., & M. J. Clancy. (1992). "The case for case studies of programming problems." *Communications of the ACM, 35*(3): 121–132.

Linn, M. C., D. Clark, et al. (2003). "WISE design for knowledge integration." *Science Education, 87*: 517–538.

Linn, M. C., C. Clement, et al. (1989). "Scientific reasoning during adolescence: The influence of instruction in science knowledge and reasoning strategies." *Journal of Research in Science Teaching, 26*(2): 171–187.

Linn, M. C., & J. Dalbey. (1985). "Cognitive consequences of programming instruction: Instruction, access, and ability." *Educational Psychologist, 20*: 191–206.

Linn, M. C., A. diSessa, et al. (1994). "Can research on science learning and instruction inform standards for science education?" *Journal of Science Education and Technology, 3*(1): 7–15.

Linn, M. C., & B. S. Eylon. (1996). Lifelong science learning: A longitudinal case study. *Proceedings of Cognitive Science Society, 1996.* Mahwah, NJ, Lawrence Erlbaum Associates: 597–602.

Linn, M. C., & B. S. Eylon. (2000). "Knowledge integration and displaced volume." *Journal of Science, Education, and Technology, 9*: 287–310.

Linn, M. C., & S. Hsi. (2000). *Computers, teachers, peers: Science learning partners.* Mahwah, NJ, Lawrence Erlbaum Associates.

Linn, M. C., & L. Muilenburg. (1996). "Creating lifelong science learners: What models form a firm foundation?" *Educational Researcher, 25*(5): 18–24.

Linn, M. C., & S. Pulos. (1983). "Aptitude and experience influences on proportional reasoning during adolescence: Focus on male–female differences." *Journal for Research in Mathematics Education, 14*: 30–46.

Linn, M. C., L. Shear, et al. (1999). "Organizing principles for science education partnerships: Case studies of students' learning about 'rats in space' and 'deformed frogs.' " *Educational Technology Research and Development, 47*(2): 61–85.

Linn, M. C., & J. D. Slotta. (2000). "WISE Science." *Educational Leadership, 58*(2): 29–32.

Linn, M. C., & J. D. Slotta. (in press). Enabling participants in online forums to learn from each other. *Using technology to enhance learning.* A. O'Donnell, C. Hmelo-Silver, & J. van der Linden (Eds.). Mahwah, NJ, Lawrence Erlbaum Associates.

Linn, M. C., & N. B. Songer. (1991). "Teaching thermodynamics to middle school students: What are appropriate cognitive demands?" *Journal of Research in Science Teaching, 28*: 885–918.

Linn, M. C., & N. B. Songer. (1993). "How do students make sense of science?" *Merrill-Palmer Quarterly, 39*: 47–73.

Linn, M. C., N. B. Songer, et al. (1996). Shifts and convergences in science learning and instruction. *Handbook of educational psychology.* R. Calfee & D. Berliner (Eds.). New York, Simon & Schuster Macmillan: 438–490.

Loucks-Horseley, S., P. W. Hewson, et al. (1998). *Designing professional development for teachers of science and mathematics.* Thousand Oaks, CA, Corwin Press.

Lovett, M. C., & J. R. Anderson. (1994). "Effects of solving related proofs on memory and transfer in geometry problem solving." *Journal of Experimental Psychology: Learning, Memory, & Cognition, 20*: 366–378.

Lundeberg, M. A., B. B. Levin, et al. (Eds.). (1999). *Who learns what from cases and how? The research base for teaching and learning with cases.* Mahwah, NJ, Lawrence Erlbaum Associates.

Maher, C. A., & A. M. Martino. (2001). "From patterns to theories: Conditions for conceptual change." *The Journal of Mathematical Behavior, 19*(2): 247–271.

Mandinach, E. B., & H. F. Cline. (1994). "Modeling and simulation in the secondary school curriculum: The impact on teachers." *Interactive Learning Environments, 3*: 271–289.

Mandinach, E. B., & M. C. Linn. (1987). "Cognitive consequences of programming: Achievements of experienced and talented programmers." *Journal of Educational Computing Research, 3*(1): 53–72.

Margel, H., B. Eylon, et al. (2003). *A longitudinal study of high school students' conceptions of the structure of materials.* Manuscript submitted for publication.

Martin, B., & E. Richards. (1995). Scientific knowledge, controversy, and public decision making. *Handbook of science and technology studies.* S. Jasanoff, G. E. Markle, J. C. Petersen, & T. Pinch (Eds.). Newbury Park, CA, Sage: 506–526.

Masters, J. (1995). The history of action research. *Action research electronic review.* I. Hughes (Ed.). Sydney, New South Wales, Australia, University of Sydney. Retrieved from http://www.behs.cchs.usyd.edu.au/arow/Reader/masters.htm

Mayberry, M. (1998). "Reproductive and resistant pedagogies: The comparative roles of collaborative learning and feminist pedagogy in science education." *Journal of Research in Science Teaching, 35*: 443–459.

McDermott, L. C. (1990). A view from physics. *Toward a scientific practice of science education.* M. Gardner, J. G. Greeno, F. Reif, A. H. Schoenfeld, A. diSessa, & E. Stage (Eds.). Hillsdale, NJ, Lawrence Erlbaum Associates: 3–30.

McHughen, A. (2000). *Pandora's picnic basket: The potential and hazards of genetically modified foods.* New York, Oxford University Press.

McLaughlin, M. W. (1987). "Learning from experience: Lessons from policy implementation." *Educational Evaluation and Policy Analysis, 9*: 171–178.

McLaughlin, M. (1990). "The RAND change agent study revisited: Macro perspectives and micro realities." *Educational Researcher, 19*(9): 11–16.

McLaughlin, M. W., & D. Mitra. (2001). "Theory-based change and change-based theory: Going deeper, going broader." *Journal of Educational Change, 2*(4): 301–323.

Means, B. (1994). *Technology and education reform: The reality behind the promise.* San Francisco, Jossey-Bass.

Means, B., & E. Coleman. (2000). Technology supports for student participation in science investigations. *Learning the sciences of the 21st century: Theory, research, and the design of advanced technology learning environments.* M. J. Jacobson & R. B. Kozma (Eds.). Mahwah, NJ, Lawrence Erlbaum Associates: 287–319.

Means, B., T. Middleton, et al. (1996). *GLOBE year 1 evaluation.* Menlo Park, CA, SRI International.

Merrill, M. D., & D. G. Twitchell (Eds.). (1994). *Instructional design theory.* Englewood Cliffs, NJ, Educational Technology Publications.

Metz, K. (2000). Young children's inquiry in biology: Building the knowledge bases to empower independent inquiry. *Inquiring into inquiry learning and teaching in science.* J. Minstrell & E. Van Zee (Eds.). Washington, DC, American Association for the Advancement of Science Press.

Metz, K. E. (1995). "Reassessment of developmental constraints on children's science instruction." *Review of Educational Research, 65*(2): 93–127.

Michotte, A. (1963). *The perception of causality.* London, Methuen.

Miller, G. A. (1956). "The magical number seven, plus or minus two: Some limits on our capacity for processing information." *Psychological Review, 63*: 81–97.

Minstrell, J. (1989). Teaching science for understanding. *Toward the thinking curriculum: Current cognitive research.* L. B. Resnick & L. E. Klopfer (Eds.). Alexandria, VA, Association for Supervision and Curriculum Development: 130–149.

Minstrell, J. (2000). Implications for teaching and learning inquiry: A summary. *Inquiring into inquiry learning and teaching in science.* J. Minstrell & E. van Zee (Eds.).

Washington, DC, American Association for the Advancement of Science Press: 471–496.

Minstrell, J. (2001). The role of the teacher in making sense of classroom experiences and effecting better learning. *Cognition and instruction: 25 years of progress.* D. Klahr & S. Carver (Eds.). Mahwah, NJ, Lawrence Erlbaum Associates: 121–150.

Mokros, J. R., & R. F. Tinker. (1987). "The impact of micro-computer based labs on children's ability to interpret graphs." *Journal of Research in Science Teaching, 24*: 369–383.

National Center for Education Statistics (NCES). (2001). "Internet access in U.S. public schools and classrooms: 1994–2000" (Publication No. NCES 2001-071). Washington, DC, U.S. Department of Education.

National Research Council. (1996). National science education standards. Washington, DC, Author.

Neilsen, J. (1994). Guerrilla HCI: Using discount usability engineering to penetrate the intimidation barrier. *Cost-justifying usability.* R. G. Bias & D. J. Mayhew (Eds.). Boston, MA, Academic.

Newton, P., R. Driver, et al. (1999). "The place of argumentation in the pedagogy of school science." *International Journal of Science Education, 21*: 553–576.

Nielsen, J. (2000). *Designing Web usability: The practice of simplicity.* Indianapolis, IN, New Riders Publishing.

Novak, J. D. (1990). "Concept mapping: A useful tool for science education." *Journal of Research in Science Teaching, 27*: 937–949.

Nussbaum, J. (1985). The earth as a cosmic body. *Children's ideas in science.* R. Driver, E. Guesne, & A. Tiberghien (Eds.). Philadelphia, Open University Press.

Osborne, J. F. (1996). "Beyond constructivism." *Science Education, 80*: 53–82.

O'Sullivan, C. Y., C. M. Reese, et al. (1997). *NAEP 1996 science report card for the nation and the states.* Washington, DC, National Center for Education Statistics.

Owens, K. S. (2001, March). *A chemist's role in design of Web-based curriculum on a current scientific controversy.* Paper presented at the National Association for Research in Science Teaching, St. Louis.

Owens, K. S., & P. Bell. (in press). Using controversy and technology to develop conceptual understanding of chemical representations. *Fifth International Conference of the Learning Sciences (ICLS).* P. Bell, R. Stevens, & T. Satwicz (Eds.).

Paepke, A., C.-C. K. Chang, et al. (1998). "Interoperability for digital libraries worldwide." *Communications of the ACM, 41*(4): 33–43.

Palincsar, A. S., & A. L. Brown. (1984). "Reciprocal teaching of comprehension-fostering and comprehension-monitoring activities." *Cognition and Instruction, 1*: 117–175.

Palincsar, A., S. Magnusson, et al. (2001). "Making science accessible to all: Results of a design experiment in inclusive classrooms." *Learning Disability Quarterly, 24*: 15–32.

Palmiter, S., & J. Elkerton. (1993). "Animated demonstrations for learning procedural computer-based tasks." *Human–Computer Interaction, 8*: 193–216.

Papert, S. (1993). *The children's machine: Rethinking school in the age of the computer.* New York, Basic Books.

Park, O., & R. Hopkins. (1993). "Instructional conditions for using dynamic visual displays: A review." *Instructional Science, 21*: 427–449.

Pascual-Leone, J., D. Goodman, et al. (1978). Piagetian theory and neo-Piagetian analysis as psychological guides in education. *Knowledge and development.* J. M. Gallagher & J. A. Easley (Eds.). New York, Plenum. Vol. 2: 243–289.

Pea, R. D. (1987). "Socializing the knowledge transfer problem." *International Journal of Educational Research, 11*: 639–663.

Pea, R. D. (1999). New media communications for improving education research and practice. *Issues in education research.* E. C. Lagermann & L. S. Shulman (Eds.). San Francisco, Jossey-Bass.

Pea, R. D., & L. M. Gomez. (1992). "Distributed multimedia learning environments: Why and how?" *Interactive Learning Environments, 2*(2): 73–109.

Pea, R. D., & L. Gomez. (1993). "Distributed multimedia learning environments: The Collaborative Visualization Project." *Communications of the ACM, 36*(5): 60–63.

Pea, R. D., & M. D. Kurland. (1987). On the cognitive effects of learning computer programming. *Mirrors of minds: Patterns of experience in educational computing.* R. D. Pea & K. Sheingold (Eds.). Norwood, NJ, Ablex: 147–177.

Pellegrino, J. W., N. Chudowsky, et al. (2001). *Knowing what students know: The science and design of educational assessment.* Washington, DC, National Research Council.

Peterson, P. (1998). "Why do educational research? Rethinking our roles and identities, our texts and contexts." *Educational Researcher, 27*(3): 4–10.

Pfundt, H., & R. Duit. (1991). *Students' alternative frameworks.* Federal Republic of Germany, Institute for Science Education at the University of Kiel.

Piaget, J. (1951). *The child's conception of the world.* London, Routledge & Kegan Paul. (Original work published 1929)

Piaget, J. (1969). *The child's conception of the world.* Totowa, NJ, Littlefield, Adams & Co.

Piaget, J. (1971). *Structuralism.* New York, Harper & Row.

Piaget, J., & B. Inhelder. (1974). *The child's construction of quantities: Conservation and atomism.* London, Routledge & Kegan Paul.

Pirolli, P., & M. Recker. (1994). "Learning strategies and transfer in the domain of programming." *Cognition and Instruction, 12*: 235–275.

Radinsky, J., L. Bouillion, et al. (2001). "Mutual benefit partnership: A curricular design for authenticity." *Journal of Curriculum Studies, 33*: 405–430.

Raghavan, K., & R. Glaser. (1995). "Model-based analysis and reasoning in science: The MARS curriculum." *Science Education, 79*: 37–61.

Rao, R., J. Pedersen, et al. (1995). "Rich interaction in the digital library." *Communications of the ACM, 38*(4): 29–39.

Recker, M., & P. Pirolli. (1995). "Modeling individual differences in students' learning strategies." *The Journal of the Learning Sciences, 4*: 1–38.

Reif, F., & J. I. Heller. (1982). "Knowledge structure and problem solving in physics." *Educational Psychologist, 17*: 102–127.

Reif, F., & J. H. Larkin. (1991). "Cognition in scientific and everyday domains: Comparison and learning implications." *Journal of Research in Science Teaching, 28*: 733–760.

Reif, F. S., & L. A. Scott. (1999). "Teaching scientific thinking skills: Students and computers coaching each other." *American Journal of Physics, 67*: 819–831.

Reigeluth, C. M., B. H. Banathy, et al. (Eds.). (1993). *Comprehensive systems design: A new educational technology.* New York, Springer-Verlag.

Reiser, B. J., W. A. Copen, et al. (1994). *Cognitive and motivational consequences of tutoring and discovery learning* (Tech. Rep. No. 54). The Institute for the Learning Sciences, Northwestern University, Evanston, IL.

Reiser, B. J., M. Ranney, et al. (1989). Facilitating students' reasoning with causal explanations and visual representations. *Artificial intelligence and education: Proceedings of the 4th International Conference on artificial intelligence and education.* D. Bierman, J. Breuker, & J. S. Sandberg (Eds.). Springfield, VA, 105: 228–235.

Reiser, B. J., J. P. Spillane, et al. (2000). Investigating the mutual adaptation process in teachers' design of technology-infused curricula. *Fourth International Conference of the Learning Sciences.* B. Fishman & S. O'Connor-Divelbiss (Eds.). Mahwah, NJ, Lawrence Erlbaum Associates: 342–349.

Reiser, B. J., I. Tabak, et al. (2001). BGuILE: Strategic and conceptual scaffolds for scientific inquiry in biology classrooms. *Cognition and instruction: Twenty-five years of progress.* S. M. Carver & D. Klahr (Eds.). Mahwah, NJ, Lawrence Erlbaum Associates: 263–305.

Repenning, A., A. Ioannidou, et al. (2001). "Using components for rapid distributed software-development." *IEEE Software, 18*(2): 38–45.

Resnick, L. B. (1987). *Education and learning to think.* Washington, DC, National Academy Press.

Resnick, L. B., M. Salmon, et al. (1993). "Reasoning in conversation." *Cognition and Instruction, 11*(3 & 4): 347–364.

Rice, D. C., J. M. Ryan, et al. (1998). "Using concept maps to assess student learning in the science classroom: Must different methods compete?" *Journal of Research in Science Teaching, 35*: 1103–1127.

Richardson, V. (1994). "Conducting research on practice." *Educational Researcher, 23*(5): 5–10.

Rieber, L. P., M. J. Boyce, et al. (1990). "The effects of computer animation on adult learning and retrieval tasks." *Journal of Computer-Based Instruction, 17*(2): 46–52.

Rifkin, J. (1998). *The biotech century: Harnessing the gene and remaking the world.* New York, Tarcher/Putnam.

Robinson, V. M. J. (1998). "Methodology and the research-practice gap." *Educational Researcher, 27*(1): 17–27.

Rodger, W. (1998, July). Power broker. *Wired Magazine, 6*(7). Retrieved from http://www.wired.com/archive/6.07/netizen.html

Rogers, E. M. (1995). *Diffusion of innovations.* New York, Free Press.

Rothkopf, E. (1966). "Learning from written instructive materials: An Exploration of the control of inspection by test-like events." *American Educational Research Journal, 3*: 241–249.

Ruiz-Primo, M. A., & R. J. Shavelson. (1996). "Problems and issues in the use of concept maps in science assessment." *Journal of Research in Science Teaching, 33*: 569–600.

Russell, J., & J. D. Slotta. (1999, March). *The scientist who went back to school: A case study of partnership in curriculum development.* Paper presented at the National Association for Research in Science Teaching, Boston.

Sadker, M., & D. Sadker. (1994). *Failing at fairness: How America's schools cheat girls.* New York, Macmillan.

Salomon, G. (1996). Studying novel learning environments as patterns of change. *International perspectives on the design of technology-supported learning environments.* S. Vosniadou, E. DeCorte, R. Glaser, & H. Mandl (Eds.). Mahwah, NJ, Lawrence Erlbaum Associates: 363–377.

Saxe, G. B., M. Gearhart, et al. (1993). Peer interaction and the development of mathematical understandings: A new framework for research and educational practice.

Charting the agenda: Educational activity after Vygotsky. H. Daniels (Ed.). London, Routledge: 107–144.

Saxe, G. B., & S. R. Guberman. (1998). "Studying mathematics learning in collective activity." *Learning and Instruction, 88*: 489–501.

Scaife, M., & Y. Rogers. (1996). "External cognition: How do graphical representations work?" *International Journal of Human–Computer Studies, 45*: 185–213.

Scardamalia, M. (1977). "Information processing capacity and the problem of horizontal decalage: A demonstration using combinatorial reasoning tasks." *Child Development, 48*: 28–37.

Scardamalia, M., & C. Bereiter. (1991a). "Higher levels of agency for children in knowledge building: A challenge for the design of new knowledge media." *Journal of the Learning Sciences, 1*: 37–68.

Scardamalia, M., & C. Bereiter. (1991b). Literate expertise. *Toward a general theory of expertise: Prospects and limits*. K. A. Ericsson & J. Smith (Eds.). Cambridge, England, Cambridge University Press: 172–194.

Scardamalia, M., & C. Bereiter. (1992a). A knowledge building architecture for computer supported learning. *Computer-based learning environments and problem solving*. E. De Corte, M. C. Linn, H. Mandl, & L. Verschaffel (Eds.). Berlin, Springer-Verlag.

Scardamalia, M., & C. Bereiter. (1992b). "Text-based and knowledge-based questioning by children." *Cognition and Instruction, 9*(3): 177–199.

Scardamalia, M., C. Bereiter, et al. (1989). "Computer supported intentional learning environments." *Journal of Educational Computing Research, 5*(1): 51–68.

Schank, P. K., M. C. Linn, et al. (1993). "Supporting Pascal programming with an on-line template library and case studies." *International Journal of Man–Machine Studies, 38*: 1031–1048.

Schank, R. C., A. Fano, et al. (1993/1994). "The design of goal-based scenarios." *Journal of the Learning Sciences, 3*: 305–345.

Scherlis, W. (1996, October). "Repository interoperability workshop: Towards a repository reference model." *D-Lib Magazine*. Retrieved from http://www.dlib.org/dlib/october96/workshop/10schleris.html

Schmidt, W. H., C. C. McKnight, et al. (1997). *A splintered vision: An investigation of U.S. science and mathematics education*. Dordrecht, The Netherlands, Kluwer.

Schmidt, W. H., C. C. McKnight, et al. (Eds.). (2001). *Why schools matter: A cross-national comparison of curriculum and learning*. San Francisco, Jossey-Bass.

Schmidt, W. H., S. A. Raizen, et al. (1997). *Many visions, many aims: A cross-national investigation of curricular intentions in school science*. Dordrecht, The Netherlands, Kluwer.

Schnotz, W., & H. Grzondziel. (1996, April). *Knowledge acquisition with static and animated pictures in computer-based learning*. Paper presented at American Educational Research Association, New York. (ERIC Document Reproduction Service No. ED 401878)

Schoenfeld, A. H. (1987). What's all the fuss about metacognition? *Cognitive science and mathematics education*. A. H. Schoenfeld (Ed.). Hillsdale, NJ, Lawrence Erlbaum Associates: 189–215.

Schon, D. (1987). *Educating the reflective practitioner*. San Francisco, Jossey-Bass.

Schunn, C. D., & J. R. Anderson. (2001). Acquiring expertise in science: Explorations of what, when, and how. *Designing for science: Implications from everyday, classroom, and professional settings*. Mahwah, NJ, Lawrence Erlbaum Associates: 83–114.

Schwab, J. (1962). The teaching of science as enquiry. *The teaching of science*. Cambridge, MA, Harvard University Press: 1–103.

Schwab, J. J. (1978). Education and the structure of the disciplines. *Science, curriculum, and liberal education*. J. J. Schwab (Ed.). Chicago, IL, University of Chicago Press: 229, 272.

Schwartz, D., X. Lin, et al. (1999). Toward the development of flexibly adaptive instructional design. *Instructional-design theories and models: A new paradigm of instructional theory*. C. Reigeluth (Ed.). Mahwah, NJ, Lawrence Erlbaum Associates: Vol. II. 183–214.

Seethaler, S. (2002, April). *Genetically modified food in perspective: An inquiry-based curriculum to help middle school students make sense of tradeoffs*. Paper presented at the meeting of the American Educational Research Association, New Orleans. Available from http://www.InternetScienceEducation.org/

Shear, L. (1998). *When science learners are language learners: Designing linguistically aware instruction to teach science "the knew way."* Unpublished master's thesis, University of California, Berkeley.

Sherwood, R., A. Petrosino, et al. (1998). Problem-based macro contexts in science instruction: Design issues and applications. *International handbook of science education*. B. J. Fraser & K. Tobin (Eds.). Dordrecht, The Netherlands, Kluwer: 349–362.

Shneiderman, B., D. Byrd, et al. (1998). "Sorting out searching: A user-interface framework for text searches." *Communications of the ACM, 41*(4): 95–98.

Shonkoff, J. P., & D. A. Phillips (Eds.). (2000). *From neurons to neighborhoods: The science of early childhood development*. Washington, DC, National Academy Press.

Shulman, L. S. (1987). "Knowledge and teaching: Foundations of the new reform." *Harvard Educational Review, 57*: 1–22.

Shymansky, J. A., & W. C. Kyle, Jr. (1992). "Establishing a research agenda: Critical issues of science curriculum reform." *Journal of Research in Science Teaching, 29*: 749–778.

Shymansky, J. A., W. C. Kyle, Jr., et al. (1983). "The effects of new science curricula on student performance." *Journal of Research in Science Teaching, 20*: 387–404.

Siegler, R. S. (1978). *Children's thinking: What develops?* Hillsdale, NJ, Lawrence Erlbaum Associates.

Simon, H. A. (1969). *The sciences of the artificial*. Cambridge, MA, MIT Press.

Singer, J., J. Krajcik, et al. (2000). "Constructing extended inquiry projects: Curriculum materials for science education reform." *Educational Psychologist, 35*(3): 165–178.

Sloane, K., & M. C. Linn. (1988). Instructional conditions in Pascal programming classes. *Teaching and learning computer programming: Multiple research perspectives*. R. E. Mayer (Ed.). Hillsdale, NJ, Lawrence Erlbaum Associates: 207–235.

Slotta, J. D. (2000, April). *Toward a WISE professional development model: Case studies from a whole-school study of teacher adoption*. Paper presented at the National Association for Research in Science Teaching, New Orleans. Available from http://www.InternetScienceEducation.org/

Slotta, J. D., M. T. H. Chi, et al. (1995). "Assessing the ontological nature of conceptual physics: A contrast of experts and novices." *Cognition and Instruction, 13*: 373–400.

Slotta, J. D., D. B. Clark, et al. (2002). Integrating Palm hand-held technology into the Web-based Inquiry Science Environment (WISE). *Computer support for collaborative learning 2002*. G. Stahl (Ed.). Mahwah, NJ, Lawrence Erlbaum Associates: 453–462.

Slotta, J. D., K. Dodson, et al. (1998, April). *Connecting school science with real science through Internet resources: Partnerships in the Knowledge Integration Environment.* Paper presented at the meeting of the National Association for Research in Science Teaching, San Diego, CA. Available from http://www.InternetScienceEducation.org/

Slotta, J. D., K. Dodson, et al. (1999, April). *Making use of existing Web resources: A partnership between KIE and the NASA Life Sciences Data Archive.* Paper presented at the meeting of the National Association for Research in Science Teaching, Boston. Available from http://www.InternetScienceEducation.org/

Slotta, J. D., & M. C. Linn. (2000a). The Knowledge Integration Environment: Helping students use the internet effectively. *Innovations in science and mathematics education: Advanced designs for technologies of learning.* M. J. Jacobson & R. B. Kozma (Eds.). Mahwah, NJ, Lawrence Erlbaum Associates: 193–226.

Slotta, J., & M. C. Linn. (2000b). How do students make sense of Internet resources in the science classroom? *Learning the sciences of the 21st century.* M. J. Jacobson & R. Kozma (Eds.). Mahwah, NJ, Lawrence Erlbaum Associates: 193–226.

Smith, J. P., A. A. diSessa, et al. (1994). "Misconceptions reconceived: A constructivist analysis of knowledge in transition." *The Journal of the Learning Sciences, 3:* 115–163.

Snir, J., C. Smith, et al. (1993, June). "Conceptually enhanced simulations: A computer tool for science teaching." *Journal of Science Education and Technology, 2:* 373–388.

Snyder, L., A. V. Aho, et al. (1999). *Be FIT! Being fluent with information technology.* Washington, DC, National Academy Press.

Songer, N. B. (1989). *Promoting integration of instructed and natural world knowledge in thermodynamics.* Unpublished doctoral dissertation, University of California, Berkeley.

Songer, N. (1996). "Exploring learning opportunities in coordinated network-enhanced classrooms—A case of kids as global scientists." *Journal of the Learning Sciences, 5:* 297–327.

Songer, N. B. (2000, October). *Scaling beyond mavericks: What do our experiments tell us?* Paper presented at the NCSA Workshop on Visual Modeling of Scientific Phenomena, Washington, DC.

Songer, N. B., H.-S. Lee, et al. (2003). "Research towards an expanded understanding of inquiry science beyond one idealized standard." *Science Education, 87:* 490–516.

Songer, N. B., & M. C. Linn. (1991). "How do students' views of science influence knowledge integration?" *Journal of Research in Science Teaching, 28:* 761–784.

Spitulnik, M. W. (1998). Using technology to support students' artefact construction in science. *International handbook of science education.* B. J. Fraser & K. G. Tobin (Eds.). London, Kluwer: 363–381.

Squire, K., J. MaKinster, et al. (2003). "Designed curriculum and local culture: Acknowledging the primacy of classroom culture." *Science Education, 87:* 468–489.

Stapp, W. (1997). *Field manual for global low-cost water quality monitoring.* Dubuque, IA, Kendall/Hunt.

Stasko, J. T., & A. Lawrence. (1998). Empirically assessing algorithm animations as learning aids. *Software visualization: Programming as a multimedia experience.* J. T. Stasko, J. Domingue, M. H. Brown, & B. A. Price (Eds.). Cambridge, MA, MIT Press: 419–438.

Staudt, C., & P. Horwitz. (2001, Spring). Reconciling conflicting evidence. *Concord Consortium newsletter, 5*(1). Retrieved from http://www.concord.org/newsletter/2001spring/evidence.html

Steed, M. (1992). "Stella, a simulation construction kit: Cognitive process and educational implications." *Journal of Computers in Mathematics and Science Teaching, 11*: 39–52.

Steele, C. (1997). "A threat in the air: How stereotypes shape intellectual identity and performance." *American Psychologist, 52*: 613–629.

Steffe, L. P., & P. W. Thompson. (2000). Teaching experiment methodology: Underlying principles and essential elements. *Handbook of research design in mathematics and science education*. A. E. Kelly & R. A. Lesh (Eds.). Mahwah, NJ, Lawrence Erlbaum Associates: 267–306.

Sternberg, R. J. (1977). *Intelligence, information processing, and analogical reasoning: The componential analysis of human abilities*. Hillsdale, NJ, Lawrence Erlbaum Associates.

Sternberg, R. J. (1985). *Beyond IQ: The triarchic theory of human intelligence*. Cambridge, England, Cambridge University Press.

Stevens, R., G. Cherry, et al. (2002). VideoTraces: Rich media annotations for learning and teaching. *Computer Support for Collaborative Learning (CSCL) 2002 Conference*. G. Stahl (Ed.). Mahwah, NJ, Lawrence Erlbaum Associates.

Stigler, J. W., & J. Hiebert. (1999). *The teaching gap: Best ideas from the world's teachers for improving education in the classroom*. New York, Free Press.

Stokes, D. E. (1997). *Pasteur's quadrant: Basic science and technological innovation*. Washington, DC, Brookings Institute.

Suppes, P. (Ed.). (1978). *Impact of research on education: Some case studies*. Washington, DC, National Academy of Education.

Tabak, I., W. Sandoval, et al. (1998, April). *BGuILE: Facilitating reflection as a vehicle toward local and global understanding*. Paper presented at the meeting of the American Educational Research Association, San Diego, CA. Retrieved from http://www.letus.org/bguile/Papers/Bguile_papers.html

Tien, L., D. Rickey, et al. (1999). "The MORE cycle: Guiding students' thinking in the laboratory." *Journal of College Science Teaching, 18*: 318–324.

Tinker, R. F. (1997). *Science learning in context: Research on technology for student field investigation*. Washington, DC, National Science Foundation.

Toth, E., D. Suthers, et al. (2002). "Mapping to know: The effects of representational guidance and reflective assessment on scientific inquiry skills." *Science Education, 86*(2): 264–286.

Toulmin, S. (1958). *The uses of argument*. Cambridge, England, Cambridge University Press.

Treloar, A. E. (1998). "Libraries' new role in electronic scholarly publishing." *Communications of the ACM, 41*(4): 88–89.

Tudge, J., & B. Rogoff. (1989). Peer influences on cognitive development: Piagetian and Vygotskian perspectives. *Interaction in human development*. M. H. Bornstein & J. S. Bruner (Eds.). Hillsdale, NJ, Lawrence Erlbaum Associates: 17–40.

Tufte, E. R. (1983). *The visual display of quantitative information*. Chelshire, CT, Graphics Press.

Tufte, E. R. (1990). *Envisioning information*. Chelshire, CT, Graphics Press.

Tufte, E. R. (1997). *Visual explanations: Images and quantities, evidence and narrative*. Chelshire, CT, Graphics Press.

Tversky, A. (1977). "Features of similarity." *Psychology Review, 84*: 327–352.

Tyack, D., & L. Cuban. (1995). *Tinkering toward utopia: A century of public school reform*. Cambridge, MA, Harvard University Press.

Tyack, D., & W. Tobin. (1994). "The 'grammar' of schooling: Why has it been so hard to change?" *American Educational Research Journal, 31*: 453–479.

Van Lehn, K. (1999). "Rule-learning events in the acquisition of a complex skill: An evaluation of Cascade." *The Journal of the Learning Sciences, 8*: 71–125.

van Zee, E., & J. Minstrell. (1997). "Reflective discourse: Developing shared understandings in a physics classroom." *International Journal of Science Education, 19*: 209–228.

Vosniadou, S., & W. Brewer. (1992). "Mental models of the earth: A study of conceptual change in childhood." *Cognitive Psychology, 24*: 535–558.

Vye, N., D. L. Schwartz, et al. (1998). SMART environments that support monitoring, reflection, and revision. *Metacognition in educational theory and practice*. D. Hacker, J. Dunlosky, & A. Graessar (Eds.). Mahwah, NJ, Lawrence Erlbaum Associates: 305–346.

Vygotsky, L. S. (1962). *Thought and language*. Cambridge, MA, MIT Press.

Vygotsky, L. S. (1978). *Mind in society: The development of higher psychological processes*. Cambridge, MA, Harvard University Press.

Walker, D. F., & J. Schaffarzik. (1974). "Comparing curricula." *Review of Educational Research*, (44): 83–111.

Warren-Little, J. (1990). "The persistence of privacy: Autonomy and initiative in teachers' professional relations." *Teachers College Record, 91*: 509–536.

Warren-Little, J. (1993). "Teachers' professional development in a climate of educational reform." *Educational Evaluation and Policy Analysis, 15*(2): 129–151.

Weinland, R. G. (1993). *Using pragmatic principles to teach eighth graders about light*. Unpublished master's thesis, University of California, Berkeley.

Welch, W. W. (1979). Twenty years of science curriculum development: A look back. *Review of research in education*. D. C. Berliner (Ed.). Washington, DC, American Educational Research Association: 282–308.

Wellesley College Center for Research on Women. (1992). *How schools shortchange girls*. Washington, DC, American Association of University Women Educational Foundation.

White, B. (1993a). Intermediate causal models: A missing link for science education? *Advances in instructional psychology*. R. Glaser (Ed.). Hillsdale, NJ, Lawrence Erlbaum Associates. Vol. 4: 177–252.

White, B. Y. (1993b). "ThinkerTools: Causal models, conceptual change, and science education." *Cognition and Instruction, 10*: 1–100.

White, B. Y., & J. R. Frederiksen. (1995). *The ThinkerTools inquiry project: Making scientific inquiry accessible to students and teachers* (Causal Models Research Group Report CM-95-02). School of Education, University of California, Berkeley.

White, B. Y., & J. R. Frederiksen. (1998). "Inquiry, modeling, and metacognition: Making science accessible to students." *Cognition and Instruction, 16*: 3–118.

White, B., & C. Schwarz. (1998). Alternative approaches to using modeling and simulation tools for teaching science. *Computer modeling and simulation in science education*. N. Roberts, W. Feurzeig, & B. Hunter (Eds.). New York, Springer-Verlag: 226–256.

White, R. T. (1988). *Learning science*. Oxford, England, Blackwell.

Wiesenmayer, R. L., & G. R. Meadows. (1997). "Addressing science teacher's initial perceptions of the classroom uses of Internet and world wide web-based resource materials." *Journal of Science Education and Technology*, 6: 329–335.

Williams, M., & M. C. Linn. (2002). "WISE inquiry in fifth grade biology." *Research in Science Education*, 32: 415–436.

Williams, S. M., & R. Bareiss. (1998, April). *Facilitating reflection and revision in design*. Paper presented at the annual meeting of the American Educational Research Association, San Diego, CA.

Williamson, V. M. (1995). "The effects of computer animation on the particulate mental models of college chemistry students." *Journal of Research in Science Teaching*, 32: 521–534.

Wilson, S. M., L. S. Shulman, et al. (1990). 150 different ways of knowing. Representations of knowledge in teaching. *Exploring teachers' thinking*. J. Calderhead (Ed.). Sussex, England, Holt, Rinehart & Winston: 104–124.

Wiser, M. (1988). The differentiation of heat and temperature: History of science and novice–expert shift. *Ontogeny, phylogeny, and historical development*. S. Strauss (Ed.). Norwood, NJ, Ablex.

Wiser, M. (1995). Use of history to understand and remedy students' misconceptions about heat and temperature. *Software goes to school*. D. Perkins, J. Schwartz, M. West, & M. Wiske (Eds.). New York, Oxford University Press: 22–38.

Wiser, M., & S. Carey. (1983). When heat and temperature were one. *Mental models*. D. Gentner & A. L. Stevens (Eds.). Hillsdale, NJ, Lawrence Erlbaum Associates: 267–298.

Wong Fillmore, L. (1989). Teaching English through content: Instructional reform in programs for language minority students. *Multicultural education and policy*. J. Esling (Ed.). Ontario Institute for Studies in Education of the University of Toronto, Canada: 125–143.

Yerushalmi, E., & B. Eylon. (2000). Teachers' approaches to promoting self-monitoring in physics problem solving by their students. *International Conference: Physics Teacher Education Beyond 2000*. P. Roser & S. Santiago (Eds.). 129–132.

Yin, R. K. (1994). *Case study research, design and methods* (2nd ed.). Newbury Park, CA, Sage.

Author Index

A

Aho, A. V., 5, 6, *376*
Alberts, B., 6, *353*
Alexander, C., 83, *353*
American Association for the Advancement of Science, 6, 55, *353*
American Association of University Women, 5, 6, 38, 41, 62, *353*
American Institutes for Research, 41, *353*
Anderson, J. R., 7, 36, 66, 67, 68, 75, 159, *353*, *365*, *369*, *374*
Andrews, J., 267, 270, *365*
Aronson, E., 61, 64, 171, *353*
Ash, D., 128, *356*
Atkinson, R. C., 35, *354*

B

Baddeley, A. D., 44, 59, *354*
Bagno, E., 31, 67, 68, *354*
Baker, L. M., 260, *354*
Banathy, B. H., 81, *372*
Barab, S. A., 7, 173, *354*

Bareiss, R., 151, *379*
Bargh, J. A., 39, *354*
Barnett, M., 7, *376*
Bass, K., 52, 59, 116, 268, 283, *366*
Bassok, M., 65, 91, 92, 93, *357*
Baumgartner, E., 149, 151, 265, *354*
Becker, H. J., 6, *354*
Belkin, N., 258, *366*
Bell, K., 84, *359*
Bell, P., 16, 19, 20, 21, 23, 38, 39, 51, 69, 74, 89, 96, 99, 109, 116, 118, 123, 124, 125, 126, 128, 130, 131, 133, 135, 136, 137, 139, 235, 237, 243, 250, 252, 255, 257, 265, 289, 323, 325, 329, 335, 342, *354*, *355*, *359*, *361*, *363*, *368*, *371*
Ben-Zvi, R., 33, *355*
Bereiter, C., 17, 30, 37, 42, 43, 61, 67, 91, 92, 99, 104, 152, *355*, *374*
Berenfeld, B., 284, *355*
Berman, B. P., 147, 152, *364*
Best, S., *361*
Biagioli, M., 241, *355*
Bielaczyc, K., 92, 94, *355*

381

Subject Index

Note: The letter *n* following a page number denotes a footnote.

About the Contributors

EDITORS

Marcia C. Linn (BA, PhD, Stanford University) is professor of development and cognition specializing in education in mathematics, science, and technology in the Graduate School of Education at the University of California, Berkeley. A fellow of the American Association for the Advancement of Science (AAAS), she investigates science teaching and learning, gender equity, and design of learning environments. In 1998, the Council of Scientific Society Presidents selected her for its first award in educational research. From 1995 to 1996 and 2001 to 2002 she was a fellow at the Center for Advanced Study in the Behavioral Sciences. In 1994, the National Association for Research in Science Teaching presented her with its Award for Lifelong Distinguished Contributions to Science Education. The American Educational Research Association bestowed on her the Willystine Goodsell Award in 1991 and the Women Educator's Research Award in 1982. Twice she has won the Outstanding Paper Award of the *Journal of Research in Science Teaching* (1975 and 1983). She has served on the board of the AAAS, the Graduate Record Examination Board of the Educational Testing Service, and the McDonnell Foundation Cognitive Studies in Education Practice board. Her publications include *Computers, Teachers, Peers: Science Learning Partners,* with S. Hsi (2000); "WISE Science" with J. D. Slotta in *Educational Leadership* (2000);

"The Tyranny of the Mean: Gender and Expectations," in *Notices of the American Mathematical Society* (1994); and *Designing Pascal Solutions*, with M. C. Clancy (1992). For more, see http://www.kie.berkeley.edu/linn.html

Elizabeth A. Davis is an assistant professor of science education at the University of Michigan. Davis received a PhD in Education in Mathematics, Science, and Technology from the University of California, Berkeley in 1998 after earning an undergraduate degree at Princeton University and working as an industrial engineer at Hewlett-Packard for several years. Her dissertation work focused on the role of reflection in knowledge integration and on ways of promoting productive reflection for middle school students working on complex science projects using the Knowledge Integration Environment (KIE). Her current research builds on this earlier work. Davis is investigating the knowledge integration processes of prospective and new elementary teachers who are learning to teach inquiry-oriented science. As part of this work, she has developed a Web-based integrated instructional resource and learning environment called Curriculum Access System for Elementary Science (CASES), intended to support prospective and new elementary teachers. Her research investigates ways in which specific features within CASES support teachers in engaging in specific knowledge integration processes. This work on the features of CASES extends her conceptual work on scaffolding for science learning. In 2001, Davis received the Presidential Early Career Award for Scientists and Engineers in recognition of the promise of her work on new science teachers' learning. For more, see http://www.umich.edu/~betsyd

Philip Bell is an assistant professor of cognition and technology in the Cognitive Studies in Education program at the University of Washington. His research investigates how innovative technologies shape human development, learning, and collaboration. Bell received his doctorate in cognition and development from the University of California, Berkeley in 1998 with an emphasis in science, math, and technology education. Prior to entering the field of education, Bell worked as a software engineer; he has a technical background in electrical engineering and computer science from his time as an undergraduate at the University of Colorado at Boulder. His educational research has focused on the design and study of scaffolded inquiry learning environments for science education, debate and argumentation in science and history classrooms, the promotion of online educational communities, the educational opportunities associated with contemporary controversies in science, the orchestration of university–school collaborative partnerships, and the nature of design-based research in education. His most recent research effort investigates the longitudinal influence of technology on human development and social interaction in this era of increasingly pervasive information and communication technologies. For more, see http://faculty.washington.edu/pbell/

AUTHORS

Eric Baumgartner is cofounder of and lead designer at Inquirium, a consulting firm specializing in the design and development of innovative learning technologies. Eric spent 1 year as research specialist at the University of California, Berkeley and 3 years as a postdoctoral fellow with the Center for Innovative Learning Technologies (CILT) prior to founding Inquirium. He has designed and built visualization and modeling technologies to support middle and high school science learning and studied the use of these tools in classroom settings. His current research interests focus on the nature of design knowledge, the process of designing innovative, technology-rich curricula, and the challenge of adapting existing innovative materials to meet local needs. Eric holds a PhD from Northwestern University's Learning Sciences program. His dissertation work examined the role of engineering design projects as a means to support student engagement in scientific inquiry and the strategies teachers used to support student inquiry within the design context. For more, see http://www.inquirium.net/people/eric.html

Douglas B. Clark is an assistant professor of science education at Arizona State University (ASU). Prior to ASU, he completed his doctorate and postdoctoral work at the University of California, Berkeley where his research on technology, depth of coverage, and conceptual change earned him the School of Education's Outstanding Dissertation Award. Before earning his doctorate, he completed his MA and teaching credential at Stanford University and taught science to Grades 6 through 12 in a variety of diverse public and private schools in Arizona and California. His current research continues to investigate computer and Internet supports for science inquiry and specifically focuses on supporting English language learners. In particular, his research investigates the use of text-based computer supported collaborative learning environments to engage language learners in the discourse and argumentation of science inquiry. Other specific continuing interests focus on comparisons of knowledge-in-pieces and knowledge-as-theory perspectives on conceptual change. For more, see http://www.kie.berkeley.edu/people/dclark.html

Bat-Sheva Eylon has an MSc in physics and a PhD in science education from the University of California, Berkeley. Since 1979, she has been a member of the science teaching department at the Weizmann Institute of Science in Israel. Currently she heads the junior high school science and technology group and the secondary physics group. She is also head of the professional national committee for physics teaching in Israel. In the last several years she has been directing a national research and development project for learning science and technology in junior high school. Her research and development interests include concept learning, problem solving, and knowledge organization in the physical sciences. In the last several years she has been also active in the area of continuing teacher development and has conducted longitudinal studies of students and teachers. In the area of problem solving, she has been concerned with the processes students use to develop strategic knowledge and in ways to enhance their problem-solving behavior. She investigated how students learn and use solved examples (learning from analogies) and examined individual differences in this area. Recently, she has explored ways to enhance students' self-monitoring processes and ability to learn from problem-solving experience. Many of her studies follow the design experiments methodology and have led to instructional methods that are used in Israeli schools. The limited success with scaling up ideas and innovations resulting from her earlier work with students and other research led her recently to focus her attention on teachers. She was one of the founders of the Israeli national teacher centers in physics and middle school science and was active in designing models of long-term, in-service teacher enhancement. Some of her recent graduate students have investigated issues associated with long-term teacher development and teacher change.

Christopher Hoadley is an assistant professor in the College of Education and the School of Information Sciences and Technology of the Pennsylvania State University at University Park. Hoadley designs and studies sociotechnical systems for learning and knowledge management from young children through adult professionals. Hoadley's research embraces the interplay between educational design, technology design, and social science research. He was the originator and director of the CILT Knowledge Network (http://www.ciltkn.org/) and founded the Design-Based Research Collective (http://www.

designbasedresearch.org/). He is a cofounder of the International Society for the Learning Sciences.

Doug Kirkpatrick, a long-time middle school science teacher, has been part of the Computer as Learning Partner, KIE, and Web-Based Inquiry Science Environment (WISE) projects at the University of California, Berkeley for the past 13 years, serving as a teacher, researcher, and mentor teacher. He is currently working full time for the WISE project coordinating professional development along with teacher support and curriculum review. Doug has been active in both national and state science teachers associations and is currently serving as a consultant to the California Academic Partnership Program.

Linda Shear is a Learning Consultant at SRI International's Center for Technology in Learning, working with clients in the public and private sectors to study and support the effectiveness of complex educational initiatives. She has served as program manager of CILT, which funds and studies cross-organizational collaborations in support of student learning. On the KIE project her research focus was collaborative curriculum development and integration projects with teachers, particularly in urban settings and with students for whom English was a second language. In a prior life, Linda was a technology consultant and executive educator with Price Waterhouse and with Lotus, with a primary focus on the business and organizational aspects of information technologies. Linda has an MA in Cognition and Development from the University of California, Berkeley, with a focus on education in math, science, and technology. For more, see http://www.sri.com/policy/ctl/

Jim Slotta is a Professional Researcher and lecturer at the Graduate School of Education at the University of California, Berkeley. An undergraduate degree in physics led to graduate work in cognitive psychology where his dissertation contributed to a theoretical framework of conceptual change in physics. As a postdoctoral scholar at the University of California, Berkeley, Slotta codirected the KIE project with Marcia Linn. His research in this project explored the use of Internet materials in inquiry science curriculum and the development of advance guidance information to help students use such materials effectively. In 1998, Slotta and Linn extended this work by creating WISE. This project sought to improve on the learning environment technologies, establish partnerships of scientists and educators, and research teacher adoption of inquiry and technology practices. WISE has grown dramatically in the past 4 years, resulting in a small library of completed activities, more than 4,000 teacher participants, and more than 50,000 students who have worked in the WISE environment. Slotta's research program has led to numerous presentations, publications, and manuscripts in preparation, with ongoing research interests in the design of inquiry activities, online community supports, international partnerships, and teacher professional development approaches. For more information see http://www.kie.berkeley. edu/people/slotta.html